Buenos Aires

timeout.com/buenosaires

Time Out Guides Ltd
Universal House
251 Tottenham Court Road
London W1T 7AB
United Kingdom
Tel: +44 (0)20 7813 3000
Fax: +44 (0)20 7813 6001
Email: guides@timeout.com
www.timeout.com

Published by Time Out Guides Ltd, a wholly owned subsidiary of Time Out Group Ltd.
Time Out and the Time Out logo are trademarks of Time Out Group Ltd.

© Time Out Group Ltd 2012
Previous editions 2001, 2004, 2006, 2008, 2010.

10 9 8 7 6 5 4 3 2 1

This edition first published in Great Britain in 2012 by Ebury Publishing.
A Random House Group Company
20 Vauxhall Bridge Road, London SW1V 2SA

Random House Australia Pty Ltd 20 Alfred Street, Milsons Point, Sydney, New South Wales 2061, Australia

Random House New Zealand Ltd 18 Poland Road, Glenfield, Auckland 10, New Zealand

Random House South Africa (Pty) Ltd Isle of Houghton, Corner Boundary Road & Carse O'Gowrie, Houghton 2198, South Africa

Random House UK Limited Reg. No. 954009

Distributed in the US and Latin America by Publishers Group West (1-510-809-3700)
Distributed in Canada by Publishers Group Canada (1-800-747-8147)

For further distribution details, see www.timeout.com.

ISBN: 978-1-84670-260-0

A CIP catalogue record for this book is available from the British Library.

Printed and bound in Great Britain by Butler Tanner & Dennis, Frome, Somerset.

The Random House Group Limited supports The Forest Stewardship Council (FSC®), the leading international forest certification organisation. Our books carrying the FSC label are printed on FSC® certified paper. FSC is the only forest certification scheme endorsed by the leading environmental organisations, including Greenpeace. Our paper procurement policy can be found at www.randomhouse.co.uk/environment

Time Out carbon-offsets its flights with Trees for Cities (www.treesforcities.org).

Contents

Introduction

Few things are for certain in Buenos Aires. But here's one of them: the words 'sleepy, orderly and peaceful' will never be used to describe the Argentinian capital. So if you're looking for a holiday that matches that description, stop reading this and go fly fishing in Patagonia instead. If, on the other hand, you're game to live like a *porteño* – whether it's for a day, week or year – there are things you need be prepared for.

Like a restless child, Buenos Aires doesn't like going to bed, standing still or being told what to do. Despite (or, perhaps, because of) economic instability, this spontaneous port city continues to surprise with free-for-all art events, pop-up restaurants, all-night warehouse parties and impromptu rooftop gigs. Yes, in the beloved home town of writer Jorge Luis Borges, creative minds will always prevail over boring red tape and financial hardship.

And while BA's European-style architecture and strong musical and literary traditions are lure enough for international culture vultures, remember that for every art nouveau palace, century-old café and tango show you see, there's a quirky alternative: an art workshop at a psychiatric hospital (*see p58*); the resurrection of a 12-metre-high Christ at the world's only religious theme park (*see p78*); or the mirrored ceilings of a love hotel (*see p92*), to name but a few.

Be warned that in Buenos Aires, with the exception of beer measures, nothing is ever done by halves. Whether quibbling over this week's price of rump steak, debating Peronism or watching a football match, it's done with passion. To fit in, gesticulate, raise your voice, make a joke, swear – and if in doubt, do all four simultaneously.

But most importantly, don't try to 'understand' BA. It's not to be 'got' but to be experienced (after all, who can explain why BA's dog walkers tie 17 canines to their waist before setting off on a bicycle?) Instead, indulge your senses in the sights, smells and soundtrack of this most sensuous of cities: the cacophony of car horns on the world's widest avenue; the intense aroma of beef roasting over hot coals; the deafening roar of 40 thousand frenzied football fans; the rattle of a graffiti artist's spray can; the thunder of hooves on the polo field; the heartbroken lament of a tango singer; the sweet first bite of an *alfajor* (Argentinian biscuit) and the bitter taste of a *cortado* (espresso cut with milk). This is Buenos Aires, in all its chaotic and unpredictable glory. And you must admit, it sounds a lot more exciting than fly fishing. Clemmy Manzo, *Editor*.

Buenos Aires in Brief

IN CONTEXT
Read up on BA's moments of grandeur and most devastating crises, punctuated by a cast of pivotal players from ruthless Juan Manuel de Rosas to political power couples Juan Domingo and Eva Perón and Néstor and Cristina Kirchner. We examine past and present porteño culture, with a close look at football — an emblematic tradition in this passionate, vibrant city.
▶ *For more, see pp13-35.*

SIGHTS
These chapters will guide you through our pick of the essentials in BA's barrios: from eclectic architecture – including La Boca's vividly painted shacks and Recoleta's French-style palaces, all recalling BA's diverse immigrant roots – to the city's historic plazas, parks, museums and public spaces that host some of the most exciting local arts and cultural events.
▶ *For more, see pp37-82.*

CONSUME
Argentinian *asado* absolutely lives up to the hype, but don't restrict yourself to steak in a city where wildly experimental culinary creations abound. The local fondness for lingering over a beer or coffee means quaint cafés and atmospheric bars are never more than a few steps away. We point you in the direction of the best, as well as selecting BA's top shops and hotels.
▶ *For more, see pp83-180.*

ARTS & ENTERTAINMENT
Take in a polo or football match, some great art at a graffiti-focused gallery, a film festival or a fashion show. By night the options are also endless: catch a tango show, a big budget production at a major theatre, or an underground, avant-garde performance. Or wind your way to a rock venue, a dimly lit *milonga* or one of dozens of pulsing, boisterous *boliches* (nightclubs).
▶ *For more, see pp181-234.*

ESCAPES & EXCURSIONS
Once you get to BA you may not want to leave, but there's a world of adventures to be had outside the city too. Escape to the countryside for a lazy stay on an estancia, or head to Uruguay's beautiful beaches. Argentina has its share of tranquil seaside towns and fine coastline as well, and there's water of the clamouring, crashing variety at the breathtaking Iguazú falls.
▶ *For more, see pp235-252.*

Buenos Aires in 48 Hrs

Day 1 Southern and Central Sights

10AM Start your day at the **Obelisco** (*see p44*) where the city's multi-lane Avenida 9 de Julio meets Avenida Corrientes. Walk four blocks south to Avenida de Mayo and stroll east down this pleasant thoroughfare to **Café Tortoni** (*see p144*). If you're lucky, you'll beat the crowds queuing to have a coffee at this atmospheric, traditional *confitería*.

Continue walking east along the avenue (or hop on the historical *subte* A underground line) to the politically charged **Plaza de Mayo** (*see p38*), where the human rights group Madres de Plaza de Mayo still marches every Thursday. In the centre is the **Pirámide de Mayo**, facing the presidential palace the **Casa Rosada**.

NOON From Plaza de Mayo, walk south along *calle* Defensa to **San Telmo**. Visit **Pasaje de la Defensa** at no. 1179 to see the inside of a *conventillo* (structures which housed immigrant families in the early 20th century), pass tango dancers deftly manoeuvring over the cobbles and look out for the abundance of antiques shops. If you're in town on a Sunday, don't miss the enormous antiques fair, **Feria San Pedro Telmo** (*see p178*), on **Plaza Dorrego**. There are plenty of bars around the plaza, and popular parrillas **El Desnivel** (*see p118*) and **Gran Parrilla del Plata** (*see p118*) are located nearby.

4PM Take a short taxi trip to **La Boca**, the barrio that was a portal to the city for thousands of immigrants and is home to legendary football team Boca Juniors. Saunter through the colourful open-air museum **Caminito** (*see p56*) with its street performers and tango memorabilia. If you're not lucky enough to be in town on a match day, the **Museo de la Pasión Boquense** (*see p57*) is your next best bet for an education in local football. The more artistically inclined shouldn't miss the **Fundación Proa** (*see p56*) art museum.

7PM Head to BA's ritzy dockland redevelopment **Puerto Madero** (*see p76*) for a walk along the water and drinks or dinner at one of the numerous bars and restaurants populating the two long promenades. If you're not ready to call it a night, zoom back to Avenida 9 de Julio and catch a show in the acoustically brilliant, beautifully restored **Teatro Colón** (*see p205*), one of the world's best opera houses.

NAVIGATING THE CITY

BA's relatively flat topography and grid system of streets makes walking around easy. Public transport is cheap. Note that the *subte* (underground system) only provides transport in central neighbourhoods and closes relatively early. Buses, known as *colectivos*, service most of the city 24 hours a day, although initially the number of routes can be bewildering. To pay, swipe your Sube card (available from locations listed at www.sube.gob.ar); otherwise carry coins for the bus, as notes are not accepted. Plan your route in advance with a **Guía T** (*see p254*) or through www.mapa.buenosaires.gov.ar, a handy website that will tell you which *colectivo* or *subte* stop you need for your destination; when in doubt ask the driver for

Day 2 Dead Presidents, Chic Shops and Essential Art

10AM Get up close and personal with BA's rich and famous – at least the ones who are dead – with a tour of the **Cementerio de la Recoleta** (*see p60*). Next door is the historic **Básilica Nuestra Señora de Pilar**, while the **Centro Cultural Recoleta** (*see p61*), one of the city's most important cultural and artistic institutions, is just a few steps away.

11AM Cross Avenida del Libertador to take in the **Museo Nacional de Bellas Artes** (*see p65*), which boasts a fine selection of 19th- and 20th-century Argentinian art. Just beyond the museum, in the Plaza Naciones Unidas is Eduardo Catalano's iconic **Floralis Genérica**, an impressive steel sculpture of a giant flower.

NOON
From the plaza, continue along Avenida Figueroa Alcorta to the **MALBA** (*see p69*) in Palermo for modern Latin American art and excellent international exhibitions. Duck into upmarket mall **Paseo Alcorta** (*see p155*) for some retail therapy, and refuel at the food court there or at the lovely café and restaurant at the MALBA.

4PM Still in Palermo, work your way west towards **Plaza Italia**, strolling through the tranquil greenery of the **Parque Tres de Febrero**. Pass the bustling plaza, cross Avenida Santa Fe and head deep into trendy Palermo Soho to explore the cutting-edge fashion and design stores. Stop off at bookshop **Libros del Pasaje** (*see p158*) for coffee and a good read in English or Spanish.

9PM It's dinner time, and in Palermo your options are endless. Try popular **Don Julio** (*see p131*) for a sizzling steak, or **Sarkis** (*see p141*) in nearby Villa Crespo for hearty Armenian fare. For dinner and a show, visit **Los Cardones** (*see p210*), where you'll experience Argentina's *folclórico* music accompanied by regional dishes. You're in one of BA's best dining and dancing districts, so if you're not ready to hit the hay, sample a cocktail at **Isabel** (*see p151*) before moving on to **Niceto Club** (*see p216*), where things really get going after midnight and well into the early hours.

---

directions. When catching cabs, always choose **radio taxis** (*see p255*).

SEEING THE SIGHTS
Buenos Aires is an enormous city, and while some central sights are close together it's best to plan days by neighbourhood, rather than running across town to see everything in one go. Many museums are subsidised by the state, and charge very low or no admission fees. Entrance to private collections and cultural events is generally more expensive.

GUIDED TOURS
A number of tours are available through agencies around town, including bus and bicycle sightseeing trips. *See p42* **Terrific Tours**.

Buenos Aires in Profile

THE CENTRE

History and business go hand in hand in the city centre. East of the Obelisco on Avenida de Mayo, a dizzying rush of office workers, tourists and protesters go about their business. At one end of this central artery is the Plaza de Mayo, the site of historical and political happenings and of the office of the president. Just steps away in Microcentro is the country's most important financial district.

▶ For more, see pp38-48.

SOUTH OF THE CENTRE

The south rewards those willing to explore. San Telmo is the obvious highlight, with its quaint cobblestone streets and Sunday market. Neighbouring Monserrat is often overlooked, but its noteworthy buildings delight history and architecture fans. The working class areas of La Boca, Barracas and Constitución reveal an even edgier side of the city.

▶ For more, see pp49-58.

NORTH OF THE CENTRE

Across gaping Avenida 9 de Julio is refined Recoleta, best known for its star-studded cemetery. Here porteños can justify the age-old claim that BA is the Paris of South America: the chic cafés and architecture are reminiscent of the European city. Palermo, BA's largest barrio, attracts families, hipsters and tourists with its expansive parks, great shops and varied gastronomic offering.

▶ For more, see pp59-70.

WEST OF THE CENTRE

Unexplored terrain for many, the west may be less than postcard perfect but it provides intriguing alternatives to the city's polished northern barrios. Boedo and Abasto are scattered with relics of tango's past; while the cast of deceased folk heroes at Chacarita's cemetery gives Recoleta's most famous residents a run for their money.

▶ For more, see pp71-75.

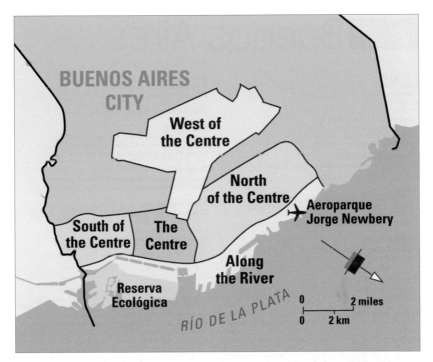

BUENOS AIRES CITY

West of the Centre

North of the Centre

Aeroparque Jorge Newbery

South of the Centre

The Centre

Along the River

Reserva Ecológica

RÍO DE LA PLATA

| 0 | | 2 miles |
| 0 | 2 km | |

ALONG THE RIVER

Puerto Madero is a spectacle on the city skyline. Fringing the old dockland, its modern high-rises house multinational businesses and well-heeled residents; and its swanky restaurants and bars contrast starkly with the nearby historical centre. Costanera Sur's ecological reserve is a delightful downtown haven, while the attractive Costanera Norte waterfront is perfect for weekend strolls.
► *For more, see pp76-78.*

FURTHER AFIELD

In Belgrano the hectic city feel is eased by wide streets and green spaces. BA's tiny Chinatown is also found here. Affluent barrio Núñez is home to River Plate's football stadium; and further north, upscale San Isidro is a leafy suburban paradise complete with bars, shops and restaurants. On the city's western edge Mataderos is a whole other world, associated with meatpacking, cowboys and cattle-dealing.
► *For more, see pp79-82.*

Time Out Buenos Aires

Editorial
Editor Clemmy Manzo
Managing Editor Mark Rebindaine
Copy Editor Janine Israel
Project Editor (London) Ros Sales
Proofreader Emma Clifton
Editorial Assistant Georgia Gray
Indexers Georgia Gray, Janine Israel
Intern Rosie Hilder

Editorial Director Sarah Guy
Management Accountants Margaret Wright,
Clare Turner

Design
Art Director (Buenos Aires office) Gonzalo Gil
Designer (Buenos Aires office) Javier Beresiarte
Senior Designer Kei Ishimaru
Guides Commercial Senior Designer Jason Tansley

Picture Desk
Picture Editor Jael Marschner
Picture Researcher Ben Rowe

Advertising
Sales Director St John Betteridge
Advertising Sales (Buenos Aires) Sara Blaylock,
Juan Faieraizen, Gustavo García Santa Cruz
Administration (Buenos Aires) Mau Banach

Marketing
Senior Publishing Brand Manager Luthfa Begum
Group Commercial Art Director Anthony Huggins
Circulation & Distribution Manager Dan Collins

Production
Group Production Manager Brendan McKeown
Production Controller Katie Mulhern-Bhudia

Time Out Group
Director & Founder Tony Elliott
Chief Executive Officer Aksel Van der Wal
Editor in Chief Tim Arthur
Group Financial Director Paul Rakkar
UK Chief Commerical Officer David Pepper
Time Out International Ltd MD Cathy Runciman

Contributors
Introduction Clemmy Manzo. **History** Matt Chesterton, Peter Hudson (*The Old Frenemy* Matt Chesterton; *The Afro-Argentinian Population* Matt Chesterton). **Buenos Aires Today** Matt Chesterton. **Football** Matt Chesterton, Dan Colasimone. **The Centre** Matt Chesterton, Brian Hagenbuch (*Terrific Tours* Clemmy Manzo, Arielle Milkman). **South of the Centre** Fiona McCann (*Spray it Loud* Janine Israel). **North of the Centre** Chris Moss (*Death Becomes Them* Chris Moss; *Walk: Palermo Park Life* Matt Chesterton). **West of the Centre** Declan McGarvey. **Along the River** Declan McGarvey, Matt Chesterton. **Further Afield** Brian Hagenbuch. **Hotels** Matt Chesterton, Daniel Neilson, Claire Rigby, Cat Scully (*Sex in the City* Daniel Neilson). **Restaurants** Ismay Atkins, Matt Chesterton, Clemmy Manzo, Daniel Neilson, Mark Rebindaine, Claire Rigby, Cat Scully (*Booze for Thought* Ian Mount; *Beef Encounter* Kristen James Henley; *On the Empanada Trail* Sorrel Moseley-Williams). **Cafés, Bars & Pubs** Matt Chesterton, Bridget Gleeson, Daniel Neilson, Cat Scully (*Melting Moments* Janine Israel). **Shops & Services** Florencia Bibas, Sophie Parker (*Made in Argentina* Vanessa Bell, Janine Israel, Clemmy Manzo, Cat Scully; *Hide and Seek* Sophie Parker). **Calendar** Melanie Kramers. **Children** Cat Scully. **Film** Brian Hagenbuch, Melanie Kramers. **Galleries** Matt Chesterton, Elizabeth Gleeson, Melanie Kramers (*Xul Solar* Sophie Parker). **Gay & Lesbian** Pablo de Luca, Jeremy Helligar, Gustavo Noguera. **Music** Brian Hagenbuch, Janine Israel (*A Little Bit of Country* Marc Rogers, Janine Israel). **Nightlife** Jack Coleman, Grant Dull, Elizabeth Gleeson. **Performing Arts** Brian Hagenbuch, Janine Israel, Melanie Kramers. **Sport & Fitness** Mark Rebindaine, Cat Scully (*Striking Out* Dan Colasimone; *Horsing Around* Clemmy Manzo, Alex Coidan). **Tango** Maggie Cowan-Hughes, Janine Israel, Chris Moss (*Tango Timetable* Jessica McGovern). **Upriver** Emma Clifton (*Chasing Waterfalls* Janine Israel, Arielle Milkman). **Country** Matt Chesterton (*Dude, Where's My Ranch?* Arielle Milkman). **Beach** Mark Rebindaine. **Uruguay** Gabriel Bialystocki, Mark Rebindaine, Cintra Scott. **Directory** Fiona McCann, Declan McGarvey.

Maps Nexo Servicios Gráficos, Luis Sáenz Peña 20, Piso 7 'B', Buenos Aires, Argentina (www.nexolaser.com.ar).

Cover Photography Photolibrary.com

Photography Adrien de Bontin (illustration on page 118 by Emiliano Guevara), except: pages 14 Archivo General de la Nación Dpto. Doc. Fotográficos, Argentina; page 14, 27 TÉLAM; 23 courtesy of Museo Histórico Nacional; 3, 43, 45, 52, 57 Felipe Martínez A; 4, 60, 63, 126 Gabriela Mac Hannaford; 5 (In Context), 8 (The Centre), 28, 37, 46, 77, 119, 122, 130, 147, 164, 176, 226, 236, 239, 240, 253 Joe Rondone; 5 (Arts and Entertainment), 215 Franco Meligene; 5 (Escapes and Excursions) courtesy of Estancia La Oriental; 8 (West of the Centre), 39, 53, 64, 67, 70, 72, 73, 74, 187 Georgia Gray; 17, 54, 55 courtesy of Graffitimundo; 31 Patricio Murphy; 33, 134 Jocelyn Mandryk; 58 courtesy of Usina de Arte; 83, 145, 157, 229, 244 Shooresh Fezoni; 91 courtesy of Patios de San Telmo; 92 courtesy of Dissors; 93, 142 courtesy of Faena Hotel + Universe; 95 courtesy of Park Hyatt; 99 courtesy of Legado Mítico; 103 courtesy of Krista; 110, 143, 149, 153, 216 Jo Castillo; 113 courtesy of Tomo I; 123 Emily Epstein; 136 Stefane San Quirce; 137 courtesy of Unik; 141 Frances Ren, courtesy of Cocina Sunae; 138, 148 Bereissa Alvarez; 154, 223 Ali Cherkis; 193 courtesy of Gachi Prieto; 197 courtesy of Rubbers; 198, 190 courtesy of MALBA; 199 courtesy of Elsi del Río; 200 courtesy of Out & About; 204 courtesy of Fabulous Weddings; 205 courtesy of Teatro Colón; 206 Alejandra Farizano; 208 courtesy of Las Kellies; 210 courtesy of NoAvestruz; 212 Lucio Alvarez; 213 Marc Van der Aa; 218, 219 courtesy of Ojalá; 220 courtesy Teatro Nacional Cervantes; 222 Cambalache; 228 Buena Onda Yoga; 230 courtesy of Rojo Tango; 235 James Kibbey; 241, 243 Ed Stocker; 242 courtesy of San Antonio de Areco tourist board; 249 Eduardo Alvares; 251 Indias Filmica; The following images belong to the Time Out archive: pages 135, 186, 201, 203, 234, 237, 238.

The Editor would like to thank: all contributors and photographers to the current and previous edition of *Time Out Buenos Aires*.

About the Guide

GETTING AROUND

The back of the book contains street maps of Buenos Aires as well as overview maps of the city and its surroundings. The maps begin on page 289; the locations of hotels (**❶**), restaurants (**❶**), and cafés, pubs and bars (**❶**) are marked on them. Most businesses listed in this guide are in the mapped areas; the grid-square references at the end of each listing refer to the maps.

THE ESSENTIALS

For practical information, including visas, disabled access, emergency numbers, lost property and local transport, please see the Directory. It begins on page 253.

THE LISTINGS

Addresses, phone numbers, websites, transport information, hours and prices are all included in our listings. All were checked and current at the time of going to press. However, business owners can alter their arrangements at any time, and fluctuating economic conditions can cause prices to change rapidly.

The best venues in the city, the must-sees and must-dos, have been marked with a red star (★). In the Sights chapters, we've also marked venues that do not charge admission with a **FREE** symbol.

THE LANGUAGE

For a language primer, see pages 264-265.

PHONE NUMBERS

The area code for Buenos Aires is 011. You don't need to use the code when calling from within Buenos Aires: simply dial the eight-digit number as listed in this guide.

From outside Argentina, dial your country's international access code (011 from the US, or 00 from the UK) or a plus symbol, followed by the Argentinian country code (54), 11 for Buenos Aires and the eight-digit number as listed. For more on phones, including information on calling abroad from Argentina and local mobile phone access, see p262.

FEEDBACK

We welcome feedback on this guide, both on the venues we've included and on any other places that you'd like to see featured in future editions. Please email us at guides@timeout.com.

Time Out Guides

Founded in 1968, Time Out has grown from humble beginnings into the leading resource for anyone wanting to know what's happening in the world's greatest cities. Alongside our influential weeklies in London, New York and Chicago, we publish more than 20 magazines in cities as varied as Beijing and Beirut; a range of travel books, with the City Guides now joined by the newer Shortlist series; and an information-packed website. The company remains proudly independent, still owned by Tony Elliott four decades after he launched *Time Out London*.

Written by local experts and illustrated with original photography, our books also retain their independence. No business has been featured because it has advertised, and all restaurants and bars are visited and reviewed anonymously.

ABOUT THE EDITOR

Based in Buenos Aires, **Clemmy Manzo** is editor of *Time Out insiders' guide to Buenos Aires* magazine. She has also contributed to various guidebooks on Argentina and the rest of South America, and regularly writes about her adopted city for various international magazines.

A full list of the book's contributors can be found opposite.

In Context

History

It's not all riots, revolutions and rogues..

The history of Argentina is too frequently compared to a 'rollercoaster ride', with the implication that this is a country more prone to ups and downs than most. It's a perspective that's both condescending and flaky. Indeed, it was precisely because they wanted to get off the 'rollercoaster' of history that millions of Europeans emigrated to Argentina in the first place.

Rather, it is events in living memory that have shaken Argentinians' faith in their country's ability to live up to the idealism of its founders, who shook off the chains of Spanish rule in 1810 to pursue liberty and prosperity. Liberty vanished during the military dictatorship of 1976-82, in which thousands of Argentinians were murdered by their own government. As for prosperity, many who lived through the financial meltdown of 2001-02 thought they'd seen the last of it.

But predictions can be as dodgy as fairground analogies. Argentina's economy has performed strongly over the past decade, while a series of recent trials have seen those responsible for the worst atrocities of the 1970s put behind bars. Facing the past has left Argentina in better shape to face the future.

TWO FOUNDINGS

For most *porteños*, the city's history began when the European conquistadors arrived in the 16th century. But the land they conquered wasn't empty. The area stretching inland from the southern shore of the estuary of the Río de la Plata (River Plate) was populated by bands of hunter-gatherer Querandí who eked out a nomadic existence on the vast, grassy pampas.

The first Europeans botched their entrance spectacularly. Juan Díaz de Solís, a Portuguese navigator employed by the Spanish crown, landed in 1516, 24 years after Columbus reached the Americas. Solís and the rest of the landing party were killed and eaten by the indigenous tribes on the eastern bank of the River Plate. Nevertheless, waves of Spanish and Portuguese explorers sparked a race to colonise the area.

Spaniard Pedro de Mendoza arrived with between 1,200 and 2,000 soldiers and settlers in February 1536. The city and port of Santa María de los Buenos Ayres that he founded was probably located near what is now Parque Lezama. But after initial friendly contact, conflicts with the indigenous inhabitants further upriver grew. Some settlers resisted, but the main force of Spanish colonisation switched northwards and, in 1541, Domingo Martínez de Irala, commander of the garrison in Asunción, ordered the abandonment of Buenos Aires.

Settlement of what is now Argentina continued with the foundation of three regional capitals in the interior: Santiago del Estero, Tucumán and Córdoba. But it became clear that a port would be necessary to service the vast area to the south of the silver deposits of Potosí, and on 11 June 1580 Lieutenant Juan de Garay replanted the Spanish flag in the soil of Buenos Aires. The city was reborn.

But with no great fanfare. Until 1610, Buenos Aires had scarcely 500 inhabitants, few of whom dared or cared to venture into the as yet unsettled and uncultivated pampas, making them dependent on supply ships for survival. Unfortunately, these were infrequent; Spain sent virtually all its goods on a circuitous route, allowing voyages to Buenos Aires only every one or two years in an attempt to cut piracy.

COLONIAL UNREST

From these humble beginnings, Buenos Aires gradually grew in importance. By the 18th century, the process of taming the pampas was under way. Hardy settlers ventured out into the fertile plains and established what would become the vast estancias (cattle ranches) of the province, and the resulting trade in leather and dried beef continued to flow through Buenos Aires. In 1776, in recognition of the port's strategic position and in a bid to regain commercial control, Spain created the Virreinato del Río de la Plata (Viceroyalty of the River Plate), comprised of what are today Bolivia, Paraguay, Argentina and Uruguay, and finally separated it from Peruvian command.

The new authorities immediately set up free-trade agreements with Chile, Peru and Spain, and during the last two decades of the 18th century the port boomed. The first of many waves of immigrants arrived from Europe. Buenos Aires became a bustling commercial centre.

But the rapid growth also brought tensions. The new pro-free trade merchant class began to face off against the Spanish-born oligarchy that favoured Spain's monopoly. The creation of the city's first newspapers and the prospect of revolution and war in Europe also inspired heated debate about the country's future.

The empire-building British had ideas of their own and began to cast a covetous eye over Spain's colonies. In 1806, under the command of General William Carr Beresford, some 1,500 British troops entered BA. The 'English Invasion' was a débacle.

With the blundering Brits sent home with their sabres between their legs, *porteño* resentment was focused once more on the Spanish rulers. Simmering tensions in the city were heightened further by news that Napoleonic forces had triumphed in Spain. The *criollos* (American-born Spanish) demanded that Viceroy Santiago de Liniers's successor, Baltasar Hidalgo de Cisneros, convene an open

IN CONTEXT

The Old Frenemy

When it comes to Anglo-Argentinian relations, it's complicated.

Argentina and Great Britain (or 'England' as many Argentinians insist on calling it) have had a relationship so unpredictable, so on-again, off-again, that the two countries make Elizabeth Taylor and Richard Burton look like a pair of devoted turtle doves.

As with all tempestuous liaisons, the tiffs and the tantrums tend to get more publicity than the periods of going steady. All Argentinian children (though few British ones) learn about the 'English Invasions' of 1806 and 1807 (*see p15*), when *porteño* militias threw the forces of perfidious Albion back into the Río de la Plata. It was the crucible in which Argentinian national identity was forged. Battle would not be rejoined until 1982, when an Argentinian invasion force seized control of the Falkland Islands, known in Spanish as Las Malvinas (*see p23*). This was a far bloodier conflict than the skirmishes of 1806-07 and one in which the British prevailed, although the issue at stake – who should have sovereignty over the islands – is far from settled. The discovery of substantial oil reserves beneath the seabed surrounding the archipelago means diplomatic relations are likely to get worse before they get better.

So much for ancient and recent history. As duelling couples in Hollywood movies are fond of saying in moments of reflection, there have been good times too. Between 1880 and 1950 in particular, the relationship between Britain and Argentina was largely one of cooperation and mutual enrichment. From 1890 until the outbreak of World War I, the British invested more in Argentina than in any other country. Around 40 per cent of this consisted of manpower, steel and iron for Argentina's nascent railway network. In other words, heavy metal – paid for with Argentinian products that

were essentially country and western, such as corn and (especially) beef.

Steel rails still criss-cross Argentina, but most of the trains that ran on them have long been decommissioned. But one British import, whose first appearance in Argentina dates back to 1868, is alive and (literally) kicking: football. And while the memory of Diego Maradona's 'Hand of God' goal in the 1986 World Cup can still bring tears to the eyes of grown Englishmen, take a look at the names of the Argentinian clubs Maradona played for: Argentinos Juniors, Boca Juniors and Newell's Old Boys. Notice anything they have in common?

meeting of the city's governing body to consider the situation. Despite attempts by Spanish loyalists to restrict the size of the meeting, the vote was conclusive. The *criollos* declared the viceroy's reign to have expired and a junta (council) was elected to replace him. This marked a revolutionary transfer of power from the Spanish elite to the *criollos*.

The loyalists made a last-ditch attempt at resistance, but a massive protest backed by the *criollo* militia units on 25 May 1810 – in the square later named Plaza de Mayo in honour of the events that took place there – convinced them of the inevitable.

This conflict, known as the Revolución de Mayo, sparked a rise in anti-Spanish feeling. Argentina formally declared its independence in the northern province of Tucumán on 9 July 1816. On this day, celebrated annually as Argentina's independence day, the new nation announced its opposition to 'any other form of foreign domination'.

FORMING A NEW NATION

Emboldened by having crushed the English invaders in the previous decade, *criollos* in Buenos Aires led the movement for independence from Spain, promising to consult the provinces later. But the city had scarcely 40,000 inhabitants, and the provinces, jealous of its power, were not easily convinced. The province of Córdoba staged a counter-revolution, led by Liniers, who was executed by the junta for his trouble.

The resulting civil war lasted ten years, during which the government sought to assume all the rights and privileges of the former Spanish colonial authorities.

This period saw the establishment of professional armed forces led by General José de San Martín and the rise of the caudillos, provincial strongmen who brutally defended regional autonomy. In the name of Federalism, the caudillos opposed centralised Unitarian rule. San Martín, the son of Spanish officials, ensured his place in Argentina's pantheon of national heroes by joining the revolutionary cause and leading an advance across the Andes to liberate Chile from Spanish control.

In 1820, provincial forces defeated the nationalist army and the centralist intentions of the city were scuppered. Thereafter the city suffered a period of turmoil. But by the end of 1820, order had been restored under Bernardino Rivadavia, who dedicated the income from the customs house to improving the city and reorganising its government and justice system.

The intellectual, architectural and economic growth of the city, which now had over 55,000 inhabitants, contrasted with underdevelopment in the provinces. Nevertheless, relations with the rest of the country improved and the city took on the responsibility for international relations as the new nation was recognised by the major foreign powers.

RED RULES WITH AN IRON FIST

Rivadavia became the first president of a united and independent Argentina in 1826, but a year later the provinces were again up in arms. Rivadavia's constitution was rejected by most of the provincial caudillos, who were led by Juan Manuel de Rosas and Juan Facundo Quiroga.

Two times governor of Buenos Aires province, Rosas consolidated his strong following in the countryside by organising an expedition to exterminate the indigenous Araucano, who competed with the wealthy ranch owners for the region's cattle. During his 17-year reign, Rosas consolidated the power of the port and province of Buenos Aires. But he also imposed rigid censorship and ruled by murder and repression. All citizens were compelled to make public their support for Rosas by wearing a red Federalist ribbon (the Unitarian colours were sky-blue and/or white), and public documents, newspapers and personal letters were required to start with the forceful slogan 'Long live the Federation and death to the savage Unitarians!'

At the end of his second governorship Rosas left a country that was isolated and economically backward. But he had also, albeit forcibly, encouraged national unity.

IN CONTEXT

La única y auténtica taquería

www.LaFabricaDelTaco.com

La Fábrica del Taco.™

Buenos Aires

Ricos Tacos

ILUSTRACIÓN CHARLES GLAUBITZ/TEAM FABRICA

AGRICULTURAL ADVANCES AND FEVERISH FLIGHT

The next two decades saw the forging of the new nation, as successive presidents worked to create a unified state. Democracy, even imperfectly administered, was an advance over the earlier despotism. Bartolomé Mitre, governor of Buenos Aires and the founder of *La Nación* newspaper, was succeeded by Domingo Faustino Sarmiento.

Despite further uprisings, the national army successfully defended the republic and was further battle-hardened during a pointless war with Paraguay that lasted from 1865 to 1870. The controversial 'Desert Campaign' of 1879, on the other hand, led by General Julio Roca was deemed a resounding success. The campaign resolved the long-running conflict with indigenous groups, and in the process opened up 605,000 square kilometres (233,500 square miles) of land for cattle farming.

Technological advances facilitated the country's first wheat exports in 1878, and a year later refrigerated meat shipments followed in their wake. Both developments would have a major economic impact in the decades to come. The bulk of the profits went to the large landowners, however, or were spent on British imports. The British also reaped handsome rewards from the construction of the railways, which grew by 2,516 kilometres (1,563 miles) from 1862 to 1880.

Characteristically, the city benefited the most from these economic advances, but the absence of water and sewage systems led to outbreaks of cholera in 1867 and yellow fever in 1871. The latter killed more than one-tenth of the city's population and encouraged the wealthy to relocate from the hard-hit southern areas to Barrio Norte.

In 1880, the city of Buenos Aires suffered its final assault at the hands of the provinces. Roca, like Rosas before him, used his slaughter of indigenous groups as a springboard for the presidency. Although backed by the provinces, he was resisted by Buenos Aires. The fighting that ensued killed more than 2,000 people, most of them *porteños*, before the national government was able to prevail. The city was then placed under central government control and separated from the province, which adopted as its capital La Plata, 60 kilometres (37 miles) to the east.

Roca was the figurehead for an oligarchy, represented by the Partido Autonomista Nacional (PAN), which held power for three decades. During this time immigration swelled the city's population from 90,000 in 1854 to 526,000 by 1890. By 1914 it was the largest metropolis on the continent, with 1,575,000 inhabitants.

BOOM AND BUST

Buenos Aires was remodelled under Torcuato de Alvear, municipal chief from 1883 to 1887 and considered to be the father of the modern city. The grand public buildings, parks and plazas date mainly from this time. British companies built tramways and gas and electricity networks, and a modern sewage system was created. Meanwhile, Argentina established its place as the world's leading grain exporter and was second only to the US as a frozen meat exporter, creating a second boom for the port city. But a rise in British interest rates led the British Baring Brothers bank – which had funnelled vast sums into the republic – to cut off its cash supply and demand repayment. In 1890 Argentina was plunged into a sudden, massive economic crisis.

If emergency measures and the general conditions at the time – including devaluation and further credit from Britain – allowed Argentina to recover, the growing urban working class enjoyed little protection against social and economic problems. Discontent made them a ready audience for revolutionary ideas imported with European immigrants, and there was a series of strikes and armed uprisings. The government controlled these with police repression and the threat of deportation.

In 1912, Roque Sáenz Peña, leader of the PAN's liberal faction, enacted compulsory universal male suffrage. Hipólito Yrigoyen, leader of the newly formed Unión Cívica Radical (the Radicals), was elected president in 1916, marking the advent of popular politics after a century of elite rule.

IN CONTEXT

'Perón's genius was to recognise the growing importance of the Argentinian working class.'

The Radicals were to rule Argentina for the next 14 years. During this time, ten per cent of the rural population moved to the cities to join an upwardly mobile middle class. But Yrigoyen did nothing to alter conservative political and economic structures. From 1914, international prices for Argentina's produce declined and growth was curtailed.

After initial conciliatory overtures to the unions, which caused heated conservative protests, the government subsequently permitted their brutal repression. In Buenos Aires, the terror reached its height during La Semana Trágica (Tragic Week) in 1919, when the government put down a metalworkers' strike with the aid of gangs organised by the employers, who also attacked Jewish immigrants.

Nonetheless Yrigoyen, in typical caudillo style, enjoyed almost reverential support as a populist demagogue who displayed a paternal interest in his supporters – especially students, for whom he opened up free university education. He also made nationalist gestures by creating the state-owned petroleum company Yacimientos Petrolíferas Fiscales to exploit the country's new oil wealth (oil had been discovered in 1907), and opposing US colonialism. But when Yrigoyen was re-elected in 1928, he was in his twilight years. The Great Depression, which started in 1929, limited his ability to buy support by dipping into state coffers. His government was overthrown in 1930 by an army that he himself had helped to politicise.

The coup was backed by the rural oligarchy, who were hardest hit by the global crisis and resented their removal from power in 1916. But it also owed much to the rise of fascist ideologies imported from Europe, which saw little use for democracy. General José Félix Uriburu's decision to dissolve Congress, censor the media and imprison political opponents in 1930, and the subsequent election of his military rival General Agustín Justo, in 1931, inaugurated a period of what some termed 'patriotic fraud' – a populist ploy to prevent the Radicals from taking power.

Justo invested heavily in public works, including trunk roads from Buenos Aires to the provinces. Three new Subte (subway) lines – B, C and E – were inaugurated between 1930 and 1936, to supplement line A, the continent's oldest, which opened in 1913. Avenida 9 de Julio was also widened and the city's administration decided to broaden every third or fourth street between *avenidas* Caseros and Santa Fe, replacing the narrow colonial streets with today's busy transport arteries.

Production flourished with the start of World War II, which stemmed the tide of European imports. Argentina stayed neutral until late in the war, but by 1943 the conservative government had lost much of its lustre and the army again intervened.

IN CONTEXT

VOICE OF THE VOICELESS

The military was now installed as a de facto political party, running government for much of the rest of the century. But it had little idea what to do once in power. The issue was resolved with the emergence of another modern-day caudillo, army colonel Juan Domingo Perón, head of the then obscure labour department. He had a keen understanding of the power of the masses, picked up during his time as a military attaché in late-1930s Italy, where European fascist movements were taking off.

Perón's genius was to recognise the growing importance of the Argentinian working class and win the support of the union movement, which remains under his spell to this day. He was soon named vice-president and war minister and eventually presidential candidate. With Argentina's produce fetching bonanza prices, the healthy state of the economy allowed Perón considerable leeway with welfare projects, including housing and health schemes and the introduction of universal pensions.

Between 1936 and 1947, Buenos Aires's population swelled from 3,430,000 to 4,724,000. Most of the new inhabitants were poor migrants from the provinces – they increased from 12 to 29 per cent of the city's population – and they formed the bedrock of Perón's support. When the oligarchy decided, in 1945, that Perón had gone too far and arrested him, it was this underclass (known in Peronist lore as the *descamisados* or 'shirtless ones') that came to his rescue. On 17 October – still celebrated by Peronists as Día de la Lealtad (Loyalty Day) – workers massed in Plaza de Mayo to defend Perón. When he appeared around midnight on the balcony of the Casa Rosada, to the cheers of 300,000 supporters, it became evident that he was too powerful to be stopped, at least for the time being.

In February 1946, Perón won the first democratic election since Yrigoyen, launching propaganda and state welfare campaigns that converted him and his young, ambitious wife, Eva, into legends. While Perón fulfilled his duties, Eva dispensed the government's welfare budget, mixing easily with the poor, while enjoying her new wealth. She also took up the campaign that enacted women's suffrage in 1947.

Massive state intervention in the economy, however, was poorly handled. The railways, which were bought from the British to popular rejoicing, cost four times their official valuation. Mismanagement of the transport, gas and phone services damaged their efficiency. Nonetheless, in 1949 a new constitution was approved, guaranteeing social rights and allowing for Perón's re-election. Perón was elected to a second term in 1951, but less than two months after retaking office, Eva died from cancer, aged 33. Although Perón remained a crucial figure until his death in 1974, the heart had gone from Peronism. Moreover, Argentina had exhausted most of its reserves of gold and foreign exchange, and two bad harvests exposed the fragility of Perón's welfare drive. He promptly abandoned the more radical economic policies and passed a law protecting foreign investment.

Yet even as the economy recovered, Perón inexplicably launched a series of barbed attacks on the church, which had previously backed him. The move fuelled a growing opposition. In 1955, Plaza de Mayo was bombed by naval planes during an attempted military uprising, killing more than 200 government supporters. In response, Peronists torched city churches. Argentina had begun to spin out of control.

DISORDER TO DICTATORSHIP

The next two decades saw a fragmentation of Argentinian society that gave rise to a period of unparalleled barbarism. In December 1955, Perón was overthrown by the military and went into exile. His Partido Justicialista was banned and persecuted.

The Radicals split, too, and Arturo Frondizi, leader of their more combative wing, was elected president in 1958. Once in power, however, Frondizi alienated those who had voted for him by reneging on campaign promises, though he won friends in the oligarchy with free-market policies. Angered by news that the president had held a secret meeting in Buenos Aires with Ernesto 'Che' Guevara, Argentinian-born hero of the Cuban revolution, the army forced Frondizi's resignation in 1962.

Arturo Illia, leader of the Radicals' more conservative wing, was elected president the following year. Although his brief rule restored economic growth, the military was once again dissatisfied and retook power in 1966. The country continued its descent into chaos with the growth of guerrilla movements, led by the Montoneros, who had Peronist origins, and, later, the Trotskyite People's Revolutionary Army (ERP).

Eventually even Perón's opponents accepted that he was the only viable alternative to military rule, even though his movement was split between left-wing nationalists and conservatives. When Perón returned to Argentina in 1973, the tension erupted into bloodshed at a massive rally to welcome him. The violent conflict between the two factions left scores dead and the party split.

The Afro-Argentinian population

In 1778, they comprised 30 per cent of the population. What happened?

Candombe federal en la época de Rosas, Martín Boneo.

Every so often, a history programme on Argentinian TV will re-enact a famous battle from the country's independence struggle. The *mise-en-scène* is pretty standard: sideburned officers on horseback barking orders at raggedy foot soldiers. It's all very convincing except in one respect. Invariably, all of the actors are white.

It is a truth not universally acknowledged that huge numbers of enslaved black men and mulattoes (as people with one black and one white parent were then known) fought Argentina's 19th-century wars. Indeed, Afro-Argentinians (as they only later came to be known) comprised around 65 per cent of the most celebrated force in the country's history – General San Martín's Army of the Andes. The 'Liberator' recognised the value of slaves... as cannon fodder. Of the 2,500 Afro-Argentinians who crossed the Andes to liberate Chile in 1817, only 150 crossed back.

Despite the 1813 'Law of Wombs', which freed the future children of enslaved parents, slavery in Argentina wasn't formally abolished until 1853. The importance of black slaves in Argentina's formative centuries can be deduced from population statistics. The 1778 census found that blacks and mulattoes comprised 30 per cent of the total population. Most were sent to work in the provinces; those who remained in BA formed ad hoc communities in barrios such as San Telmo.

But as Argentina grew, the Afro-Argentinian community declined. The census of 1887 found that only two per cent (8,000 out of 433,000) of Argentinians were black or mulatto. So what had happened?

Historians have advanced several theories to explain the collapse of the Afro-Argentinian population, and there's probably some truth to all of them. Many freed slaves migrated to neighbouring countries such as Brazil and Uruguay, where black communities were larger and better organised. Thousands of others lost their lives in the murderous war with Paraguay (1864-70). Intermarriage was another factor: while black men were dying in border conflicts, black women were marrying white men and starting families with them. Their children's children's children would be more or less indistinguishable from the 'European' population.

This last factor raises the question of whether Afro-Argentinians are as 'absent' as they commonly thought to be. In a pilot census carried out in 2006, five per cent of respondents claimed that, to the best of their knowledge, one or several of their ancestors had African heritage. Extrapolated to the population as a whole, this means that around two million Argentinians know themselves to be descended from African slaves. To quote the title of a book on the subject by American historian George Reid Andrews, the Afro-Argentinians are forgotten, but not gone.

IN CONTEXT

After his election as president the same year, Perón sided with the right, forcing the Montoneros to abandon the movement after he harangued them at the May Day rally in 1974. He died two months later at the age of 74, leaving the country in the incapable hands of his third wife, Isabel. She in turn was dominated by José López Rega, whom Perón had promoted to minister of social welfare. López Rega is famous as the founder of the Triple A, a shadowy paramilitary organisation dedicated to the murder of political opponents. As the violence spiralled and the economy collapsed, much of the population breathed a sigh of relief when Isabel was replaced in 1976 by a military junta, led by General Jorge Rafael Videla.

The satisfaction was short-lived. The Proceso de Reorganización Nacional (known as *el Proceso*), presided over by Videla, imposed order by eliminating the regime's opponents and killing as many as 30,000 people, according to the estimates of human rights groups. A minority of those killed had taken part in the armed struggle, but the majority were trade unionists, political activists, rebellious priests and student leaders.

Most were kidnapped, taken to torture centres and then 'disappeared': buried in unmarked graves or heavily sedated and thrown from aircraft over the River Plate. In the face of such horrors, many Argentinians emigrated or were forced into exile – although many more stayed and feigned ignorance.

The military government introduced radical free-market policies, reducing state intervention and allowing a flood of imports, much to the detriment of local industry. The deregulation of financial markets created a speculative boom, while spiralling national debt left a legacy from which Argentina has yet to recover. Inflation soared again and the regime sought ways to distract the population. The 1978 World Cup, staged in Argentina, was one such distraction.

But although Argentina triumphed on the football field, growing opposition encouraged political parties and the church to raise their voices. The greatest courage was displayed by human rights groups, particularly the Mothers of the Plaza de Mayo, who marched in front of the Casa Rosada on a weekly basis to demand information on their missing children.

On 2 April 1982, under the leadership of General Leopoldo Galtieri, the military made one last desperate attempt to flame popular support, invading the Falkland Islands/Islas Malvinas, occupied by the British since 1833.

OFF TO WAR

Britain had earlier shown little interest in preserving the Falklands/Malvinas, even downgrading the British citizenship of the islands' 1,800 inhabitants. But the British prime minister Margaret Thatcher's unpopularity at home meant a tide of patriotic passion was as much in her interests as the junta's. On 1 May, a British submarine attacked and sank the Argentinian cruiser *General Belgrano*, killing almost 400 crew members. The ship was outside the 200-mile 'exclusion zone' that the British had imposed around the islands and was steaming away from them, although the Admiralty claimed that it might have intercepted British ships on their way to join the conflict. In retaliation, the Argentinians sank the British destroyer HMS *Sheffield*, killing 20.

A peaceful settlement was now impossible. Galtieri had trusted in US support, which never materialised; Washington eventually backed the British. The junta had an equally poor understanding of the military side of the conflict. After the sinking of the General Belgrano, the navy sat out the rest of the conflict, and Argentinian forces, badly led and composed largely of ill-equipped conscripts, were no match for a professional British task force. The defeat was the final nail in the regime's coffin. It was also a shock to a society that had been convinced by its press that Argentina was winning the war until the moment of surrender. Celebrated Argentinian writer Jorge Luis Borges famously stated that the Falklands/Malvinas war 'was a fight between two bald men over a comb'.

'Sovereignty of the Falklands/Malvinas is an unwaivable goal of the Argentinian people.'

Defeat brought the population back to its senses, although the issue has by no means gone away. Most Argentinians believe that '*las Malvinas son argentinas*' and the 1994 constitution ratified Argentina's claim to the islands, specifying that the recovery of sovereignty is an unwaivable goal of the Argentinian people. The islands appear on all Argentinian maps as Argentinian territory.

NUNCA MÁS
Democracy returned in 1983 with the election of Radical leader Raúl Alfonsín, one of the few political leaders to have maintained his distance from the military and opposed the Falklands War. The momentous changes afoot were described at the time as '*una fiesta de democracia*' and a party atmosphere prevailed.

But the new president lacked a majority in Congress and faced a range of vested corporate interests. He also faced stiff military opposition to the investigation of abuses committed during *el Proceso* – although he was helped by the publication in 1984 of *Nunca Más* (*Never Again*), a harrowing report of human rights abuses during the military government, identifying 9,000 victims. In the ensuing public outcry, the three juntas that presided over the Guerra Sucia (Dirty War) were tried in 1985 and stiff sentences handed down, including life for Videla – one of few cases of Latin American military leaders being imprisoned for their crimes. But in the face of military pressure, the government passed the Punto Final (Full Stop) law in 1986, limiting the trials.

Another military uprising during Easter Week in 1987 was met by impressive public demonstrations in support of democracy. But after persuading the rebels to lay down their arms, Alfonsín then caved in to the military's demands, passing the Obediencia Debida (Due Obedience) law, which excused the vast majority of the accused officers on the grounds that they were only following orders.

Among the trade unions Alfonsín initially attracted hostility with a failed attempt to introduce new labour laws. But 13 general strikes later, he capitulated and appointed a senior union leader as labour minister. He did little better with the economy. After initial economic stabilisation as a result of the Plan Austral in 1985, the government's nerve again failed when faced with serious restructuring.

MENEM'S MIRACLE ECONOMY
With the Peronist opposition gaining strength, Alfonsín finished his term in rout. His successor, Carlos Menem, was forced to take office five months early as the economy spun out of control, monthly inflation hit 197 per cent and looters raided supermarkets. Once in office, Menem abandoned his electoral promises and embraced neo-liberalism.

Under convertibility, introduced by finance minister Domingo Cavallo in 1991, the peso was pegged to the dollar at one-to-one. Privatisation resolved the problem of a bloated state sector, with handsome rewards for the business oligarchy. International capital was appreciative, too; the brisk opening of the economy left virtually all leading companies and financial institutions in foreign hands. Menem's decade in office saw total growth of around 35 per cent, and inflation was vanquished.

Menem ruled largely by decree and with little regard for constitutional niceties. But he finally dominated the military, and the mutiny by army rebels in December 1990 was the last of its kind. Although he dismayed human rights campaigners by granting an amnesty to the jailed junta leaders, he also starved the armed forces of funds, leaving

IN CONTEXT

them operationally incapable of another coup. Menem negotiated a constitutional amendment allowing him to win re-election in 1995, although the opposition extracted some changes in return, including elected authorities for Buenos Aires city.

But Menem's second term could not sustain the impetus of his first. Local industry largely collapsed under foreign competition, turning the industrial belt around Buenos Aires into a wasteland, populated by an increasingly bitter and impoverished underclass. Real wages dropped and the gulf between the rich and poor steadily widened. Menem's flamboyant style and love of showbiz glitter – la farándula, as Argentinians call it – went hand in hand with numerous high-profile corruption scandals.

In the 1991 'Yomagate' or 'Narcogate' scandal, various Menem officials were accused of links to money laundering and the illegal drugs trade. Menem's association with Alfredo Yabrán (a shadowy businessman implicated in the murder of journalist José Luis Cabezas in 1997), and allegations that his Middle Eastern connections (he is of Syrian descent) had hampered official investigations into the terrorist attacks on the city's Jewish communities in 1992 and again in 1994, were sufficient to give Argentinians the impression that every injustice led back to the presidential palace.

Tired of such excesses, the population turned to Fernando de la Rúa, head of Buenos Aires's city council and self-styled antithesis of Menem. Running at the head of the Alliance, formed by the Radicals and Frepaso, a smaller left-wing party, de la Rúa was elected president in December 1999. For some, the rise of such an unexceptional man to the head of a coalition government marked the death of the caudillo and a new period in Argentinian politics. In retrospect, the de la Rúa years can be seen as little more than a period in which international financiers demanded payback for investing in Menem's chimerical new economy. Throughout his term, de la Rúa maintained an image of calm – soporific even – government, but the manner with which the Alliance led the country to economic meltdown was devastating.

CHAOS AT THE BANK

The beginning of the end was a scandal over alleged vote-buying in the Senate, which dominated the media throughout the spring of 2000. The subsequent resignation of his popular vice president Carlos 'Chacho' Alvarez left de la Rúa weak and isolated. By this time, Brazil's decision to devalue its currency by 30 per cent the year before had caused Argentinian exports, still pegged to the dollar, to plummet. The ensuing crisis was met by severe austerity measures, but the recession worsened and eight billion dollars of emergency aid was sought from the International Monetary Fund.

It was not enough. The economic situation atrophied as unemployment rose to 20 per cent in Buenos Aires and far higher levels in many provinces. Argentina's credit rating fell to a historic low, its national bonds were designated as junk stock, and the dithering, quiet-mannered president was ill-equipped to reverse the inevitable economic disaster. In October 2001, the Peronist opposition took control of both houses in congress and began to lead a takeover. On 19 December, protests segued into full-scale riots and looting, prompting heavy-handed police repression; de la Rúa declared a state of emergency. On 21 December, de la Rúa resigned after massive rallies took to the streets and over 20 people were killed when riot police (and some shopkeepers) opened fire on looters, protesters and bystanders.

For Christmas 2001, Argentinians were gifted four presidents in just 11 days, the largest ever default in history – around US$150 billion – and the contempt of the IMF. When de la Rúa stood down, Ramón Puerta took over as caretaker between 20 and 23 December; Adolfo Rodríguez Sáa ruled between 23 December and 30 December but was ousted by fellow Peronists when he made it clear that he wanted more than an interim role; Puerta became caretaker again for 30 December and Eduardo Camano stood in between 31 December and 1 January.

The man then chosen by Congress to run Argentina until the next elections, Eduardo Duhalde, was a populist Peronist known for his opposition to neo-liberal ideology.

Riots, December 2001.

IN CONTEXT

For 15 months he managed, with the aid of his appointed finance minister, Roberto Lavagna, to contain the crisis, further exacerbated by the January 2003 devaluation of the peso. Slowly, a semblance of calm and order was restored in BA and across the country, although more than half of the population was left in poverty. Duhalde supported his successor, the modern and outgoing Néstor Kirchner.

A DYNAMIC DUO

Argentinians from across the political spectrum welcomed the arrival of Néstor Kirchner, who took office on 25 May 2003. Kirchner's no-nonsense populism was regarded as an asset, though his electoral mandate – just 22 per cent of the popular vote – was far from strong.

Opinion is divided over whether Kirchner was a good president, but he was unquestionably a lucky one. The mid-noughties commodities boom, and in particular China's insatiable demand for soya beans, helped push the Argentinian economy into overdrive, with annual growth averaging an impressive 7.7 per cent from 2004 to 2010. Kirchner used the proceeds to fund redistributive social programmes, which had the dual effect of boosting domestic consumption and shoring up his political power base. Kirchner's critics grew to deplore what they perceived as his authoritarian instincts and 'jobs for the boys' cronyism, but there is little doubt that he would have won the 2007 presidential election had he chosen to contest it.

Instead, he handed the baton to his wife, lawyer-turned-senator Cristina Fernández de Kirchner, who cruised into the Casa Rosada with an impressive 45 per cent plurality. Néstor, who hadn't retired in order to potter around the garden, continued to be an influential figure at the heart of government. Marked by high-profile conflicts with Argentina's agricultural sector and several media conglomerates but also by consistent economic growth, Cristina's first term was a qualified success.

Whether a refreshed Néstor would have re-run for office in 2011 is now a moot point. He died of a heart attack in October 2010, leaving behind a wife whose conspicuous grief was only matched by her determination to extend and solidify the Kirchner legacy. Cristina's opponents found themselves running against a popular president and an even more popular ghost – 'Néstor lives!' chanted the crowds at election rallies – and were duly crushed. Fernández de Kirchner secured a second term in office with an absolute majority of 54 per cent.

Buenos Aires Today

One foot in the past and another in the future for this city at a crossroads.

TEXT: MATT CHESTERTON

At the right time and in the right place – the pavement terrace of a steakhouse on a warm spring night, say, with the almost narcotic aroma of barbecue in your nostrils and the properly narcotic effect of half a bottle of malbec smoothing the edges from your skepticism – Buenos Aires seems like the greatest place on earth.

Porteños will happily admit to having a love-hate relationship with their city but of the two emotions, it's clearly love that burns strongest. However their affection has been tested by the fact that the decade of spectacular economic growth enjoyed by Argentina since the 2001/2002 economic crisis has not been mirrored in any spectacular improvement to their urban environment. The Buenos Aires that tourists adore, the city of glorious municipal buildings and monument-studded avenues, is real, brilliant and beautiful. But *porteños* are more concerned about the schools their children will attend than with the palaces their great-grandparents built.

Put another way, nostalgia just ain't what it used to be. It's all too obvious where Buenos Aires is coming from. But where is it going?

MEET THE PEOPLE

We can't talk about Buenos Aires without talking about *porteños*. Which is fine, because *porteños* – and they will confirm this – are worth talking about.

It won't hurt to rehash a couple of stereotypes. Not all of the 2,891,082 *porteños* counted by the 2010 census are in psychoanalysis, but those who do seek therapy are spoilt for choice: the city has 789 shrinks for every 100,000 *porteños*, the highest number per capita in the world. Even so, you're more likely to find a *porteño* in a steak house than on a couch. There are 800 licensed *parrillas* in the federal capital, plus any number of ad hoc 'steak shacks', which are little more than plastic awnings attached to barbecues. The average Argentinian consumes around 58 kilos (128 pounds) of beef per year. Only Uruguayans are more carnivorous.

But the times they are a-changin' and some beloved caricatures will have to change with them. The aforementioned beef consumption figure, for example, is on a downward trend, reflecting inflation's impact on the *porteño* diet as well as a growing preoccupation with healthier, more 'balanced' lifestyles.

If that's the yin of globalisation, the yang is the growing homogeneity of the city's high streets. Starbucks and Wal-Mart are replacing, respectively, the traditional cafés where the waiters are as old and weathered as the furniture, and the corner *almacénes* (general stores) where neighbours meet to exchange gossip and flash photos of their grandkids. In general, however, the disappearance of such places irks tourists more than it does *porteños*, who understandably fail to see why their city should be some kind of olde worlde theme park for jaded first worlders.

Jaded is not an adjective routinely applied to *porteños*. Passionate, freewheeling, voluble, convivial, tolerant, erudite, nocturnal, a little over the top from time to time (they will confirm this too) – yes. Whether it's down to nature, nurture or all those hours in therapy, *porteños* are easy to love and difficult to forget. The challenge has always been to build a city in which such people can not only live, but thrive.

MAKING BUENOS AIRES

Like all cities, Buenos Aires is a work in progress. The city government chose wisely, then, when they picked the slogan 'Haciendo Buenos Aires' or 'Making Buenos Aires'. You'll see it everywhere, in big black type on yellow billboards, marking roadworks, construction sites and other municipal projects. Whether the government lives up to this no-nonsense, we've-got-our-sleeves-rolled-up mantra is a matter for fierce debate. But it has at least succeeded in stating the mission, which is to make Buenos Aires a city fit for the 21st century.

In many respects the city has improved tangibly over the last decade and has become a tourist hotspot. A decade ago, many streets that had knolls of garbage steaming in the sun now have wheelie dumpsters. The smoke-free laws, widely derided as unenforceable when first floated, have proved to be... eminently enforceable. Violent crime, covered in lurid detail by the evening news bulletins, is less of a problem here than in supposedly sleepy Montevideo and booming São Paulo. If man's best friend still leaves pedestrians' worst nightmare on the pavement, more and more owners are wielding poo bags.

Some of these trends are global, of course. As regards the other achievements, there is no shortage of people who will say, 'What's a smoking ban and some dog poop amelioration compared to 160,000 people living in shanty towns, 4,000 families living in squats without gas or electricity, and many thousands of others living in fire-trap tenements?' Fair enough. So let's focus for a moment on one aspect of Buenos Aires that most everyone, irrespective of political affiliation or socio-economic status, agrees needs improving: transportation.

TRAINS, BIKES AND AUTOMOBILES

If we were living in the 1950s, Buenos Aires's mass transit network would be perfectly satisfactory. But we aren't, and it isn't. Argentina's breakneck economic growth in the noughties caused a spike in car ownership, with more and more vehicles entering circulation. Clearly, a swift and massive investment in the capital's creaking public transport system was needed to persuade some of these motorists to leave their rides in the garage and take the subway instead.

Clear to everyone except the powers that be, who have spent the last decade dragging their feet and squabbling among themselves. The Subte (as the Buenos Aires metro network is known) dates back to 1913, and the fleet of trains that runs on it is the oldest in the world. It carries 1,300,000 passengers per day but comprises a mere 52 kilometres (32 miles) of track, with six more kilometres under construction. To put this in perspective, New York City has 1,354km (841 miles) of track and London 402km (249 miles). In BA, some kind of strike action takes place every fortnight, with mass wildcat walkouts on the flimsiest of pretexts commonplace. On days like these the crescendo of honking car horns can probably be heard in Tierra del Fuego.

Much to the delight of environmentalists and bicycle manufacturers, mayor Mauricio Macri, like his London counterpart Boris Johnson, has made the promotion of sustainable transport one of the cornerstones of his administration. He's had some success, too. One hundred kilometres (62 miles) of protected and integrated bicycle lanes are either under construction or in operation. As of June 2012, 51,000 cyclists were registered in the Mejor en Bici (Better by Bike) programme, enabling them to book in advance one of the 700 free-to-use yellow bikes currently in circulation which they can then collect from stations scattered across the city. A study in 2012, commissioned by *La Nación* newspaper, found that getting from A to B by bicycle in the city took on average half the time it did by car.

Welcome though the success of Mejor en Bici is, only the most ardent pedalhead would suggest that the expansion of the city's bicycle lane network is any substitute for the modernisation of its subway system. But progress on the latter is frustratingly slow. One problem is that the city government took it for granted that everyone in the city would fancy the idea of having a subway station on their doorstep. This has not proved to be the case: work on the flagship Plaza Francia station, the first Subte stop in Recoleta and part of the 'H' line that will eventually link the south of the city with Retiro, had to be halted after the well-heeled burghers of the barrio, who want the station moved to a different location, obtained a court injunction. Plaza Francia was slated to be inaugurated in 2015, but at time of writing no one is sure when – or even where – the work will recommence.

STATE OF THE NATION

The federal capital is not an island, though both *porteños* and those who live in the interior of the country sometimes give the impression they'd like to dig a moat around the city. The Autonomous City of Buenos Aires (to give it its official name) is only autonomous in certain respects. National policies continue to shape the lives of citizens in a way most local policies do not. In periods of economic stability, people will gather around the water-cooler to discuss the new bicycle lane they rode on during their commute, as well as how blessed the nation is to have a footballer such as Lionel Messi; in periods of uncertainty the topics of such fat chewing sessions are more likely to be inflation, unemployment and currency controls.

In mid 2012, the shadow of uncertainty is darkening over both Argentina and Buenos Aires. The government claims that annual inflation is hovering at around ten per cent; independent economists and opposition politicians put the figure at more like 24 per cent: the average shopper simply knows that things are getting more expensive and that last year's staples are this year's luxuries.

Inflation is something Argentinians have lived with for years and is, in any case, the inevitable consequence of the kind of strong economic growth the country has experienced over the past decade. But the import restrictions and currency controls

IN CONTEXT

The First Family

Argentina's democratic dynasty shows little sign of abating.

The one thing we can say almost for certain about the current government led by Cristina Fernández de Kirchner, is that it will cease to exist in October 2015, when a new head of state must be elected (no Argentinian president can serve more than two successive terms). We say 'almost' because several mid-ranking *kirchneristas* have floated the idea of altering the constitution to allow Cristina to run for re-re-election.

So who's up next? High profile contenders include Daniel Scioli, former vice president of the nation and current governor of Buenos Aires province, and Mauricio Macri, the mayor of Buenos Aires city. But it's just as likely that Cristina will try to handpick her successor: someone who can be trusted with her legacy; someone obscure. After all, her late husband, Néstor, a dark horse who galloped all the way from Patagonia to the Casa Rosada, was such a candidate in 2003.

These are troubled waters, and in order to cross them, Cristina needs a bridge. As we go to print, *la presidenta* is still emotionally and sartorially in mourning for her husband, and relies increasingly on the man who she regards as the next best thing: her son.

Pale and rather pudgy, with an unruly shock of dark hair already streaked with grey, Máximo Kirchner looks more like a heavy World of Warcraft user than an Argentinian politician. However, if reports are to be trusted – Máximo doesn't even go on the record with sympathetic reporters, let alone speak at public events – Cristina and Néstor's eldest (born in 1977) has inherited his parents' sharp political instincts, along with their preference for establishing power bases outside of Argentina's traditional party political structures. La Cámpora, the pro-Kirchner youth movement Máximo established in 2003 to support his father, has grown from

something that resembled a Boy Scout troop with left-wing slogans into an influential and aggressive (albeit non-violent) wing of the ruling Frente de la Victoria (Victory Front) party – which is, of course, led by Máximo's mum.

Most pundits assume that Máximo will run for congress in 2015 – and after that, who knows? The idea of a Kirchner 'dynasty' excites some Argentinians and alarms others. Critics of the government have begun to highlight what they allege is the infiltration of La Cámpora activists into the higher echelons of state-run enterprises, most notably the national airline Aerolíneas Argentinas. Even Cristina's very conspicuous mourning – she often refers to 'he' or 'him' in her speeches, glancing upwards as she does so – has begun to draw flak: James Neilson of the English-language *Buenos Aires Herald* compared her to an 'old-fashioned Sicilian widow.'

Not every Kirchner has a passion for power. Cristina and Néstor's other child, Florencia, born in 1990, is as likely to be photographed on the beach as she is at one of her mother's rallies. Rumour has it she brushes off would-be suitors in nightclubs with a curt, 'You wouldn't be trying to chat me up if you knew who my mother was.' All things considered, she's probably right.

being ratcheted up at time of writing are something else entirely. It's one thing not to be able to buy an iPhone in Argentina: that's been the case for several years now. It's quite another (from the point of view of the privileged middle classes at least) when your supply of Parma ham is suddenly cut off due to a new import restriction. And it's something else entirely when the government announces that henceforth all applications to convert pesos to US dollars must be authorised by AFIP, Argentina's equivalent of the IRS or HM Revenue & Customs. With no access to global capital markets since its record-breaking default in December 2001, the Argentinian government needs the dollars to stay in the country so that it can pay its public debt and continue to finance its expensive state welfare programmes.

It's too early to judge whether the good times are over, or even to say that they are ending. It's instructive, however, to dig into newspaper archives from early 2002 and re-read what was being written then about Argentina, in the immediate aftermath of the country's economic crisis. 'I'm crying for Argentina!' wailed the average headline, and beneath it there'd be all manner of morose prognostications about the country's future (or lack of it). And what about Buenos Aires, one of the world's great cities? If you'd believed the pundits back then, you'd have thought it was about to disappear beneath the waves. But both the country and the city bounced back then, and whatever happens next, they will surely bounce back again.

Buenos Aires by Numbers

12.8 million population of greater BA (2,891,082 in the federal capital).
163,587 number of people who live in *villas* (slums) in BA's federal capital.
144 number of bus lines in BA.
4th BA's ranking in list of the world's noisiest cities.
90 percentage of BA's population composed of immigrants in 1890.
32 percentage of Argentinians who have visited a psychoanalyst at some point in their lives.
1 in 30 number of Argentinians who have undergone plastic surgery since 1970.
1 in 10 number of teenage girls in Argentina suffering from an eating disorder.
30 percentage of porteñas who are on a diet at any one time.
25.3 percentage of adults in BA who smoke.
20 percentage of Argentinians who are practising Roman Catholics.
33 Evita's age when she died of cancer.
7th Argentina's world ranking for wine consumption.
98 percentage of Argentinian households in which maté is drunk.
1st Argentina's world ranking for soy meal and soy oil exports.

1947 year Argentinian women were given the right to vote.
1987 year divorce became legal in Argentina.
2010 year same-sex marriage was legalised in Buenos Aires.
73.9 Argentinian male life expectancy.
80.54 Argentinian female life expectancy.
9.9% Argentina's official inflation rate in 2012, according to the government.
24% Argentina's inflation rate in 2012, according to independent economists.
50,000 estimated number of tangos ever composed.
14,000 number of left-wing dissidents 'disappeared' under the 1976-83 military rule according to official reports.
30,000 number of left-wing dissidents 'disappeared' according to human rights groups.
338 number of streets in Buenos Aires named after military figures.
58 number of streets in Buenos Aires named after women.
283 number of tree species growing in Buenos Aires.
4,780 number of tombs in Recoleta cemetery.
29 number of merry-go-rounds in BA.

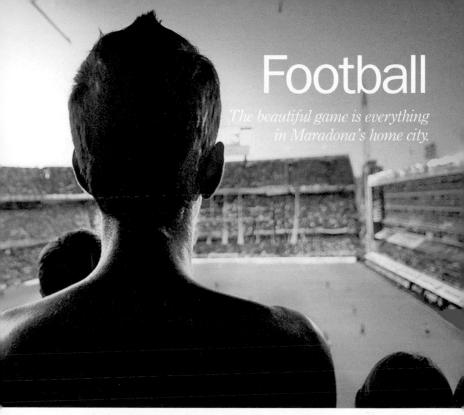

Football

The beautiful game is everything in Maradona's home city.

Football. Soccer. *Fútbol*. Call it what you will. Just don't call it insignificant. In Argentina, it's not just an immensely popular game, it's a perennial mania that envelopes the nation. It's omnipresent on the television, radio, in printed media and local websites. The topic pops up in conversation so frequently that if you're unable to offer an opinion on Boca's backline or Lionel Messi's best position, you risk becoming a social outcast. If you have nothing to say about River's relegation or the latest refereeing controversy, you're likely to be subjected to suspicious rear-view glances from your taxi driver and dispirited sighs from your building's doorman. Haven't adopted a team of your own yet? Make your selection as soon as possible, even if you have little knowledge of the league. You may already have a favourite club; otherwise you could choose the one with the closest stadium or with the shirt colours that look best on you. But remember: once you've chosen your club, there's no switching of allegiances allowed. From there, it should only be a matter of time before you find yourself sucked in to the loony, polemical, fascinating and ridiculously entertaining world of Argentinian *fútbol*.

A NATIONAL PASSION

It was British sailors in the 1860s who first introduced football to Buenos Aires, their shore leave kick-abouts on the city's dusty plazas attracting first the attention and then the participation of locals. By the end of the 19th century, amateur clubs had been founded and the game began its rise from fringe pastime to national pursuit. So speedy was this process that, in 1930, Argentina reached the final of the first World Cup, losing to hosts Uruguay. The *selección* (as the Argentinian national team is known) gave an early demonstration of the two contrasting elements that always seem to define their play: brilliant skill and murky controversy. Unable to agree on which type of ball to use for the match, it was decided that an Argentinian brand would be used in the first half and a Uruguayan one in the second. At half-time, Argentina were leading 2–1; by the end they had lost 4–2. Still muttering about 'rigged balls', Argentinian footballers turned professional the following year.

Achievement and notoriety would continue to bless and dog Argentinian football in equal measures. In the famously ill-tempered quarter-final between Argentina and England in the 1966 World Cup, Alf Ramsey's 'wingless wonders' beat the South Americans 1–0. After Argentinian captain Antonio Rattín had been sent off for dissent, the match degenerated into a scrappy, dirty affair, and a rivalry was born that endures to this day. Argentina finally got their hands on the World Cup trophy in 1978 when, playing on home turf, they beat the Netherlands 3–1. For the ruling military junta, it was a public relations coup to add to their military one of two years before. However, there were rumours that the Peruvian team was bribed to throw their group match against Argentina, allowing the latter to reach the final ahead of Brazil.

But 1986 in Mexico was a different ball game. The record states that Argentina won the World Cup by edging out West Germany 3–2 in the final. Far more memorable, however, was the quarter-final against England, illuminated by the divine talent and devilish opportunism of Diego Maradona. 'El Diez' (after his shirt number) scored one goal through pure skill – often cited as the best ever – and another through sheer cheek, knocking the ball past a floundering Peter Shilton with his hand – the infamous 'Hand of God' goal. It was sweet revenge for 1966; some – Maradona included – have also referred to the win as payback for the Falklands/Malvinas conflict of 1982.

Argentina made the final again in 1990, but since then the team has largely failed to impress on the big stage, despite consistently entering the tournament as one of the favourites. In the 2010 World Cup, Maradona attempted to inspire the side to glory once again, this time as coach. Despite some quirky team selections, bizarre sideline antics and an almost complete disregard for tactics, Diego guided his team to the quarter-finals with several entertaining displays. Unfortunately for Messi and co, a powerful German team exposed the flaws in the scheme and routed Argentina 4–0 to brutally put a stop to talk of another Maradona miracle.

With the 2014 tournament being held in neighbouring Brazil, Argentina will once more be regarded as a serious title contender. Whether it's a tale of joyous victory or agonising defeat, there's no doubt that another major chapter in the history of the *selección* is about to be written.

TOP TOURNAMENTS

All professional football in Argentina comes under the aegis of the Argentinian Football Association (AFA). The only significant hiatus in top-flight action comes during the summer months of December and January when the Torneo de Verano (Summer Tournament) is held. This is a chance for the bigger clubs to give their second-rung players a run out; nonetheless, the matches, held in cities like Mar del Plata, still attract big crowds.

For teams in the *primera división*, the rest of the year is divided into two distinct seasons: the *clausura* (closing) tournament from the end of January to May; and the *apertura* (opening) from August to December. If you're wondering why the *clausura* comes at the beginning of the year, take a deep breath and then forget about it.

The system of relegation and promotion is an even harder nut to crack. Teams move between divisions in accordance with their average points score over a three-year period. So it's theoretically possible to win the *primera* and be relegated from it on the same day. Cynics (that is to say, everyone bar the AFA) believe this system was introduced to make it virtually impossible for the bigger teams to be relegated (which highlights just how dismal River Plate were over a number of years to be relegated).

THE RIVALRIES
Possibly the biggest story in the last 100 years of Argentinian football was the relegation from the first division of River Plate in June 2011. In terms of success and popularity, River, along with their arch-rival Boca Juniors, are the biggest club in the land. However, after years of financial mismanagement by club directors, at the end of the 2011 *clausura* the team was forced into a play-off against second division side Belgrano de Córdoba for the right to remain in the top flight. The giants from the neighbourhood of Núñez defied all expectations and somehow managed to lose the play-off, sparking tears – and riots – from distraught fans across the country. It took one soul-destroying year in the second division for River to regain their place in the *primera*. Thus, after a year's hiatus, the *superclásico*, Boca versus River, is back on the agenda – now with extra spice added as Boca fans will certainly not let their opponents forget their little foray into lower division purgatory. This bucket-list encounter is one of the world's great sporting spectacles. If you get the chance to go to one of these matches, don't pass it up.

STRAIGHT SHOOTERS
Argentina is known throughout the footballing world as a tremendous producer of talent. Argentinian footballers can be divided into two categories; those who play for big bucks overseas and those who play in the local league for less-big bucks.

At the very top of the tree sits Lionel Messi, the freakishly talented forward who plays his club football for Barcelona and notches up World Player of the Year awards at the same rate that the rest of us achieve birthdays. The shy, diminutive goal-getter is captain of Argentina's national team and is already considered by some to be the greatest footballer of all time. The one gap in his resume is a World Cup – and 42 million Argentinians are watching that space very intently.

There are a bevy of other superstars playing in Europe who are the proud bearers of Argentinian passports, among them Sergio Agüero (Manchester City), Javier Mascherano (Barcelona), Gonzalo Higuaín and Ángel di María (Real Madrid).

FOOTY ETIQUETTE
On match day, follow the well-honed rituals of any Argentinian football fan. 1) Wake up to the sound of non-stop football punditry on the radio, shower with team-branded soap, then pop on your retro 1972 top. 2) Pick up a copy of the daily sporting paper *Olé* and head to a preordained bar for a Quilmes beer while deconstructing the team line-up. 3) Get to the stadium early and chant derogatory songs at the fenced-off visiting fans, buy a *choripán* (sausage sandwich) – possibly the most dangerous custom – and a fluffy, naff hat. 4) After the *barra brava* (frenzied fans) have slipped past the police to the stadium, make your way through various friskings into the stand to the overwhelming sight of 40,000 bouncing, singing fans. 5) Boo and whistle as the referee walks on to the pitch (it doesn't matter that he hasn't made a decision yet), and scream the worst word you know in Spanish as the opposition appear. As your team walk out, throw the pile of ripped newspaper you were just handed into the air for a spectacular ticker-tape effect. 6) Spend the next 90 minutes shouting yourself hoarse, enjoying the thrilling game and gawping at the unique spectacle that is the fans of Argentinian football.

Sights

Puerto Madero. *See p76.*

The Centre

Palaces, plazas and protests in the city's bustling centre.

French-style palaces, wide avenues and green plazas meet choking traffic, scuttling office workers, flocks of tourists and clamorous protestors: the city's historic and commercial nerve centre, *el Centro*, is where reminders of an erstwhile splendour and utopian dream compete with the grittier, more cynical realities of the 21st century.

The city's contrasts and contradictions are more evident here than anywhere else: by night, *cartoneros* (cardboard collectors) haul their carts and sift through rubbish, while just a stone's throw from such poverty is the affluence surrounding Plaza San Martín.

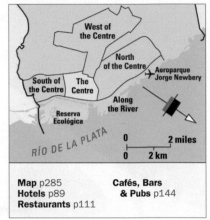

West of the Centre

North of the Centre

Aeroparque Jorge Newbery

South of the Centre

The Centre

Along the River

Reserva Ecológica

RÍO DE LA PLATA

0   2 miles
0   2 km

Map p285
Hotels p89
Restaurants p111

Cafés, Bars
& Pubs p144

PLAZA DE MAYO

Subte A, Plaza de Mayo or D, Catedral/bus 9, 10, 17, 39, 45, 93, 152.

Tradition and convention both dictate that if you want to do something big in Buenos Aires, you do it in **Plaza de Mayo**. Despite being shabby and overrun with pestiferous pigeons and tiresome souvenir hawkers, BA's central square remains the cockpit of Argentina's remarkable narrative. On its palm-bowered stage have strutted, preened and fretted revolutionaries, reactionaries, human rights icons, rock stars, visionaries, lunatics, demagogues and Madonna.

The original *plaza mayor* (main square), was laid out by the city's founder Juan de Garay in the 1580s, shortly after the successful foundation of Buenos Aires. Garay still stands as a bronze statue in a tiny square just metres north-east of the plaza, beside an oak tree from his Basque motherland.

The colonial plaza became Plaza de Mayo to commemorate 25 May 1810, when the masses assembled there to celebrate the deposition of the Spanish viceroy and the swearing in of the Primera Junta (First Council). Famously, it was the site of the great gatherings of the *descamisados* or 'shirtless ones' under Perón and was bombed by the military in 1955 (to oust the aforementioned general); bullet holes

are visible in the walls of the **Ministerio de Economía** building on Hipólito Yrigoyen next to Avenida Paseo Colón. The Madres de Plaza de Mayo still march here every Thursday at 3.30pm to protest the 'disappearance' of their loved ones during the last military government, which itself announced the invasion of the Falklands/Malvinas islands (a last-ditch attempt to revive its flagging popularity) in early 1982, in front of vast crowds in the Plaza.

At the plaza's centre is the **Pirámide de Mayo**, an obelisk raised in 1811 for the anniversary of the May revolution. The Madres' internationally famous symbol – a white headscarf that alludes to motherhood and to the nappies of their lost children – is painted on the tiles circling the pyramid. To the east is a statue of independence patriot Manuel Belgrano – the only national hero to be honoured with a statue in the plaza.

Glowing like a psychedelic fantasy, especially at sunset, the **Casa Rosada** (Pink House) is the presidential palace (not the residence, which is out in the sticks in Olivos). Built between 1862 and 1885, it stands where Buenos Aires's 17th-century fort, later the viceroy's palace, used to be. The splendour of its European Renaissance-style façade came together in several stages. The emblematic rosy hue originated during Sarmiento's 1868-74 presidency: it was then

Plaza de Mayo.

SIGHTS

common practice to add ox blood to whitewash
to provide colour and thicken the mix.

The central balcony has been the soapbox
of diverse demagogues and dictators, although
the Peróns used the lower balcony, to be 'closer
to the people'. This was also used by Madonna
in the filming of Alan Parker's *Evita*, despite
protests by Peronists who felt the material
girl was tarnishing the memory of Saint Evita.

Surrounding the Plaza de Mayo are a
number of important buildings. On the corner
of Avenida Rivadavia and 25 de Mayo is the
Banco de la Nación, the country's state
bank. The present building, constructed
between 1940 and 1955, is topped by an
enormous, neo-classical dome.

Heading west on Avenida Rivadavia is the
neoclassical **Catedral Metropolitana** (*see
below*). The Plaza's other main building, the
Cabildo, was HQ of the city council from 1580
to 1821, and the place where revolutionaries
took the first steps towards independence.
Today it houses the **Museo Histórico
Nacional del Cabildo y de la Revolución
de Mayo** (*see p41*).

FREE Catedral Metropolitana
*Avenida Rivadavia, y San Martín (4331 2845).
Subte A, Plaza de Mayo or D, Catedral or E,
Bolívar/bus 24, 64, 130.* **Open** 7.30am-6.30pm
Mon-Fri; 9am-7pm Sat, Sun. **Admission** free.
Map 285 E11.
On the north side of the plaza is this neoclassical
cathedral, whose strictly-by-the-book columns and
cornices look rather incongrous amid all the chaos.
The cornerstone for the original church was laid by
Juan de Garay in 1580 (perhaps he did a poor job of
it as the structure has collapsed five times since
then). The plan for the present cream-coloured
building, the sixth cathedral on this site, was
hatched in 1753; the first façade was blessed in 1791
and the final touches were added in 1910. The high
baroque interior arches create a sombre atmosphere,
while the rococo main altar and the organ (dating
from 1822) stand out. The right-hand nave houses
the mausoleum containing – since 1880 – the
repatriated remains of the Liberator José de San
Martín (who died in France in 1850). The most
striking feature of the building's Greco-Roman
exterior is the frontispiece, depicting the reunion of
Jacob and his sons with Joseph in Egypt.

AN IRISH POSTCARD IN BUENOS AIRES

Happy Hour & Promotions all day long
6,00 p.m. to 8,00 p.m.

Live bands and dj's play
everyday around 11,30 p.m.

Best Irish food
in town

Six differents
premium draught beers

Whiskey Club with more
than 80 brands

Major credit cards
accepted

THE KILKENNY
Irish Pub & Restaurant
BUENOS AIRES

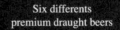

M.T. de Alvear 399 • Downtown Buenos Aires • Tel. (54-11) 4312-7291/9179
E-mail: thekilkenny@thekilkenny.com.ar

Museo Histórico Nacional del Cabildo y de la Revolución de Mayo

Bolívar 65, entre Avenida de Mayo y Hipólito Yrigoyen (4334 1782). Subte A, Plaza de Mayo or D, Catedral or E, Bolívar/bus 28, 56, 105, 126. **Open** 10.30am-5pm Wed-Fri; 11.30am-6pm Sat, Sun. **Admission** AR$6; free under-12s. Free Fri. **No credit cards. Map** p285 E10.

The Cabildo was HQ of the city council between 1580 and 1821, and was where the seeds of Argentina's revolution were sown. Seemingly the oldest building on the plaza, it recovered its colonial style only in the 1940s, several decades after six of its original 11 arches were lopped off to make room for Avenida de Mayo and Avenida Julio A Roca. The museum comprises a number of austere rooms in which you'll find valuable items such as a magnificent gold and silver piece from Oruro (Bolivia); one of the country's first printing presses; and a number of items relating to the English invasions. Behind the building is a shaded colonial patio, the site of a handicrafts fair on Thursdays and Fridays.

AVENIDA DE MAYO

Subte A, Plaza de Mayo/bus 39, 60, 64, 168.

Opened in 1894, the grand Avenida de Mayo, its spacious pavements dotted with plane trees, is the most obvious example of Buenos Aires trying to emulate the wide boulevards of Paris. In reality, though, it's more closely associated with Spain, due to the large numbers of Spanish immigrants who settled in the neighbourhood.

Newly elected presidents make their way down this avenue to the Casa Rosada after being sworn in at the Palacio del Congreso. Common folk travel below, on Latin America's oldest underground railway, opened in 1913, just nine years after New York's subway started rolling. Although the Subte's *línea* A is losing its old lustre to modernisation, the retro posters and fittings at Perú station (Avenida de Mayo between Bolívar and Perú) recalls the Argentina that used to be.

Despite run-down sections, modern towers and some of the more faded-looking Spanish restaurants along and around the avenue, fine European-style buildings with exquisite architectural details still abound. The best example of art nouveau, richly decorated with elements from the natural world, is the **Hotel Chile**, on the corner of Santiago del Estero.

Heading west from Plaza de Mayo, the first highlight is the Gallic *La Prensa* newspaper building, from 1896, now the city government's **Casa de la Cultura** (*see right*).

The avenue's outstanding edifice and one of the city's notable buildings is the **Palacio Barolo** (*see right*). It was built as, and remains, office space, but you can enter its ground floor passageway with its gargoyles, Latin inscriptions and several kiosks that look like they were stolen from the set of *Brief Encounter*. Another stunning building marks the avenue's west end. With its two slender domes the **Edificio de la Inmobiliaria**, built in 1910 for an insurance company, is a nattily eclectic celebration of several styles including Italianate balconies and Eastern motifs. From here it's a few steps to the Plaza del Congreso.

FREE Casa de la Cultura

Avenida de Mayo 575, entre Perú y Bolívar (4323 9669). Subte A, Perú or D, Catedral or E, Bolívar/bus 24, 29, 64, 86, 105, 111. **Open** *Temporary exhibitions only* 9am-8pm Mon-Fri. Tours 4pm, 5pm, Sat; every hr 11am-4pm Sun. Closed Jan. **Admission** free. **Map** p285 F10.

Built in 1896, this was once the headquarters of *La Prensa* newspaper but now belongs to the city government. This building's French feel goes beyond the façades – the impressive Salón Dorado, inspired by the Palace of Versailles, hosts chamber music concerts each Friday at 7pm (entry is free), tango concerts on Sunday evenings and the odd temporary exhibition during the week. A siren on top, sounded at crucial moments in the city's history, was last heard in 1983 when democracy was restored. (But curiously not in 1986 when Argentina won the World Cup.)

Palacio Barolo

Avenida de Mayo 1370, entre San José y Santiago del Estero. Subte A, Sáenz Peña/bus 12, 37, 64, 86. **Map** p285 F9.

One of the city's finest and most emblematic buildings, this 1923 construction is a neo-Gothic allegorical tribute to the 100 cantos of Dante's *Divine Comedy*. Hell is on the ground floor: Latin inscriptions taken from nine different literary works represent the nine infernal circles and are engraved on the entrance hall's nine vaults. Above, the first 14 floors comprise Purgatory (and if you get stuck in one of the picturesque but temperamental lifts, you'll know what it's like to be a soul in waiting), while Paradise can be found in the upper reaches. At the very top is a domed lighthouse, representing God. Ask at the desk about guided tours, some of which are led by English-speaking guides.

CONGRESO & TRIBUNALES

Subte A, Congreso or B, Uruguay/bus 60, 102, 168, 180.

Plaza del Congreso is the popular name for the three squares filling the three blocks east of the Palacio del Congreso. Rundown in recent years by protestors, vagrants and metal thieves who hijack commemorative plaques, all that's left of its once stately elegance are the shady jacarandas, *tipa* and *ceibo* trees (whose red

SIGHTS

Terrific tours

Buenos Aires for one and all.

FOR THE TANGO-LOVER
Carlos Gardel is practically a saint
in Buenos Aires and with María Leila
Ivancovich's **Caminos de Gardel** tour
(http://marialeliadebsas.com.ar)
visitors get to retrace some of his
favourite haunts, most of which are
in the neighbourhood of Abasto.
You'll also visit Gardel's mausoleum
in the Cementerio de Chacarita. If
you want to don your dancing shoes,
then let BA-based travel operators
Tango Focus (www.tangofocus.com)
arrange classes or take you to the
city's best *milongas*.

FOR THE INTELLECTUAL
The **Argentinian Labyrinth** tour by
Eternautas (www.eternautas.com)
documents the city's political ups and
downs from past to present and covers
any questions you may have regarding
politics, history and culture. Guides are
university professors or students with
a penchant for history and foreign
languages. Other tours offered by
Eternautas include **Images of Buenos
Aires, Evita and Peronism, Paris of
South America** and, if you're looking
for an out-of-town experience, **San
Isidro and Tigre**.

FOR THE PEDALHEAD
Biking Buenos Aires (www.bikingbueno
saires.com) makes good use of BA's new
cycle paths on its half- and full-day city
highlights tours. Friendly guides strike
just the right balance of peddling, walking,
talking and eating. For a breath of fresh
air, **Urban Biking** (www.urbanbiking.com)
offers all-day cycling and kayaking tours
out of town to Tigre and the Delta on
eco-friendly bamboo bikes.

FOR THE LOAFER
If you're tired from the long flight to BA,
Opcion Sur (www.opcionsur.com.ar) is
geared towards non-walkers and uses
audio-visuals. Its tour bus is air-conditioned
and stops at all the city's must-sees,
showing passengers archive footage of
the epoch-defining events that took place
in the barrio the bus is passing through at
the time. It's a spoon-fed approach but
no less enjoyable for that.

FOR ARTY TYPES
Happy snappers looking to explore
less well-known barrios will enjoy **Foto
Ruta**'s (www.foto-ruta.com) twice-weekly
interactive photography tours, run by
friendly pros. Highly recommended.
The **Graffitimundo** team (www.graffiti
mundo.com), meanwhile, are the city's
authorities on all things street art.
Bilingual guides steer you around
the sprayed, painted and stenciled
streets of BA on a three-hour tour.
On Sundays they run graffiti tours
on two wheels with Biking Buenos
Aires (*see left*).

FOR THE CHEAPSKATE
Proving that the best things in life can be
free, **BA Free Tour** (www.bafreetour.com)
offers guided walks around the downtown
area, stopping off at landmarks such as
the Obelisco, Casa Rosada and Congreso.
Meanwhile, newcomers on a budget will
appreciate the induction to the Subte
and bus systems given by the English
guide who runs **Buenos Aires Local
Tours** (www.buenosaireslocaltours.com),
taking in Palermo, Abasto and the
city centre. Tips are appreciated on
both tours.

FOR A SLICE OF JEWISH LIFE
Ernesto Yattah from **Jewish Buenos Aires**
(4811 0108) shows you the city through
a Jewish frame on fascinating five-hour
tours exploring Plaza de Mayo, Once and
Belgrano. He takes you inside synagogues,
to the sites of terrorist attacks and explains
Jewish life today, while examining the role
Sephardic crypto-Jews, Eastern European
immigrants and Jewish gauchos have
played in Argentinian history.

FOR THE BEATNIK
If you're looking for something out of the
ordinary, **Cultour**'s (www.cultour.com.ar)
Buenos Aires Traces tour explores the
essence of the city by deconstructing
some iconic lives and events. Guides
associated with the University of Buenos
Aires will spark your interest in the city's
recent history by examining the scars
left by bomb shrapnel as well as
plaques marking the locations
where protesters fell.

Palacio del Congreso

blossom is the national flower) that colour the plaza in spring. The plaza contains a version of Rodin's *Thinker* and a statue of Mariano Moreno, one of the May revolutionaries.

The western section of the plaza is dominated by the **Monumento a los Dos Congresos**, in remembrance of the first constitutional assembly held in 1813 and the Declaration of Independence three years later in Tucumán. The monument's centrepiece is the statue of the republic, propped up by a plough and waving a victorious laurel branch.

Like Argentina's federal constitution, which was inspired by the US model, the Greco-Roman **Palacio del Congreso** (*see p44*) is a dome-and-column affair resembling Washington's bicameral legislature. Completed in 1906, its extravagant interior can be visited with a guided tour (no access when in session).

On the corner to the right of the palace is a historical *confitería* (closed since 1996) where politicians used to sip their espressos between sessions. It's called **El Molino**, a reference to the windmill above its entrance. The small **Teatro Liceo** (*see p219*), on the corner of Rivadavia and Paraná, is one of the oldest playhouses in Buenos Aires. It opened in 1876 and has been the stage for many of the country's greatest thespians. It's also where a struggling young actress named Eva Perón once performed.

To visit the rest of civic Buenos Aires, a good starting point is **Diagonal Norte** (*photo p46*) running north-west from Plaza de Mayo. The avenue is a masterpiece of urban harmony;

every building is ten storeys tall with a second-floor balcony, though a rigidly monumental style dominates many of its edifices. Empty on weekends, the Diagonal's finest architecture is on the corner of *calle* Florida where Bank Boston shows off its decorative façade and heavily decorated gilt ceiling of the inner hall (visible during bank opening hours only).

Diagonal Norte links the Plaza de Mayo with the barrio of Tribunales, where the law courts are surrounded by solicitors' offices, law firms and kiosks selling legal pamphlets. The avenue's disappointing dead-end is the **Palacio de Justicia**, seat of the Supreme Court and another popular venue for public protest. Stretching out in front as far as Avenida Córdoba is the **Plaza Lavalle**, an attractive green spot rich in history and sprawling *ceibo* trees. Its focal point is a monument to Juan Lavalle, one of the military heroes who crossed the Andes with San Martín. Also look out for *La Fuente de los Bailarines* (Dancers' Fountain), a simple and touching memorial to two dancers from the Teatro Colón killed in a plane accident in 1971. Across the Plaza, and filling a whole block, is the **Teatro Colón** (*see p205*) itself. With its regular lines and tempered classicism, it's a key landmark and an internationally renowned venue for opera and classical music.

On the corner of Avenida Córdoba and Libertad, is the **Teatro Cervantes** (*see p219*), the capital's grand old lyric theatre. Unveiled in 1921, its façade is a near replica of the university at Alcalá de Henares in Spain, where Don Quixote's creator was born. Equally

SIGHTS

impressive inside, the building also houses the **Museo Nacional del Teatro** (*see below*), a tribute to Argentina's thespian history.

It's just a short walk from here to the grand asphalt canyon of Avenida 9 de Julio and its iconic monument, the **Obelisco** (*see below*).

🆓 Museo Nacional del Teatro

Avenida Córdoba 1199, y Libertad (4816 7212). Subte D, Tribunales/bus 23, 39, 109. **Open** 10am-6pm Mon-Fri. **Admission** free. **Map** p285 H10.

Right next to the Teatro Cervantes, BA's Museum of Theatre offers the stage-struck visitor a fascinating insight into Argentina's thespian heritage, from the earliest colonial times up until the present day. Among the exhibits are costumes and personal effects, photographs of celebrated actors, writers and directors, programmes and documents.

▶ *If you're inspired to tread the boards, The Actors Studio (see p220) runs workshops.*

El Obelisco

Avenida 9 de Julio, y Avenida Corrientes. Subte B, Carlos Pellegrini or C, Diagonal Norte/bus 6, 7, 9, 10, 56, 67, 70, 100, 105. **Map** p285 G10.

The Obelisco was built to mark four of the city's key historical events: the first and the final foundation of Buenos Aires; the 1880 declaration of the city as the country's federal capital; and to mark the site of the demolished church of San Nicolás where the national flag was first flown. When the 68-metre (223-foot) obelisk was completed in 1935, the critics went to town, describing it as an undignified, phallic, cement spike. Radical feminist groups suggested lopping it in half, and three years after its inauguration the city's parliament voted for its demolition. The decision was ignored and the Obelisco became, over time, the city's postcard emblem and a symbol of its self-conscious monumentalism.

▶ *A 67-metre red condom wrapped the phallic symbol on World AIDS Day in 2005.*

🆓 Palacio del Congreso

Hipólito Yrigoyen 1849, entre Entre Ríos y Combate de los Pozos (4010 3000). Subte A, Congreso/bus 12, 37, 60, 102. **Guided tours** *Spanish* 10am, 11am, 5pm, 7pm Mon, Tue, Thur, Fri. *English* 11am, 4pm Mon, Tue, Thur, Fri. Closed sometimes Jan. **Admission** free. **Map** p285 G9.

Argentina's constitution was inspired by its US equivalent. In a similar spirit of benign plagiarism, the Palacio del Congreso is a dome-and-column affair designed to resemble Washington's bicameral legislature. Depending on your architectural and/or political preferences, the Palace is either an awe-inspiring shrine to the democratic principle or an over-elaborate wedding cake. Completed in 1906, the Congress building's very extravagant interior, which includes an extensive network of basements and bunkers, can be visited by guided tour. (The advertised tour schedule is notoriously unreliable; call in advance if you want to arrange a guided visit.) Note that all 72 Senate seats have a button for direct calls to the cafeteria. *Photo p43.*

MICROCENTRO

Subte B, Florida or D, Catedral/bus 4, 20, 56, 93, 152.

It's every claustrophobe's worst nightmare – on weekdays during business hours the whole downtown district becomes a maelstrom of porteños shopping, working, running, shouting, flouting traffic laws, shouting some more, and generally fulfilling their big-city stereotype.

The district was once known as 'the 20 blocks that rule the country'. It has the largest concentration of financial institutions in the country, extending almost the entire length of *calles* Florida, San Martín and Reconquista (named after the reconquest, when Buenos Aires repelled the English in 1806-07). Many of the banks were built during the first half of the 20th century, at a time when affluent Argentinians had money to deposit. A good example is the former **Banco Tornquist**, at Bartolomé Mitre 559, on the first section of street to be paved in BA. A financially-themed museum is the excellent **Museo Histórico y Numismático del Banco de la Nación Argentina** (*see p45*).

To see how affluent porteños lived during the economic boom of the late 19th century, step into the **Museo Mitre** (*see p46*) – home of former president and founder of *La Nación* newspaper, Bartolomé Mitre. It contains his rich library specialising in American history.

At the corner of Reconquista and Perón, protected by wonderful wrought-iron gates, is the 18th-century **Basílica Nuestra Señora de la Merced**, the richly decorative façade of which was restored in 1905. Next door, the **Convento de San Ramón**'s patio contains small attractive shops and hidden lunchtime eateries overlooking an attractive garden.

Along the west side of Avenida Leandro N Alem, more commonly called *el bajo* – meaning the low place – runs an almost uninterrupted arcade packed with banks, cafés, the stock exchange and, on its eastern side, the colossal **Correo Central**, located at Sarmiento 151. Inaugurated after 41 years of construction in 1928, the Central Post Office is one of BA's best examples of French-inspired classical architecture. Philatelists will want to check out the little museum inside. Diagonally opposite the post office's north-east corner is **Luna Park** (*see p208*), where Carlos Gardel's funeral was held in 1935 and where in 1944 Perón met Eva. It's now a music venue.

SIGHTS

El Obelisco.

Though once an elegant thoroughfare, Florida is now unashamedly commercial. However, amid the street vendors, you can still find traces of its refined past.

As Florida's old glamour wanes, more modern variations on retail sophistication spring up. **Galerías Pacífico** (*see p155*) is the city's most aesthetically inspired mall. In its south-east corner (with an entrance at the corner of Viamonte and San Martín) is the **Centro Cultural Borges** (*see right*), built in memory of one of Argentina's greatest writers, and a thriving venue for the arts. Behind it on the opposite corner of San Martín and Viamonte is the 18th-century church of **Santa Catalina**.

Lavalle, for pedestrians only between San Martín and Carlos Pellegrini, makes Florida look chic and classy. It's packed with cinemas, fast-food outlets, evangelical churches and seedy, subterranean girly bars.

Close by, but extending beyond the Microcentro, is Avenida Corrientes. Though it's been an *avenida* since 1936, people still fondly call it a *calle* (street). Until the 1970s it was the mecca for tango artists and BA's Broadway, and home to a coffee-drinking, literature-loving

nocturnal scene, where bohemians would meet to talk revolution and rock 'n' roll.

★ Centro Cultural Borges

Galerías Pacífico, Viamonte y San Martín, (5555 5359, www.ccborges.org.ar). Subte C, San Martín/ bus 10, 17, 152. **Open** 10am-9pm Mon-Sat; noon-8pm Sun. **Admission** AR$20; AR$15 reductions. **No credit cards. Map** p285 G11.

Named after Argentina's most famous writer, Jorge Luis Borges, the centre lives up to its namesake's upper-crust reputation by charging an admission fee (most cultural centres are free). Nevertheless, this *centro* is the site of some of the city's most interesting and eclectic arts and film programming. It has hosted many of the must-see shows of recent years, including the annual World Press Photo exhibition.

FREE Museo Histórico y Numismático del Banco de la Nación Argentina

1st Floor, Bartolomé Mitre 326, entre 25 de Mayo y Reconquista (4347 6277). Subte B, Florida/bus 93, 109, 132. **Open** 10am-3pm Mon-Fri. **Admission** free. **Map** p285 F11.

A real mouthful of a museum, mainly of interest to anthropologists and those who enjoy staring at money they'll never be able to spend, this

Diagonal Norte. See p43.

financially themed centre was inaugurated in 1966 to mark the 75th anniversary of Argentina's central bank. It exhibits exotic early bank notes (from as far back as 1820) featuring dogs, goats, cows and even a kangaroo, as well as gold and silver coins.

Museo Mitre

San Martín 336, entre Corrientes y Sarmiento (4394 7659/www.museomitre.gov.ar). Subte B, Florida/bus 93, 99, 152. **Open** 1-5.30pm Mon-Fri. *Library* 2-5.30pm Wed. **Admission** AR$5. **No credit cards. Map** p285 F11.
This gorgeous colonial mansion, dating from 1785, was, between 1860 and 1906, the home of former president and founder of *La Nación* newspaper, Bartolomé Mitre. The library is the main attraction; it holds some of the region's most important books as well as documents on Latin American history and some unique photographic exhibits.

RETIRO

Subte C, Retiro/bus 6, 20, 93, 152.
For centuries this area – a natural point on the river – was the northern edge of the town, and was once the refuge of a hermit known as 'la ermita de San Sebastián'. When a late 17th-century Spanish governor built a country

house in the area for his retirement, and called it El Retiro – *retiro* means retreat – the district took its name. Today the area's main attraction is its open space, the well-shaded green swathe that is the lovely **Plaza San Martín**, the city's second most important plaza.

This natural bluff stretches down to three railway terminals, beyond which lie a jumble of official buildings and the docks. The plaza is named after José de San Martín, who trained his troops here. The Liberator is still revered. According to protocol, all visiting dignitaries must lay a wreath at the **Monumento al Libertador General San Martín**, the city's most important monument. It's a heroic marble and bronze equestrian affair created in 1862 by French sculptor Louis Joseph Daumas.

Sun-worshipping office workers lunch in the plaza, while an inordinate number of couples locked in marathon kissing sessions loll underneath overhanging branches or lie exposed to the sun on the windy vantage point of the green slopes.

The first block of Florida leading off the plaza was called '*la manzana loca*' (the crazy block) in the 1960s for the avant-garde art experiments held at the Instituto Di Tella at Florida 940 (now a multi-brand shop with a small art space). The district is still arty, with numerous galleries such as the **Fundación Federico Jorge Klemm** (*see p48*), regular gatherings among the creative set at traditional cafés such as **Florida Garden** (*see p144*) and some great bars like expat favourite **Dadá** (*see p144*).

Several impressive buildings surround Plaza San Martín. On the south-west side is the gargantuan **Palacio Paz**, the largest private residence in the country and formerly the home of José C Paz, founder of the once important (but now derided) *La Prensa* newspaper. Since 1938, by which time the Paz empire had shrunk to insignificance, military officers have luxuriated in part of the palace, renamed the **Círculo Militar** (to see inside, you have to join a 75-minute guided tour; 4311 1071, www.circulomilitar.org). One wing now houses the **Museo de Armas de la Nación** (*see p48*) which comprises a sizeable collection of arms and military uniforms, some of which date from as far back as medieval times, plus a room of ancient Oriental weapons.

At the edge of the plaza, the **Palacio San Martín** (Arenales 761, 4819 8092) – until recently home of the Argentinian foreign ministry – was built between 1909 and 1912 for the mega-rich Anchorena family. Nowadays, it's mostly used for official galas, although it opens for bilingual guided tours, which include a view of the garden containing a section of the Berlin Wall and an excellent collection of pre-Columbian Argentinian art.

On the opposite side of the plaza, the **Basílica del Santísimo Sacramento**, at San Martín 1039, regularly plays host to society weddings. Also built with Anchorena money (before they lost it all in the Depression) and consecrated in 1916, the Basílica's French exterior hides an inner sanctum combining Flemish and Italian handiwork with French and North African raw materials. Mercedes Castellanos de Anchorena, the woman who used some of her savings to build the church and lived at the Palacio San Martín, rests in expensive peace in an ornate marble vault in the crypt. The **Edificio Kavanagh** next door also points heavenward – at 120 metres (394 feet) it was South America's tallest building when completed in 1935, the project bankrolled by Irishwoman Corina Kavanagh. At the time of its construction, this apartment block was admired by rationalist architects the world over and is still considered an art deco landmark. Next door, the luxurious Plaza Hotel – now part of the Marriott chain – was built in 1908 by Alfred Zucker, architect of Saint Patrick's Cathedral in New York.

At the very foot of the plaza is a black marble cenotaph to those who fell in the Falklands/ Malvinas War, watched over by two soldiers in traditional uniforms who perform a stiff changing of the guard several times a day.

Across the road from this sombre memorial, in an ironic twist of history, stands a Big Ben lookalike. The British-designed and built clock tower used to be known as the Torre de los Ingleses – it was presented as a gift to Argentina by local Anglo-Argentinians for the 1910 centennial celebrations. Since the war with the UK in 1982, though, the authorities have insisted on using its official name, **Torre Monumental** (*photo p48*) though most locals are too stubborn to hop on the patriotic bandwagon. Likewise, the land around it, formerly called the Plaza Británica, was renamed **Plaza Fuerza Aérea Argentina**. For a panoramic view of the plaza and the English-built railway stations, you can take a lift to the sixth floor – 35 metres (115 feet) up (though opening hours are irregular). There are occasional exhibits in the small photo gallery inside.

Shattering the peace is the endless din from horn-honking lorries on Avenida del Libertador leading to the railway stations. Though everyone says they are going 'to Retiro' to get a train or bus, there are, in fact, three separate train terminals plus a bus station along Avenida JM Ramos Mejía. The largest, English-built terminal, the **Mitre**, dates from 1915, and stands out as one of South America's best examples of Crystal Palace-inspired architecture. A plaque on an arch of its iron structure reads 'Francis Morton & Co Ltd – Liverpool'. Although renovated, the station still retains a hue of the golden age of railways in objects such as a tobacco-stained map of Argentina's once 45,000-kilometre (27,000-mile) network, the largest in South America.

Surrounding the terminals, food stands and market stalls add to the general noise and chaos, making for a colourful though stressful walk, especially in rush hours. The **Paseo del Retiro** handicrafts fair, created to give some life to the uninviting wasteland opposite the bus station, runs every weekend.

Just north of the bus terminal is **Villa 31**, the capital's best-known shantytown. The reason for the slum's notoriety is the community's refusal to move from this potentially prime real estate until the city offers it something better. The adjacent badlands consist of run-down military and other buildings. You should avoid this area, especially after dusk.

A couple of blocks up Avenida del Libertador in an old railway building is the nostalgic **Museo Nacional Ferroviario** (*see right*). Just a hop across the road and up the incline

SIGHTS

at Suipacha 1422 is one of BA's cultural gems, the **Museo de Arte Hispanoamericano Isaac Fernández Blanco** (*see right*), housed in a beautiful Peruvian-style mansion.

The **Plaza Embajada de Israel** lies on the corner of Suipacha and Arroyo streets. A bomb destroyed a previous Israeli embassy on this site in 1992. Each of the 29 trees represents a victim of the blast. At Suipacha 1333, Argentina's main English-language teaching organisation runs the **British Arts Centre** (BAC; *see below*), while many important Argentinian and international art pieces are housed in **Fundación Federico Jorge Klemm** (*see right*), on Marcelo T de Alvear.

British Arts Centre

Suipacha 1333, entre Juncal y Arroyo, (4393 6941, www.britishartscentre.org.ar). Bus 59, 61, 93, 130, 152. **Open** 3-9.30pm Tue-Sat. Closed Jan. **Admission** varies. **No credit cards. Map** p285 H11.
A bit of Blighty in the heart of Buenos Aires, the British Arts Centre, created in 1997, is devoted to promoting Argentinian and British culture. It puts on loads of free events such as plays and films in English as well as jazz, Celtic and classical concerts, and photo and art exhibits and workshops.

Torre Monumental. *See p47.*

FREE Fundación Federico Jorge Klemm

Basement, Marcelo T de Alvear 626, entre Maipú y Florida, (4312 4443, www.fundacionfjklemm.org). Subte C, San Martín/bus 10, 17, 70, 152. **Open** 11am-8pm Mon-Fri. Closed Jan.
Admission free. **Map** p285 G11.
This important gallery houses many key Argentinian works (including some Berni pieces) and an impressive international collection (Picasso, Dalí, Warhol, Mapplethorpe). At the back, the creations of founder Jorge Klemm (imagine an even more self-obsessed version of Andy Warhol) along with his collection of 20th-century pop arcana – costumes worn by Nureyev and dresses owned by Evita – are on permanent display.

Museo de Armas de la Nación

Avenida Santa Fe 750, entre Maipú y Esmeralda (4311 1071). Subte C, San Martín/bus 10, 17, 152. **Open** 1-7pm Mon-Fri. **Admission** AR$10. **No credit cards. Map** p285 G11.
Founded by President Roca in 1904, this well-curated weapons museum moved to its current location in the Palacio Retiro in 1940. It houses a collection of arms and military uniforms, some dating from the 12th century, spread over 17 rooms.

Museo de Arte Hispanoamericano Isaac Fernández Blanco

Suipacha 1422, entre Arroyo y Avenida del Libertador (4327 0228, www.museofernandez blanco.buenosaires.gov.ar). Bus 93, 130, 152. **Open** 2-7pm Tue-Fri; 11am-7pm Sat, Sun. **Admission** AR$1. Free Thur. **No credit cards. Map** p285 H12.
This white baroque building houses a collection of Spanish American paintings, religious objects and silverware. And to add a bit of spice to a visit, there's a story that the ghost of a lady in white is said to inhabit the house. Classical music recitals are often held on Friday, Saturday and Sunday evenings at 7pm, usually featuring the museum's own baroque chamber orchestra. If you've time, wander about the mansion's peaceful, ivy-lined Andalusian courtyard.

FREE Museo Nacional Ferroviario

Avenida del Libertador 405, y Suipacha (4318 3343). Subte C, Retiro/bus 62, 93, 152. **Open** noon-6pm Mon-Fri. **Admission** free. **Map** p285 H12.
Housed in an old railway building, this tribute to trains comprises an intriguing hotchpotch of exhibits from a railway era that puts car-obsessed governments to shame. Alongside the museum is the cluttered workshop of Carlos Regazzoni, an internationally respected sculptor whose creations are made from the scrap he finds in railway yards.

SIGHTS

South of the Centre

Crumbling colonial mansions and artistic charm.

With his trademark blend of nostalgia and irony, Jorge Luis Borges wrote 'the South is the original substance from which Buenos Aires is made.' Its crumbling façades, narrow passageways and sepia-toned cafés still breathe history, and the area has shed little of its lyrical melancholy.

Barrios San Telmo and La Boca, in particular, are tourist magnets: the former is often touted as the heartland of tango – though neighbourhoods like Boedo and Abasto have more historical associations with the dance – while the latter is the home of the Boca Juniors football club. These southern barrios remain run-down and slightly seedy, although recent gentrification is bringing big changes to their cobbled streets.

Map pp284-285	**Cafés, Bars**
Hotels p91	**& Pubs** p144
Restaurants p115	

MONSERRAT

Subte A, Plaza de Mayo or E, Bolívar/bus 39, 60, 86, 105, 111, 126.

For those who are interested in Argentinian history (both the pre- and post-independence eras) or who simply enjoy mooching around and exploring the city's old churches, Monserrat is an education and a delight that shouldn't be missed. While the barrio attracts fewer tourists than neighbouring San Telmo, its architecture and heritage are in a class of their own.

INSIDE TRACK
EAT, SLEEP, DREAM FOOTBALL

If a trip down to Boca Juniors' hallowed turf has left you wanting more, check into the high-end **Hotel Boca** (Tacuarí 243, San Telmo, 4896 6359, www.hotel bocajuniors.com) for a football-tastic stay in the city. Doors are blazoned with paintings of Boca stars, football games are screened in the lobby and there's even a Boca-blue pool. It's the real Boquense deal.

Bounded by Alsina, Bolívar, Moreno and Perú streets is a complex of historical buildings filling the whole city block and known as the **Manzana de las Luces** (Block of Enlightenment; *see p50*). The illumination moniker was coined in the early 19th century in allusion to the wisdom garnered by the leading lights who were educated here.

The block's **Iglesia de San Ignacio**, on the corner of Alsina and Bolívar, dates from 1734 and is the oldest church in the city. Hidden behind the church is the brick-walled patio of the **Procuraduría de las Misiones**, accessed on Avenida Julio A Roca (also known as Diagonal Sur), which cuts into the block, via a small handicrafts market. This was the HQ of the Jesuits who ran the New World conversion programme in the 18th century.

On the opposite corner from the church is the **Librería de Avila**, the city's oldest bookshop, dating from 1785. There's another bookish haunt a few blocks south: the old **Biblioteca Nacional** building on México 564, now a research centre for musicologists, is where Jorge Luis Borges served as library director for 17 years. On the corner of Alsina and Defensa is the charming 1894 chemist **La Estrella**, whose mahogany interior has barely been touched. At lunchtime, office workers file in to test its two-metre Toledo, Ohio-made iron weighing scale, reputed to be the most accurate in the city. Directly above is the **Museo de la Ciudad** (*see right*).

Opposite the chemist's is the **Iglesia de San Francisco**, begun in 1730 by Jesuit architect Andrés Blanqui, who also worked on the Pilar church, in Recoleta, and the Cabildo. Inside, there is a startlingly gaudy 20th-century tapestry of St Francis by Argentinian artist Horacio Butler, evidently a fan of psychedelic flowers and cartoon animals.

Adjacent to this church is the smaller **Parroquia San Roque** (Saint Roque parish church), built in the 1750s. Opposite, the **Plazoleta San Francisco** contains four statues, moved here from Plaza de Mayo in 1972. They depict geography, sailing, astronomy and industry – in short, all of the disciplines that have tested belief in the God worshipped across the road.

In the middle of all these Roman Catholic ramparts and monuments to post-colonial ambition, the **Museo Etnográfico** (*see right*) delivers a salutary reminder that before the arrival of the Europeans, Argentina had such a thing as an indigenous population.

The **Basílica de Santo Domingo** and the adjoining **Basílica Nuestra Señora del Rosario**, at Defensa and Belgrano, are two other important 18th-century centres of worship. One of the towers of the former was punctured by bullets during the English invasions of 1806-07. The flags seized from the vanquished invaders are on display in the far corner to the left of the altar, and even the street name Defensa pays homage to this first popular local resistance against foreign forces.

On the edge of Montserrat is the **Museo del Bicentenario** (*see right*), which displays the personal effects of former Argentinian presidents, as well as some amusing – and often quite pointed – caricatures of said heads of state by leading cartoonists of their era. There are some real curios too, including a black doll given to poor kids by Evita's charity.

Manzana de las Luces

Perú 272, entre Moreno y Alsina (4343 3260, www.manzanadelasluces.gov.ar). Subte A, Plaza de Mayo or D, Catedral or E, Bolívar/bus 24, 29, 86, 126. **Open** 10am-9pm daily. *Tours (Spanish)* 3pm Mon-Fri; 3pm, 4.30pm, 6pm Sat, Sun. **Admission** free. *Guided tours* AR$12; free under-6s. **No credit cards. Map** p285 E10.

The 'Block of Enlightenment' is a complex of historical buildings occupying an entire city block. The complex has been, inter alia, a Jesuit school and residence, a marketplace, a university library, and the representative chamber from where

Buenos Aires province was governed until 1880. You can take a tour of the semi-circular chamber, the patios and a series of 18th-century tunnels that used to link the building to the coast. The block's church, the Iglesia de San Ignacio, dates from 1734.

Museo del Bicentenario

Paseo Colón 100, y Hipólito Yrigoyen (4344 3802, www.museo.gov.ar). Subte A, Plaza de Mayo or D, Catedral or E, Bolívar/bus 29, 64, 129. **Open** 10am-6pm Wed-Sun. **Admission** free. **Map** p285 E10.

Situated behind the Casa Rosada, this museum opened in 2011 (it was meant to open in 2010 to mark 200 years of Argentina's independence) and delivers a heavy hit of pro-government propaganda. The impressively restored space is in the city's former fort, and artefacts, artworks, campaign posters and videos are used to explore the nation's political history. Notable exhibits include the mural *Ejército Plástico* (Plastic Army) by Mexican artist David Siqueiros and the bloodied headscarf of Madres de Plaza de Mayo leader Hebe de Bonafini following blows she received during a protest rally.

Museo de la Ciudad

Defensa 219, entre Alsina y Moreno (4331 9855, www.museodelaciudad.buenosaires.gob.ar). Subte A, Plaza de Mayo or D, Catedral or E, Bolívar/bus 24, 29, 64, 86, 152. **Open** 11am-7pm daily. **Admission** AR$1; free under-12s. Free Mon, Wed. **No credit cards. Map** p285 E10.

Created as a labour of love in 1968 by José María Peña, a leading authority on architecture in Buenos Aires, the objective of this museum is to conserve and investigate the physical structures and social customs of the city. Among the exhibits are photographs, blueprints, furniture, toys, magazines, and an interesting collection of door jambs with art nouveau detailings.

Museo Etnográfico

Moreno 350, entre Balcarce y Defensa (4345 8196/www.museoetnografico.filo.uba.ar). Subte A, Plaza de Mayo or D, Catedral or E, Bolívar/bus 24, 29, 64, 152. **Open** 1-7pm Tue-Fri; 3-7pm Sat, Sun. Closed Jan. **Admission** By donation. **No credit cards. Map** p285 E10.

This museum's small but rather fascinating collection includes head-dresses, masks and cooking implements, as well as panels describing Argentina's indigenous tribes. The moving stories of the Yamana tribe of Tierra del Fuego are part of the display, and include the astonishing tale of Jemmy Button, a young man kidnapped and forcibly transported to England in 1830 as a living exemplar of what Rousseau had termed the 'noble savage'. A wood-carved Japanese Buddhist altarpiece is the museum's most valuable object.

San Telmo

'HÆC EST DOMUS DOMINI'

SAN TELMO

SIGHTS

Subte C, Independencia or San Juan/bus 20, 59, 67, 93, 98, 126, 152.

For visitors, San Telmo is enchanting: its cobblestoned streets and crumbling mansions echo old European quarters long since swept away by municipal clean-ups, Olympic bids and the best efforts of the Luftwaffe and Royal Air Force. Unfortunately, this somewhat romanticised vision is lost on locals; ask a porteño and they'll probably tell you that San Telmo is dirty, rundown and unsafe.

But San Telmo is changing. It is becoming more glamorous and less faded. A regeneration spurred by the arrival of antique dealers and restaurateurs – and more recently hostel owners and a thriving gay scene – has brought the area into the 20th century, if not yet the 21st.

Heading to San Telmo from **Plaza de Mayo**, Defensa and Balcarce are the most pleasant streets to walk along. The former is full of antique shops and considered to be the barrio's main vein, while the latter is a quieter, cobblestoned street lined with tango venues and tiny cafés. While walking you will pass by several of the tattered mansions and drooping balconies that give San Telmo its unmistakable appearance. Most were occupied by grand families until a mass flight from cholera and yellow fever took place over a century ago.

Subsequently, the old houses were turned into tenements – called *conventillos* – with poor immigrant families occupying what were formerly single rooms round the main patio. As these humble abodes are still very much lived in, no matter how open the doors look, the general public are not welcome. To see the inside of an 1880 house, visit the lovely **Pasaje de la Defensa** (Defensa 1179), a refurbished two-storey building originally owned by the Ezeiza family, and now hectic with souvenir and bric-a-brac shops.

The surrounding streets are also of interest, with bars and restaurants punctuating the houses. The quaint **Pasaje San Lorenzo** and **Pasaje Giuffra** – their cobbles harking back to a more attractive city from the 1930s and 1940s – were once streams running down to the river where Avenida Paseo Colón now pullulates. San Lorenzo 380 is the location of the strikingly ultra-thin colonial house **Casa Mínima**, the narrowest house in the city at just two metres wide – but 50 metres (165 feet) long. According to local legend, the house was built by freed slaves in 1800 on a sliver of land bestowed by their master next door.

Casa Mínima is part of the same conservation initiative that rescued **El Zanjón de Granados** (*see p53*), a beautifully restored colonial mansion capturing three centuries of urban living, which is situated round the corner where San Lorenzo butts against *calle* Defensa.

Down on Avenida Paseo Colón is Rogelio Yrurtia's bronze monument **Canto al Trabajo** (Song to Work) on the plaza of the same name (at Avenida Independencia).

SIGHTS

Plaza Dorrego

The rest of Avenida Paseo Colón is dominated by a series of serious-looking public buildings, three of them – the army's **Edificio del Libertador**, the **Aduana** (headquarters of the customs service) and the **Secretaría de Agricultura** (Ministry of Agriculture) – built along French Academic lines. The Libertador building is fronted by tanks, cannons and a statue of an Unknown Soldier. The soldier has a hole in his chest, a symbol of those who died in the Falklands/Malvinas war, who, although not buried on the islands, left their hearts there.

The fourth public building is the University of Buenos Aires's **Facultad de Ingeniería** (Faculty of Engineering), a harsh classical building that originally housed the Fundación Eva Perón, the charity created by Evita. Far more attractive is the tall, slim red-brick **Iglesia Dinamarquesa** at Carlos Calvo 257. A Lutheran church built in 1931, its modern Gothic style is at odds with everything else in San Telmo.

On Sundays, **Plaza Dorrego**, one of the few Spanish-style plazas in the city where you can drink beer and coffee in the open air, is taken over by traders, tango and tourists. Although the Sunday *feria* is a genuine, fully functional and ever-expanding antiques market, it also provides one of BA's most popular days out for both visitors and locals, especially when the sun is shining.

For fashion victims only, there's an enjoyable small museum – **Museo del Traje** (*see p53*) – tracing Argentinian fads and fashions from 1850 to the present. The **Museo de Arte Moderno (MAMbA**, Avenida San Juan 350, 4342 3001) is no Tate Modern or MoMA but it serves as a vital proving ground for contemporary Argentinian artists working in a variety of mediums. The museum, housed in a recycled tobacco warehouse, has no permanent exhibits. Instead it hosts excellent temporary shows, as well as various music and video events. Opening at the time of going to print, and located adjacent to the MAMbA in an area the city government is calling the Polo Cultural Sur (southern cultural pole), is the new **Museo de Arte Contemporáneo de Buenos Aires** (MACBA; www.macba.com.ar), which aims to study and promote 20th century and contemporary art from around the world.

At the southern end of San Telmo, **Parque Lezama** is a dramatic patch of greenery on the bluff of the old city, which, for many historians, is the location of the initial settlement of Buenos Aires. A monument at the Brasil and Defensa corner commemorates Pedro de Mendoza's hypothetical landfall at this spot in 1536, and on the park's southern side is the **Monumento a la**

Confraternidad (Monument to Brotherhood), expressed as a neo-industrial boat.

Outside the terracotta-coloured mansion that houses the **Museo Histórico Nacional** (Defensa 1600, 4307 1182), the park is a dramatic cliff covered in palms and yellow-flowered tipa trees. Musicians and market stalls fill the park at weekends and the wonderfully out-of-place **Iglesia Ortodoxa Rusa**, topped with blue onions in the Russian style, adds further colour to the scene.

FREE Museo del Traje

Chile 832, entre Tacuari y Piedras (4343 8427, www.funmuseodeltraje.com.ar). Subte C, Independencia/bus 45, 59, 70, 103. **Open** *Jan-Nov* 3-7pm Tue-Sun. *Guided tours (Spanish)* 5pm Sat, Sun. **Admission** free. **Map** p285 E9.

Fashionistas who've spent the morning twisting and twirling in front of three-way mirrors can take a quick post-lunch break – and appreciate some of BA's design history – at this small but entertaining museum. True, the bald mannequins posed like cocktail partygoers are creepy, but the intricately crafted dresses they're wearing are gorgeous and perfectly preserved.

★ El Zanjón de Granados

Defensa 755, entre Chile e Independencia (4361 3002). Bus 29, 93, 152. **Tours** 11am-3pm Mon-Fri; 1-6pm Sun. **Admission** *Mon-Fri* AR$60; *Sun* AR$40. Free under-10s. **Map** p285 E10.

Part archaeological museum, part event space, El Zanjón is a beautifully restored residence encapsulating three centuries of urban living. Although the façade dates from 1830, traces from an earlier patrician home – an open-air cistern, a look-out tower and a 1740 seashell-mortared wall – have been excavated by amateur historian Jorge Eckstein, who started dredging the 166m (545ft) of tunnels beneath his property in 1985. Eckstein has unearthed a trove of workaday but eclectic objects from the colonial era, including French tiles, African pipes and English china. An underground hit.

LA BOCA

Bus 20, 25, 29, 53, 64, 152.

In both space and spirit, La Boca is as far south as Buenos Aires gets. Divided from the vast suburbs of greater BA by the dark and toxic gloop of the Riachuelo river, this working class barrio was until the late 19th century the

San Telmo.

Spray It

Tagging the town.

In the last decade, street art has transformed Buenos Aires into one of the world's most spectacular outdoor galleries. Since the 2001 economic meltdown, the city has gone up in a blaze of colour, with local and international graffiti artists taking advantage of a grey area in the law to paint the town with witty stencils, large-scale murals and surreal paintings.

Neglected buildings, drab public squares and even entire residential streets have been revamped. And while in most corners of the globe graffiti is synonymous with urban decay and gang warfare, in Buenos Aires street art has become a sign of beauty, creativity and gentrification. It's not uncommon to see artists painting away in broad daylight while police stroll nonchalantly by. The rest of the world is taking notice too, with artists like Ever, Gualicho and Jaz having been invited to spray or exhibit in Europe and North America.

In BA, graffiti artists are increasingly the first port of call for rundown neighbourhoods in dire need of revitalisation. In 2011, when residents of La Boca wanted to revamp the derelict Garibaldi passageway linking tourist-friendly Caminito with Boca Juniors's La Bombonera stadium, they invited well-established street artists to unleash their spray cans, latex paints and stencils.

This wasn't the first time street art had been used to brighten up a desolate southern barrio. In 2001, in the adjacent barrio of Barracas, a local artist, Marino Santa María, began adorning homes in *calle* Lanín (*see p58*) with abstract mosaics and paint swirls. His labour of love attracted UNESCO funding and transformed the street into a tourist attraction.

The residents of Casacuberta street in nearby Parque Patricios took inspiration from *calle* Lanín's success when, in 2011, they offered prominent BA stencil artists BsAs.Stncl, Run Don't Walk and Stencil Land paint, aerosols and biscuits in exchange for using the façades of their homes as blank canvases. The result is the stuff of Banksy's wildest stencil dreams (*see pictures*).

If you're interested in seeing the city's latest ephemeral magnum opus's up close and personal, Graffitimundo (*see p42*) are the all-round experts in all things street art, running excellent three-hour tours. If you want to go home with your own piece of local graffiti, many artists sell prints of their work at the Hollywood in Cambodia (*see p197*) gallery in Palermo. If you fall in love with a piece on the street, note that artists sometimes leave their email address next to their work, so unlike the elusive Banksy, there's no reason you can't contact them directly and put a face to the urban canvas.

SIGHTS

obligatory entry point to the city for both goods and immigrants – hence the name (literally 'the mouth'). But when the docks moved north, decline set in, and today all that's left of the once bustling port are a few abandoned hulks and some crepuscular warehouses. The crime, unemployment and poor housing statistics have been trending upwards for decades. It's best not to go looking for the charismatic *compadrito* of yore, immortalised in countless tangos: you're more likely to bump into a furtive kid in a hoodie. That said, those who cherish La Boca, whether for its history, its lack of Paris-of-South-America pretentiousness or its cheap rents, really cherish it. The barrio's waterfront in particular is enjoying a mini-renaissance, in part thanks to a booming tourist trade that has more and more people making the trek down to the tiny, multicoloured Caminito.

The barrio stretches from the river right up to the roundabout where Avenida Paseo Colón becomes Avenida Martín García, and where a mast and a 3-D frieze announce that you are entering the 'República de la Boca'.

Set back from the river, on Brandsen, is the reason why people who have never been to BA have heard of La Boca. The port a thing of the past, the communal heart now beats at the **Estadio Alberto J Armando** (*see p225*), aka La Bombonera, where top-flight football team Club Atlético Boca Juniors has held court for nearly a century. The blue and yellow of the team strip is ubiquitous on walls and balconies throughout the neighbourhood. The team's on-field exploits have fomented any number of off-field brand extensions, the most important of which is the **Museo de la Pasión Boquense** (*see p57*), located at the stadium's entrance.

From the museum's entrance a disused railway track runs down Paseo Garibaldi and comes out two blocks later at the back end of **Caminito** (*see right*), a short, banana-shaped pedestrianised theme street recognised as Argentina's only open-air museum.

La Vuelta de Rocha, the road that follows the bend in the river at the opening to Caminito, is marked by a mast and rigging. A painting at the **Museo Nacional de Bellas Artes** (*see p65*) in Recoleta bears the same name, and its stylised portrayal of this corner is an acknowledgement of the near-mythical status the area has for porteños.

However, it's not all nostalgia in La Boca. **Fundación Proa** (*see right*) is one of the city's premier spaces for contemporary art and a great reason to visit the area, as is hipster favourite, **POPA** (*see p193*) – the most recent addition to La Boca's art scene. The area's other outstanding gallery is housed in the buildings donated to La Boca

by painter Benito Quinquela Martín (1890-1977). The **Museo de Bellas Artes de La Boca** (*see p57*) contains works by Quinquela Martín and other Argentinian artists, while creepy wax portrayals of famous public figures can be found in Argentina's one and only **Museo de Cera** (*see p57*).

Three bridges at the northern end of Avenida Pedro de Mendoza connect the capital with the province. The oldest is the **Puente Transbordador** (transporter bridge), a massive iron contraption not used since 1940.

Caminito
Bus 29, 53, 64, 152. **Map** p284 A8.
This street's name – literally 'little walkway' – comes from a 1926 tango by legendary composers Gabino Coria Peñaloza and Juan de Dios Filiberto, the lyrics of which are inscribed on a wall plaque. The corrugated zinc shacks stacked up on each side of the street owe their resplendent colours to the imaginative, but impoverished, locals who begged incoming ships for spare tins of paint. These days the street is thronged with tango dancers, small-time grifters and tourists, but Caminito's colour and chaos continue to charm.

★ Fundación Proa
Avenida Pedro de Mendoza 1929, entre Magallanes y Rocha (4104 1000/ www.proa.org). Bus 25, 29, 46, 53, 64, 152. **Open** 11am-7pm Tue-Sun. **Admission** AR$12. **Map** p284 A8.
The phenomenal Proa is flourishing in its stunning waterfront building, just off the tourist hub of Caminito, and features expanded industrial exhibition spaces, the city's best art library and bookstore, and a third-floor café with a harbour view. With a gravitational pull strong enough to reel in sculptor and confessional art pioneer Louise Bourgeois, found-object works by French mastermind Marcel Duchamp, and a comprehensive look at the Futurist movement, Proa packs in a full schedule throughout the year, complete with related film cycles, lectures, performances and theatre productions.

Museo de Bellas Artes de La Boca Benito Quinquela Martín
Avenida Don Pedro de Mendoza 1835, entre Palos y Del Valle Iberlucea (4301 1080). Bus 20, 25, 29, 33, 46, 53, 64, 86, 129, 152, 159. **Open** 10am-6pm Tue-Fri; 11am-6pm Sat, Sun. **Admission** AR$8. **No credit cards.** **Map** p284 A9.
In the 1930s, over-excited local critics compared Quinquela Martín's canvases, with their character-istic spatula marks, to those of Vincent Van Gogh. The artist's vibrant collection is organised around three themes: fire (once a constant hazard for La Boca's wood-framed warehouses), port workers and ships' graveyards.

La Boca.

SIGHTS

Museo de Cera

Del Valle Iberlucea 1261, entre Magallanes y Aráoz de la Madrid (4301 1497, www.museo decera.com.ar). Bus 29, 53, 64, 152. **Open** 10.30am-6pm Mon-Thur; 10.30am-4pm Fri; 11.30am-6pm Sat, Sun. Times subject to change Jan & Feb). **Admission** AR$15; free under-8s. **Map** p284 A8.

Argentina's only waxworks museum brings to life (well, sort of) some of the pioneers and personalities most closely associated with La Boca. Sculptor Domingo Tellechea founded the museum in 1980, adapting a colourful Italian-style mansion – which was incidentally one of the first cement constructions in the city – that dates back to 1904. As well as famous faces, there are tableaux scenes of cock fights, gaucho gatherings and *compadritos* dancing tango in its earliest, earthiest form.

Museo de la Pasión Boquense

Brandsen 805, y Juan de Dios Filiberto (4362 1100, www.museoboquense.com). Bus 10, 20, 22, 24, 25, 29, 33, 39, 46, 53, 64, 70, 74, 86, 93. **Open** 10am-6pm daily. Closed on match days. **Admission** AR$45 museum only; AR$50 museum & tour (11am-5pm on the hour). **Credit** AmEx, DC, MC, V. **Map** p284 B8.

For the real *pasión* you should visit the Bombonera on a match day; but for everything else Boca, this modern museum hits the back of the net. There are loads of audio-visual widgets and gizmos to twiddle with, mountains of facts and figures to absorb and, naturally, tributes galore to Boca's greatest hero, Diego Maradona, including a bronze statue that is the museum's top photo-opportunity. In the gift shop you can buy your souvenirs in any colour you like – so long as they're blue and yellow.

Usina del Arte

Avenida Don Pedro de Mendoza y Caffarena (4343 5356, www.lausinaculturalbarracas. blogspot.com.ar). Bus 29, 129, 130, 152, 168, 195. **Box office** hours vary. **Shows** varies. **Admission** varies. **No credit cards.** **Map** p284 A9.

Down-and-out La Boca received an injection of grandeur when this former power plant was reincarnated as a 15,000sq m cultural centre in May 2012. The impressive building – in the style of a Florentine palace – boasts a 1,200-seat concert hall with world-class acoustics as well as a cinema, and hosts all manner of cultural activities, including dance performances and art exhibitions. *Photo p58.*

CONSTITUCION & BARRACAS

Subte C, Constitución/bus 20, 37, 45, 148. Constitución is a rundown barrio that most porteños prefer to avoid, but without its railway station, BA would never have reached its late-19th century economic zenith. Neighbouring Barracas was once a hotbed for working-class protest movements but lately shows some signs of gentrification. Still, the barrio shares a dodgy after-dark reputation with nearby Constitución. If you want to visit either area, the safest option is to go with a local or an organised tour.

Dominating **Plaza Constitución**, the **Estación Constitución** is an imposing 1880s construction. Built to shuttle the rich to the Atlantic resort of Mar del Plata, it now shuttles weary commuters southwards. The forecourt is a whirl of vagrants, vendors and commuters, with numerous bus lines terminating here too, just to add to all the chaos.

The name Barracas refers to the warehouses that clustered here from the late 18th century onwards; cheap housing and brothels completed the picture by the early 1900s. The barrio's current gentrification effort is converting many of the crumbling warehouses and grand relics into affordable housing and offices. An early anchor of the renewal is the **Centro Metropolitano de Diseño** (*see right*).

Usina del Arte.
See p57.

Among the artists breathing new life into Barracas is Marino Santa María. Since 2001, on *calle* Lanín, Santa María has been spearheading an imaginative public-art project he calls the postmodern version of La Boca's **Caminito**. Every house on the curved two-block street is painted with colourful, abstract streaks resembling psychedelic tiger stripes. Santa María's studio can be visited at Lanín 33. The Graffitimundo tour *(see p42)* to the south of the city stops at *calle* Lanín.

FREE **Centro Metropolitano de Diseño**
Algarrobo 1041, y Villarino (4126 2950, www.cmd.gov.ar). Train to Hipólito Yrigoyen/ bus 12, 93, 195. **Open** 9.30am-6pm Mon-Fri. **Admission** free.
This city-run incubator for young designers was set up in 2001 in a remodelled facility that once housed the city's fish market. Conferences and classes for up-and-coming artists are currently held, as well as free tours hosted by architects at 3pm every Friday, by appointment only (visitas-guiadascmd@gmail.com).

North of the Centre

Park life, palaces and Parisian flair in BA's grandest neighbourhoods.

The greenest and most pleasant parts of the city are concentrated in the affluent neighbourhoods of Recoleta, Barrio Norte and Palermo. It was here that the Buenos Aires aristocracy fled to in 1871, escaping the yellow fever epidemic that swept through the previously well-to-do southern barrios.

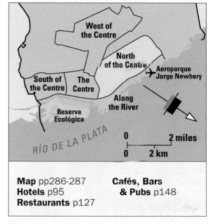

Map pp286-287	**Cafés, Bars**
Hotels p95	**& Pubs** p148
Restaurants p127	

Today these northern neighbourhoods are characterised by European-style architecture, monumental boulevards and parks – thanks in great part to the vision of French landscaper Charles Thays, who designed the **Jardín Botánico** (*see p68*) and the **Parque Tres de Febrero** (*see p68*).

Besides its chichi shops, Recoleta is also home to the impressive cemetery that's the resting place of Eva Perón. And if Buenos Aires is the city that doesn't sleep, then the greatest insomniac of all is Palermo, which has the biggest and best concentration of restaurants and stylish drinking holes.

RECOLETA

Bus 17, 60, 92, 93, 102.

It's BA's most exclusive patch of real estate – but nobody lives there. We refer of course to the **Cementerio de la Recoleta** (*see p60*), one of the world's great necropolises.

The plazas outside the cemetery walls were once on the banks of the river. Though barely a bump in its present landscaped form, the mount was of sufficient size to serve as a hiding place for bandits in the 17th century. Between 1716 and 1730, a French chapter of the Franciscans, known as the Padres Recoletos, chose the area to build a chapel and convent as a place of retreat. At the same time, the Jesuits, already established as missionaries and merchants in northern Argentina, Paraguay and Brazil, settled in Recoleta. The building of their **Basílica Nuestra Señora del Pilar** (Junín 1904, 4803 6793) began in 1716 and the church site was consecrated in 1732.

The plain-looking façade, the whiteness barely interrupted but for the sky-blue Pas-de-Calais ceramic tiles that decorate its upper reaches, is reminiscent of many colonial churches found in remote northern provinces. Inside is a superlative baroque altar, featuring Incan and other pre-Hispanic motifs. The altar was brought along the mule trails from Peru, the heart of colonial South America, and given a wrought-silver frontal in Jujuy in north-west Argentina. You can visit the cloisters, the crypt beneath the church and adjoining tunnels, thought to connect with tunnels in Monserrat, on guided tours.

To the north of the Pilar church, on the site of the Franciscan convent, is the **Centro Cultural Recoleta** (*see p61*). It promotes contemporary visual arts and contains several performance rooms. There is also a film projection room and an interactive science museum for kids, the **Museo Participativo de Ciencias** (*see p187*). From the roof terrace you can view the surrounding plazas.

It's not all high culture and high church, though: a specialised mall, **Buenos Aires Design** (*see p179*), has two floors showcasing designer furniture and interiors. The mall's terraces are lined with cafés and restaurants,

SIGHTS

Cementerio de la Recoleta.

while on Vicente López at the south-west of the cemetery is the Recoleta Mall (which also houses the Village Recoleta cinema), providing incongruous shopping and entertainment options on the dead's doorstep.

In the pleasant grassy spaces in front of the Centro Cultural, stretching down to Avenida del Libertador, are three giant *gomero* (rubber) trees that provide shade for loungers and dog walkers. **Plaza Francia**, directly north-east of the cultural centre, is commandeered on weekends by a handicraft fair, which draws tourists, stragglers and neo-hippies.

Across Posadas street is the belle époque **Palais de Glace** (*see 61*), which was an ice-rink, a ballroom and an important tango salon in the 1920s, run by aristocrat Baron de Marchi. It was in this circular building that tango was officially embraced by the bourgeoisie.

In front of the Palais de Glace stands a monument to Carlos María de Alvear, an officer who founded the horse guards regiment in 1812 with San Martín, and was the first in a line of Alvears to play an important part in the city's history. Opposite are the monument and plaza dedicated to Carlos María's son, Torcuato de Alvear, the first governor of the city of Buenos Aires and an important urban planner.

The pedestrian walkway **RM Ortiz**, which runs from the corner of Junín and Vicente

López to Avenida Quintana, is one of BA's most popular strips for the time-honoured evening stroll known as *el paseo* – though the trend of restaurant staff pestering passers-by to come and eat is annoying. At the corner of Avenida Quintana is the classy and predictably overpriced café **La Biela** (Avenida Quintana 596, 4804 0449, www.labiela.com). Opposite the café, its tentacle-like bowers casting a shadow over the outdoor terrace, is a magnificent rubber tree known as the *Gran Gomero*.

★ Cementerio de la Recoleta

Junín 1760, entre Guido y Vicente López (4803 1594). Bus 10, 17, 60, 67, 92, 110. **Open** 7am-5.45pm daily. *Guided tours* (English) 11am Tue, Thur. **Admission** free (to the living). **Map** p286 J11.

Originally conceived by Bernardino Rivadavia and designed by Frenchman Prosper Catelin, the cemetery was opened in 1822. The narrow passages and high walls make comparisons with the real city outside inevitable. Entrance to the cemetery is through a Doric-columned portico designed in 1886 by Juan Buschiazzo, one of Argentina's most important architects. The cemetery is home to hundreds of illustrious corpses, laid out in a compact maze of granite, marble and bronze mausoleums – most of the materials came from Paris and Milan – and a slow walk down its avenues and alleyways is one of BA's undisputed delights.

Originally a public cemetery on the fringes of the city – nearby Avenida Callao marked the limit of Buenos Aires until the 1880s – it is now even harder to move into than the posh flats that surround it. Seafarers and freed slaves were once given their final berths in Recoleta, but now ordinary folk can only get in alive. Many Argentinian presidents are entombed here, though most visitors come to see the resting place of María Eva Duarte de Perón, better known as Evita. There are also impressive collective tombs (housing fallen soldiers), great pantheons and cenotaphs inches away from one another. Assorted architectural styles are arranged side by side, from distinguished chemist Dr Pedro Arata's diminutive Egyptian pyramid to aristocrat Dorrego Ortiz Basualdo's monumental sepulchre, decorated with 'prudent virgins' and topped by a great candelabra. Among the patrician families here, residing in a style befitting one-time mansion dwellers, are the Alvears, the Estradas, the Balcarces and the Alzagas, together with members of the Paz clan. *See also p63* **Death Becomes Her**.

★ Centro Cultural Recoleta

Junín 1930, y Avenida Alvear (4803 1040, www.centroculturalrecoleta.org). Bus 10, 17, 60, 67, 92, 110. **Open** 2-9pm Mon-Fri; noon-9pm Sat, Sun. **Admission** free. **Map** p286 J11.
The Centro Cultural Recoleta is a much-loved standard on the Buenos Aires art scene: numerous versatile exhibition spaces host works ranging from art produced by psychiatric patients to displays of traditional textiles. It's also the site of major shows – such as the captivating *Fuerzabruta* – and is a great place to catch retrospectives. For those who want to get a bit more involved, the centre holds various arts workshops that generally begin in March and August.

FREE **Espacio Fundación Telefónica**

Arenales 1540, entre Montevideo y Paraná (4333 1300, www.fundacion.telefonica.com.ar). Bus 10, 37, 59. **Open** 2-8.30pm Mon-Sat. *Guided tours* 5pm. **Admission** free. **Map** p286 I10.
This two-floor contemporary arts centre, owned by the Telefónica foundation, has educational and

---

THE BEST CULTURAL CENTRES

Centro Cultural Borges
The CC Borges hosts everything from art exhibitions to tango shows. *See p45.*

Centro Cultural Recoleta
Stop off at this great cultural centre while visiting the nearby sights. *See left.*

Centro Cultural Ricardo Rojas
Visit for theatre, indie cinema and a range of courses. *See p191.*

Centro Cultural San Martín
Independent theatre and dance, and workshops (www.ccgsm.gov.ar).

---

artistic ambitions. Sophisticated multimedia technology is used to present the visual arts alongside social projects and research. There are media labs and educational activities, such as conferences, and information about social justice in Latin America, as well as the exhibition space.

FREE **Palais de Glace**

Posadas 1725, y Schiaffino (4804 1163, www.palaisdeglace.gob.ar). Bus 17, 67, 92, 130. **Open** noon-8pm Tue-Fri; 10am-8pm Sat, Sun. **Admission** free. **Map** p286 J11.
French speakers won't have to guess the original function of this elegant belle époque building; Palais de Glace, which opened its doors to skaters in 1910, means 'Ice Palace'. The grand circular structure also housed a landmark tango salon before being declared a national monument in 2004. Today, the palace hosts major exhibitions of fashion and the visual arts. The two-level space, complete with decorative reliefs and a huge dome, is a suitably grand setting for the diverse roster of large-scale paintings, contemporary photography, engravings, sculpture and video installations that are shown here. Free tours in Spanish are held on Saturdays at 5pm and 6pm.

SIGHTS

Palais de Glace.

Death Becomes Them

Cementerio de la Recoleta: who's who in BA's most exclusive burial ground.

Almost every major Argentine hero and villain is buried in Recoleta's glorious necropolis. Along with Evita are several high-profile presidents including the two 19th-century arch-enemies – educator Domingo Sarmiento and tyrant Juan Manuel de Rosas – and Julio A Roca. National personages laid to rest here include San Martín sidekick Tomás Guido, in his grotto-like pile of stones, and La Rioja *caudillo* Juan Facundo Quiroga. Assassinated during the bloody war in the 1830s, Quiroga is buried standing up – a sign of courage, or as the cemetery's sub-director puts it, 'So he can get his sabre out quickly if need be.'

Irish freedom fighter and naval hero William Brown spends his afterlife beside a green mast bearing a frigate. His daughter Elisa is also buried here. She was found drowned in her wedding dress in the Riachuelo river. Legend has it she killed herself out of grief for her Scottish lover, who died helping her father foil Brazil's imperial ambitions.

Another sad story is that of Rufina Cambaceres, a rich kid buried alive after a cataleptic attack. When she woke up, she managed to prise the coffin open but died during the night from a heart attack. She is buried in an art nouveau tomb stylishly decorated with much-admired wrought iron.

Someone who could have punched his way out is Luis Angel Firpo, heavyweight boxer, who nearly beat Jack Dempsey in 1923. A statue of the boxer by the eminent sculptor Luis Perlotti stands on Firpo's granite tomb.

LOOK OUT ALSO FOR
Stylish patricians Carlos de Alvear, Familia Dorrego Ortiz Basualdo, Familia Leloir.
Noble-looking leaders and politicians Manuel Dorrego, Lucio López, Juan Lavalle, Pantheon of the Fallen in the Revolution – Leonardo M Alem, Hipólito Yrigoyen and Arturo Illia.
Key artists and writers José Hernández, Vicente López y Planes, Miguel Cané, Eduardo Mallea, Adolfo Bioy Casares, Victoria Ocampo.

SIGHTS

Monumento de los Españoles. *See p68.*

SIGHTS

Avenida del Libertador

Beyond the cluster of life, leisure and style that has sprung up around the necropolis, Recoleta has other public spaces and venues along Avenida del Libertador. At the centre of **Plaza Francia**, at Libertador and Pueyrredón, is a baroque marble monument to Liberty, which was presented to Argentina by France as part of the centenary celebrations in 1910.

Across the avenue from the **Palais de Glace** is the newest patch of urban landscaping, **Parque Carlos Thays**, which boasts a heroic bronze *Torso Masculino* by Colombian sculptor Fernando Botero. At Libertador and Callao is the **Museo de Arquitectura** (4800 1888), located in a former railway water tower dating from 1915. Exhibitions trace the evolution of Buenos Aires and general matters of design and architecture.

On Avenida Figueroa Alcorta, behind the **Museo Nacional de Bellas Artes** (*see p65*), is the **Facultad de Derecho** (Law Faculty), thronged all year round by students. Plazas Urquiza, Uruguay and Naciones Unidas are plain public spaces.

Eduardo Catalano's **Floralis Genérica** is a popular, striking steel and aluminium sculpture. Its petals are meant to open and close daily at sunrise and dusk but mechanical problems with one of the petals immobilised the flower in early 2010, with no resolution yet as to who will foot the US$125,000 bill to fix it.

Occasionally, a building or two gets in the way of the greenery – such as the Bauhaus-style, state-owned ATC Channel 7 TV studios, built in 1978 to broadcast the World Cup; but there are open spaces all the way to Palermo and beyond on the river side of Libertador.

Back across the road, the plazas don't stretch as far, but they are more dramatic. At the top of **Plaza Mitre**, a great red granite pedestal is adorned with lively allegorical and lyrical figures in marble, above which rides a stern bronze of Bartolomé Mitre, president from 1862 to 1888 and founder of *La Nación* newspaper.

The next patch of grass, the **Plaza Rubén Darío**, named after the Nicaraguan poet and philosopher, is brooded over by the jutting upper half of the extremely functional-looking **Biblioteca Nacional** (*see p65*), designed in the 1960s by three prominent architects,

Clorindo Testa, Alicia Cazzaniga de Bullrich and Francisco Bullrich. Building work dragged on for years, and the library only opened to the public in 1992.

Before the controversial concrete block of the library was conceived, this was the land of the Unzué family, and for a time the site of the presidential residence, where the Peróns lived and Evita died on 26 July 1952. The military tore down the mansion to erase the memory of Peronism, unswayed by the fact that Juan Domingo Perón had risen from within its very own ranks.

At the Palermo end of Recoleta, at Avenida del Libertador 1902, is the beautiful mansion Palacio Errázuriz, which houses the **Museo Nacional de Arte Decorativo** (*see below*).

Biblioteca Nacional

Agüero 2502, entre Avenida del Libertador y Las Heras (4808 6000, www.bn.gov.ar). Bus 59, 60, 93, 102. **Open** 9am-9pm Mon-Fri; noon-7pm Sat, Sun. **Admission** free. Map p286 K11.

Most of the library's two million books and manuscripts are kept in the underground vaults, so there's not much to see except for occasional exhibits. Current and back issues of periodicals and newspapers are available, however: go to the Hemeroteca in the basement, with photo ID.

Museo Nacional de Arte Decorativo

Avenida del Libertador 1902, y Pereyra Lucena (4801 8248, www.mnad.org). Bus 10, 59, 60, 67, 130. **Open** *Jan-Feb* 2-7pm Tue-Sat. *Mar-Dec* 2-7pm Tue Sun. Closed 1st 2 wks Jan. **Admission** AR$5; AR$3 reductions. Free Tue. **Map** p286 K11.

This stunning building was converted into a museum in 1937, and its majestic ballrooms, bedrooms and hallways today display over 4,000 pieces of decorative art, plus works by well-known artists such as El Greco and Manet. Tours in English are offered at 2.30pm and 4.30pm from Tuesday to Saturday, and the museum has a good bookshop in the basement.

FREE Museo Nacional de Bellas Artes

Avenida del Libertador 1473, y Pueyrredón (5288 9900, www.mnba.org.ar). Bus 17, 62, 93, 130. **Open** 12.30-8.30pm Tue-Fri; 9.30am-8.30pm Sat, Sun. **Admission** free. **Map** p286 J11.

The MNBA has 24 rooms, several sculpture patios, a library and an auditorium. It houses the country's biggest collection of 19th- and 20th-century Argentinian artworks, which, after the property's extensive refurbishment in 2004-5, are now on permanent display. Displays include outstanding works by Ernesto de la Cárcova and Cándido López. The collection includes 20th-century pieces from all the major names in Argentinian art, including

Eduardo Sivori, Antonio Berni, Xul Solar and Guillermo Kuitca. The international collection on the ground floor includes works by El Greco, Rubens, Rembrandt and Goya, among other names. There is also a permanent display of indigenous art. An audio guide service in English and Spanish is available.

BARRIO NORTE

Subte D, Pueyrredón/bus 39, 64, 152, 188. When alluding to the overcrowded, middle-class residential area between Avenida Las Heras and Avenida Córdoba, most *porteños* use the term Barrio Norte. The nickname is often associated with the *chetos* (social-climbers) and *paquetes* (also poseurs, but with the confidence of older money) who live here. Evita, in one of her many fiery speeches to seduce the working classes, declared an ambition to 'bomb Barrio Norte'. The neighbourhood's main consumer corridor and a Barrio Norte symbol par excellence, is Avenida Santa Fe, which is lined with big-name brand shops and boutiques.

If you take a stroll down this commercial thoroughfare, slip inside the former theatre at number 1860 that now houses the **Ateneo** (*see p158*) bookshop. Just a few blocks from here, between Callao and Pueyrredón, is one of BA's most vibrant gay scenes.

Literary pilgrims should check out the **Museo Casa de Ricardo Rojas** (*see below*). Rojas (1882-1957) was an influential writer and one of Argentina's most important educators, teaching Argentinian literature at the state university before becoming its rector in 1926. Another cultural highlight in the area is the **Museo Xul Solar** (*see p67*), two blocks from Avenida Santa Fe.

Museo Casa de Ricardo Rojas

Charcas 2837, entre Anchorena y Laprida (4824 4039). Subte D, Agüero/bus 12, 39, 152. **Open** 11am-5pm Tue-Fri. **Admission** (suggested) AR$1. **Map** p286 K9.

Undergoing renovation at the time of writing and due to reopen later in 2012, this museum preserves the original furnishings and household objects of writer Rojas, as well as more than 20,000 volumes from his personal library. Rojas intended that his house, built in 1927 and donated to the state in 1957 by the writer's widow, should be a visual expression of the contending forces that have enriched and disfigured the Argentinian experience: civilisation versus barbarism, South America versus Europe, city versus country, and so on. Consequently, the design of the building, by architect Angel Guido, is an attempt to harmonise a number of eclectic influences, including a Spanish-colonial façade (reminscent of buildings in Rojas's native province of Tucumán) and a patio that incorporates Incan ornamental motifs.

SIGHTS

SIGHTS

Walk Palermo Park Life

Take a stroll – and a breath of fresh air – in Palermo's green expanses.

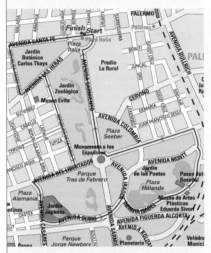

Spend enough time in BA's traffic-choked city centre and you'll begin to wonder if the city shouldn't be rechristened. To really breathe 'good airs', you need to head north, to the parks and gardens of Palermo.

This walk takes you through some of the most attractive spaces in this bucolic patch of the city. Meander as often as time allows and smell the roses along the way.

Start in **Plaza Italia**. You won't want to linger long here: it's one of the city's noisiest junctions and a far cry from the lawned idylls that punctuate the area.

Head east along Avenida Santa Fe, in a downtown direction. Turning left on to *calle* República Arabe Siria, and then left again on to Avenida Las Heras, you'll skirt around the **Jardín Botánico Carlos Thays** (*see p68*), full of monuments, fountains, ferns, orchids and cacti. There's also a botanical library, but the main attraction is the calm offered by this hedged-in triangle.

As you head north-east along *calle* República de la India, the calm is broken by the howls and yelps emanating from the **Jardín Zoológico** (*see p187*) on your left. On your right is the exclusive sub-barrio of Palermo Chico, home to diplomats, TV stars and corporate expats. It's a tranquil if largely soulless neighbourhood.

Turning left on to busy Avenida del Libertador you'll begin to pass through

and around **Parque Tres de Febrero** (*see p68*). The park (sometimes known as the Bosques de Palermo, or Palermo Woods) is named after the date in 1852 when the forces of General Urquiza defeated the despotic General Rosas at the Battle of Monte Caseros. Using land formerly owned by Rosas, President Sarmiento – who razed Rosas's mansion – envisioned the park as a way for BA to resemble more closely the capitals of Europe. Statues of a dashing Rosas and a saturnine Sarmiento face off at the Libertador-Sarmiento crossroads, the latter's monument (by Auguste Rodin) on the site of the flattened house.

Continuing along Avenida Casares and then Avenida Berro, you'll pass another glorious spot for greenfingered visitors: the **Jardín Japonés** (*see p68*). The garden is awash with artificial lakes brimming with weirdly anthropomorphic giant koi, ornate bridges, a fine Japanese restaurant that is open in the evenings, and – in the pagoda – an attractive all-day tearoom serving green teas and cakes. Botanical species include black pines, sakura and ginkgo and there are regular bonsai exhibitions.

Your zen moment over, continue through the park on Avenida Berro and then Infanta Isabel. The highlight on this stretch is the delightfully pretty **Rosedal** (Rose Garden – entered at *avenidas* Iraola and Presidente Montt); within it lies the **Jardín de los Poetas**, with its peaceful fountains surrounded by busts of literary giants, a lovely, tiled Patio Andaluz and a shaded pergola by the lake. In these well-planted spaces, look out for native bird life, such as the *hornero* (oven bird – it has an oven-shaped nest) and the yellow and black *cabecita negra*, not to mention the common, or garden, sparrow, introduced from Europe by Sarmiento as yet another 'civilising' presence. Non-birders and kids may prefer to float on the lake (pedalos and boats are available for hire opposite the excellent **Museo de Artes Plásticas Eduardo Sívori**; *see p69*).

Turning back on to Avenida del Libertador once more, walk along the southern fringe of the park until you reach the striking **Monumento de los Españoles** (*see p68*). You'll now have Plaza Italia back in your sights, at the southern end of the broad, Parisian Avenida Sarmiento.

Museo Xul Solar

Laprida 1212, entre Mansilla y Charcas (4824 3302, www.xulsolar.org.ar). Subte D, Agüero/ bus 12, 39, 64, 152. **Open** *noon-6pm Tue-Sun.* **Guided tours** *4pm Tue, Thur; 3.30pm Sat.* **Admission** *AR$10; AR$4 reductions.* **Credit** *AmEx.* **Map** *p286 J9.*

This museum is installed in the house in which the city's most eccentric self-proclaimed visionary, sailor turned painter, astrologer, mathematician, writer and philologist Agustín Alejandro Schulz Solari (1887-1963), or Xul Solar lived. Conceived by him in the late 1930s but only built in 1986, after his death, the museum exhibits 86 of his own self-selected works, alongside a collection of esoteric objects and weird instruments. Solar also invented his own languages (Neocriollo and Panlengua) and lived in his own personal time zone (in Buenos Aires the latter is less of an eccentricity than it sounds). The main draw, though, is perhaps not Solar's art, but the building in which it is kept, his home having been completely remodelled to reflect his own peculiar 'cosmovision', resulting in an award-winning modern space. (*See also p198* **Xul Solar**).

PALERMO

Subte D, Plaza Italia/bus 15, 39, 60, 93, 152.
As Walt Whitman might have said, Palermo is large; it contains multitudes. It's comfortably the biggest barrio in the city, and the famous parks, gardens and lakes make it also the greenest and most pleasant. There is space to jog, cycle, stroll and picnic; at times the air is almost fresh enough to breathe. The fact that

the neighbourhood also contains a Japanese garden, a mosque and a cricket club – not to mention an airport that is knuckle-whiteningly close to all of the above – gives the impression that Palermo is a city within a city.

Helpfully – or perhaps confusingly – the neighbourhood contains a number of sub-divisions, some of which are semi-official, and others of which could only have been dreamed up by estate agents. Most people recognise three basic areas: Palermo Chico (bordering Recoleta), for embassies and the filthy rich; leafy Palermo Viejo (comprising Palermo Hollywood and Palermo Soho), for global cuisine and funky boutiques; and Palermo for all the rest, including the expanses of greenery.

From the little street called Cavia to Monroe in Belgrano (the next barrio along), there's a patchwork of plazas and parks congregating round the Parque Tres de Febrero, formerly a flood plain drained in the late 16th century by the barrio's namesake, Italian farmer Giovanni Domenico Palermo. At the northern limit of the park is the **Hipódromo Argentino** racecourse (*see p225*), but walkers and cyclists can skirt this by heading towards the river and continuing on to Núñez and the River Plate football stadium.

Although you may stroll into Palermo as a continuation of your wanderings through Recoleta, the most usual point of access is **Plaza Italia**. The monument to Italian hero Giuseppe Garibaldi at the centre of the plaza is the only static figure in this hectic scene.

The **Jardín Botánico Carlos Thays** (*see right*), in between Avenida Santa Fe, Las Heras

Palermo.

Jardín Botánico Carlos Thays

shopping centre. But the area's most important cultural venue is the Museo de Arte Latinoamericano de Buenos Aires, or **MALBA** (*see p69*), a contemporary space paid for, and stocked by, art collector Eduardo Costantini.

Back on Aveninda del Libertador, on the way towards the centre, is the refurbished **Museo de Arte Popular José Hernández** (*see p69*), named after the author of Argentina's national epic verse-novel, *Martín Fierro* (1873).

Heading back to Recoleta from the park, or vice versa, you can slip off Avenida del Libertador into **Palermo Chico** (aka Barrio Parque). This tiny, upmarket patch of suburbia is where national television stars like Susana Giménez and diplomats park their bulletproof jeeps. There are no shops or even *kioscos* to spoil the views, just plenty of grand architecture to admire. One exception: at the roundabout where Sánchez de Bustamante hits Rufino de Elizalde is the **Monumento San Martín Abuelo**, a rare effigy of the general without his horse. *Abuelo* means 'grandfather', and this likeable likeness of the Liberator shows him in his later years, dispensing advice to his granddaughters.

FREE Jardín Botánico Carlos Thays
Avenida Santa Fe 3951 (4831 4527). Subte D, Plaza Italia/bus 39, 93, 152. **Open** *Apr-Aug* 9am-6pm Mon-Fri; 9.30am-6pm Sat, Sun. *Sept-Mar* 8am-8pm Mon-Fri; 9.30am-7pm Sat, Sun. **Admission** free. **Map** p287 M9.
Laid out by celebrated French landscaper Charles Thays and inaugurated in 1898, BA's botanical garden is a slightly shabby but nonetheless tranquil space, full of fascinating flora. Thousands of species flourish here, and fountains, orchids, cacti, ferns and spectacular trees make this a paradise for anyone who likes to potter around a garden. Monuments include a Venus, Saturnalia and Romulus and Remus. Check out the old stagers playing cards and chess for money on the adjacent square. And if for any reason you need a dozen stray cats in a hurry, this is the place to come.

Jardín Japonés
Avenida Casares, y Figueroa Alcorta (4804 4922, www.jardinjapones.org.ar). Bus 10, 37, 57, 67, 102, 130, 161. **Open** 10am-6pm daily. **Admission** AR$16; free under-12s. **No credit cards. Map** p287 M11.
Created in 1967 as a token of thanks from the local Japanese community, BA's Japanese garden is one of the largest in the world outside Japan. You'll find over 150 species of flora here, many brought specially from the mother country; some are on sale at the small shop next to the entrance. Once you've fed the ravenous ornamental carp (they can jump like Kobe Bryant), you can refresh yourself at the all-day tearoom, which serves green teas and cakes.

and Gurruchaga, is more peaceful. The **Jardín Zoológico** (*see p187*) is across the road.

Beyond the zoo, at the busy junction of *avenidas* Sarmiento and del Libertador, is the bleached-white **Monumento de los Españoles** (*photo p64*). A centenary gift from the Spanish, the four bronzes represent Argentina's four main geographical regions: the Pampas, the Andes, the Chaco and the River Plate.

Designed and overseen by Thays, the **Parque Tres de Febrero** – which locals call Los Bosques de Palermo (the Palermo Woods) – boasts well-kept lawns, beautiful jacarandas and palms, and a lake, as well as cafés and a good art gallery, the **Museo de Artes Plásticas Eduardo Sívori** (*see p69*). A particular highlight is the delightfully pretty **Rosedal** rose garden, accessible from *avenidas* Iraola and Presidente Montt. After dusk this is the city's de facto red-light district for transvestite prostitutes, despite the strenuous efforts by many local residents to get them moved on. 'The function of oral sex in a public space is incompatible with the function of a historic rose garden', explained one city legislator. Less contentious spaces in the Rosedal include the Jardín de los Poetas, with its peaceful fountains surrounded by busts of literary giants, and a tiled Patio Andaluz. If you prefer a lazy float on the lake, hire a pedalo.

Along Avenida Figueroa Alcorta are a number of facilities, including **Paseo Alcorta** (*see p155*)

MALBA.

There's also a highly regarded Japanese restaurant. The highlight of each day is the Tea Ceremony, which takes place at 5pm and is open to all.

▶ *For another taste of Asia in Buenos Aires, visit the Belgrano neighbourhood's small but vibrant Chinatown (see p79).*

★ MALBA: Colección Costantini

Avenida Figueroa Alcorta 3415, entre Salguero y San Martín de Tours (4808 6500, www.malba. org.ar). Bus 10, 37, 67, 92, 102, 110, 128, 130. **Open** noon-8pm Mon, Thur-Sun; noon-9pm Wed. *Guided tours* (Spanish & English) by arrangement. **Admission** AR$25; AR$12 reductions and on Wed. **Credit** AmEx, MC, V. **Map** p286 L11.

With consistent rave reviews in both the local and foreign media, MALBA would be many people's pick for best museum in the city. Frida Kahlo and Diego Rivera, Tarsila do Amaral and other illustrious painters share the walls with wonderful Argentinian modern masters such as Antonio Berni and Jorge de la Vega, who are well respected but not well known internationally. There is also an excellent café and terrace restaurant, plus a small cinema specialising in cult and arthouse retrospectives. The museum shop stocks top local design and a great range of books. The building itself is smaller than Costantini originally wanted, and can house only 40 per cent of his collection. To solve this he has funded an expansion project that will add several new exhibition areas in an underground space beneath Plaza República de Perú.

Museo de Artes Plásticas Eduardo Sívori

Avenida Infanta Isabel 555, in front of the bridge into the Rosedal (4774 9452, www.museosivori.org.ar). Bus 10, 34, 37, 57, 130, 160, 161. **Open** noon-8pm Tue-Fri, 10am-8pm Sat, Sun. **Admission** AR$1. Free Wed, Sat. **No credit cards. Map** p287 N10.

Located in Parque Tres de Febrero, and named for the realist painter Sívori, this excellent museum houses a major collection of Argentinian paintings and sculpture from the 19th century to the present day. If that doesn't appeal, at least have a coffee on the grass patio inside.

Museo de Arte Popular José Hernández

Avenida del Libertador 2373, entre San Martín de Tours y Coronel Díaz (4803 2384, www.mujose.org.ar). Bus 10, 37, 59, 60, 92, 93, 102, 118, 128, 188. **Open** 1-6.30pm Wed-Fri; 10am-7pm Sat, Sun. **Admission** AR$1; free under-12s, reductions. Free Sun. **No credit cards. Map** p286 L11.

The museum's main collection comprises gaucho motifs and other elements of Argentina's rural past. Two buildings off a patio are hung with maté gourds, spurs, weapons (especially knives) and other gaucho paraphernalia. There's also a reconstruction of a *pulpería*, the tavern-cum-grocer's shop that was the focal point of 19th-century country life. The museum also features exhibits inspired by matters of Argentinian history.

SIGHTS

SIGHTS

Museo Evita

Lafinur 2988, entre Gutiérrez y Avenida Las Heras (4807 9433, www.museoevita.org). Subte D, Plaza Italia/bus 37, 59, 60, 102. **Open** 11am-7pm Tue-Sun. **Admission** AR$15 (AR$25 with guided tour). **No credit cards. Map** p287 M9.
This museum is housed in an aristocratic residence that Perón expropriated to convert into a women's shelter for his wife's welfare agency. It's worth a visit to see the range of myths Evita has inspired in Argentina. Paintings, posters and busts are displayed alongside fabulous outfits she wore on tours of Europe. The two star pieces are the dresses designed by Paco Jamandreu that she wore for her audiences with the Pope, and her *libreta cívica* (identity document) – No.0.000.001. Arguably better than the museum itself is the adjoining restaurant and outdoor terrace.

Palermo Viejo

Comprising Palermo Soho and Palermo Hollywood (Soho is south-east of Avenida Juan B Justo and Hollywood is north-west), Palermo Viejo was run down and romantic until the early 1990s. The area has since been thoroughly transformed by restaurants and boutiques. While modern tower blocks are increasingly peppering the area, many of the homes here are still just one or two storeys high, and the townhouses – many of them revamped into urban lofts – come with terraces. There's a literary past here – witness the street called Borges and the **Plazoleta Cortázar** (at the junction of Borges and Honduras – better known still by its former name, Plaza Serrano), but thanks to an influx of nightclubs and bars, these days there's more emphasis on high jinks than high culture.

East European and Armenian communities made Palermo Viejo their home in the early 20th century, and cuisines from all over the world are served in the area's many restaurants. Although it's not particularly attractive, Plazoleta Cortázar is hugely popular for alfresco drinking beneath the lime trees among Argentinians and those who find the pseudo-bohemian bars too expensive.

Elsewhere in Palermo

Fringed by the polo ground and racecourse is a buzzing residential and dining district known as **Las Cañitas** (the name comes from the sugar canes that once grew wild here). It's a popular focal point for the monied socialites of Palermo and Belgrano, with little historical interest by day. The area made the news big time when former president Carlos Menem gave the Saudis land on which to build the city's mega-mosque and religious centre, the **Centro Islámico Rey Fahd** at *avenidas* Bullrich and del Libertador. For information on guided tours (Spanish only), and other activities, such as Arabic language classes, call 4899 1144.

One of Palermo's more amusingly-monikered unofficial sub-barrios, just south of Plaza Italia, is **Villa Freud**; the name makes reference to the number of psychoanalysts working there. Sharing the area with the shrinks are several spiritual centres, including a Buddhist cemetery, a mosque and the **Basílica del Espíritu Santo** on Plaza Güemes (at the corner of Mansilla and Medrano). This sturdy church, built between 1901 and 1907, is known by locals as Guadalupe, after the 16th-century Mexican Virgin who later became an icon of that country's independence struggle.

Palermo.

West of the Centre

The city's wild west: heartland of tango and for many, the 'real' BA.

The western neighbourhoods best reflect BA's rich immigrant traditions. What they lack in European-style mansions, they make up for in homely bakeries, serious milongas, barbershops, avant-garde theatres and shops that sell 1980s video game consoles. In short, here is the unpretentious Buenos Aires where most *porteños* live, work, play and die.

The barrio of Once is a riotous commercial hub, and the place to go if you're in the market for tinsel, tights or textiles, while Abasto and Boedo are both famed for their tango heritage. Traditionally residential areas like Caballito and Almagro offer parks as well as historic bars and cafés for the fringe-friendly tourist. Leafy Villa Crespo is fast becoming the barrio of choice among hipster locals, thanks to the volume of new down-to-earth bars and restaurants offering a refreshing alternative to Palermo's night scene.

West of the Centre

North of the Centre

Aeroparque Jorge Newbery

South of the Centre

The Centre

Along the River

Reserva Ecológica

RÍO DE LA PLATA

0   2 miles
0   2 km

Map pp282-283 & pp285-286   **Restaurants** p138
Hotels p105   **Cafés, Bars & Pubs** p153

ONCE & ABASTO

Subte A, Plaza Miserere or C, Carlos Gardel/ bus 24, 68, 88, 104, 168, 188, 194.
The neighbourhood of Once (pronounced 'ON-say'), about 20 blocks west along Avenida Corrientes from the Microcentro, is the city's most hectic commercial district, a warren of wholesale and retail outlets, the origin of whose wares it is best not to ask about. Visitors who have bought into the cliché of Buenos Aires being the 'Paris of South America' should take a detour here – Once has all the subtlety and sophistication of a Guatemalan bus station, but it's a heck of a lot more fun than the Champs-Elysées. Historically associated with the city's large Jewish population, it now has sizeable Korean and Peruvian communities.

The barrio is named after the ugly 11 (Once) de Septiembre railway station – which commemorates an 1852 battle between the provinces and the capital. The station was the scene of carnage in February 2012 when a train failed to stop in time, crashing into a platform barrier and killing 51 passengers. The adjacent **Plaza Miserere** (usually called Plaza Once), for years a rubbish-strewn hub

for transport, the sex trade and preachers foretelling the apocalypse, is now also home to the monument to those who died in the Cromañón nightclub fire of 2004. On the corner of Bartolomé Mitre and Ecuador is a mural in their honour.

Avenidas Rivadavia and Pueyrredón are Once's main arteries, but the neighbourhood's pulse is found in the blocks to the north and east of their intersection. Here, Latin dance beats blast out from every other store, with the tack and trash sold inside spilling on to the streets. If you like sterile shopping malls, forget Once, though it certainly deserves a quick jaunt to experience what local author Álvaro Abós calls a 'branch of hell'.

As for Jewish Once, the **Congregación Sefardi**, a Moorish-style Sephardic synagogue at Lavalle 2400, is worth a visit. Two blocks away, at Paso 400, is the elegant **Ashkenazi Templo de Paso**. The synagogues are best visited with a tour, but access has been restricted since the 1990s Jewish-targeted terrorist attacks. Victims of the 1994 car bomb attack on Once's **AMIA Jewish Welfare Centre** are remembered by the moving **Monumento de Homenaje y Recordación a las Víctimas**

El Abasto de Buenos Aires.

del Atentado a la AMIA, situated in the courtyard of the reconstructed building, at Pasteur 633. Tour agencies require 48 hours' notice to arrange visits here.

Once is, in fact, part of a barrio officially known as Balvanera, with its northern limit at Avenida Córdoba. At Córdoba 1950 is the striking **Palacio de Aguas Corrientes** (Palace of Running Water), occupying a whole block. It's home to the capital's water works, which were run by private company Aguas Argentinas until the government intervened in 2006. Constructed between 1887 and 1895, this flamboyantly decorated building, with its vivid colours and jigsaw of architectural styles, is a real one-off among the city's civic piles.

Just up from Once, at Avenida Corrientes and Anchorena, is the beautiful **Mercado de Abasto** building, a curvaceous art deco masterpiece built between 1930 and 1934 as a wholesale market. It was neglected for decades, and the building's powerful, but empty, decaying presence became symbolic of the Abasto neighbourhood's own downward spiral into a seedy scene of blues, booze and cocaine.

In 1998, the market building was the first in the barrio to see rejuvenation, converted into a shopping centre known as **El Abasto de Buenos Aires** (*see p155*). Inside the mall is the interactive children's museum **Museo de los Niños** (*see p187*), full of educationally-minded displays about the commercial and industrial activities of Buenos Aires.

Speaking of commerce, Once's **Museo de la Deuda Externa** (*see p73*) provides a deeper explanation of the maddening rollercoaster that is Argentina's economy.

If one regards La Boca as the cradle of tango, Abasto can be thought of as its nursery. Seminal composers like Osvaldo Pugliese and Aníbal Troilo either lived or were born in the neighbourhood. But no *tanguero* is more closely

associated with this barrio than the greatest of them all, '*el morocho*' Carlos Gardel, who lived here for most of his life. The small but neat **Museo Casa Carlos Gardel** (*see below*) offers a peep into the domestic life of the legendary crooner. Tangophiles should also visit **Pasaje Zelaya**, a two-block street whose buildings are adorned with tango lyrics written by Alfredo Le Pera, and five colourful portraits of Gardel by the artist Marino Santa María.

At the intersection of Sarmiento and Jean Jaurès is the multi-purpose **Ciudad Cultural Konex** (*see p221*), a vast and very popular arts complex. The building's exterior echoes the geometric design of El Abasto's art deco style, and inside there are various performance spaces. With a programme inspired by the Pompidou Centre in Paris, it's the nerve centre of the influential **Fundación Konex**.

Museo Casa Carlos Gardel

Jean Jaurès 735, entre Zelaya y Tucumán, Abasto (4964 2015/www.museocasacarlosgardel. buenosaires.gob.ar). Subte B, Pueyrredón or Carlos Gardel/bus 29, 99, 140. **Open** 11am-6pm Mon, Wed-Fri; 10am-7pm Sat, Sun.
Guided tours Spanish and English on request.
Admission AR$1. Free Wed. **No credit cards.**
Map p286 J8.

A tribute to one of the 20th century's greatest exponents of popular song, the Gardel museum is located in the house – a classic *casa chorizo* ('sausage house') in which all rooms open out on to a central patio – purchased by the singer in 1927. He lived here, in his beloved barrio, with his beloved mother, until 1933. The museum preserves and exhibits various items and memorabilia that either belonged to or were connected to the tango legend who tragically died young in a plane crash in Colombia while on tour. Among the museum's activities are free tango classes (call to check times) and screenings of films that the tango king acted – and of course, sang – in.

FREE Museo de la Deuda Externa

Centro Cultural Ernesto Sábato, Facultad de Ciencias Económicas, Uriburu 763, entre Viamonte y Avenida Córdoba, Once (4370 6105/www.museodeladeuda.com.ar). Subte D, Facultad de Medicina/bus 39, 68, 152. **Open** 9am-8pm Mon-Fri. **Admission** free. **Map** p286 I9.

A topical museum sounds like a contradiction in terms, but the Museum of Foreign Debt, run by the (itself permanently debt-stricken) University of Buenos Aires (UBA), harks back not only to the city's golden age but also to a very recent and far less glittering era – the economic crisis of 2001-02. Opened in 2005, the museum charts the course of the country's overdraft from the first default of 1827 to the chaos of December 2001. It all sounds pretty grim, but despite, or perhaps because of, the downbeat subject matter, the exhibits are suffused with the dark humour porteños are famous for. A visit is probably best avoided if you work for the International Monetary Fund. Audio guides in English are available on request.

BOEDO

Subte E, Boedo/bus 75, 88, 97, 160.
Street corners hold a unique status in Buenos Aires life. According to tangos, illicit encounters and knife fights always happen on *esquinas*, and corner cafés are the settings for last coffees with lovers, or sorrowful binges. These days, plaques decorated in the traditional *fileteado* style appear on hundreds of corners around the city, commemorating anything from tango singers to long-gone bars. Nowhere is this more evident than in one of the bona fide barrios of tango, Boedo. Signs seem to hang

from every corner around here, but one of these intersections is probably more famous than any other in the city: San Juan and Boedo.

When lyricist Homero Manzi scribbled his extraordinary ode to the city's poorer south, 'Sur', in 1948, he was already lamenting the loss of the neighbourhood's golden period as if it were a lover who'd just jilted him for another *tanguero*. 'Ancient San Juan and Boedo, lost sky ... Sorrow for the barrio that has changed/ and bitterness for a dream that died.'

Were he alive today, Manzi would be aggrieved to discover that his beloved bar on this corner, where musicians and poets once gathered, is now a tango-for-tourists venue. He would be more encouraged, however, to see a new crop of genuinely bohemian bars, art cafés and guesthouses springing up, prompting whispers that Boedo is becoming the 'new' Palermo. Whether or not this would be a desirable fate for the moody, old-school barrio is a matter for debate.

In Boedo, as elsewhere, Avenida Rivadavia marks the boundary between the wealthier north and the poorer south. Heading south from here is Avenida Boedo, named after Dr Mariano Boedo, a brilliant lawyer born in 1782 who fervently supported the Argentinian drive for independence. A series of sculptures stretch down Avenida Boedo from Avenida Independencia – a classic example of how the artistic and political traditions of Buenos Aires are often so tightly interwoven.

At Boedo 745, only a plaque marks the location of the **Café Dante**. This 100-year-old bar, closed in 2003, was frequented by players and fans of top-flight football team, San Lorenzo, whose red and blue stripes can

Mural of Carlos Gardel, Abasto.

SIGHTS

SIGHTS

Fabulous Fileteado

Colourful, swirly and cool, this uniquely porteño art form is famous in Abasto.

Buenos Aires, the city that talks up tango and brags about Borges, is surprisingly bashful about promoting its unique contribution to the visual arts, the decorative style known as *fileteado*. When asked about it, many *porteños* will reward you with a blank stare. Which is strange when you consider that it's a fundamentally public and popular art genre. It was never meant for museum walls. The originators of *fileteado*, who lived in BA in the late 19th century weren't even artists. They were Italian immigrants employed as engineers and bodywork finishers in the city's transport workshops. They weren't paid to paint, but, upon deciding that their vehicles should look good as

well as run smoothly, paint they did, using cheap acrylics and their own ingenuity. With the side panels of *colectivos* (city buses), handcarts and delivery vans as their canvases, workers like Salvador Venturo and Vicente Brunetti developed the signature style of *fileteado*: brightly coloured decorative whorls and vortices, flower motifs, calligraphic flourishes and tendril-like lines that resolve themselves into the heads of fabulous creatures. Pithy phrases and maxims were often incorporated into the design, making *fileteado* a sophisticated precursor of the bumper sticker. Up until the mid 1970s, the main audience for *fileteado* consisted of commuters. It was steadfastly ignored by the *porteño* art elite – perhaps because it wasn't elitist enough. Then, showing the same disregard for aesthetics as they did for human rights, the military dictatorship banned the use of fileteado on city buses. Buenos Aires entered a darker period in more ways than one.

But the good news for lovers of colour is that *fileteado* has made a comeback. Once dismissed for being grassroots and native (there is a parallel with tango here), the *fileteado* is now lauded for exactly those reasons. It is reappearing on the walls of

concert venues, on book covers, in ad campaigns and as part of interior design schemes. Even uber-trendy Faena Hotel + Universe has a part *fileteado* floor in its El Mercado restaurant. The artist commissioned by Faena and the leading contemporary exponent of *fileteado* is Alfredo Genovese. A passionate cheerleader for the art form, he has published a book about it, also available in English, and hosts *fileteado* workshops (see www.fileteado.com.ar).

To see examples of this unique *porteño* art, head to Abasto and take a stroll along the Paseo de Fileteado on Jean Jaurès. The block between Zelaya and Tucumán was selected as the open-air canvas for a competition entitled '*Abasto y el fileteado*', organised by the Museo Carlos Gardel in 2004 – the year *fileteado* was officially declared part of Argentina's *patrimonio cultural* (cultural heritage). Six contemporary artists, including Horacio Vega and Marcos Inza, were allocated a house upon which to unleash their imaginations, transforming the block into a landmark bursting with colourful curlicues and bold brushwork, which stands testament to the expertise and endurance of this emblematic art form.

be seen hanging from balconies around the barrio. Across the road is the compact **Museo Monte de Piedad** (*see below*).

A block further along is the aforementioned **Esquina de Homero Manzi**. No longer a 'blacksmith's corner' scented with 'weeds and alfalfa', this busy junction offers zero nostalgia. Better to head off Avenida Boedo to admire the many beautifully restored – or re-imagined – 18th- and 19th-century townhouses.

FREE Museo Monte de Piedad

2nd Floor, Avenida Boedo 870, entre Estados Unidos y Carlos Calvo, Boedo (1932 4680). Subte E, Boedo/bus 88, 160. **Open** 10am-5pm Mon-Fri (guided tours only, on demand, in English and Spanish). **Admission** free. **Map** p282 I2.

Essentially a history of how a municipal pawnbroker for immigrants became the city bank, this museum also provides a glimpse into the city at the turn of the 20th century. It includes a partly recreated Café Biarritz, which once stood on this spot and was the meeting place of the Boedo Literary Group, an assembly of socialist and anarchist writers, poets and playwrights active during the 1920s. Brutal, colloquial works by local novelists like Roberto Arlt – who influenced writers such as William Burroughs and Irvine Welsh – reflect the Group's working-class roots.

▶ *One old-school café still standing is atmospheric Café Margot (Avenida Boedo 857, 4957 0001).*

ALMAGRO, CABALLITO & VILLA CRESPO

Subte B, Medrano, Angel Gallardo or Malabia; Subte A, Castro Barros, Río de Janeiro, Acoyte or Primera Junta/bus 24, 55, 160, 168.

West of the Abasto neighbourhood, Almagro, Caballito and Villa Crespo are three districts with particularly proud residents and a real neighbourhood air. **Parque Centenario**, in Caballito, serves as the sole park for these densely populated barrios, and fills up on weekends with market stalls and hordes of families.

The main crowd-puller, and great for kids, is the **Museo Argentino de Ciencias Naturales Bernardino Rivadavia** (*see p187*), with plenty of fossils as well as several enormous Patagonian dinosaur skeletons.

Caballito is also a reminder of a gentler era in Buenos Aires, when the tram was king. Now, this is the only barrio that keeps the soothing clankety-clank alive, with a 25-minute service departing from Emilio Mitre and José Bonifacio every 15 minutes on Saturday afternoons and Sunday mornings and afternoons. For times, check the website of the **Asociación Amigos del Tranvía** (www.tranvia.org.ar).

Almagro and Villa Crespo are traditional residential neighbourhoods, although the latter, in particular, is becoming increasingly gentrified, in large part due to its proximity to hip Palermo. Life in both of these barrios revolves around the main *avenidas* Corrientes and Córdoba; off these traffic-choked thoroughfares you'll find quieter side streets where a number of small bars and restaurants offer decent inexpensive drinks and meals.

CHACARITA

Subte B, Federico Lacroze/bus 39, 65, 93, 168.

Like many one-time outlying barrios, Chacarita – originally the location of an important Jesuit farming community, hence the name (*chacra* is Spanish for small farm) – developed around a railway station, **Federico Lacroze**. The terminus, opened in 1880, is now just a commuter hub. Far more interesting is the **Cementerio de la Chacarita** (*see below*) on the other side of Avenida Guzmán. The cemetery was conceived as a resting place for the staggering number of individuals who died from the yellow fever outbreak of 1871.

The zone around Lacroze station is lively, bordering on chaotic, with numerous pizza parlours and primitive *parrillas* servicing the commuters, and plenty of pavement florists servicing tomb-bound mourners. Otherwise, Chacarita is quiet, pretty and solidly middle class – much as Palermo was before it became expensive and fashionable. The analogy has not been lost on local estate agents, who have begun to dub the barrio 'Palermo Dead' – either because they think an apartment within a stone's throw of a graveyard is automatically a des res, or because they just can't help themselves.

FREE Cementerio de la Chacarita

Avenida Guzmán 680, y Federico Lacroze (4553 0041). Subte B, Federico Lacroze/ bus 39, 93, 111. **Open** 7am-6pm daily. **Admission** free. **Map** p283 O2/P2.

Now far more expansive than Recoleta's exclusive necropolis, with numbered streets and car access to its thousands of vaults, this cemetery is largely for ordinary folk. Still, a number of popular heroes have also wound up here, including Carlos Gardel, Alfonsina Storni and aviation pioneer Jorge Newbery. Until 1939, Chacarita also held the cemeteries of the Jewish, British and German communities. After the middle of the 20th century, with Hitler affecting relations even in far-off Argentina, the Jews left for a new site west of the city, and the Brits and Germans built walls to separate their dead.

Along the River

Riverside promenades, designer docks and a 12-metre-high Jesus.

It's big, it's brown and without it Buenos Aires simply would never have happened. We're talking about the massive Río de la Plata – 200 kilometres wide at its broadest point.

Beside it, you'll find the yachts and yuppies of chichi Puerto Madero with the unpretentious Costanera Sur nearby – the site of the popular nature reserve filled with kissing couples, cyclists and young families sipping maté on the weekends.

On the Costanera Norte, the gloriously kitsch **Tierra Santa** religious theme park (yes, really; *see p78*) attracts hordes of visitors, while the **Parque de la Memoria** (*see p78*) is an important and tasteful site of remembrance dedicated to the thousands of victims of the 1976-1983 military dictatorship; stone tablets bear the names of the 'disappeared'.

Map pp284-285	Restaurants p115
& pp287-288	Cafés, Bars
Hotels p91	& Pubs p147

PUERTO MADERO & COSTANERA SUR

Subte B, LN Alem/bus 26, 61, 93, 152, 159.
The appearance of Puerto Madero – the dockland area to the east of Plaza de Mayo, divided into two lengthy promenades on either side of the dock, Puerto Madero Oeste (west) and Puerto Madero Este (east) – is the embodiment of BA's self-image as a grand, European-style city. The red-brick port buildings and grain warehouses, built between 1889 and 1898, were the first view of BA seen by immigrants, and the city fathers wanted to impress them with a modern skyline.

Yet as early as 1911, a new harbour was being built, the narrow rectangular wharves having proved hopelessly inadequate. Puerto Nuevo, as it is known, is still where container ships load up north of Retiro. Meanwhile, Puerto Madero went into decline, and the dream docks became rat-infested husks. It was only in the late 1980s that the area began to get some love from the powers-that-be. The Puerto Madero Oeste development was officially unveiled in 1996, with a new-look quayside, flashy restaurants and high-rent apartments. Only relatively recently has

the riverside zone gained some depth, with projects of a civic, cultural and commercial slant springing up along the promenades of BA's youngest barrio.

One of the most important of these is the **Colección de Arte Amalia Lacroze de Fortabat** (*see p77*), a glass and concrete structure shaped like a giant claw. Amalia Lacroze de Fortabat was, until she died in 2012, Argentina's richest woman, and judging from the size and quality of her art collection, was something of a Peggy Guggenheim *manquée*. The museum is mostly dedicated to Argentinian art; one very notable exception is a portrait of Fortabat herself by Andy Warhol.

The location of the museum couldn't be more appropriate. Real estate prices in the Madero Este zone are now among the highest in Latin America. This is a world created for the rich and beautiful. Although unabashed in celebrating the finer things in life, much of Puerto Madero is, curiously, also dedicated to struggle, as all its streets are named after women who fought for female emancipation in Argentina. Encarnación Ezcurra, wife of 19th-century caudillo Juan Manuel de Rosas, and Azucena Villaflor, founder of the Mothers of Plaza de Mayo, are among those honoured.

Puerto Madero.

For evidence of the area's maritime history, visit the impeccable **Corbeta Uruguay**, moored further down on Dique 4 at Alicia Moreau de Justo and Corrientes. A museum vessel of Argentina's Naval Academy dating back to 1874, the Uruguay would apppear to have been above regular warfare, and instead distinguished itself in revolutions, expeditions and search-and-rescue missions. At Dique 3 is the even more impressive **Fragata Presidente Sarmiento** (*see right*).

Stretching in front of the Sarmiento is the elegant **Puente de La Mujer**, a pedestrian bridge designed by the renowned Spanish engineer Santiago Calatrava. Opened to acclaim in December 2001, the bridge's US$6 million construction costs were covered by Alberto R González, late owner of much of Madero Este and its Hilton Hotel. The Hilton, however, faces competition from the striking **Faena Hotel + Universe** (*see p91*), an über-stylish Philippe Starck-designed hotel, which opened the **Faena Arts Centre** (*see p78*) in 2011.

Beyond Madero Este is an altogether earthier experience, the Río de la Plata's other urban jungle: the **Reserva Ecológica Costanera Sur** (*see p78*), BA's biggest – free – wilderness on the edge of the city. The long esplanade skirting the reserve is one of the city's most pleasant spaces for walking and sunbathing. A lavish 1927 *bierkeller*, the **Cervecería Munich** houses the **Centro de Museos** (Avenida de los Italianos 851, 4516 0944), from where all the city's museums are administered. A guided tour of the picturesque former pub shows how good life used to be for the city's wealthy weekenders.

Just south, at the centre of a roundabout near the reserve's entrance (Avenida Tristán

Achaval Rodríguez y Padre ML Migone), is an eye-catching fountain, executed in 1902 by Tucumán-born artist Lola Mora. The **Fuente de las Nereidas** is a marble allegory set in a clam shell, depicting erotic female forms (worth a look if mermaids are your thing).

One block south, you'll find many cheap parrillas (most of them in the guise of small, technically mobile vans known as *carritos*), making this a popular weekend lunch spot.

Buque Museo Fragata Presidente Sarmiento

Alicia Moreau de Justo 900, y Belgrano, Dique 3, Puerto Madero (4334 9336). Subte B, LN Alem/bus 4, 93, 152. **Open** 10am-7pm daily. **Admission** AR$2; free under-5s. **No credit cards.** **Map** p285 E11.

This frigate, built in Birkenhead, was used as a training ship from 1897 to 1961. Its second life is as a wonderful museum, full of photos, maps and domestic objects, with the original cabins and dining rooms restored and intact. The vessel was a floating witness to numerous important occasions of state, including the coronations of Kings Edward VII and George V of Britain, the opening of the Panama Canal, and the 100th anniversary of Mexican independence. Photographs of these and other events are displayed on board.

Colección de Arte Amalia Lacroze de Fortabat

Olga Cossettini 141, Puerto Madero (4310 6600, www.coleccionfortabat.org.ar). Subte B, LN Alem/bus 4, 26, 152. **Open** noon-9pm Tue-Sun. **Admission** AR$25; AR$10 reductions. **Credit** AmEx, MC, V. **Map** p285 F12.

SIGHTS

This, the private treasure trove of the late Amalia Lacroze de Fortabat, who held the status as Argentina's wealthiest woman, is housed in a stunning glass and steel airplane hangar-type edifice in front of Dique (dock) 4 on Puerto Madero's rapidly developing waterfront. The collection of both Argentinian and international works includes the psychologically complex paintings of Carlos Alonso and the highly versatile work of the painter of the people, Antonio Berni. Don't miss the Dalí, the Turner or the Brueghel pieces, or Warhol's silkscreen of Amalia Lacroze de Fortabat herself. Guided tours in Spanish are at 3pm and 5pm from Tuesday to Sunday, or call in advance to arrange a tour in English.

Faena Arts Centre

Aimé Paine 1169, y Azucena Villaflor, Puerto Madero (4010 9233, www.faenaartscentre.org) Bus 2, 64, 111, 152. **Open** 11am-7pm Tue-Sun. **Admission** AR$22. **Map** p284 D11.
The Faena Hotel + Universe (*see p91*) has added another landmark to its Puerto Madero empire, opening the city's hottest new contemporary art space inside a restored flour mill. It has all the glamour of the hotel, complete with majestic marble stairs and high ceilings that lend themselves to large-scale installations.

Reserva Ecológica Costanera Sur

Avenida Tristán Achaval Rodríguez 1550 (4893 1588/freephone 0800 444 5343). Bus 2, 4. **Open** *Apr-Oct* 8am-6pm Tue-Sun. *Nov-Mar* 8am-7pm Tue-Sun. **Admission** free. **Map** p284 C11.
Within this nature reserve's boundaries, four lakes, giant *cortaderas* (foxtail pampas grass), willows and shrubs provide habitats for more than 200 bird species, not to mention a bit of privacy for cruising gay men. Iguanas scuttle across the hard earth, but on weekends you're more likely to see joggers, cyclists and picnickers among the 15,000 or so visitors who descend on the reserve. Moonlight tours are organised one night per month, whenever the moon is fullest; phone ahead to book your place.

COSTANERA NORTE

Bus 33, 37, 45, 130.
North of town, skirting the **Aeroparque Jorge Newbery** – the city airport that, rather impressively, runs the length of Palermo – is a traditional promenade. One of the few places where the mud-coloured river laps close to the land, the paved thoroughfare has a few restaurants and is thronged on any given Sunday with anglers, walkers, cyclists and maté-supping, picnic-eating day trippers. The main road – Avenida Costanera Rafael Obligado – hums with traffic heading out of

the city, and the airliners zooming overhead make the noise pollution almost comical. But it's dramatic in an urban jetsetter kind of way. The city's beach and sports clubs, where thousands of porteño families go to beat the heat during the sweltering summer months, dot the avenue.

At the southern end of the airport is the chalet-style **Club de Pescadores**, a private fishing club of which Carlos Gardel was once a member. The pier is for the club's anglers, but visitors can dine in the airy restaurant, accessed via the oak and marble entrance hall. The area around the club is currently being redeveloped.

North of the airport is wacky religious theme park **Tierra Santa** (*see below*), curiously one of BA's most popular attractions since opening at the turn of the millennium.

On the final northern curve of the Costanera Norte, close to the Ciudad Universitaria, is the **Parque de la Memoria** (Avenida Costanera Norte Rafael Obligado 6745, 4787 0999, www.parquedelamemoria.org.ar), which has been developed in remembrance of Argentinian victims of human rights abuses under the 1976-1983 military dictatorship. Completed in 2005 and opened in 2007, the park features a sombre centrepiece, the Monumento a las Víctimas del Terrorismo de Estado, which contains stone tablets bearing the names of Argentina's 'disappeared', many of whom were drugged and then thrown to their deaths from planes into the Río de la Plata. The Plaza de Acceso includes works by noted American sculptors Dennis Oppenheim and William Tucker.

Tierra Santa

Avenida Costanera Rafael Obligado 5790 (4784 9551/www.tierrasanta-bsas.com.ar). Bus 33, 37, 42, 160. **Open** *May-Nov* 9am-9pm Fri; noon-10pm Sat, Sun. *Dec-Apr* 4pm-midnight Fri-Sun. **Guided tours** Spanish every 30-40mins. **Admission** AR$50; AR$20 under-11s. **Credit** MC, V. **Map** p288 R11.
Modestly touted by its creators as 'a chance to visit Jerusalem all year round', Tierra Santa is the kind of project that might have been realised had Walt Disney and Billy Graham put their heads together. This Holy Land experience begins with a son-et-lumière extravaganza celebrating the Nativity. As the Angel of the Annunciation descends from a neon-lit sky, locals in Middle Eastern drag herd visitors into the 'world's largest manger'. But the pièce de résistance is undoubtedly the Resurrection, re-enacted every 45 minutes, when a 12-metre haloed Christ rises from the depths of a plastic Mount Golgotha to a series of 'Hallelujahs'. Another highlight are the shawarmas sold in the park's cafés.

SIGHTS

Further Afield

Into museums and urban rodeos? Then the 'burbs is where it's at.

Not many visitors venture far off BA's well-beaten tourist circuit, but those who do are rewarded with some of the city's most distinctive and diverse sights and sounds.

Belgrano hides notable historical and art museums, and its plush homes, modern tower blocks and leafy parks seem a world away from the small yet energetic Barrio Chino (Chinatown) in the same northern neighbourhood.

Fancy rubbing shoulders with Buenos Aires high society and enjoying a spot of aqua diversion? Then head to Zona Norte. Or else, go west to Mataderos on the weekend for an unmissable colourful fair that sees gauchos showing off their skills on horseback and couples of all ages dancing in the central square to live folkloric music (*see p80*).

Tigre

San Isidro

BUENOS
AIRES
PROVINCE

RÍO DE LA PLATA

Olivos
Vicente López

Saavedra
Nuñez

Liniers

BUENOS
AIRES
CITY

0   10 km

0   10 miles

Map p288	**Cafés, Bars**
Hotels p107	**& Pubs** p154
Restaurants p141	

BELGRANO & NÚÑEZ

Subte D, Juramento/bus 60, 65, 152, 168.
From the north–south downtown axis, all roads initially lead west, but *avenidas* Santa Fe, Córdoba and Corrientes eventually fan out to the smarter north-western neighbourhoods in the conurbation of Belgrano. Those who live there rave about it, but it's essentially a residential and commercial district. Named after independence hero General Manuel Belgrano, it was originally a city in its own right, but its incorporation into the capital in 1887 turned the area into a des res option for affluent *porteños*. Though the Subte from the centre gets you there in a matter of minutes, it still feels like a separate town and its main thoroughfare, Avenida Cabildo, is as important and as horribly busy as any downtown.

The most attractive parts of Belgrano are a block from the commercial epicentre; the two museums on Plaza General Belgrano are definitely worth a visit. The **Museo de Arte Español Enrique Larreta** (*see p80*) is housed in a neo-colonial mansion that once belonged to wealthy Uruguayan exile Enrique Larreta. Across the road is the **Museo**

Histórico Sarmiento (*see p80*), dedicated to one of America's greatest educators, Domingo Sarmiento. Also worthwhile is the **Museo Casa de Yrurtia** (*see p80*) a few blocks away, which showcases the work of its former resident, sculptor Rogelio Yrurtia.

Calle Juramento runs north to the verdant *barrancas* (slopes) bordering the Belgrano C railway station (on the Mitre line from Retiro). On and around Arribeños, running parallel to the railway line, is BA's diminutive **Chinatown**, populated by mainland Chinese and especially Taiwanese immigrants who arrived in several waves after World War II and own most of the restaurants and supermarkets in the area. At **Chinese New Year** (*see p184*), the community takes its celebrations to the streets.

Avenida Cabildo runs on into Núñez, which borders BA province. Again, this is largely a residential district, with the smartest houses encircling the huge 100,000-spectator **Estadio Monumental** (*see p225*), home to River Plate football club and the venue for the 1978 World Cup final – which Argentina won amid rumours of bribery and protests about atrocities being committed under military dictator Jorge Rafael Videla. Nearby, at

SIGHTS

Avenida del Libertador 8000-8500, is what was until recently known as the Ex-Escuela Mecánica de la Armada, or ESMA. It has been renamed to the long-winded **Espacio para la Memoria y para la Promoción y Defensa de los Derechos Humanos** (4704 4958, www.institutomemoria.org.ar) and was the country's most notorious torture centre and death camp of the 1970s, where 5,000 men and women were clandestinely held under suspicion of 'subversion'. This museum is not permanently open to the public, but call or email visitasguiadas@ espaciomemoria.ar to arrange a guided tour in Spanish or English.

Flanking Núñez is Saavedra, where Parque Saavedra and Parque Sarmiento provide urban dwellers with cleaner air and greenery. The **Museo Histórico Cornelio de Saavedra** (*see below*) is located in the former residence of Luis María Saavedra (descendant of the museum's namesake who was one of the heroes of Argentinian independence).

Museo de Arte Español Enrique Larreta

Juramento 2291, y Vuelta de Obligado (4783 2640). Subte D, Juramento/bus 55, 60, 65. **Open** 1-7pm Mon-Fri; 10am-8pm Sat, Sun. **Admission** AR$1. Free Thur. **No credit cards. Map** p288 S8.
The varied collection here, in the 19th-century edifice that was at one point the residence of Argentinian writer Enrique Larreta, includes Renaissance and modern Spanish art, which is displayed among stunning furniture, tapestries and silverware. Equally eye-catching are the gardens, a riot of flowering and climbing plants skirting a large native *ombú* tree that's more than 200 years old.

Museo Casa de Yrurtia

O'Higgins 2390, y Blanco Encalada (4781 0385/www.casadeyrurtia.gov.ar). Bus 29, 59, 60, 152. **Open** 1-7pm Tue-Fri; 3-7pm Sat, Sun. **Admission** AR$5. Free Tue. **No credit cards. Map** p288 S8.
This was the home of sculptor Rogelio Yrurtia (1879-1950), who is responsible for a great number of monuments around the city, including the *Canto al Trabajo* bronze on Paseo Colón. The museum includes a lush garden as well as numerous small sculptures and casts of major works.

Museo Histórico Cornelio de Saavedra

Crisólogo Larralde 6309, y Medeyros (4572 0746). Train to Villa Urquiza, then bus 176/ bus 28, 110, 111, 176. **Open** 9am-6pm Tue-Fri; 10am-8pm Sat, Sun. **Admission** AR$1; free under-12s. Free Tue, Wed. **No credit cards.**

In addition to 18th- and 19th-century furniture, silverware and arms, the museum records daily life and highlights the fashions used in the old city. Guided tours (in Spanish and English) are offered by arrangement on Saturdays and Sundays.

Museo Histórico Sarmiento

Juramento 2180, entre Cuba y Arcos (4781 2989/www.museosarmiento.gov.ar). Subte D, Juramento/bus 60, 68, 152. **Open** Apr-Nov 1-6pm Mon-Fri; 3-7pm Sat, Sun. Dec-Mar 1-5.30pm Mon-Fri. **Admission** AR$5. Free Thur. **No credit cards. Map** p288 R8.
Domingo Sarmiento was Argentinian president from 1868 to 1874. He was also a writer; his work, *Facundo*, was a treatise – somewhat reminiscent of Matthew Arnold's *Culture and Anarchy* – on the need for Argentinians to stop being gauchos. The museum, housed in a neoclassical building that once served as Belgrano's city hall, contains documents, old books and household objects.

MATADEROS & LINIERS

Bus 21, 28, 36, 141, 143.
In the far west, the barrios get noticeably poorer, with occasional shantytowns dotting the gloomscape of high-rise 'mono-blocks'. People tend to be friendlier and calmer in the outer reaches, but some streets are dodgy and night strolls are not recommended. This is definitely the case at the outer city limits in the barrio of Mataderos, named after its slaughterhouses and formerly known as Nueva Chicago for the cattle carnage theme it shares with the Windy City.

On Sundays (Saturday evenings and into the night in summer), the place is brightened up by a rural-style fair, the **Feria de Mataderos**. Also open on Sundays is the **Museo Criollo de los Corrales** (*see p81*), which displays gaucho artefacts.

In nearby Liniers, another barrio linked closely with the meatpacking business, the country's second most important saint (after the Virgin of Luján) has his shrine. Proletarian pilgrims flock each month to worship San Cayetano, a 15th-century Venetian priest and the patron saint of bread and work.

★ FREE Feria de Mataderos

Lisandro de la Torre y Avenida de Los Corrales (information Mon-Sat 4342 9629/Sun 4687 5602/www.feriademataderos.com.ar). Bus 55, 80, 92, 126. **Open** Jan-mid Mar 6pm-1am Sat. Mid Mar-Dec 1-7pm Sun. **Admission** free.
Every weekend (Saturday evenings in summer, Sunday afternoons during the rest of the year), the central square of Mataderos is taken over for this fair, with a craft market, traditional music and folk dancing. Restaurants lay out tables under the

arcade of the 100-year-old administration building of the former Mercado Nacional de Hacienda, a massive livestock auction house. On the southern spoke of Lisandro de la Torre, brilliant horsemen take each other on at spearing the *sortija* – a small ring dangling on a ribbon – while standing high on criollo breed horses.

Museo Criollo de los Corrales

Lisandro de la Torre y Avenida de Los Corrales (4687 1949). Bus 55, 80, 92, 126. **Open** *Mar-Dec* noon-6.30pm Sun. Guided tours (Spanish) by arrangement. **Admission** AR$2.
No credit cards.
The entrance to this museum is beneath the same arcade as the market. Exhibits include farming implements and country artefacts, along with cartoons by Argentina's most famous painter of gaucho life, Molina Campos, and a reconstruction of a *pulpería* (rural bar/grocer's store).
▶ *For more pulperías and gaucho life, visit the town of San Antonio de Areco; see p241.*

ZONA NORTE

Tren de la Costa (various stations)/bus 60, 168.
Originally home to the grand quintas (or summer houses) of BA's 19th-century aristocracy, the riverside neighbourhoods of Zona Norte, stretching from Olivos to San Isidro, still exude exclusivity – elegant abodes, private country clubs and a wealthy minority renowned for its love of the 'upper-class' sports of rugby, windsurfing and yachting.

To lord it with the privileged, take the **Tren de la Costa** (*see p188*), which skirts the River Plate all the way up to Tigre. The train departs from Olivos's Maipú station, and three blocks from here is **La Quinta Presidencial**, the presidential residence. The quinta's main entrance is at the intersection of Maipú and Libertador, but its grounds cover nine blocks; it's so big that ex-President Carlos Menem kept a private zoo here. Views of the residence are obscured by tall perimeter walls.

Feria de Mataderos.

For dramatic vistas head towards the river, to **Puerto Olivos**, situated between Corrientes and Alberdi streets. This private yacht club's 200-metre (656-foot) public pier offers a stunning panorama spanning the River Plate and BA's city skyline to the south.

Windsurfers and kiteboarders should hop off at Barrancas Station – serving the *barrios* of both Martínez and Acassuso – five minutes up the line from Olivos. The **Perú Beach** (*see p228*) complex opposite the station has numerous wet and dry sports activities and is a popular place to hang out. These areas are both favourites with kite-flyers and rollerbladers too.

Far removed from nature, but perfect for shopaholics, is Martínez's **Unicenter** (Paraná y Panamericana, Martínez, 4733 1166, www.unicenter.com.ar), Argentina's biggest shopping centre. For dining, try the riverside bars or Acassuso's strip on Avenida del Libertador, between Roque Sáenz Peña and Almafuerte.

Another eating strip is developing on Dardo Rocha, which runs inland alongside the grassy expanses of the **Hipódromo de San Isidro** racetrack (*see p225*) and the Jockey Club.

Sticking to the coastal train, the next stop is San Isidro, the most exclusive and enchanting of all the riverside neighbourhoods. Highlights are dotted around the main square, **Plaza Mitre**, located in front of the station and home to an artisans' fair every Sunday. At the square's far end is the neo-Gothic **Catedral de San Isidro**. Situated opposite are the area's tourist office and the **Museo del Rugby** (*see right*). Located on the same corner is the **Museo Biblioteca y Archivo Histórico Municipal** (*see below*).

Beccar Varela, one of several cobbled streets wending from Plaza Mitre, leads visitors to the **Mirador de los Tres Ombúes**, which offers breathtaking views across the Río de la Plata to the lush islands of Tigre's delta.

Three blocks east is the **Museo Histórico Municipal Juan Martín de Pueyrredón** (*see right*), the Spanish-colonial style quinta of one of the heroes of Argentinian independence. Another mansion where ghosts of the past linger is the masterfully eclectic **Villa Ocampo** (*see right*), former residence of literary luminary and arts patron Victoria Ocampo.

FREE Museo Biblioteca y Archivo Histórico Municipal

Avenida del Libertador 16362, San Isidro (4575 4038). Train Mitre or de la Costa to San Isidro/ bus 60, 168. **Open** *Museum* Dec, Feb, Mar 10am-6pm Tue, Wed; 3-7pm Sat, Sun. April-Nov 10am-6pm Tue, Thur; 2-6pm Sat, Sun. *Library* Feb 9am-2pm Mon-Fri. Mar-Dec 10am-6pm Mon-Fri. **Admission** free.

Named a national monument in 2007, this colonial era building houses six exhibition areas dedicated to San Isidro's rich history and culture. As well as important documents, the exhibits include all kinds of odds and ends donated by important local families over the past couple of centuries – magazines, furniture, toys, paintings and so on. The library holds over 12,000 volumes and is open to both serious historians and the casual browser.

FREE Museo Histórico Municipal Juan Martín de Pueyrredón

Rivera Indarte 48, entre Roque Sáenz Peña y Rubén Darío, San Isidro (4512 3131/ www.museopueyrredon.org.ar). Train Mitre or de la Costa to San Isidro/bus 60, 168. **Open** 10am-6pm Tue, Thur; 2-6pm Sat, Sun. *Guided tours:* 4pm Sat. **Admission** free.

This Spanish colonial-style mansion was home to, and is named after, one of the heroes of Argentinian independence who lived here up until his death in 1850. It was here that Generals Pueyrredón and San Martín plotted the defeat of the Spanish while – as legend has it – sitting beneath a carob tree in the glorious gardens. The building, with its white-washed brickwork and iron-grilled windows, has been lovingly preserved.

FREE Museo del Rugby

Juan B de Lasalle 653, y Almirante Brown, San Isidro (4732 2547/www.museodelrugby.com). Train Mitre or de la Costa to San Isidro/bus 60, 168. **Open** 10am-6pm Tue-Sun. **Admission** free. Situated in the Tren de La Costa station, this museum – a modern, interactive shrine to the oval ball – is stacked with jerseys of famous rugby players, narrative displays and memorabilia. Rugger buggers will love it of course; but even if you're not a fan, it's still worth a look. You might just be converted.

▶ *To watch a match, try catching local teams Club Atlético de San Isidro (CASI) or San Isidro Club (SIC) in action; see p225.*

Villa Ocampo

Elortondo 1837, y Uriburu, San Isidro (4732 4988/www.villaocampo.org). Train Mitre or de la Costa to San Isidro/bus 60, 168. **Open** 12.30-6pm Wed-Sun. *Guided tours* 2.30pm, 4.30pm Wed-Sun. **Admission** AR$15 Wed-Fri; AR$22 Sat, Sun.

This is the former residence of arts patron Victoria Ocampo. The guest lists for the parties Ocampo threw here read like a roll-call of the 20th century's most influential ink-slingers – Borges, Camus, Huxley, Greene and many others. This national monument was partially destroyed by fire in 2003 before being restored by UNESCO. The Franco-Victorian-style exterior has been repainted in its original hue, while the ground-floor rooms have been filled with the things that survived the fire, including Ocampo's piano and some of her art collection.

Consume

Piola. *See p125.*

Hotels

Check in to a bijou boutique hotel.

You know exactly what you're getting when you bunk down in an international chain hotel. But Buenos Aires is also home to characterful boutique hotels, concentrated around the trendy neighbourhoods of Palermo and San Telmo.

Chic quarters can also be found in upmarket Recoleta or Puerto Madero, where a bed will cost you quite a chunk of change. However, those on a budget need not worry: BA's youth hostel boom reflects the city's ascendancy to the backpacker party capital of South America.

Short-term apartment rental agencies provide an alternative for visitors seeking more independence, and can offer everything from compact pieds-à-terre to expansive penthouses.

STAYING IN THE CITY

With a little forward planning you can find some excellent accommodation, no matter what your budget or reasons for visiting BA.

There are hotels for wannabe oenologists (**Miravida Soho**; *see p103*) and tango aficionados (**Mansión Dandi Royal**; *see p89*), stylish gay hotels (**Axel Buenos Aires**, *see p201*) and places for those seeking the utmost in luxury (**Faena Hotel + Universe**, *see p91* and the **Algodon Mansion**, *see p93*).

Local design creativity, combined with renowned Argentinian hospitality, come together successfully in the boutique hotels that are listed in this chapter, which by their nature tend to be small and to get booked up quickly. They are often refurbished old houses, the best of them retaining some of their previous grandeur and boasting their own spas, pools, bars and restaurants. Palermo and San Telmo are two of the most popular areas for boutique retreats. Downtown and the exclusive Recoleta areas are dominated by larger hotels, though a glut of hostels and some budget hotels can be found here too. Most lodgings have Wi-Fi and air-conditioning (a necessity in summer), and while a few hotels have smoking rooms, the majority only permit smoking in outdoor spaces, and others not at all.

Prices & booking

We have noted price categories by using one to four peso signs ($-$$$$) and our listings follow these categories: **Deluxe** $$$$ (over US$350/AR$1,500 for a double); **High-end** $$$ (US$200-$350/AR$900-$1,500); **Moderate** $$ (US$100-$200/AR$450-$900); **Budget** $ (US$50-$100/AR$225-$450). Most hotels quote their rack rates in US dollars. The prices in this chapter are the high season rates for the cheapest double room as quoted to us by hotels, and include VAT (called 'IVA' and charged at 21 per cent) and breakfast, though it's best to check what's included when you reserve. Doing some online research before booking is recommended, as better deals can often be had by booking through third-party websites. For apartment rentals, *see p107*; for hostels, *see p109*.

❶ Red numbers given in this chapter correspond to the location of each hotel on the street maps. *See pp279-288.*

INSIDE TRACK
UNPREDICTABLE PRICES

Argentina is a country where anything is possible, including 25-30 per cent annual inflation. We've listed hotel rates as general ranges because they change incredibly frequently.

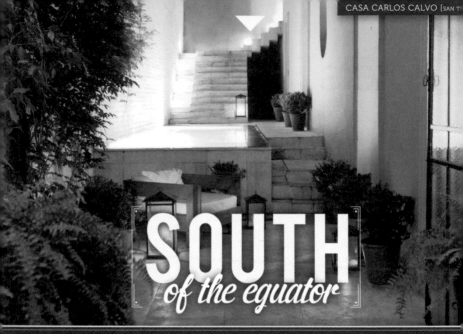

CASA CARLOS CALVO [SAN T

SOUTH
of the equator

THE CENTRE
High-end

Casa Calma
Suipacha 1015, entre Avenida Santa Fe y Marcelo T de Alvear, Retiro (5199 2800, www.casacalma.com.ar). Subte C, San Martín/ bus 17, 59, 61, 62, 75, 92, 100, 130, 152. **Rates** $$$ double. **Rooms** 17. **Credit** AmEx, MC, V. **Map** p285 G11 **❶**
Offset your carbon guilt with a stay at this eco-friendly hotel, complete with living walls and bamboo bicycles for guest use. The bright, spacious rooms have a Scandinavian air, and there has been no skimping on luxury facilities for the sake of saving the planet. Deluxe suites come with a mini sauna, while all rooms are fitted out with four-jet showers and jacuzzis large enough to bathe a harem. The 'calm house' delivers serenity through small touches: yoga mats in rooms, balconies draped with vines and healthy breakfasts served straight to your bed.
Bar. Concierge. Disabled-adapted rooms. Internet: wireless & shared terminal (free). No-smoking hotel. Room service. TV: DVD.

Marriott Plaza Hotel
Florida 1005, y Marcelo T de Alvear, Retiro (4318 3000, www.marriottplaza.com.ar). Subte C, San Martín/bus 93, 130, 152. **Rates** $$$ double. **Rooms** 318. **Credit** AmEx, DC, MC, V. **Map** p285 G11 **❷**
If grand and traditional suits you better than boutique, this might be the place for you. The Plaza Bar is a glorious, Bauhaus-esque design treat, while the Plaza Grill is reminiscent of the banquet hall of an Austro-Hungarian count, with a colonial twist – note the fabulous velvet mechanical fans. The hotel's location, overlooking Plaza San Martín, is arguably the best in the city, plus there is a fine fitness centre and a terrace pool surrounded by vegetation.
Bar. Business centre. Concierge. Disabled-adapted rooms. Gym. Internet: wireless (AR$79). No-smoking rooms. Pool (outdoor). Restaurants (3). Room service. Spa. TV: DVD.

Moderate

Castelar Hotel & Spa
Avenida de Mayo 1152, entre Salta y Lima, Congreso (4383 5000, www.castelarhotel. com.ar). Subte A, Lima/bus 39, 64, 86. **Rates** $$ double. **Rooms** 151. **Credit** AmEx, MC, V. **Map** p285 F10 **❸**
In business since 1929, this hotel is a successful combination of period atmosphere and modern amenities. The integrity of the original design is intact – one of the rooms even doubles as a museum to the memory of the renowned Spanish poet and playwright Federico García Lorca, who spent a year in

exile living at the Castelar. Some of the interior rooms have limited light and are a tad melancholic – fine for an exiled poet, perhaps; other guests may prefer one of the rooms overlooking the tree-lined Avenida de Mayo. Meanwhile, there's a fine Turkish spa in the basement, with steam rooms, a sauna and massage facilities for men and women. Open to non-residents too, this is one of BA's more reasonably priced spas; *see p117.*
Bar. Concierge. Gym. Internet: wireless (free). No-smoking rooms. Restaurant. Room service. Spa. TV.

La Cayetana Historic House
México 1330, entre San José y Santiago del Estero, Congreso (4383 2230, www. lacayetanahotel.com.ar). Subte E, Independencia/ bus 39, 103, 168. **Rates** $$ double. **Rooms** 11. **Credit** AmEx, MC, V. **Map** p285 F9 **❹**
Opened in 2005, this thoughtfully restored 1820s home is nestled on a back street, and a buzz-to-enter policy only adds to the sense of sanctuary. Owners Estela Fitere and Silvina Tarrio found the hotel's name following hours of searching through documents to discover the house's original owner, Doña Cayetana Casanova. Beyond the ivy-clad courtyard and its 200-year-old *higuera* (fig tree) are 11 suites that are full of charm, finding inspiration in early 19th-century post-colonial stylings.
Internet: wireless (free). No-smoking rooms. Room service.

Moreno Hotel
Moreno 376, entre Balcarce y Defensa, Monserrat (6091 2000, www.morenobuenosaires.com). Subte E, Bolívar/bus 29, 56. **Rates** $$ double. **Rooms** 39. **Credit** AmEx, DC, MC, V. **Map** p285 E10 **❺**
A stunning art deco exterior forms the shell of this seven-floor boutique hotel, with an interior that runs along minimalist lines interspersed with dazzling touches left over from the roaring 1920s, such as glazed wall-tiles, stained-glass windows and wrought-iron lifts. Breakfast can be taken on the terrace, which is also home to an open-air jacuzzi with wonderful views of surrounding San Telmo and Monserrat. The bedrooms are generously sized, with original art in the best, whirlpool baths and either a balcony or views of the church dome next door. Gastronomes shouldn't miss the chance to dine in the hotel's hyper-modern restaurant, Aldo's (*see p113*).
Bar. Internet: wireless (free). No-smoking rooms. Restaurant. Room service. TV.

Rooney's Boutique Hotel
Sarmiento 1775, y Avenida Callao, Tribunales (5252 5060, www.rooneysboutiquehotel.com). Subte B, Callao/bus 12, 37, 124. **Rates** $$ double. **Rooms** 14. **Credit** AmEx, MC, V. **Map** p285 G9 **❻**

CONSUME

This lovely boutique hotel was once the residence of the writer and poet Leopoldo Lugones. Today, 14 rooms and suites still contain original wood floors, gilded mirrors, high ceilings and pretty chandeliers. Designer Paula Piatti reworked the original style with a palette of cream and soft green to create a calm, downtown haven in a neighbourhood filled with theatres and tango dancehalls. Guests have access to a lounge bar, café and tango patio, where lessons are held.

Bar. Concierge. Internet: wireless (free). Room service. TV.

Budget

Gran Hotel Hispano

Avenida de Mayo 861, entre Piedras y Tacuarí, Monserrat (4345 2020, www.hhispano.com.ar). Subte A, Piedras or C, Avenida de Mayo/bus 10, 17, 64. **Rates** $ double. **Rooms** 60. **Credit** AmEx, DC, MC, V. **Map** p285 F10 **❼**

Located in the heart of downtown, not far from classic *confitería* Café Tortoni (*see p144*), this family-run, classic city hotel has been around since the 1950s and retains its original Spanish-style architecture. While most of the hotel's small, modest rooms are located around a beautiful three-storey inner courtyard, a few of the premium rooms have small, private balconies that open out on to the street.

Internet: wireless (free). TV.

SAN TELMO & SOUTH OF THE CENTRE

Moderate

Bonito B&B

Avenida Juan de Garay 458, entre Defensa y Bolívar, San Telmo (4362 8451, www.bonitobuenosaires.com). Bus 24, 29, 39, 93, 143, 152. **Rates** $$ double. **Rooms** 7. **Credit** AmEx, MC, V. **Map** p284 D9 **❽**

A cliché it may be, but the expression 'home away from home' applies perfectly to Bonito B&B – if you're used to living in beautiful art nouveau buildings with winding staircases and a labyrinth of attractive outdoor spaces, that is. Friendly staff create a family feel, and guests have free reign of the kitchen as well as the parrilla on the wood-decked roof terrace. Artist-owner Yanina has put her creative flair to work, and the seven rooms have been decorated by different local artists.

Internet: wireless (free). Room service. TV.
Other location Bonito Hotel Boutique, 3rd floor, Chile 1507, San Telmo, 4381 2161.

Hotel Babel

Balcarce 946, entre Estados Unidos y Carlos Calvo, San Telmo (4300 8300, www.hotelbabel. com.ar). Bus 10, 29. **Rates** $$ double. **Rooms** 9. **Credit** AmEx, MC, V. **Map** p284 D10 **❾**

INSIDE TRACK ROOFTOP BAR

On a balmy summer night, the **Hotel Pulitzer**'s rooftop Sky Bar is one of the hippest places in BA to sink a drink and catch a DJ set (Maipú, 907, Microcentro, 4316 0800, www.hotelpulitzer.com.ar).

Once home to a multinational community of late 19th-century immigrant families, this renovated *conventillo*-style house continues to welcome visitors from all parts of the globe, maintaining the tradition of a hodge-podge of languages that inspired the hotel's name. Located within walking distance of Plaza Dorrego, this intimate lodging has all the charm and personalised attention of a guesthouse. The nine air-conditioned rooms surround a small patio and are compact and pared-down. Flat-screen televisions and chic bathrooms add a touch of sophistication.

Bar. Concierge. Internet: wireless (free). TV.

Mansión Dandi Royal

Piedras 922/936, entre Estados Unidos y Carlos Calvo, San Telmo (4307 7623, www.mansiondandiroyal.com). Bus 10, 24, 29. **Rates** $$ double. **Credit** AmEx, MC, V. **Map** p285 E9 **❿**

Just like a sultry *tanguero*, the Mansión Dandi Royal is a bit of a dark horse from the outside, set on an unlikely-looking city block. But once you're inside, the sumptuously polished wood, murals and the gorgeous period details make it a perfect choice if you want a stay that's heavy on tango and charm, drenched in the romantic spirit of Buenos Aires. There's a compact but inviting heated rooftop pool, plus two pretty, tiled patios. And though you could perfectly well enjoy a stay here without even catching a glimpse of tango, why would you? The speciality of the *casa* – the hotel is owned by a world-famous tango dancer and instructor – is the beautiful dance, and there are classes available daily.

Bar. Concierge. Internet: wireless (free). No-smoking rooms. Pool (outdoor). Room service. TV: DVD.

Mansión Vitraux

Carlos Calvo 369, entre Defensa y Balcarce, San Telmo (4300 6886, www.mansionvitraux.com). Bus 10, 22, 29, 126. **Rates** $$ double. **Rooms** 12. **Credit** AmEx, DC MC, V. **Map** p284 D10 **⓫**

The 12 rooms of this decidedly sophisticated hotel range from zen-like havens of minimalism to an opulent oriental-inspired boudoir and a glamorous black-walled den of decadence fitted with a projector. Wine-tasting sessions are held in the intimate wine cellar, where gourmet cuisine is also served, and you can work off the results of your

CONSUME

indulgence in the gym or the terrace pool, equipped with a counter-current swimming system.
Gym. Internet: wireless (free). No-smoking hotel. Pool (1 outdoor; 1 indoor). Room service. Spa.

Patios de San Telmo

Chacabuco 752, entre Independencia y Chile, San Telmo (4307 0480, www.patiosdes antelmo.com.ar). Subte C, Independencia/bus 10, 24, 17, 86, 129, 126. **Rates** $$ double. **Rooms** 30. **Credit** AmEx, DC MC, V. **Map** p284 9E ⓬
If San Telmo is romantic, bohemian and steeped in history, then this restored *conventillo* (tenement-style structure) has done its barrio proud. The poor immigrant families who crammed into this very building in the 19th century would be dazzled by its latest incarnation. Light streams through high windows into luxurious suites, a series of palatial tiled patios ensures there's space in spades, and Baroque motifs are paired with contemporary elegance for a result that's pure sophistication. The architect owners have topped off their three-storey stunner with a sleek rooftop sundeck and swimming pool. There's also a ground-floor café.
Concierge. Disabled-adapted rooms. Gym. Internet: wireless (free). Pool (outdoor). Restaurant. Room service. TV.

PUERTO MADERO

Deluxe

Faena Hotel + Universe

Martha Salotti 445, Dique 2, Madero Este (4010 9000, www.faenahotelanduniverse. com). Subte B, LN Alem/bus 2, 130, 152.
Rates $$$$ double. **Rooms** 105. **Credit** AmEx, DC, MC, V. **Map** p284 D11 ⓭
Exotic and contemporary, there's simply nowhere else like the Faena Hotel + Universe. Designed by Philippe Starck, this opulent hotel was built inside the shell of a disused red-brick grain silo. It includes a spectacular restaurant, El Bistro, and El Mercado, which serves more traditional but equally delicious Argentinian food. The cabaret theatre, Library Lounge (*see p210*), pool bar, spa and hammam are all open to mere mortals. *Photo p93.*
Bar. Business centre. Concierge. Disabled-adapted rooms. Gym. Internet: wireless (free). No-smoking rooms. Pool (outdoor). Restaurants (2). Room service. Spa. TV: DVD.

High-end

Hotel Madero

Rosario Vera Peñaloza 360, Dique 2, Madero Este (5776 7777, www.hotelmadero.com). Subte B, LN Alem/bus 2, 130, 152. **Rates** $$$ double. **Rooms** 193. **Credit** AmEx, DC, MC, V. **Map** p284 D11 ⓮
Inconspicuously tagged on at the far end of Puerto Madero Este, this swanky hotel is aimed at the discerning business traveller, although couples and families will be equally happy with its attractive features, which include the sensational Rëd Restó & Lounge. There's also a tricked-out spa and health club, a heated indoor pool, massage room and solarium, and the upper floors afford stunning views of the barrio.
Bar. Business centre. Concierge. Disabled-adapted rooms. Gym. Internet: wireless (free). No-smoking hotel. Pool (indoor). Restaurant. Room service. Spa. TV: DVD.

Patios de San Telmo.

CONSUME

Sex in the City

Get a room at one of BA's love hotels.

Argentinians are an amorous bunch. Never shy of a little plaza-side nooky, whatever their age or sexual preference, there is, nevertheless, a limit to what even liberal-minded porteños can stomach. So when the petting gets a little too hot and heavy, couples are often spied sneaking through a garishly lit doorway marked only with the words '*albergue transitorio*'.

These 'temporary lodging' hotels, known in *porteño* backslang as *telos*, exist for the sole but honourable purpose of clandestine copulation. Frequented by horny teenagers and illicit lovers with no shag shack of their own, *telos* offer rooms by the *turno* (around AR$150 for two hours).

Every barrio will have several *telos*, but since anonymity is paramount, they are supposed to be tricky to spot. In reality, the giveaway signs – random bushes outside doorways, neon lights guiding cars to a hidden garage and a plastic Venus de Milo standing guard – are about as subtle as their names (Eros, Kiss Me, and the wonderful Pussy-Cats are just a few random examples). Once inside there is a choice between an often bewildering menu of room types. After selecting whatever takes you and your partner's fancy, a studiedly disinterested (they've seen it all before) receptionist behind a smoked-glass window will throw some keys at you, and off you head through the dimly lit corridors.

Even the most basic rooms will have mirrored ceilings, a see-through shower and porn on the telly; many also bafflingly advertise live cable football. More exotic options will include water beds, medieval looking 'sex chairs' and, occasionally, a covered outdoor garden. For the final preparations, room service can bring up drinks, condoms and sex toys, all served through a hole in the wall.

If it all sounds a little seedy, it is. And that's all part of the fun. *Telos* are to Argentina what motels are to North America and the back of Ford Fiestas are to the UK. Nevertheless, an Argentinian who claims never to have visited one is either a man of the cloth, lying through his teeth, or both. The *telo* is an indispensable part of a culture where people often live at home with their parents until the day they marry, and quite often beyond. But they can also offer a precious moment of privacy for couples with kids, or couples without 'sex chairs'. Leaving the sprogs at the in-laws with the statement 'we're going to the cinema' often implies a couple of hours 'quality time' where the only movies will be from the low-budget Swedish collection.

Another point to note about *telos* is that they are usually kept incredibly clean – you've got more chance of, um, coming across a soiled sheet in a standard three-star than in a love hotel.

For a comprehensive list of *telos* in BA, log on to www.alberguesonline.com.ar, where you can search by location, price and in-room extras. If it's Swedish 'porn set' minimalism that you are after, the erotically titled **Rampa Car** (Angel J Carranza 1347, Palermo Hollywood, 4773 6964, www.hotelrampacar.com) is a good bet. Should the urge take you among the steel and glass erections of Retiro, walk through the subtle doors of **Kansas City** (Talcahuano 844, 4813 6860) where couples wanting to experiment with a 'sex chair' should ask for the 'Especial' suite. Further afield in Núñez, the well-established **JJ Hotel** (Avenida del Libertador 7900, 4701 4800, www.hoteljj.com.ar) has seen satisfied punters come and go for over 35 years. And those who venture out of town for some extramural hanky-panky are richly rewarded at the upmarket **Dissors** (Colectora de Avenida General Paz 900, 4653 0314, www.dissorshotel.com.ar), where you can fornicate in five-star facilities. Sophisticated yet saucy, this *telo*'s stylish rooms feature premium porn, complimentary blindfolds, feathers and lube tubes.

Faena Hotel + Universe. *See p91.*

RECOLETA & BARRIO NORTE
Deluxe

Algodon Mansion
*Montevideo 1647, entre Guido y Quintana
Recoleta (3530 7777, www.algodonmansion.com).
Bus 17, 39, 110, 124, 150, 152.* **Rates** $$$$
double. **Rooms** 10. **Credit** AmEx, MC, V.
Map p286 I11 ⑮
When only gilded ceilings and your own private
butler will do, this sumptuous hotel delivers the
goods. Each of the ten impeccably-styled suites in
this 1912 belle époque mansion comes with a pala-
tial bed and opulent bathroom, four of which have
an iPod-synchronised hydrotherapy massage tub.
The roof terrace has an inviting pool, lounge
and bijou bar. A spa, cognac bar and the James
Bond-worthy Chez Nous restaurant complete the
decadent package.
*Bar. Business centre. Concierge. Gym. Internet:
wireless (free). No-smoking rooms. Pool (outdoor).
Restaurant. Room service. Spa. TV: DVD.*

★ Alvear Palace Hotel
*Avenida Alvear 1891, entre Avenida Callao
y Ayacucho, Recoleta (4808 2100, www.alvear
palace.com). Bus 67, 93, 130.* **Rates** $$$$
double. **Rooms** 210. **Credit** AmEx, DC,
MC, V. **Map** p286 I11 ⑯
The Alvear reeks of money and old-school class.
Filling half a block of Avenida Alvear, the rooms are
an ocean of opulence in rich burgundies, with
antique French furniture and lashings of space. The
lobby is a cathedral to power and riches, with gra-
cious staff who never make you feel like an imposter
in paradise, even if you clearly are. High tea in the
spectacular L'Orangerie is probably the most accessible way for non-guests to soak up the ambience.

*Bars (2). Business centre. Concierge. Disabled-
adapted rooms. Gym. Internet: wireless (free). No-
smoking rooms. Pool (indoor). Restaurants (2).
Room service. Spa. TV: DVD.*

Four Seasons Hotel
*Posadas 1086, y Cerrito, Recoleta (4321 1200,
www.fourseasons.com). Bus 67, 130.* **Rates** $$$$
double. **Rooms** 138. **Credit** AmEx, DC, MC, V.
Map p286 I11 ⑰
This 13-storey monument to taste and elegance is
draped in class, from the recently refurbished tango-
inspired *intérieur* to the immaculate garden, complete with an outdoor pool. The spa provides
tranquility in a bottle and a masseur's touch, and the
27 suites are light-drenched, spacious gems. And
then there's the historic Mansión. Set apart from the
main hotel, this jewel looks and smells of Old World
grandeur, with four gold-leafed reception rooms,
seven luxurious suites and one imposing staircase.

THE BEST HOTEL POOLS

Home Hotel
Splash about in the garden pool then
treat yourself to a massage and a cocktail.
See p97.

Faena Hotel + Universe
The most lavish pool in the city, complete
with ostentatious fountains, royal-red
sunloungers and fresh juices. *See p91.*

Ultra
After a dip in the rooftop infinity pool, sit
back and enjoy the Palermo views from a
sun-lounger. *See p101.*

CONSUME

Bar. Business centre. Concierge. Disabled-adapted rooms. Gym. Internet wireless (free). No-smoking rooms. Pool (outdoor). Restaurant. Room service. Spa. TV: DVD.

Mio Buenos Aires
Avenida Quintana 465, entre Avenida Callao y Ayacucho, Recoleta (5295 8500, www.miobuenos aires.com). Bus 10, 37, 60, 110. **Rates** $$$$ double. **Rooms** 30. **Credit** AmEx, MC, V. **Map** p286 J11 ⑱
Owned by the Catena clan – Argentina's most famous family of winegrowers – this Recoleta hotel is filled with viticultural touches. Both wine buffs and interior design fanatics will appreciate the gorgeous French oak barrel doors, the champagne dispenser and selection of wines in every room. There's a spa and pool on the eighth floor, but opt for a terrace suite if you want your very own outdoor jacuzzi.
Bar. Business centre. Disabled-adapted rooms. Gym. Internet wireless (free). No-smoking hotel. Room service. Spa. TV: DVD.

Park Hyatt Buenos Aires
Avenida Alvear 1661, entre Montevideo y Rodríguez Peña, Recoleta (5171 1234, www.buenosaires.park.hyatt.com). Bus 93, 152. **Rates** $$$$ double. **Rooms** 165. **Credit** AmEx, DC, MC, V. **Map** p286 I11 ⑲
In true belle époque style, the entrance to the Park Hyatt is a vision of neoclassical columns, marble floors and cast-iron gates, while the rooms themselves, simple and modern, speak of a very 21st-century sensibility. The hotel boasts a *vinoteca* with over 3,000 bottles of local wines (including some of the best malbecs ever produced), a cheese room (yes, a cheese room), a spa and three restaurants.
Bar. Business centre. Concierge. Disabled-adapted rooms. Gym. Internet: wireless (free). No-smoking rooms. Pool (indoor). Restaurants (3). Room service. Spa. TV: DVD.

High-end

Ulises Recoleta Suites
Ayacucho 2016, entre Avenida del Libertador y Posadas, Recoleta (4804 4571, www.ulises recoleta.com.ar). Bus 62, 93, 130. **Rates** $$$ double. **Rooms** 26. **Credit** AmEx, MC, V. **Map** p286 J11 ⑳
This hotel's prime selling point is indisputably its location: ask for a room facing the street, so you can look out at the regal Alvear Palace Hotel and the high-end designer stores, just a couple of blocks from the cultural centre and the shops. The elegant and comfortable rooms are equipped with kitchenettes. The duplexes have bathrooms on each level for extra privacy, and the penthouse suite features a lustrous living room topped off with a skylight.
Concierge. Internet: wireless (free). No-smoking rooms. Parking. Room service. TV.

Park Hyatt Buenos Aires.

Urban Suites Recoleta
Junín 1727, entre Guido y Vicente López, Recoleta (4803 2300, www.urbanrecoleta.com). Bus 10, 37, 59. **Rates** $$$ double. **Rooms** 34. **Credit** AmEx, MC, V. **Map** p286 J11 ㉑
Situated opposite Recoleta Cemetery, Urban Suites Recoleta is a good place to come if you fancy spoiling yourself. Contrasting nicely with the historic landmark opposite, it's a modern, minimalist boutique hotel with 34 roomy, comfortable suites. After a long day in the city you can treat yourself in the 'U spa' which includes a small gym and balcony jacuzzi; for a less virtuous but equally relaxing end to your day, enjoy a cocktail and an impressive view from the solarium.
Bar. Concierge. Disabled-adapted rooms. Gym. Internet: wireless. No-smoking hotel. Room service. Spa. TV.

PALERMO
High-end

★ 1555 Malabia House
Malabia 1555, entre Gorriti y Honduras, Palermo Soho (4833 2410, www.malabiahouse.com.ar). Bus 39, 55, 168. **Rates** $$$ double. **Rooms** 15. **Credit** AmEx, DC, MC, V. **Map** p283 M5 ㉒
Much imitated though perhaps still not bettered, this establishment was at the vanguard of the boutique hotel wave in Palermo Soho. This former convent – once home to the ladies of San Vicente Ferrer, who would scarcely recognise its contemporary incarnation – benefits from its owner's inherent flair for design. Three mini gardens combine to create a

relaxed oasis – few travellers leave these premises unimpressed. Of the 15 tasteful rooms, all have air-conditioning and one has its own balcony. Though the building has undergone a transformation scarcely imaginable in 1896, it truly remains an urban sanctuary and the warmth of your reception will likely tempt you to linger.

Bar. Concierge. Internet: wireless (free). Room service. TV.

Atempo

Arévalo 1564, entre Gorriti y Cabrera, Palermo Hollywood (5297 3333, www.atempo hotel.com). Bus 140, 168, 151. **Rates** *$$$ double.* **Rooms** 28. **Credit** AmEx, MC, V. **Map** p283 O5 ㉓

Fancy your own two-storey loft apartment? How about a swimming pool out back? Atempo delivers the Palermo Hollywood dream at prices that can't be beat, complete with peaceful courtyard and in-house bar. The 20 suites and eight sleek lofts in this ten-storey block come with kitchenettes, office space, balconies and bathrooms large enough to practise your tango moves.

Bar. Concierge. Disabled-adapted room. Internet: wireless (free). No-smoking rooms. Pool (outdoor). TV: DVD.

Bo Bo Hotel

Guatemala 4882, y Thames, Palermo Soho (4774 0505, www.bobohotel.com). Subte D, Plaza Italia/bus 36, 55, 60, 64, 93, 152. **Rates** $$$ double. **Rooms** 7. **Credit** AmEx, DC, MC, V. **Map** p283 M6 ㉔

Bo Bo helped pave the way in Palermo for boutique hotels, and the consistently high standard of service here is exemplary. The hotel's piano gets a tune-up when one of Bo Bo's musically-inclined clients comes to stay and guests can enjoy weekly wine tastings. The hotel's brilliant contemporary restaurant and excellent location close to Palermo Soho's bars and boutiques crank up the appeal even more.

Bar. Internet: wireless (free). Restaurant. Room service. TV: DVD.

Fierro Hotel

Soler 5862, entre Ravignani y Carranza, Palermo Hollywood (3220 6800, www.fierrohotel.com). Bus 39, 60, 93, 152, 161. **Rates** $$$ double. **Rooms** 27. **Credit** AmEx, DC, MC, V. **Map** p283 O5 ㉕

Fierro Hotel has all the amenities of a five-star hotel yet still retains an intimate boutique feel. The spacious rooms are kitted out with iPod docks and suite guests have iPads at their disposal, but for something really special, book the terrace suite with its own parrilla and outdoor jacuzzi. The rooftop pool is small but sweet, complete with hydro-massage beds, yet the highlight is the lovely garden surrounded by palm trees – a perfect spot for a pre-dinner cocktail before dining at star chef Hernán Gipponi's restaurant *(see p135)* on the ground floor.

Bar. Concierge. Disabled-adapted rooms. Gym. Internet: wireless (free). Pool (outdoor). Restaurant. Room service. Spa. TV.

Glu

Godoy Cruz 1733, entre Honduras y Gorriti, Palermo Soho (4831 4646, www.theglu hotel.com). Subte D, Palermo/bus 34, 39, 55, 140, 151, 168. **Rates** $$$ double. **Rooms** 3. **Credit** AmEx, MC, V. **Map** p283 N5 ㉖

At the Glu the smallest room measures around 375sq ft (35sq m), and is decorated in irreproachably minimalist style. Immaculate rosewood furnishings, buff leather sofas and spotless linen bedclothes are all pleasing to the eye and to the touch. It's a pleasure to see a place paying attention to the smallest of details and getting them right, like the rooftop jacuzzi and spa downstairs, complete with a sauna and an invigorating Scottish shower.

Bar. Concierge. Internet: wireless (free). Room service. Spa. TV: DVD.

★ Home Hotel Buenos Aires

Honduras 5860, entre Carranza y Ravignani, Palermo Hollywood (4778 1008, www.home buenosaires.com). Bus 39, 93, 111. **Rates** $$$ double. **Rooms** 18. **Credit** AmEx, MC, V. **Map** p283 O5 ㉗

It's not, truth be told, very homely at all at Home. Unless your house looks out on to an exquisite garden complete with an azure pool, boasts flawless design and attracts the effortlessly hip and lovely, that is. Each of the rooms at this boutique hotel has its own look, which includes the vintage wallpaper that British owner Tom collects. Drop by the bar *(see p151)* for a drink, or drift into the restaurant to tuck into weekend brunches.

Bar. Concierge. Internet: wireless (free). No-smoking hotel. Pool (outdoor). Room service. Restaurant. Spa. TV: DVD.

★ L'Hôtel Palermo

Thames 1562, entre Honduras y Pasaje Soria, Palermo Soho (4831 7198, www.lhotelpalermo.com). Bus 34, 39, 55, 140, 151, 168. **Rates** $$$ double. **Rooms** 23. **Credit** AmEx, MC, V. **Map** p283 N5 ㉘

This little slice of Provence in Palermo boasts weeping willow branches draped over cobbled pathways and restored antique furniture that could be straight out of a grand château. The garden – a secluded oasis with a pool, manicured lawn and high, ivy-covered walls – is the perfect place to hide from the paparazzi, and they'd never suspect you were just one block from perpetually buzzing Plaza Serrano. L'Hôtel's tasteful suites are spaced across two buildings, and despite the proximity to BA's nightlife hub, deliver a surprisingly silent night.

Bar. Concierge. Disabled-adapted rooms. Internet: wireless (free). No-smoking hotel. Pool (outdoor). Room service. TV.

CONSUME

Ilum

El Salvador 5726, entre Bonpland y Carranza,
Palermo Hollywood (4776 8667, www.ilum
hotel.com). Bus 39, 93, 108, 111. **Rates** $$$
double. **Rooms** 12. **Credit** AmEx, DC, MC, V.
Map p283 N5 **㉙**

When you can't decide between a city break in
Buenos Aires or a relaxing retreat on a Thai island,
Ilum delivers the best of both worlds. Buddha statues
adorn this luminous boutique hotel, where a
cascading waterfall descends into the lobby and a
serene back garden transports you light years
away from the urban cacophony. There are just 12
elegant rooms here, spaced well enough apart that
you don't feel like you're going to bed with your
neighbour. Sweeping views of the barrio can be
enjoyed from the outdoor Nordic-style jacuzzis, or
take the muscle-melting bliss indoors with an
in-room massage.

Concierge. Disabled-adapted rooms. Internet:
wireless (free). Spa. TV: DVD.

Jardin Escondido

Gorriti 4746, entre Armenia y Malabia, Palermo
Soho (from USA 800 746 3743, from outside
USA 501 824 4085, www.coppolajardin
escondido.com). Bus 15, 55, 57, 168. **Rates**
$$$ double. **Rooms** 7. **Credit** AmEx, MC, V.
Map p283 M5 **㉚**

Francis Ford Coppola's property is composed of two
sections built around the *jardín escondido* (hidden
garden) that inspired the hotel's name. The house can
be rented in its entirety or by sector, or occasionally
by room. The concierge can arrange for an *asador* to
fire up the parrilla and make you a barbecue you'll
never forget; or order some top-notch takeaway and
watch one of the 150 DVDs in Coppola's collection.

Concierge. Internet: wireless (free). Pool
(outdoor).

Legado Mítico

Gurruchaga 1848, entre Costa Rica y
Nicaragua, Palermo Soho (4833 1300,
www.legadomitico.com). Bus 15, 34, 39, 55,
168. **Rates** $$$ double. **Rooms** 11. **Credit**
AmEx, MC, V. **Map** p283 M5 **㉛**

The designers of Legado Mítico have created a
themed hotel that doesn't sacrifice comfort and
style for gimmickry. Each of its spacious rooms is
devoted to a famous figure from Argentinian his-
tory and decorated with relevant books, pho-
tographs and posters. Don't worry, there's plenty
of stuff for boneheads too, including large-screen
TVs, a fast Wi-Fi connection, a bar and breakfast
room and a terrace with loungers.

Bar. Concierge. Disabled-adapted room. Internet:
wireless (free). Room service. TV: DVD.

Magnolia

Julián Álvarez 1746, entre Costa Rica y Soler,
Palermo (4867 4900, www.magnoliahotel.com.ar).
Bus 15, 36, 39, 57, 110, 111, 141, 160, 188.
Rates $$$ double. **Rooms** 8. **Credit** AmEx, V.
Map p282 L6 **㉜**

Hidden along a cobbled street in Palermo, the cosy
Magnolia Hotel offers excellent accommodation and
friendly service. All eight rooms in the early 20th-
century property are named after trees native to
Argentina. The beautiful stained-glass windows,
quaint patios and a lovely magnolia tree are
definitely eye-pleasing, but what makes this hotel
go from pretty to pretty darn great is the exceptional
attention of the employees.

Bar. Concierge. Disabled-adapted room. Internet:
wireless (free). Room service. TV: DVD.

Mine Hotel Boutique

Gorriti 4770, entre Malabia y Armenia, Palermo
Soho (4832 1100, www.minehotel.com). Bus 15,
55, 140, 168. **Rates** $$$ double. **Rooms** 20.
Credit AmEx, DC, MC, V. **Map** p283 M5 **㉝**

This first-class hotel is decked out in brown and
neutral tones and cool furniture that looks like it
came straight out of a swinging 1960s bachelor pad.
Mine is retro without feeling antique and original
without trying too hard. Jetted baths in all rooms
add a spot of postmodern flair, and there's also an
attractive outdoor swimming pool, though it's more
suited to lounging around in deck chairs with a
drink in hand than to taking a plunge in.

Bar. Concierge. Internet: wireless (free). Pool
(outdoor). Room service. TV: DVD.

Nuss

El Salvador 4916, entre Borges y Thames,
Palermo Soho (4833 8100, www.nusshotel.com).
Bus 34, 55, 166. **Rates** $$$ double. **Rooms** 22.
Credit AmEx, MC, V. **Map** p283 M5 **㉞**

This elegant former convent is located just steps
away from the lively Plaza Serrano: despite your
serene accommodation choice, your stay here will
most likely be more about hedonism than asceticism.
But if you're determined to remain cloistered away
for a weekend of uninterrupted rest and relaxation,
Nuss's comfortable, contemporary rooms are ideal.
A small gym and sauna are complemented by a
rooftop terrace, where you can soak up the sun.

Bar. Concierge. Disabled-adapted room. Gym.
Internet: wireless (free). TV: DVD.

Own Palermo Hollywood

Cabrera 5556, entre Humboldt y Fitz Roy, Palermo
Hollywood (47728100, www.ownhotels.com). Bus
21, 93, 111, 140. **Rates** $$$ double. **Rooms** 16.
Credit AmEx, MC, V. **Map** p283 N5 **㉟**

A stay at Own feels like an attentive and stylish
friend has lent you their hip hangout. Even the
smallest rooms are spacious for a hotel, and if you
opt for the deluxe or master suites you get a private
patio or balcony. Besides flat-screen TVs, DVD and
CD players, thoughtful details include Havaianas
flip-flops and a handy set of notes with useful phone

CONSUME

numbers, a list of local attractions, a Subte map and personalised suggestions for your visit to BA. An intimate ground-floor lounge hosts nightly drinks. *Bar. Concierge. Disabled-adapted room. Internet: wireless (free). No-smoking hotel. TV: DVD.*

Palermitano

Uriarte 1648, entre Honduras y El Salvador, Palermo Soho (4897 2100, www.palermitano.biz). Bus 34, 39, 55, 140, 151, 168. **Rates** $$$ double. **Rooms** 16. **Credit** AmEx, MC, V. **Map** p283 M5 ㊱

As slick and stylish as it is well-run and friendly, the Palermitano marks itself out from the pack with lavish details like marble bathrooms in each of its 16 rooms. And there's something satisfyingly egalitarian in the fact that the only major difference between the two suites and the rest of the rooms is size – everything else remains the same. *Bar. Concierge. Disabled-adapted room. Internet: wireless (free). No-smoking hotel. Pool (outdoor). Restaurant. Room service. TV: DVD.*

Palermo Place

Nicaragua 5865, entre Carranza y Ravignani, Palermo Hollywood (3220 9600, www. palermoplace.com). Subte D, Carranza/ bus 39, 60, 93, 111, 161, 152, 194. **Rates** $$$ double. **Rooms** 26. **Credit** AmEx, MC, V. **Map** p283 O5 ㊲

There's space and tranquillity in spades at this boutique hotel situated in an unassuming apartment block on a pretty, tree-lined street. The plush, modern rooms come with kitchenettes and French balconies from where you can take in expansive views over the low-rise neighbourhood. A small gym, coin-operated laundry and rooftop terrace

with *parrilla* (grill) are all the amenities you need for that live-like-a-local experience. *Concierge. Internet: wireless (free). No-smoking hotel. TV.*

PuroBaires

Niceto Vega 4788, entre Armenia y Malabia, Palermo Soho (4139 0100, www.purobaires. com). Bus 15, 110, 140, 151, 168. **Rates** $$$ double. **Rooms** 11. **Credit** AmEx, MC, V. **Map** p283 M4 ㊳

PuroBaires' particular brand of classiness is all in the detail, with quality dark wood combined with cream leather and the odd chandelier to give classic touches to what is overall a modern residence. Each room comes with a plasma TV, double glazing and a balcony facing the interior patio or the street. *Concierge. Disabled-adapted room. Gym. Internet: wireless (free). Pool (outdoor). Spa. TV.*

Soho All Suites

Honduras 4762, entre Malabia y Armenia, Palermo Soho (4832 3000, www.sohoallsuites. com). Bus 15, 110, 150, 151, 168. **Rates** $$$ double. **Rooms** 21. **Credit** AmEx, MC, V. **Map** p283 M5 ㊴

A boutique hotel for people who are wary of boutique hotels, Soho All Suites is unpretentious, stylish and a bit of a find. The Superior suites, which can sleep up to four people, have balconies facing the street, and the penthouse has its own terrace, while a sunny rooftop terrace open to all guests has a jacuzzi. The staff are happy to share local knowledge with guests, and the location is close to the barrio's hottest shops, restaurants and bars. *Bar. Concierge. Disabled-adapted rooms. Internet: wireless (free). Room service. Spa.*

CONSUME

Legado Mítico.

Ultra Hotel

Gorriti 4929, entre Gurruchaga y Serrano, Palermo Soho (4833 9200, www.hotelultra.com). Bus 15, 55, 57, 140, 151, 168. **Rates** *$$$ double.* **Rooms** *13.* **Credit** *AmEx, MC, V.* **Map** *p283 M5* ⓪

With a large, well-planned ground floor that lets hotel guests and visitors circulate through its eclectic spaces and come full circle, Ultra has a level of design nous other boutique hotels would kill for, shifting harmoniously between the trendy lobby, the dark wood and leather of the library lounge, and a bright, shabby-chic conservatory-style restaurant. Spacious rooms, exceptionally helpful staff and a rooftop terrace with a pool are the cherry on the cake. *Bars (2). Internet: wireless (free). Pool (outdoor). Restaurant.*

★ Vitrum Hotel

Gorriti 5641, entre Bonpland y Fitz Roy, Palermo Hollywood (4776 5030, www.vitrumhotel.com). Bus 39, 93, 111, 161. **Rates** *$$$ double.* **Rooms** *16.* **Credit** *AmEx, MC, V.* **Map** *p283 N5* ④

This cool hotel is recognisable from the street due to the colourful patchwork tiles on its façade; inside, design trends, up-to-the-minute technology and avant-garde art spice things up further. The rooms and suites come with their own espresso machines and L'Occitane bath goodies. Vitrum is also home to the SushiClub Restaurante. *Bar. Gym. Internet: wireless (free). Restaurant. Spa. TV: DVD.*

Moderate

5411 Soho Hotel Boutique

Thames 1565, entre Gorriti y Soría, Palermo Soho (4833 9233, www.5411soho.com). Subte D, Plaza Italia/bus 39, 60, 93, 154. **Rates** *$$ double.* **Rooms** *11.* **Credit** *AmEx, DC, MC, V.* **Map** *p283 M5* ④

5411 Soho Hotel Boutique is tucked away just a block from pumping Plaza Serrano, though once inside the property you can escape the crowds: the hotel is a sanctuary for those who value privacy, as there's plenty of space. The somewhat strident colour scheme may not be as conducive to relaxation, but the hotel has spa facilities, and there's an outdoor area with a pool where cocktails can be enjoyed. *Bar. Concierge. Internet: wireless & shared terminal (free). Pool (outdoor). Spa. TV: DVD.*

Abode Buenos Aires

Costa Rica 5193, y Godoy Cruz, Palermo Soho (4774 3331, www.abodebuenosaires.com). Subte D, Palermo/bus 34, 39, 60, 152. **Rooms** *4.* **No credit cards.** **Map** *p283 N5* ④

A great option in the value-for-money B&B market, this British-run home away from home in the heart of Palermo Soho provides all the niceties at affordable prices. In four large bedrooms, antique beds,

en-suite bathrooms, air-conditioning and cable TV come as standard, and the public areas include a huge sun-drenched terrace where *asados* and a proper English breakfast are served. *Internet: wireless (free).*

BA Sohotel

Paraguay 4485, y Borges, Palermo Soho (4832 4474, www.basohotel.com). Bus 34, 55, 161. **Rates** *$$ double.* **Rooms** *33.* **Credit** *AmEx, MC, V.* **Map** *p283 M5* ④

Fresh flowers, Chesterfield sofas, plasma screens and a convivial atmosphere greet you as you walk through the glass doors of this friendly Palermo Soho hotel, which adjoins its own restaurant, Rietti. The pea-green and vermilion colour scheme runs throughout the hotel, as do the contemporary paintings by local artists (some a little on the spooky side). Spacious, modern bedrooms have lovely balconies with vistas of Palermo, but if you want even more space, the 7th floor 'premium' suites come with private terraces. While the event rooms and efficient service cater to a business clientele, the wooden decked terrace with heated pool and jacuzzi and the *parrilla* on the rooftop attract guests who are in Buenos Aires simply to relax.

Craft Hip Hotel

Nicaragua 4583, entre Armenia y Malabia, Palermo Soho (4833 0060, www.crafthotel.com). Bus 34, 55, 93, 161. **Rates** *$$ double.* **Rooms** *9.* **Credit** *AmEx, MC, V.* **Map** *p283 M5* ④

The works of contemporary artists such as feminist photographer Fabiana Barreda are featured in this cool, all-white art space and hotel. A creative sensibility has been applied to each of the nine rooms with themes like Song (featuring a mini record player – vinyl LPs are available in the lobby) and Park (boasting great views over the plaza below). The rooms are a bit small, but innovative interior design uses the space wisely. And once you've had your fill of looking at works of art, you can discuss them over an afternoon cocktail on the sun-splashed roof. Hip indeed. *Internet: wireless (free).*

Cypress In

Costa Rica 4828, entre Borges y Thames, Palermo Soho (4833 5834, www.cypressin.com). Bus 34, 36, 93, 161. **Rates** *$$ double.* **Rooms** *13.* **Credit** *AmEx, MC, V.* **Map** *p283 M5* ④

Aptly named for its cypress trees, one of the few features that remain from the original old house once owned by tango musician Juan D'Arienzo, Cypress In is just minutes from Plaza Serrano. There's a cosy dining area, a living room complete with plush leather couches and plasma TV, and a rooftop terrace. While the rooms (each named after a Zen garden element) are a little on the small side, they have all the necessities for travellers who don't plan on spending all their time holed up in the hotel. *Concierge. Internet: wireless (free). TV: DVD.*

CONSUME

Krista Hotel Boutique.

Esplendor Palermo

Guatemala 4931, entre Thames y Uriarte, Palermo Soho (5217 5700, www.esplendor palermosoho.com). Subte D, Plaza Italia/bus 36, 93, 152. **Rates** $$ double. **Rooms** 27. **Credit** AmEx, MC, V. **Map** p283 M6 ⑰

This boutique hotel is relatively petite, but it's big enough that you'll be spared the intimacy of constantly meeting the same fellow guests in the lobby whenever you head out into town. The 'concept' rooms feature large flat-screen TVs and private balconies facing out over the tree lined street, while larger 'superior' rooms boast reading areas with sleek chaises longues.

Bar. Concierge. Disabled-adapted room. Internet: wireless (free). No-smoking rooms. TV.

Other location Esplendor de Buenos Aires, San Martín 780, Microcentro, 5217 5799.

Hotel Costa Rica

Costa Rica 4137/39, entre Gascón y Acuña de Figueroa, Palermo (4864 7390, www.hotel costarica.com.ar). Bus 36, 110, 160, 188. **Rates** $$ double. **Rooms** 25. **No credit cards. Map** p282 L5 ⑲

Nestled away in a quiet area of Palermo but close enough to the buzz, Hotel Costa Rica is a find to be smug about. Friendly staff are on hand to offer local advice as you enjoy a coffee or glass of *vino tinto* at the lobby-cum-lounge's elegant but understated bar. Cosy and comfortable rooms have been recently renovated and the small but perfectly formed communal areas – such as the inviting upstairs terrace – play host to those memorable story-swapping encounters normally found in a more laid-back, hostel-like environment.

Bar. Disabled-adapted room. Internet: wireless (free).

Krista Hotel Boutique

Bonpland 1665, entre Gorriti y Honduras, Palermo Hollywood (4771 4697, www. kristahotel.com.ar). Bus 39, 93. **Rates** $$ double. **Rooms** 10. **Credit** AmEx, MC, V. **Map** p283 N5 ⑲

Eschewing the hip and trendy template that some boutique properties adhere to so rigidly, Krista's owners have managed to maintain the sort of understated elegance that befits the style of this early 20th-century building. Many of the structure's original features have been kept intact, and the large, comfortable bedrooms – a number of which open on to interior patios – combine calming colour schemes and classic furnishings like bijou chandeliers and footed baths with modern comforts. The hotel's location close to a gastronomic hub means that there are plenty of dining options within strolling distance.

Concierge. Internet: wireless (free). Room service. Spa. TV: DVD.

Miravida Soho

Darregueyra 2050, entre Guatemala y Soler, Palermo Soho (4774 6433, www.miravida soho.com). Bus 55, 60, 93. **Rates** $$ double. **Rooms** 6. **Credit** AmEx, MC, V. **Map** p283 M6 ㊿

With original features and plenty of old-fashioned charm, this six-room converted house has character, as well as the full set of modern conveniences. All the rooms are bright and breezy, with high ceilings and private balconies, and Miravida stands out from other boutique hotels in featuring a very handsomely stocked wine bar and cellar. Just in case you should happen to overdo it on the grape juice of an evening, soak up the hangover with a proper fry-up the following morning.

CONSUME

Bar. Disabled-adapted rooms. Internet: wireless (free). No-smoking rooms. Room service. TV: DVD.

Rendez-Vous Hotel
Bonpland 1484, y Cabrera, Palermo Hollywood (3964 5222, www.rendezvoushotel.com.ar). Bus 39, 93, 140, 11, 168. **Rates** $$ double. **Rooms** 11. **Credit** AmEx, MC, V. **Map** p283 N4 **5**

Guest rooms at this elegant, early 20th-century edifice are small but comfortable, with a full-on feng shui colour scheme designed by impassioned owner Frédéric Dubois. For a little extra space, ask for the Campo junior suite, or the sultry red-suffused Tango deluxe suite. Take a simple breakfast of espresso and chocolate croissants in the bright dining salon; sunny afternoons are best spent on the intimate rooftop terrace.
Bar. Disabled-adapted room. Internet: wireless (free). No-smoking hotel.

Vain
Thames 2226/8, entre Charcas y Paraguay, Palermo Soho (4776 8246, www.vain universe.com). Subte D, Plaza Italia/ bus 34, 36, 39, 55, 93. **Rates** $$ double. **Rooms** 15. **Credit** AmEx, MC, V. **Map** p283 M6 **5**

The friendly folk at Vain believe there's nothing narcissistic about pampering yourself every now nd then. When you check in to this tranquil 15-room boutique hotel located a short stroll away from Palermo's Plaza Italia, you're offered a complimentary drink, and in case this isn't enough to totally de stress, the 'senior' rooms are all equipped with hydromassage tubs. And since you're indulging in deadly sins, add a little gluttony to the list: don't miss the delicious, varied breakfast, which should set you up a treat for a day of strolling in the surrounding area.
Bar. Concierge. Disabled-adapted rooms. Internet: wireless (free) & shared terminal. TV.

Budget

Bernarda House
Uriarte 1942, entre Soler y Nicaragua, Palermo Soho (mobile 15 3227 1111, www.bernardahouse.com.ar) Subte D, Plaza Italia/Bus 34, 36, 39, 55, 57, 108, 166. **Rates** $. **Rooms** 6. **No credit cards**. **Map** p283 N6 **5**

Six rooms are spread over three floors in this charming B&B on a tree-lined street. The converted house's hard-wood floors, exposed brick and vintage furniture add to its appeal, as does the artwork, painted by the owner. Guests can soak in an antique claw-foot tub or take a relaxing dip in the pool. The owner also offers guests private, tailor-made city tours.
Internet: wireless (free). Pool (outdoor).

LAS CAÑITAS
Moderate

248 Finisterra
Báez 248, entre Arguibel y Arévalo (4773 0901, www.248finisterra.com). Subte D, Carranza/bus 55, 60, 64, 152, 160. **Rates** $$ double. **Rooms** 11. **Credit** AmEx, MC, V. **Map** p287 O9 **5**

Chic and cosmopolitan, Finisterra is rather like the neighbourhood in which it's located. From the contemporary decor – offset by a sensible smattering of antique objects – to the exterior hardwood deck complete with a hot tub, Las Cañitas cool infuses this smart boutique hotel. The area may attract plenty of beautiful people with its dynamic drinking and dining scene, but the atmosphere at Finisterra is warm and friendly, and the helpful staff will happily offer advice on eating and sightseeing options.
Bar. Concierge. Disabled-adapted rooms. Internet: wireless (free). Room service. TV.

ALMAGRO
Moderate

Racó de Buenos Aires
Yapeyú 271, entre Hipólito Yrigoyen y Avenida Belgrano (3530 6075, www.racodebuenosaires. com.ar). Subte A, Castro Barros/bus 5, 103, 128, 132. **Rates** $$ double. **Rooms** 12. **Credit** AmEx, MC, V. **Map** p282 I3 **5**

'Off the beaten track' is frequently a euphemism for darn tricky to get to, but this intimate hotel is tucked conveniently close to the Subte and bus stops on busy Avenida Rivadavia. Named after the Catalan word for 'corner' in homage to owner Julián's time in Barcelona, and filled with great artwork by local artists, Racó is located in Almagro, home to the charming Las Violetas café and pleasant residential streets. The hotel's 12 comfortable rooms are all decorated in contrasting styles – a duplex, for example, recreates the aesthetic of La Boca's iconic, colourful buildings. Opt for breakfast in your bedroom or, in fine weather, on the patio.
Bar. Internet: wireless (free).

VILLA CRESPO
Moderate

Pop Hotel
Juan Ramírez de Velasco 793, y Gurruchaga, (4776 6900, www.pophotelsbuenosaires.com). Subte B, Malabia/bus 15, 24, 34, 55, 110, 127, 168. **Rates** $$ double. **Rooms** 44. **Credit** MC, V. **Map** p283 M3 **5**

With its bold colour scheme, psychedelic wall patterns and Roy Lichtenstein-inspired reception, Pop Hotel is an ode to all things pop. Although it may sound like an oxymoron, this 'budget boutique'

CONSUME

hotel does exactly what it says on the Campbell's tomato soup tin: comfort with a bright splash of style, and for less. All rooms have plasma TVs, iPod docks and kitchenettes, and some have their own balconies.
Concierge. Internet: wireless (free). TV.

Querido B&B
Juan Ramírez de Velazco 934, entre Thames y Serrano (4854 6297, www.queridobuenos aires.com). Subte B, Malabia/bus 15, 110, 168. **Rates** $$ double. **Rooms** 4. **Credit** AmEx, MC, V. **Map** p283 M3 ⑤⑦
This stylish bed and breakfast is run by an Anglo-Brazilian couple who have created a modern but homely lodging. Although it's been beautifully renovated, the building still retains some original features. Each double room has an en-suite bathroom and a balcony, and a basket of baked goods awaits you for breakfast each morning. The owners are experienced travellers, and the cosy living area contains books about South American travel.
Internet: wireless (free). TV.

COLEGIALES
Moderate

Matienzo Haus
Benjamín Matienzo 2596, y Ciudad de la Paz (4771 2749, www.matienzohaus.com.ar). Subte D, Carranza/bus 67, 68, 152. **Rates** $$ double. **Rooms** 5. **No credit cards. Map** p283 P5 ⑤⑧
This welcoming guesthouse has the sort of history and atmosphere lesser hotels can only envy. A fantastic wooden staircase leads to five classic, comfortable rooms, each with en-suite bathrooms; and the whole place is permeated by a family ambience. And it's no gimmick – on the landing of this magnificent and slightly austere-looking 1916 family home is a set of engaging family photographs.
Internet: wireless (free).

SAN ISIDRO
High-end

Hotel del Casco
Avenida del Libertador 16170 (4732 3993, www.hoteldelcasco.com.ar). Train to San Isidro from Retiro. **Rates** $$$ double. **Rooms** 20. **Credit** AmEx, MC, V.
San Isidro is an irresistibly quaint neighbourhood that has been a popular short excursion from BA's bustle ever since the 18th century. It has been more attractive than ever since this 19th-century house was made into a hotel. With its whitewashed porticoes, wrought-iron lanterns and interior glass-ceilinged patio, the hotel is charming.
Business centre. Concierge. Gym. Internet: wireless (free). Pool (outdoor). Room service. Spa. TV.

APARTMENT HOTELS
Art Suites
Azcuénaga 1465, entre French y Juncal, Recoleta (4821 6800, www.artsuites.com.ar). Subte D, Pueyrredón/bus 10, 12, 39, 61, 64, 152, 188. **Rates** $$ double. **Rooms** 15. **Credit** AmEx, MC, V. **Map** p286 J10 ⑤⑨
There's no sterile lobby here; just a round-the-clock doorman and a lift to whisk guests to huge suites fitted with whirlpool baths and soundproof glass doors opening on to private terraces. Premium apartments, each containing two bedrooms and two bathrooms, can comfortably accommodate five people. Guests might forget they're in a hotel until the doorbell rings in the morning, and a tray piled high with *medialunas* and steaming coffee is delivered to their dining room table.
Internet: wireless (free).

Hollywood Suites & Lofts
Nicaragua 5490, y Humboldt 1915, Palermo Hollywood (5276 6100, www.hollywoodsuites ba.com.ar). Bus 39, 93. **Rates** $$$ double. **Rooms** 34. **Credit** AmEx, MC, V. **Map** p283 N5 ⑥⓪
This upscale aparthotel's 17 floors feature a range of large bi-level lofts with concrete floors, leather furniture, black-out curtains, fully equipped kitchens and balconies. The communal spaces, including a rooftop pool with glassed-in terrace, are modern and inviting.
Concierge. Gym. Internet: wireless (free). Pool (outdoor).

APARTMENT RENTAL
Temporary apartment rental is big business in Buenos Aires, and furnished properties are available for anything from a few nights to several months. Numerous agencies offer this service and rates vary greatly, but you can expect a month's rental to start from around US$800. Note that not all agencies accept credit card payment.

For Rent Argentina (4822 5912, www.4rentargentina.com) and ByT Argentina (4876 5000, www.bytargentina. com) can arrange lets in fully furnished apartments all over the city, from just the basics to truly palatial digs. My Space BA (4793 3496, www.myspaceba.com) and Oasis BA (4777 3692, www.oasis collections.com) tend towards the more luxurious end of the scale. The latter also owns the exclusive Oasis Clubhouse in Palermo with three rooms to rent and use of one of BA's loveliest pools. Also in Palermo, Art House (Charcas 5006, 4899 2502, www.arthousebuenosaires.com) has four

CONSUME

sleek self-contained apartments to rent. **BA House** (4815 7602, www.bahouse.com.ar) has apartments in some of the city's smarter neighbourhoods, as well as in Uruguay's Punta del Este. **Buenos Aires Habitat** (4815 8662, www.buenosaireshabitat.com) offers short-term rental options and can also provide property management and advice on purchasing properties. A number of other businesses, such as **Nancy Landi International Properties** (mobile 15 5240 6369, www.nancylandi.com) have properties for sale as well as for rent. **BAires Apartments** (4833 3319, www.bairesapartments.com) rent out apartments all over town (available on a daily, weekly or monthly basis), and if you're in the market to buy your own Palermo pad, they have a range of properties on their books.

YOUTH HOSTELS

América del Sur
Chacabuco 718, entre Independencia y Chile, San Telmo (4300 5525, www.americahostel.com.ar). Subte E, Independencia/bus 10, 22, 29, 195. **Rates** $ per person dorm; $ double. **Credit** MC, V. **Map** p285 E9 ③
This clean, sleek and impressive property is one of the city's most pleasant hostels. There's excellent disabled access throughout plus a room specially designed for wheelchair access.

Casa Esmeralda
Honduras 5765, entre Bonpland y Carranza, Palermo Hollywood (4772 2446, www. casaesmeralda.com.ar). Bus 39, 93, 111. **Rates** $ per person dorm. **No credit cards. Map** p283 N5 ②
An unpretentious and comfy hostel run by amiable Franco-Argentinian Sebas. It enjoyed a past life as a Buddhist retreat, and a zen-like atmosphere still prevails in the shady garden. The hostel has four doubles, two dormitories and a large communal kitchen.

Chill House
Agüero 781, entre Tucumán y Zelaya (4861 6175, www.chillhouse.com.ar). Subte B, Carlos Gardel/bus 24, 26, 29, 140, 168. **Rates** $ per person dorm; $ double. **No credit cards. Map** p282 J6 ③
In a charming 1907 dwelling, the Chill House has a sociable atmosphere and comfortable shared and private rooms. Weekly *asados* are held on the roof terrace.

Circus
Chacabuco 1020, entre Carlos Calvo y Humberto Primo, San Telmo (4878 7786,

www.hostelcircus.com). Subte C, San Juan/ bus 10, 29. **Rates** $ per person dorm; $ double. **Credit** AmEx, MC, V. **Map** p284 D9 ④
Circus includes the kind of amenities that are usually found in hotels, while friendly staff maintain a welcoming hostel vibe. Every room has air-conditioning and en-suite bathrooms, and there's an in-house restaurant, cosy lounge area and a heated outdoor pool.

Eco Pampa Palermo
Guatemala 4778, entre Borges y Gurruchaga, Palermo Soho (4831 2435, www.hostelpampa.com). Subte D, Plaza Italia/bus 34, 36, 39, 55, 161. **Rates** $ per person dorm; $ double. **Credit** DC, MC, V. **Map** p283 M6 ⑤
This well-located boutique hostel has been tastefully renovated and its minimalist interior has been furnished with energy-efficient chandeliers. The rooftop terrace has an organic herb garden and solar panels.

Milhouse
Hipólito Yrigoyen 959, entre Tacuarí e Irigoyen, Monserrat (4345 9604, www.milhousehostel.com). Subte A, Piedras or C, Avenida de Mayo/bus 39, 64, 86. **Rates** $ per person dorm; $ double. **No credit cards. Map** p285 F10 ⑥
This three-tiered 1890 house was built from materials shipped over from Europe. Nowadays, it's a lively and popular hostel: book well in advance. Milhouse also offers tango classes and tours.
Other location Milhouse Avenue, Avenida de Mayo 1249, Congreso (4383 9383).

Ostinatto Hostel
Chile 680, entre Perú y Chacabuco, San Telmo (4362 9639, www.ostinatto.com). Bus 2, 9, 10, 28, 29, 86. **Rates** $ per person dorm; $ double. **No credit cards. Map** p285 E9 ⑦
This hostel has won praise for its clean, minimalist design. At first sight the interior looks a little like an Escher sketch, but this place actually comes complete with an art gallery, microcinema and piano bar.

Terrazas Estoril
6th floor, Avenida de Mayo 1386, entre Uruguay y Talcahuano, Congreso (4382 9073, www.hostelestoril.com.ar). Subte A, Sáenz Peña/bus 2, 5, 7, 24, 151. **Rates** $ per person dorm. **No credit cards. Map** p285 F9 ⑧
Bright and airy dorms, attentive staff and a prime position on Avenida de Mayo combine to make this one of the best hostels in BA. In summer, the rooftop bar and terrace becomes a stage for sultry nights against the backdrop of the impressive Palacio Barolo building.

CONSUME

Restaurants

The thrills and grills of dining out in the Argentinian capital.

There are few more enjoyable things in life than whiling away an evening over a steak and a bottle of wine. And in Buenos Aires, you're guaranteed good steak, wine... and most often the whiling away part too. But although service is generally not what it is in most European or North American cities, the meat really *is* all that and is always worth the wait. However, vegetarians need not despair: you can find much more than an artfully arranged lettuce leaf to nibble on, particularly in Palermo where many of the city's best restaurants cluster. International cuisine is now widespread, with Peruvian–Japanese fusion food being particularly popular. If you like your food very spicy though, you're in the wrong city.

For a memorable dining experience, book ahead at one of the capital's exciting closed-door restaurants, but also remember that there's always an inviting pizza joint that's anything but trendy on most city blocks – BA's staple eateries are still going strong.

EATING IN BUENOS AIRES

Cow is king in this carnivorous capital, where the world's best cuts slowly grill to perfection in the city's countless parrillas (steakhouses). The other two ubiquitous Ps – pasta and pizza – remain stubborn staples of the porteño diet, but these days you no longer have to scour the gastrosphere to also find molecular gastronomy, gourmet vegetarian food and Peruvian-Japanese fusion restaurants. Recent years have also seen the rise of seriously sexy contemporary Argentinian cuisine, where local ingredients are lifted by modern techniques and expertly paired with home-grown wines.

Despite the glut of culinary options, restaurant prices aren't what they were five years ago, or even last month, with inflation putting Buenos Aires on a par with North America and Europe. Set lunchtime menus are still fantastic value though, offering two or

❶ Blue numbers given in this chapter correspond to the location of each restaurant on the street maps. *See pp279-288.*

three courses for the price of a main. If you still have room for dinner, note that *porteños* tend to eat late – restaurants don't get full until after 10pm.

Service can be (very) slow in this unrushed capital, although warmth and character usually compensate for what is lacking in speed and efficiency. A minimum ten per cent tip (*propina*) will be greatly appreciated by underpaid restaurant staff.

Many small restaurants only accept cash, and it's always best to make sure up front that the credit card facilities are in full working order.

For a comprehensive guide to the restaurants of Buenos Aires, visit the Spanish-language website Guía Oleo (www.guiaoleo.com.ar).

ABOUT THE LISTINGS

Prices in this section are represented by peso signs. $ indicates a range of roughly AR$30-AR$49 for main courses, although some restaurants have special dishes on their menus that can be much more expensive. $$ is AR$50-AR$69, $$$ is AR$70-AR$99 and $$$$ is AR$100 and above. Prices given here do not include extras such as wine, starters, dessert or coffees. The $ symbol indicates good value dining options. The ★ indicates our favourites.

CONSUME

Filo. See p113.

CONSUME

THE CENTRE

★$ Chan Chan
*Hipólito Yrigoyen 1390, entre San José
y Santiago del Estero, Congreso (4382 8492).
Subte A, Sáenz Peña/bus 39, 60, 168.*
Open noon-4pm, 8pm-12.30am Tue-Sun.
Main courses $. No credit cards.
Map p285 F9 ❶ Peruvian
Tucked behind the magnificent Palacio Barolo (*see
p41*), sweet and kitsch Chan Chan continues to
wow punters with its brilliant, spicy Peruvian food
at affordable prices. Among a long list of Andean
classics, look out for the excellent *chicharrón de
pescado* (fried fish), the *ceviche mixto* and the *causa
de salmón ahumado* – a colourful stack of salmon-
and-potato-based joy. Also popular are daily specials such as *anticuchos de salmón* (pink salmon
served on kebab sticks) and *anticuchos de langosti-
nos* (shrimp).

Club del Progreso
*Sarmiento 1334, entre Talcahuano
y Uruguay, Congreso (4372 3350). Subte B,
Uruguay/bus 29, 60, 102.* **Open** noon-3.30pm,
8.30pm-12.30am Mon-Sat. **Main courses** $$$.
Credit AmEx, MC, V. **Map** p285 G10 ❷
Argentinian (traditional)

Dating from 1852, this hidden treasure in the heart of
Congreso features a menu based on traditional dishes
that have been reinvented for modern times and are
served in an unassuming paradise. In fine weather,
relaxing in the lovely garden – which is equipped
with a mud oven – is an excellent option. Try the
suckling pig or ribs served with gizzards, cooked in
this outdoor oven; or opt for the Patagonian trout or
pacú, a fish from the north of the country. Traditional
Argentinian desserts are another house speciality.

D'Oro
*Perú 159, entre Hipólito Yrigoyen
y Adolfo Alsina, Microcentro (4342 6959,
www.doro-resto.com.ar). Subte A, Perú or
E, Bolívar or D, Catedral/bus 22, 24.* **Open**
9am-midnight Mon-Fri; 7pm-12.30am Sat.
Main courses $$$$. **Credit** AmEx, MC, V.
Map p285 E10 ❸ Italian
Both locals and foreigners come to D'Oro for risottos,
pastas and fresh salads (enough for two), and for the
smart sommeliers, who can recommend the perfect
wine to accompany your dish. Pull up a stool at the
tiled bar for happy hour (5-8pm), and order some
crisp focaccia with a glass of Michel Rolland's Clos
de los Siete; or settle down for main courses like ravi-
oli in malbec sauce, or fig and cognac penne – a
savoury treat prepared as you watch.

Filo

San Martín 975, entre Marcelo T de Alvear y Paraguay, Retiro (4311 0312, www.filoristorante.com). Subte C, San Martín/bus 10, 93, 130, 152. **Open** *noon-1am daily.* **Main courses** $$$. **Credit** AmEx, MC, V. **Map** p285 G12. ❹ Italian

Filo is a popular lunchtime restaurant – come 1pm, even the bar stools are occupied by rows of financial advisers chowing down on pizzas, pasta or grilled vegetables. With a cool, urban interior accented by slashes of red and yellow, a lengthy menu, oversized bread baskets on every table, and a traditional brick oven, it's an obvious contender for one of the best places to grab a bite downtown. Brie, spinach, mushrooms, fat olives, rocket – choose whatever takes your fancy. Pair your pizza with a salad made from delicious, flavoursome steamed vegetables. *Photo p111.*

Status

Virrey Cavellos 178, entre Hipólito Yrigoyen y Alsina, Congreso (4382 8531). Subte A, Sáenz Peña/bus 39, 60, 168. **Open** *noon-midnight daily.* **Main courses** $$. **No credit cards. Map** p285 G9. ❺ Peruvian

Just a hop, skip and a jump from the grand, domed Congreso building, this immaculate Peruvian restaurant serves nicely spicy starters and abundant platters of rabbit, chicken and lamb as well as very good ceviche. The latter is made from fresh *tiburón* (small shark) caught off Mar del Plata, well-seasoned and served under a heap of red onions, with potatoes, egg and toasted corn on the side. Busy during the day with an eclectic, and happy-looking clientele, the restaurant is often packed by 9pm (expect to queue).

Tomo I

Hotel Panamericano, Carlos Pellegrini 521, entre Lavalle y Tucumán, Microcentro (4326 6695, www.tomo1.com.ar). Subte B, Carlos Pellegrini/bus 10, 17, 29. **Open** *noon-3pm Mon-Fri; 7.30pm-midnight Mon-Sat.* **Main courses** $$$$. **Credit** AmEx, DC, MC, V. **Map** p285 G10. ❻ Argentinian (modern)

Those hankering after the good ol' days when eating out was more about quality than keeping up with trends need to pay a visit to the ever-reliable Tomo I. This elegant restaurant serves up what might just be the best tasting menu in the city, with the likes of quail on a bed of endives and Patagonian langostines sautéed in brandy on the menu. Mood lighting and jazz tunes make this a romantic place for a tête-à-tête, while its proximity to the Teatro Colón means you'll likely see opera singers in their glad rags swanning in for a post-performance feast. Start off with the house punch, a spice and passionfruit concoction, or save yourself for the excellent wine list; reds are served in crystal decanters by suited staff.

INSIDE TRACK
ONE PRICE THIS WEEK ...

... a significantly higher one the next. Estimates suggest Argentina's unofficial inflation rate is at 25 to 30 per cent. The food industry is heavily affected, which is why we've listed prices in general ranges in this chapter. Expect them to rise!

SOUTH OF THE CENTRE

Aldo's Vinoteca y Restorán

Moreno 372, entre Defensa y Balcarce, Monserrat (5291 2380, www.aldosvinoteca.com). Subte A, Perú/bus 29, 64, 111, 152. **Open** *11am-midnight daily.* **Main courses** $$$. **Credit** AmEx, MC, V. **Map** p285 E10. ❼ Argentinian (modern)

At this Russian doll of a restaurant within a wine store within a hotel (the Moreno, *see p87*), celebrity sommelier Aldo Graziani has made *vino* the star of the show. Sure, the wall-length mirrors, soft brasserie-style lighting and a striking central bar make this place stand out, but it's the wine from more than 500 quality labels adorning the modern art-deco restaurant that have got everyone talking. Best of all, the bottles – all selected at blind tastings – are sold at retail price. An exquisite modern Argentinian menu includes slow-cooked lamb in a rich malbec jus, and of course, a perfect sirloin steak. *Photo p136.*

CONSUME

Tomo I.

A CLASSIC

CREATIVE ARGENTINE CUISINE - CHEF: ALDO BENEGAS
HAPPY HOUR EVERY DAY OF WINES AND COCKTAILS
LARGE SELECTION OF ARGENTINE WINES - SUSHI.

OPEN EVERY DAY
MONDAY TO FRIDAY FROM 7 PM
SATURDAYS, SUNDAYS AND HOLIDAYS FROM 8 PM
WE CLOSE LATE

GRAN BAR
DANZON
RESTAURANT
WINE BAR & COCKTAILS
LIBERTAD 1161 • 4811-1108
DANZON@GRANBARDANZON.COM.AR
WWW.GRANBARDANZON.COM.AR

Amici Miei

Defensa 1072, entre Humberto Primo
y Carlos Calvo, San Telmo (4362 5562,
www.amicimiei.com.ar). Bus 22, 29.
Open noon-4pm, 8pm-midnight Tue-Sat;
noon-5pm Sun. **Main courses** $$$. **Credit**
AmEx, MC, V. **Map** p284 D9. ❽ Italian
At this upmarket Italian eaterie overlooking Plaza
Dorrego, bakers in starched hats knead dough in a
glass-encased kitchen, while attentive waiters
serve up pasta that puts the overcooked spaghetti
masquerading as Italian cuisine in many BA
restaurants to shame. The black truffle carpaccio
and the risotto with prosciutto and asparagus
stand out, as do the salads. Pick an outdoor table
in fine weather.
▶ *Don't miss the chance to browse in the lovely*
gallery downstairs, the Solar de French.

Booze for Thought

Time Out talks red and white with wine lover and author Ian Mount.

First up, is malbec really all that?
Like all grapes, it can be crap. But like
only the best varietals, it can be all that
(and then some). Much like a good
Argentinian, it fled Old World poverty
(in France, in its case) and found its
fortune in the New World. The dry sun
of the Andes is its preferred habitat,
and when it's grown on pruned-back
low-yield vines, with enough altitude
that it doesn't burn into a rough-and-
ready alcohol bomb, it can be amazing.

**I've got 30 pesos to my name. What can
I buy that doesn't taste like vinegar?**
Trapiche stepchild Las Moras makes
some good wines for the price, such
as Finca Las Moras, Alma Mora and
Marianne. Séptima is also good value.
And if you want white, the Etchart Privado
torrontés is a classic for low-budget,
high-palate alcoholics.

**I don't drink red wine but I love red meat.
Will I get the evil eye for ordering white
with my steak?**
White wine with red meat gives me the
twitches, to be honest. So, I would give you
the curious eye. But I shouldn't say that.
Wine is like clothing; wear what you like. If
it's, err, 'fashion-forward' and people stare
at you, it doesn't matter if you're happy.

**Apart from torrontés and malbec,
which other Argentinian wines
should I be quaffing?**
Bonarda is the third child. Forgotten,
perhaps, but independent and a high-
achiever. Fruity and great with pasta.

**Can you recommend a good Argentinian
bottle of bubbly for a special occasion?**
In general I like Argentina's very dry
Extra Brut bubblies. For something other
than the ever-present Chandon – which
is quite nice for everyday drinking – and
something that doesn't break the bank,
try Salentein's Extra Brut. For a smaller
bodega, the Hom sparkling is a good find.

**I'm shallow: I judge a wine by its label.
Are there any bottles with snazzy labels
or silly names?**
There are plenty, though thankfully
Argentina hasn't gone in for the 'Big
Ass Red' or 'Ball Buster' style wine
names that almost make me worry that
marketing skill and wine quality come
in inverse proportions. Here, there's
Animal, Pura Sangre (Pure Blood), and
Dos Minas (Two Girls).

**I need to impress my father-in-law (and
he knows a thing or two about wine).
What can I get to take back that will
make me look good?**
Roberto de la Mota, the winemaker at
Mendel, is an artist. Try the Mendel Unos.

**And where should I go to get a little
tipsy on the good stuff?**
Don Julio (*see p131*) has an excellent
list of the bigger and better-known
bodegas, while Las Pizarras (*see p136*)
has a lot of really good boutique wineries
on its list. Neither marks their bottles
up too much. As for tastings, Anuva
Wines (www.anuvawines.com) does
a nice tasting, as does 0800-VINO
(*see p174*) and, of course, Time Out
(www.winetourtimeoutba.com.ar).

Complete the following:
For a fruity bonanza, go for...
...a bonarda, maybe the Lamadrid.
For an oaky experience, go for...
... Altocedro Reserva Malbec.
For something lovely and light, go for...
... Bodega Atamisque Sauvignon Blanc.
For a robust red, go for...
... Colomé's Amalaya. If you've got cash
(and like a lot of booze), go for the San
Pedro de Yacochuya.

Ian Mount is the author of The Vinyard at
the End of the World *(www.ianmount.com).*

CONSUME

El Baqueano

Chile 495, y Bolívar, San Telmo (4342 0802, www.restoelbaqueano.com). Subte C, Independencia/bus 10, 22, 29, 86. **Open** 8pm-midnight Tue-Sat. **7-course set menu** $$$$. **Credit** AmEx, MC, V. **Map** p285 E10. ❾ Argentinian (modern)

Despite rave reviews from food critics from around the world, as well as from film director Francis Ford Coppola, this red-hued restaurant remains something of a secret on the Buenos Aires gastronomic scene. Why? Possibly because chef and owner Fernando Rivarola has ignored the obvious choice of beef and filled his menu with creative dishes prepared from some of Argentina's most exotic fauna: *yacaré* (caiman) comes spiked on a kebab stick; and llama is served in slivers of carpaccio.

Brasserie Petanque

Defensa 596, y México, San Telmo (4342 7930, www.brasseriepetanque.com). Bus 29, 93, 152. **Open** 12.30-4pm, 8.30pm-midnight Tue-Sun. **Main courses** *Lunch* $$. *Dinner* $$$. **Credit** AmEx, MC, V. **Map** p285 E10. ❿ French

The menu at this honest-to-goodness French brasserie with a marvellously light and airy atmosphere bristles with the sort of Gallic standards it's hard to tire of, including an exceptional boeuf bourguignon, steak tartare and, of course, *escargots*, served by a corps of efficient and friendly waiters. The gigot of lamb stuffed with dried tomatoes, fennel and fresh herbs is a star, as is the seafood risotto; and a parade of daily specials makes a look at the online menu a good plan.

La Brigada

Estados Unidos 465, entre Bolívar y Defensa, San Telmo (4361 4685). Bus 22, 29, 126. **Open** 12.30-4pm, 8pm-midnight daily. **Main courses** $$$. **Credit** AmEx, MC, V. **Map** p284 D10. ⓫ Argentinian (traditional)

This San Telmo institution is a refined version of the traditional parrilla, all immaculate linen and sparkling glasses, serving up excellent cuts of meat alongside spicy chorizo, grilled provoleta cheese, various salads and crispy vegetable fritters. Regulars swear that the offal selection is among the best in the town, particularly the crispy kid *chinchulines* (chitterling).

Café Rivas

Estados Unidos, y Balcarce, San Telmo (4361 5539, www.caferivas.com.ar). Bus 22, 24, 29, 64, 152. **Open** 10am-midnight Tue-Sat; 11am-8pm Sun. **Main courses** $$. **Credit** AmEx, V. **Map** p284 D10. ⓬ Argentinian (modern)

Set on possibly the prettiest corner in San Telmo, across a wide cobbled crossroads, Café Rivas has the air, somehow, of a tearoom. Inside, it's all retro wood and cake stands, and the occasional dramatic flash of fire as the chef does his thing in the open

kitchen. The no-nonsense menu is a mix of classic Argentinian and comfort food – think pastas, risottos and neat beef medallions, served with a smile. But the place really comes into its own as a haven from the teeming streets of San Telmo on a Sunday afternoon – dart here, a block away from *calle* Defensa, for a break from the street market madness over coffee and cake.

★ Café San Juan

Avenida San Juan 450, entre Bolívar y Defensa, San Telmo (4300 1112). Subte C, San Juan/ bus 10, 24, 28, 29. **Open** 12.30-4pm; 8pm-midnight Tue-Sun. **Main courses** $$$$. *Tapas* $-$$$$. **No credit cards.** **Map** p284 D9. ⓭ Spanish

During the daily lunch rush, chef Leandro Cristobal fashions inventive tapas and pastas from the likes of sun-dried tomatoes, brie and seasonal vegetables. The daily menu is scrawled on chalkboards that are hauled around from table to table, resplendent with homely dishes like cured ham with mushrooms, or a courgette-rich fettuccine. Dinner comprises more substantial fare like *bife de chorizo* (sirloin steak), salmon and occasional rarities like *liebre* (hare) in a thick wine sauce. *Photo p119.*

Caseros

Avenida Caseros 486, entre Bolívar y Defensa, San Telmo (4307 4729, www.caserosrestaurante.com.ar). Bus 10, 29, 39, 70, 195. **Open** noon-3.30pm Mon-Sat; 8.30pm-12.30am Tue-Sat. **Main courses** $$. **Credit** AmEx, MC, V. **Map** p284 C9. ⓮ Argentinian (modern)

There's nothing equivocal about this sophisticated yet understated brasserie. Owner-chefs Santiago Leone and Silvina Trouilh know what it's all about: simple, flavoursome food. If menus came with sound effects, Caseros's *carta* would open to the thrum of a bustling market and the sound of grannies humming at their chopping boards. The fish and meat are both fresh and locally sourced, and don't miss childhood favourites like layered pancakes.

▶ *If Caseros is full, try Club Social Deluxe or Hierba Buena, both just steps away on Avenida Caseros.*

CONSUME

El Desnivel

Defensa 855, entre Avenida Independencia y Estados Unidos, San Telmo (4300 9081). Subte C, Independencia/bus 24, 29. **Open** 12.30-4pm, 8pm-midnight daily. **Main courses** $$. **No credit cards. Map** p284 D10. ⑮
Argentinian (traditional)
High on the list of fun things to do in BA is a late-night steak blowout at this legendary San Telmo parrilla. Staffing the grill are bloody-apron-wearing, knife-wielding cooks (think Sweeney Todd meets Joe Pesci). The even mix of expatriates, tourists and locals makes for a boisterous and friendly scene. Make sure you get a table in the main restaurant (rather than in the annex) to feel part of the action.

★ Gran Parrilla del Plata

Chile 594, y Perú, San Telmo (4300 8858, www.parrilladelplata.com.ar). Bus 10, 26, 29. **Open** 12.30-3.30pm, 8pm-1am daily. **Main courses** $$$. **Credit** AmEx, MC, V. **Map** p285 E10. ⑯ Argentinian (traditional)

All the Fun of the Parrilla

Menu decoder: knowing an arse from an elbow.

MEAT, GLORIOUS MEAT

Asado barbecue(d); **tira de asado** rack of ribs; **bife de chorizo** rump/sirloin steak; **bife de costilla** T-bone steak; **bife de lomo** tenderloin steak; **bondiola** shoulder of beef or pork; **chimichurri** spicy sauce for meat; **chinchulín** intestine; **chivito** kid; **choripán** sausage sandwich; **chorizo** sausage; **chuleta** chop; **cuadril** rump steak; **cordero** lamb; **entraña** skirt steak; **hígado** liver; **lechón** suckling pig; **lengua** tongue; **matambre** flank steak; **milanesa** breaded cutlet; **molleja** sweetbread; **mondongo** tripe; **morcilla** blood sausage/black pudding; **ojo de bife** rib-eye steak; **parrillada** small table grill; **riñones** kidneys; **ternera** veal; **vacío** flank.

HOW DO YOU LIKE IT?

A la parrilla grilled; **al horno** baked; **al vapor** steamed; **asado** roast; **frito** fried; **hervido** boiled; **picante** spicy/hot; **salteado** sautéed; **muy jugoso** rare; **jugoso** medium rare; **a punto** medium; **cocido** well done; **muy bien cocido** between well done and shoe leather.

SIDE DISHES

Ensalada mixta tomato, onion and lettuce salad; **espinacas a la crema** creamed spinach; **puré de calabaza** puréed squash; **puré de papas** mashed potato; **papas fritas** chips.
For more on Argentinian meat, see p122 **Beef Encounter.**

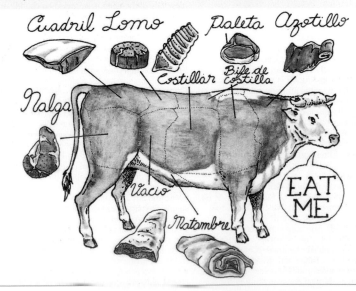

CONSUME

Café San Juan. *See p117.*

With a great location on a picturesque city corner, and fine cuts of beef and classy rustic decor to go with it, the Gran Parrilla del Plata has established itself as a barrio classic and gets packed out most nights of the week. All the cuts of meat are exquisite; but it's the *ojo de bife* (rib-eye) and the tasty *entraña* (skirt steak – a novelty to most foreigners) that are most recommended. Combine them with the baked potatoes with bacon and cream cheese and a fresh salad. Classy but affordable, this joint is always reliable.

Manolo
Bolívar 1299, y Cochabamba, San Telmo (4307 8743, www.restaurantmanolo.com.ar). Bus 10, 24, 29, 39. **Open** noon-1am Tue-Sun. **Main courses** $$. **Credit** AmEx, MC, V. **Map** p284 D9. ⓱ Argentinian (traditional)
This friendly neighbourhood joint is buzzing most nights with a loyal clientele who come to feast on the excellent parrilla standards, and the parrilla standards with a twist – a ham and mozzarella-stuffed steak, for example, or a selection of great steak sauces. There's a sprinkling of criollo cuisine (try the hearty stew *locro*), and chicken prepared in a dozen different ways, including the *suprema* Gran Manolo – a breaded chicken breast topped with ham, egg, cheese and olives.
Other location Perú 1480, San Telmo (4300 3548).

Il Matterello
Martín Rodríguez 517, y Villafañe, La Boca (4307 0529). Bus 29, 64, 86, 152. **Open** 12.30-3pm, 8.30pm-midnight Tue-Sat; 12.30-3pm Sun. **Main courses** $$$. **Credit** AmEx, DC, MC, V. **Map** p284 B9. ⓲ Italian

The food takes centre stage in this crisp, clean, cantina-style La Boca eaterie. A mixed plate of warm and cold antipasti serves to liven the taste buds in preparation for al dente tagliatelle with a puttanesca sauce and a truly sumptuous *fazzoletti alla* carbonara. Top service and unpretentious decor help to accompany, but not out-twinkle, the star here, which shines brightly from the kitchen.

M Buenos Aires
Balcarce 433, entre Avenida Belgrano y Venezuela, San Telmo (4331 3879, www.mbuenosaires.com.ar). Subte E, Belgrano/bus 2, 152. **Open** noon-3.30pm Mon-Fri; 7.30-11.30pm Mon-Sat. **Main courses** $$$. **Credit** AmEx, MC, V. **Map** p285 E10. ⓳ Peruvian–Japanese
Blessed with the kind of grand façade they just don't build any more, M Buenos Aires is as dramatic in its decor as it is bold in its cuisine and mixology. Kick off with a cocktail – the sweet tomato bloody mary is a revelation – then launch straight in to the exquisite Peruvian–Japanese fusion food. The *tiraditos* – fish strips – with dried Japanese lime and yellow pepper sauce are delicious, as are the wok-fried scallops and langostines, all served by spot-on staff.

Miramar
Avenida San Juan 1999, y Sarandí, Constitución (4304 4261). Subte E, Entre Ríos/bus 37, 53, 126. **Open** noon-4pm, 8pm-midnight Tue-Sun. **Main courses** $$$. **Credit** AmEx, MC, V. **Map** p285 F7. ⓴ Argentinian (traditional)
Beloved by its barrio, Miramar is an unpretentious eaterie boasting a well-stocked wine cellar and

CONSUME

amiable waiters. For lunch, try rabbit in white wine, Spanish tortilla, frogs' legs, Spanish-style oysters or shrimps in garlic. The justly famed *rabo de toro* (oxtail stew) has a limb-warming quality that's nigh on narcotic. You can also tuck into *centolla* (king crab) and other deep-sea delicacies, or keep it light (well, light-ish, you are in Argentina after all) and devour a cheeseboard over a bottle of wine.

Moreneta de Monserrat

Moreno 477, entre Bolívar y Defensa, Monserrat (4331 1428, www.moreneta.com.ar). Subte A, Plaza de Mayo/bus 152. **Open** 7.30am-7pm Mon-Fri; noon 5pm Sun. **Main courses** $$. **Credit** MC, V. **Map** 285 E10. ㉑ Argentinian (modern)
Porteña Luciana Corte and Italian Sebastián Raggiante met in the kitchen of the two-star El Bulli Hotel Hacienda Benazuza in Seville before bringing their culinary passion to Buenos Aires in 2010. A stream of ravenous suits flocks to their luminous resto-bar every lunchtime, scarcely believing their luck to be enjoying cuisine of such quality at such modest prices. As you'd expect from alumni of Ferran Adrià, everything arrives impeccably presented. The *fagottini de remolacha* – beetroot-filled pasta pockets – are perched in a blue cheese salsa that's plate-lickingly good, while foccacias and hamburgers keep things down to earth.

La Panadería de Pablo

Defensa 269, entre Alsina y Moreno, Monserrat (4331 6728, www.lapanaderiadepablo.com). Subte A, Plaza de Mayo/bus 29. **Open** 8am-7pm Sun-Thur; 8am midnight Fri. **Main courses** $$$. *Lunch* AR$75. **Credit** AmEx, MC, V.
Map 285 E10. ㉒ Argentinian (modern)
Set out by leading designer Horacio Gallo, this venue, complete with gorgeous patio, is the picture of elegance: huge leather sofas blend perfectly with the wooden tables and chairs, while the open kitchen bustles with young chefs under the guidance of co-owner and chef Pablo Massey. As is to be expected of a Massey venture, the menu is elegant and concise, with a special emphasis on bruschettas and fresh salads, with a rib-eye steak placed judiciously for foreigners hankering after Argentinian beef. Equally good are the desserts – the lemon tart with crème praline being the pick of a very fine selection.

$ El Obrero

Agustín Caffarena 64, entre Ministro Brin y Caboto, La Boca (4362 9912). Bus 25, 29, 68, 130. **Open** noon-4.30pm, 8pm-1am Mon-Sat.
Main courses $$. **No credit cards.**
Map p284 B10. ㉓ Argentinian (traditional)
El Obrero (literally 'the worker', which tells you a fair bit about the ambience of this joint) is one of the city's most famous restaurants, and celebrities from Bono to Wim Wenders have eaten at this living,

thriving museum piece in the heart of the old port neighbourhood. (The area is gritty, verging on lawless, so go with company, and take a taxi there and back.) The decor is busy with photos of boxing and soccer stars, the paint is peeling and the toilet is a glorified outhouse, but this is a classic spot for a three-hour lunch or dinner.

PUERTO MADERO

El Mercado

Faena Hotel + Universe, Martha Salotti 445, Dique 2 (4010 9200, www.faenahotel anduniverse.com). Subte B, LN Alem/bus 2, 130, 152. **Open** 7am-noon, 12.30-3.30pm, 8pm-midnight daily. **Main courses** $$$$.
Credit AmEx, DC, MC, V. **Map** p284 D11. ㉔ Argentinian (modern)
The Philippe Starck-designed El Mercado is a favourite of Argentina's select and selected. Inside, glittered portraits of local pop idol Sandro, Maradona and Che Guevara sit effortlessly against a collection of porcelain toy soldiers. But behind all the beauty, an open kitchen dishes up traditional Argentinian food, from squid-based starters to juicy tenderloin steaks. *Photo p142.*

Cabaña Las Lilas

Alicia Moreau de Justo 516, Dique 4 (4313 1336, www.laslilas.com.ar). Subte B, LN Alem/bus 62, 93, 130, 152. **Open** noon-1am daily. **Main courses** $$$$.
Credit AmEx, MC, V. **Map** p285 F12. ㉕ Argentinian (traditional)
Eating steak at Cabaña Las Lilas is a little like taking tea at the Ritz. You know it's a tourist trap, you know you're being overcharged, but somehow you're still glad you came. The atmospheric dockside location helps, as does the exemplary service and jumbo wine list. But what really matters is the meat. Every chop, chump and chorizo is sourced from the company's own estancias and the award-winning thoroughbred cattle that graze there. And whatever ends up on the plate will be cooked as requested and unforgettably tender.

I Central Market

Pierina Dealessi, y Macacha Güemes, Dique 4 (5775 0330, www.icentralmarket.com.ar). Bus 2, 103, 152, 195. **Open** 8am-midnight daily.
Main courses $$$$ (*Deli & tearoom* $$).
Credit AmEx, MC, V. **Map** p285 E12. ㉖ Argentinian (modern)
This jack-of-all-trades Puerto Madero multispace is designed to keep everybody happy, whether it be with an artisanal ice-cream, a lunchtime salad box, a freshly baked bagel or a five-star meal in the main restaurant. Quality is the name of the game at i-central (the 'i' pronounced 'ee', meaning 'to eat' in Mapuche), and whatever you go for it's guaranteed to be fresh and additive-free. Park yourself at

CONSUME

Beef Encounter

How to have your steak and eat it.

When hunger strikes in Argentina, one and all worship the sacred cow. Peckish local construction workers convert their wheelbarrows into pavement parrillas; visiting vegetarians wonder if, just this once, they could get away with murder; and the sounds of the suburbs are sizzling chorizos, fat hissing on hot coals and popping corks. So believe the hype: the best beef in the world is Argentinian.

Just as crucially, the Argentinians know how to cook it. While the British boil it down and the French sauce it up, Argentinians prefer their meat to arrive on the plate pretty much as it left the cow. Only the intervention of direct heat is required, using either the *al carbón* (charcoal) or *a la leña* (wood) methods. Most commonly, the cuts are laid out on a grill (*a la parrilla*) and cooked slowly to retain the natural juices. More exotically, the eviscerated carcass can be hung on cross-poles over a pit of glowing embers, a style known as *al asador*. This latter method (still seen in several of the city's traditional steakhouses and on country estancias) is a throwback to the gaucho era: a survival technique that has morphed into a gourmand's fantasy.

Once you've made friends with a local (a process that can take anything up to ten minutes) there's a fair chance he or she will invite you to an *asado* (barbecue), a supremely important ritual in which the whole canon of Argentinian social habits is played out. Look for the person who is attending the parrilla, cranking the height-adjustment handle like he is fine tuning an Aston Martin. This person will, of course, be a man (the complexities of putting meat on a grill and turning it over once in a while are thought by the locals to be too profound for the female mind to fathom).

Never offer advice to the *asador*. Should he set fire to the shed, it is only because he meant to do so. But lend an ear and he will tell you everything you need to know about the art of *asado* and plenty besides. Spices and marinades are regarded as effete fripperies, but occasionally your new best friend will throw some salt in the general direction of the meat or perhaps douse it in a little lemon juice.

As the wine starts to flow, you'll probably be handed a *choripán* (sausage sandwich), which is often served with *chimichurri* (a tasty chilli and herb sauce). Make sure you don't fill up as this is just the prologue. A dizzying procession of offal and prime cuts will follow. Very little food is wasted; one could almost reassemble the cow at the table as if it were a jigsaw puzzle.

Extras will include green salads, plenty of bread and gallons of wine. Like a python, you should put enough away to last you several days, while keeping in mind Miss Piggy's advice to never eat more than ou can lift.

All of the above, plus the famous Argentinian steaks can, of course, be enjoyed in a parrilla restaurant. Many tourists will head for the more sophisticated and pricey joints in the Puerto Madero and Recoleta districts. Don't get hooked on these establishments though, since the laid-back, local-frequented eateries found in every neighbourhood, while slightly more intimidating for the novice, are a lot cheaper, often tastier and much more fun. (For menu guidance, see p118 **All the Fun of the Parrilla**).

CONSUME

the bar for a cheeky something; or settle at one of the picturesque waterside tables and watch the denizens of Puerto Madero do their thing as you pick delicately at a smoked salmon and couscous salad, or some thyme-rubbed scallops.

▶ *Nearby, the i Fresh Market, at Azucena Villaflor and Olga Cossettini, has excellent, if pricey pastries.*

RECOLETA & BARRIO NORTE·

Casa SaltShaker

Address provided when you reserve, Barrio Norte (mobile 15 6132 4146, www.casasalt shaker.com), Subte D, Pueyrredón/bus 10, 59, 60, 95, 101, 118. **Open** from 9pm Thur Sun. **Set menu $$$$. No credit cards.** Puerta Cerrada: eclectic

Probably the city's best-known *puerta cerrada*, Casa Saltshaker is the creation of chef and sommelier Dan Perlman. Every weekend, Dan creates a menu that might include anything from shish kebabs to clam chowder – the menu is usually loosely themed around an anniversary or event. Wine can be ordered by the bottle from a shortlist, but your best bet is to go for the wine-pairing option, where each course is matched with an appropriate wine.

▶ *For more on food, life and mouthwatering recipes, have a look at Dan's blog, www.saltshaker.net.*

$ El Cuartito

Talcahuano 937, entre Marcelo T de Alvear y Paraguay, Recoleta (4816 1758). Subte D, Tribunales/bus 152, 111. **Open** 12.30pm-1am Mon-Thur, Sun; 12.30pm-2amFri, Sat . **Main courses $. No credit cards.**Map p285 H10. ㉗ Pizza

This pizza joint dates from 1934 and is still one of the best in town. The walls are covered with ancient photos of everyone from Diego Maradona to a host of local boxing greats. Grab a table under Bruno versus Tyson or stand at the pizza bar and sprinkle your slice with the sundry dried toppings to hand.

$ Cumaná

Rodríguez Peña 1149, entre Avenida Santa Fe y Arenales, Recoleta (4813 9207). Bus 10, 37, 39, 101, 124, 152. **Open** noon-midnight daily. **Main courses $. No credit cards. Map p286 I10.** ㉓ Argentinian (traditional)

Surrender to Cumaná's onslaught of tantalising aromas, settle in at one of the rustic tables, and order some *locro* (a thick Argentinian stew) and home-made empanadas. With excellently priced food served piping hot from the *horno de barro* (a domed adobe oven used in the north of Argentina) this country kitchen is hard to beat – in fact, it's excellent. Popularity like this comes at a cost, though: be prepared to queue for around an hour at weekends, when the place fills up with a young, fun crowd. *Photo p138.*

★ Gran Bar Danzón

Libertad 1161, entre Avenida Santa Fe y Arenales, Recoleta (4811 1108, www.granbar danzon.com.ar). Subte D, Tribunales/bus 39, 102, 152. **Open** from 7pm Mon-Fri; from 8pm Sat, Sun. **Main courses $$$$. Credit** AmEx, DC, MC, V. **Map** p285 H11. ㉙ Argentinian (modern)

Gran Bar Danzón's contemporary, cosmopolitan menu includes dishes like duck confit with a crisp coating, streaked with a blueberry and balsamic reduction; and a selection of sushi and very good salmon sashimi. Pumpkin ravioli with lamb and caramelised pears is another highlight, as is the grilled salmon over a king crab omelette, with cream of fennel and lemon confit. An extensive wine menu includes plenty of good options by the glass. We recommend you try one of the famed cocktails at the bar before sitting down to eat. *Photo p129.*

Tegui. *See p137.*

Las Pizarras. *See p136.*

CONSUME

Nootarine

*Vicente López 1661, entre Montevideo y
Rodríguez Peña, Recoleta (4813 6993,
www.nectarine.com.ar). Bus 10, 37, 59, 110,
124.* **Open** 12.30-3.30pm, 8pm-midnight Tue-Fri;
8pm-midnight Sat. **Main courses** $$$$. **Credit**
AmEx, V. **Map** p286 I11. ③⓪ French

Nectarine is a peach of a destination for a special
Buenos Aires evening. Hidden in a tiny pedestrian
alley in the centre of an upmarket neighbourhood,
the small interior is sophisticated without being
formal, providing the ideal setting for a romantic
tryst. Both the wine list and the menu are rich in
options and flavours, and the well-trained staff will
help you match the one with the other.

Oviedo

*Beruti 2602, y Ecuador, Barrio Norte
(4822 5415, www.oviedoresto.com.ar).
Subte D, Pueyrredón/bus 12, 64, 152.*
Open noon-1am Mon-Sat. **Main courses**
$$$$. **Credit** AmEx, DC, MC, V. **Map**
p286 J10. ③① Spanish

Oviedo has a clubbish atmosphere and is a
favourite with businessmen and political hacks.
But never mind the clientele: feel the quality. Here,

classic Iberian dishes are prepared with great care
and attention to detail. *Tortilla a la española*, goat's
cheese croquettes, grilled *chipirones* (baby squid),
baked clams, and oven-baked white fish are
savoury reminders of the old country.

Piola Pizzerie Italiane

*Libertad 1078, entre Avenida Santa Fe y
Marcelo T de Alvear, Recoleta (4812 0690,
www.piola.it). Bus 39, 102, 152.* **Open**
noon-3am Mon-Fri; 7pm-3am Sat; 7pm-2am
Sun. **Main courses** $$$. **Credit** AmEx,
MC, V. **Map** p285 H11. ③② Pizza

With locations scattered across both the Americas,
this Treviso-born Italian pizzeria chain has got
gourmet pie-tossing down to a science: roll the
dough to make the thinnest crust possible, top it
with fresh greens and sharp cheeses, and serve it
in a slick space lit by vibrantly coloured lanterns.
Salads and pasta are on the menu too, but your
best bet is a signature pizza – smoked salmon and
ricotta-topped Rimini perhaps, or the leafy Praga,
a white pizza piled high with rocket, chicken and
parmesan shavings.
Other location Gorriti 5751, Palermo
Hollywood (4777 3698).

On the Empanada Trail

An introduction to Argentina's puffy pockets of pastry.

CONSUME

So much more than a Cornish pasty dressed up in light-blue-and-white stripes, the seemingly simple empanada is actually quite complex foodstuff.

Essentially beef, potatoes and boiled egg artfully enveloped in pastry, even the most basic empanada *de carne* poses a host of questions. Should it be fried or oven-baked? Seasoned with chillies from Salta or lemons from Tucumán? Made using Juan's granny's secret recipe or by a tried-and-trusted high-street chain?

Despite this being a nation of die-hard carnivores, beef isn't the only available filling. Chicken or ham and cheese are popular too, while vegetarians are catered for courtesy of *humita* (sweetcorn and béchamel sauce), cheese and onion, *de verdura* (spinach and béchamel) or capresse (mozzarella, tomato and basil).

Argentina's most socially acceptable food, said to originate in Galicia and whose lexical root comes from the Spanish verb *empanar* (to bread), also puts in regular appearances at birthdays, bar mitzvahs, sporting events and even funerals. The empanada can seamlessly take the starring role at mealtimes as the main course – estimate two dozen, or four pies each, for a group of six – while it is equally happy to come in from the wings as a fast-food fix for those on the hoof.

But what cements the empanada's popularity is its ability to bring together friends and family – even if there is a row over where to order them from – in a touchy, feely, eating experience. Hungry hands simultaneously grab a menu to figure out the flavour by its *repulgue* (distinctive

crimped edges and shapes to indicate flavours) while diving into the cardboard takeaway box, eager for a little package of savoury goodness.

Available on every other block, from pizzerias, *kioscos* and even featuring on the menu of high-end restaurants, sorting the wheat from the chaff can be quite the mission in the search for the perfect empanada, so buyer, beware. If the only option for heating it up is in a microwave, step away from the counter and move on down the street. Here's our pick of BA's top five empanada joints:

El Desnivel *Defensa 855, San Telmo*
Look past the vast slabs of sizzling meat and refuel with a fried beef empanada.

El San Juanino *Posadas 1515, Recoleta*
Even high-end chefs love an empanada or six. Try the cheese-and-onion number, lauded by Federico Heinzmann, chef de cuisine at the Park Hyatt (see p95).

La Americana *Avenida Callao 83, Congreso*
One of the few restaurants in BA to use ample spice for a mouth-tingling experience.

Ña Serapia *Las Heras 3357, Barrio Norte*
For a *salteña* experience – flaky pastry encasing hand-cut steak – head to this tiny establishment run by Héctor Yepez, muse to photographer Marcos López.

Santa Maria *Corrientes 6801, Chacarita*
Classic neighbourhood pizzeria whose empanadas outweigh the cheesy pies.

Sette Bacco

Agüero 2157, entre Peña y Pacheco de Melo,
Recoleta (4808 0021, www.settebacco.com.ar).
Subte D, Agüero/bus 93, 152. **Open** 12.30-3pm
Mon-Fri; 8.30pm-midnight daily. **Main courses**
$$$. Credit AmEx, MC, V. **Map** p286 K10. ⬤
Italian

Tucked away on a tree-lined street in Recoleta is one
of the city's most romantic restaurants: Sette Bacco,
an intimate lamp-lit Italian restaurant that has won
a loyal complement of local regulars. This is mainly
due to owner-chef Daniel Hansen's paean-to-the-
motherland menu – a journey through Italy's
regional specialities that features familiar risotto and
pasta dishes, but also provides for the more gastro-
nomically curious. Try the eye-rollingly good *cen-
tolla* (king crab) and pasta main course, and nab a
table on the upstairs terrace in fine weather.

Sirop Folie

Units 11 & 12, Vicente López 1661, y
Rodríguez Peña, Recoleta (4813 5900,
www.siroprestaurant.com). Bus 37, 124.
Open 11am-midnight Mon-Sat; 11am-8pm
Sun. **Main courses** $$$. **Credit** AmEx,
MC, V. **Map** p286 I11. ⬤ French

There are surprisingly few sophisticated restaurants in Recoleta, but this is one of them, set
in a Parisian-style alleyway – a fantastic place for
alfresco dining, at lunch or at dinner. Prepare to be
spoiled by the exemplary staff and the varied
wine list and menu, with a compact set of dishes
including an excellent duck in cassis. Beautifully
decorated, with charming interior touches and
plenty of light, it's the ideal spot for lunch, brunch
or afternoon tea.

PALERMO

$ Arevalito

Arévalo 1478, y Cabrera, Palermo Hollywood
(4776 4252). Bus 39, 93, 111, 161. **Open**
9am-midnight Mon-Fri; 10am-midnight Sat.
Main courses $. **No credit cards.**
Map p283 O4. ⬤ Vegetarian

Vegetarians should make a pilgrimage to this
divinely cramped bohemian café in Palermo – or pull
up a seat in the street for more enjoyable, spacious
viewing. Arevalito stands out for its homemade food
and for its daily sandwich special – fit for a king's
picnic. Starring roles go to the four daily dishes on
a menu that changes between lunch and dinner, with
support from a vegetable tart, a salad of the day and
nine desserts. The pastry on the leek and potato tart
is close to perfect.

Artemisia

Gorriti 5996, entre Ravignani y Arévalo,
Palermo Hollywood (4776 5484, www.
artemisianatural.com.ar). Bus 39, 93, 111,
161. **Open** 12.30-4pm, 8.30pm-midnight

Artemisia.

Tue-Thur; 12.30pm-2am Fri, Sat. **Main**
courses $$. **No credit cards.** Map p283 O5.
⬤ Vegetarian

With decor that includes deliberately mismatched
crockery and a pantry-style counter laden with
homemade breads and muffins, this eaterie has
become an instant hit with the barrio's brunch set.
Try starting your meal with an atypical *picada* –
instead of the usual ham and cheese, it includes
bruschetta with dips, and beetroot marinated in gin-
ger, honey and thyme. Main courses include polenta
lasagne and Thai-style haddock in a marinade of
lemongrass and coconut milk.
Other location Cabrera 3877, Palermo (4863 4242).

Astrid & Gastón

Lafinur 3222, entre Juan F Segui y Cerviño,
Palermo (4802 2991, www.astridygaston.com).
Bus 10, 37, 59, 60, 110. **Open** 12.30-3pm, from
8.30pm Mon-Sat. **Main courses** $$$$. **Credit**
AmEx, MC, V. **Map** p287 M10. ⬤ Peruvian

Peruvian–Asian fusion food is no longer a new sen-
sation in Buenos Aires, and certainly not to chef
Gastón Arcurio, who has been experimenting with
these flavours for years in his international empire
of 38 restaurants. The question on everyone's lips
when his protégé Roberto Grau took the reins here

CENT*i*RAL MARKET

RESTO - CAFE - MARKET

let the crusty decor put you off. Ultra-friendly, wildly camp chef Antos Yaskowiak and his trusty staff serve delicious rollmops, stews and goulash, each course punctuated by a sharp vodka and informative chat.

$ Club Eros
Uriarte 1609, y Honduras, Palermo Soho (4832 1313). Bus 39, 55, 111. **Open** noon-3.30pm, 8.30pm-midnight daily. **Main courses** $. **No credit cards. Map** p283 M5. ○ Argentinian (traditional)
Unless you get sexually aroused by the sight of laconic waiters in shabby tuxedos serving up fried food in a setting redolent of a 1970s union soup kitchen, Club Eros only half lives up to its name (the dining room is an adjunct to various indoor sports facilities). So why is this cantina crammed full with greedy punters for lunch and supper? It's the economy, stupid. You can get steak, chips and a brimming tumbler (cork fragments and all) of Vasco Viejo, Argentina's most popular plonk, without breaking the bank.

Cluny
El Salvador 4618/22, entre Malabia y Armenia, Palermo Soho (4831 7176, www.cluny.com.ar). Bus 15, 39, 55. **Open** from noon Mon-Sat. **Main courses** $$$$. **Credit** AmEx, MC, V. **Map** p283 M5. ○ Argentinian (modern)
The chefs at this fashionable, relaxed spot in trendy Palermo have made quite a name for themselves by consistently turning out simple ideas, artfully executed. The huge portions make it essential to arrive hungry, ready to pace yourself through a menu studded with standouts like the excellent grilled octopus starter – crisp on the outside and more tender inside than an octopus has any right to be; or the creamy parmesan risotto with mushrooms topped with a melting chunk of beef, cooked for hours on end in red wine.

★ Crizia
Gorriti 5143, entre Uriarte y Thames, Palermo Soho(4831 4979, www.crizia. com.ar). Bus 34, 55, 166. **Open** 7pm-midnight Mon-Sat. **Main courses** $$$$. **Credit** AmEx, MC, V. **Map** p283 M5. ○ Argentinian (modern)
A high-ceilinged, New York-style dining room, sophisticated cocktails and a long oyster bar set the scene for a *Sex and the City*-style get-together. If you're here with someone special, the mellow tunes and soft lighting keep things thoroughly romantic, while the wonderful aromas wafting from the open kitchen are so seafood-centric you can almost hear the waves lapping against the shore. The food – each dish a work of art – is Mediterranean-Argentinian fusion with a hint of oriental. If oysters aren't your thing, then go for the seared red tuna steak with a tangy lime dressing.

Freud & Fahler. *See p133.*

Dashi
Fitz Roy 1613, y Gorriti, Palermo Hollywood (4776 3500, www.dashi.com.ar). Bus 39, 93, 111, 166. **Open** 12.30-3pm, 8pm-12.30am Tue-Fri; from 8pm Sat. **Main courses** $$$. **Credit** AmEx, MC, V. **Map** p283 N5. ○ Japanese
Sashimi and sushi plus sleek decor isn't an original formula, especially in a city in which Japanese fusion restaurants are multiplying by the minute. Dashi remains near the top of the heap, though, thanks to Jorge, the charismatic world traveller who runs the show. The sophisticated, light-filled interior is done up in black lacquer and white linen with the occasional rose-coloured splash, creating a minimalist backdrop for superb sushi rolls, crafted from red porgy, octopus and salmon.
Other locations Salguero 2643, Palermo (4806 4900); Arribeños 2302, Belgrano (4783 1070); Montevideo 1059, Recoleta (5811 3353).

★ Don Julio
Guatemala 4691, y Gurruchaga, Palermo Soho (4831 9564). Bus 35, 55, 93, 111, 161. **Open** noon-4pm, 7.30pm-1am daily. **Main courses** $$$. **Credit** AmEx, MC, V. **Map** p283 M6. ○ Argentinian (traditional)

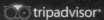

It's reassuring to know that certain bastions of familiarity remain in this fast-changing barrio: trends come and go, but Don Julio remains standing on the corner of a cobbled street, doing what it always does, and doing it very well. Owner Pablo is a stickler for succulent meat and formal service: the beef is carefully selected from the local market, and waiters are drilled in wine selection. The quality is a cut above average and although there are a few other dishes on the menu, such as pasta and salads, it's close to a crime not to order the perfectly cooked *entraña* (skirt steak) or juicy *bife de chorizo* (rump steak) here. The decor is rustic-chic, and the leather tablecloths and exposed brick walls stacked up with signed wine bottles add to the warm and pleasant atmosphere.

La Dorita
Humboldt 1892, y Costa Rica, Palermo Hollywood (4773 0070, www.parrillaladorita. com.ar). Bus 39, 93. **Open** noon-1am daily. **Main courses** $$$. **No credit cards.** **Map** p283 N5. ❹ Argentinian (traditional)
La Dorita is snug and intimate, a place where families rub elbows with local celebs, but the A-list star here is the meat. A *tabla de carnes* (three beef cuts of your choice) arrives sizzling in its own juices. Grilled provolone cheese – crisp on the outside, oozing within – makes a perfect side dish. If your tastebuds are tired of meat, head just across the road to the colourful and pescatarian-friendly La Pescadorita, by the same owners.
Other locations Arce 901, Belgrano (4776 4190).

★$ La Fábrica del Taco
Gorriti 5062, entre Thames y Serrano, Palermo Soho (4832 0815, www.lafabrica deltaco.com). Bus 15, 55, 140, 151, 168. **Open** from 1pm Tue-Sun. **Main courses** $. **No credit cards.** **Map** p283 M5. ❺ Mexican
Colourful Mexican kitsch shines down on happy punters keen to spice up their lives with tonsil-tingling tomato salsas and a selection of three hot sauces (one for Argentinians, one for Mexicans and one for daredevils). One of the house specialities, Tacos al Pastor, is a filling combination of marinated pork and homemade sauce that gets diners coming back for more. Another favourite is Volcán, a crispy tortilla with meat, cheese and guacamole on top. The mouthwatering quesadillas don't disappoint either. After dark, the backyard area under a glass roof is a brilliant spot to enjoy drinks specials and excellent margaritas at any time of the year, or head to colourful bar La Adorada opposite, the newest addition to the fun Fábrica family.

Forneria
Malabia 1825, entre Costa Rica y Nicaragua, Palermo Soho (4831 5447, www.forneria.com.ar). Bus 39, 55, 160, 168. **Open** 9am-1.30am daily. **Main courses** $$. **No credit cards.** **Map** p283 M5. ❺ Argentinian (modern)

Located on the less ventured side of Plaza Armenia, this industrial-chic style restaurant has carved out a niche for itself as a refuge from the busy fashionista thoroughfares. With its elegant French-style bar, open brickwork and duck-egg blue simplicity, Forneria attracts the laptop-affixed workaholic by day and an unaffected Palermo crowd by night. You simply can't go wrong with one of the elaborately garnished wood-oven pizzas or a gourmet salad. For a mid-morning pick-me-up, try the tangy lime cheesecake accompanied by the signature white-chocolate frappucino.

Freud & Fahler
Cabrera 5300, y Godoy Cruz, Palermo Soho (4771 3652, www.freudandfahler.blogspot.com). Bus 39, 55, 151, 168. **Open** 12.30-3.30pm, 8.30pm-midnight Mon-Fri; 12.30-4pm, 8.30pm-1am Sat. *Pastelería* 11.30am-8pm Mon-Fri. **Main courses** $$$$. **Credit** AmEx, MC, V. **Map** p283 M5. ❺ Argentinian (modern)
There's a neighbourhood feel to this restaurant and patisserie on a pretty Palermo corner. The decor is elegant in its simplicity: a 1950s flip clock from an Italian train station hanging on the wall is one example of the restaurant's semi-industrial aesthetic. Stop by for a wickedly good *torta húmeda de chocolate* or treat yourself to the exotic dishes inspired by chef Pablo Lykan's travels, such as the llama steak, fresh from Jujuy in the north, or a Patagonian lamb dish. *Photo p131.*

Il Gran Caruso
El Salvador 5805, y Carranza, Palermo Hollywood (4777 6633, www.grancaruso.com.ar) Bus 10, 21, 108, 111. **Open** 8pm-1am Mon-Fri; noon-4pm, 8pm-1am Sat, Sun. **Main courses** $$$$. **Credit** AmEx, MC, V. **Map** p283 O5. ❺ Italian
At this family restaurant with 100 per cent Italian food, you're invited to enjoy delicious dishes that combine pure Italian tradition with modern influences. The homemade pastas absolutely steal the

CONSUME

Hernán Gipponi Restaurante.

show, but you can also try delicacies such as the *carpaccio de salmón*; exquisite seafood or meat dishes; sophisticated salads named after Italian movie stars (your only opportunity to devour the likes of Sophia Loren); and irresistible desserts, such as the Marquisse Romanola.

Green Bamboo
Costa Rica 5802, y Carranza, Palermo Hollywood (4775 7050, www.green-bamboo.com.ar). Bus 34, 55, 93, 108, 111. **Open** 8.30pm-midnight Mon-Thur, Sun; 8.30pm-2am Fri, Sat. **Main courses** $$$$. **Credit** AmEx, MC, V. **Map** p283 O5. 54 South-east Asian
This well-established Vietnamese restaurant balances the five essential elements of sweet, salty, bitter, spicy and acidic tastes in a way that's likely to keep even the most sophisticated palate interested. Tuck into a seafood-based menu of starters including prawns fried in sesame seeds and curry, and ginger and sweet chilli squid tentacles, then get stuck into the fish of the day marinated with tamarind, basil and shallots wrapped up in a bamboo leaf and barbecued.

Guido Restaurant
Cerviño 3943, entre República de la India y Lafinur, Palermo (4802 1262). Subte D, Plaza Italia/bus 29, 39, 152, 188. **Open** from 7pm Tue-Sun. **Main courses** $$$. **Credit** AmEx, MC, V. **Map** p287 M10. 55 Italian

A narrow stairway leads up to this intimate space, a little piece of Italy on a quiet street in the heart of Palermo, where red checkered tablecloths, mismatched wall art and Italian tunes help pull the scene together. Inviting you to *'mangia sano, mangia italiano'*, the menu's great selection of pastas, creative sauces and pizzas ensures just that: good, healthy Italian dining. A standout on the menu (also in English) is the *homenage a Carlos Soto*, a small pizza made with the perfect amount of mozzarella, sauce, rocket, parma ham and parmesan cheese. There's live music some nights and a pretty outside patio for warm evenings.

Guido's Bar
República de la India 2843, entre Cabello y Gutiérrez, Palermo (4802 2391). Subte D, Plaza Italia/bus 29, 39, 152. **Open** 8am-1am Mon-Fri; 7am-4pm Sat. **Main courses** *Lunch* $$$; *Evening tasting menu* $$$$. **No credit cards. Map** p287 M10. 56 Italian
This pea-sized trattoria is the kind of place one always looks for but rarely finds in Italy. Owner Carlos commands a regiment of waiters who will feed you a parade of colourful appetisers followed by homemade pasta and dessert until you say *'basta!'* (enough!). With every inch of the letterbox-red walls plastered in movie poster kitsch, featuring real Italians (Mastroanni and Caruso) alongside honorary ones (John Lennon and Sammy Davis Jr), Guido's is as much an evocation of an era as it is a culture.

Hernán Gipponi Restaurante

*Soler 5862, entre Carranza y Ravignani,
Palermo Hollywood (3220 6820). Bus 39,
60, 67, 111, 161.* **Open** noon-midnight
Tue-Sat; noon-4pm Sun, Mon. **Main courses**
$$$$. **Credit** AmEx, MC, V. **Map** p283 N6. ⑤⑦
Argentinian (modern)

Hernán Gipponi Restaurante, at Fierro Hotel (*see
p97*), has made its mark on the BA culinary scene
since opening in 2010. Argentinian chef Gipponi,
who worked in Spain's Michelin-starred restaurant
Quique Dacosta, has brought some of that Michelin
magic back to BA with him with tapas-style dishes
such as goat's sweetbreads with lemongrass stock,
fennel and potato purée. An open kitchen keeps
things interesting and the few tables outside in the
garden are lovely on a balmy evening. Time Out
recommends the *menú degustación*, comprising
nine courses, matched with wine picked out by
none other than the president of the Argentinian
Sommelier Association, Andrés Rosberg himself.
▶ *Don't miss the fantastic nine-course weekend
brunch from 12.30pm.*

Little Rose

*1st Floor, Armenia 1672, entre Honduras
y El Salvador, Palermo Soho (4833 9496).
Bus 39, 55, 93, 168.* **Open** 12.30-4pm,
8.30pm-12.30am Mon-Sat. **Main courses**
$$$. **No credit cards. Map** p283 M5. ⑤⑧
Japanese

At this chic and sexy first-floor restaurant, you'll be
dining in an intimate, low-lit, black-painted interior,
watched over by slightly spooky pictures of pale
little girls. At night, it's romantic in a somewhat
gothic way; if Edgar Allan Poe were alive and kick-
ing and craving a Philadelphia roll, you might just
make him out in the dim dining room. Thankfully,
Little Rose is not an example of style over substance;
the sushi here is delicious.

El Manto

*Costa Rica 5801, y Carranza, Palermo Hollywood
(4774 2409, www.elmanto.com). Subte D,
Carranza/bus 39, 93, 111, 161.* **Open** 8pm-
midnight daily. **Main courses** $$$. **Credit**
AmEx, MC, V. **Map** p283 O5. ⑤⑨ Middle Eastern

Maybe it's the fortune teller in the confessional
booth, waiting to read the dregs of your thick, post-
dinner coffee – but there's something mysterious
about El Manto. Whatever it is, there's little secret
to its success and the huge regard in which the
restaurant is held by its regulars. The authentic
Armenian and Middle Eastern cuisine is arguably
the best in the city. You'll find your favourites here
– houmous, kibbe, kefte, kebabs, pilaf, tabouleh and
more. Low-lit and lovely – and did we say mysterious? You get the picture: it's romantic!
▶ *In fine weather, head to the bar at fashionable
Home Hotel (see p97) for chilled-out Friday night
DJ sets.*

Miranda

*Costa Rica 5602, y Fitz Roy, Palermo Hollywood
(4771 4255, www.parrillamiranda.com). Bus 39,
168, 151.* **Open** 9am-1am Mon-Thur, Sun; 9am-
2am Fri, Sat. **Main courses** $$$. **Credit** AmEx,
MC, V. **Map** p283 N5. ⑥⓪ Argentinian (traditional)

This fashionable contemporary parrilla is a steak-
house for the trend-conscious carnivore: instead of
chips or mashed potatoes, the *solomillo de cerdo*
(pork loin) and thick-cut *lomo* come with caramelised
vegetables and fruits. The Jacinta salad, tossed with
grilled chicken and squash, is another one of the
huge, highly recommendable dishes on offer. The
young, mostly male staff is easy on the eyes, though
aesthetics have a price – locals say the service used
to be a good deal more efficient.

Olsen

*Gorriti 5870, entre Carranza y Ravignani,
Palermo Hollywood (4776 7677). Bus 39, 93,
111.* **Open** noon-3.30pm, 8.30pm-midnight Tue,
Wed; noon-3.30pm, 8.30pm-1am Thur-Sat. **Main
courses** *Dinner* $$$. *Sunday brunch* $$. **Credit**
AmEx, MC, V. **Map** p283 O5. ⑥① Scandinavian

Guido's Bar.

Some quandaries are more enjoyable than others. For example, how do you choose between 50 brands of vodka? Tackle this and other conundra at Olsen, Germán Martitegui's hugely popular Scandinavian bar-restaurant where the atmosphere is as chilled as the drinks. It's hard to say which stands out more – the wooden sculptures and ivy covered garden or the fried oysters and platters of exotic starter combos, which go down great with a sampler of vodka and aquavit shots. Sunday brunch is the perfect way to wind down from an extended Saturday night.

★ Osaka
Soler 5608, y Fitz Roy, Palermo Hollywood (4775 6964, www.osaka.com.pe). Bus 21, 111, 161. **Open** *12.30-4pm, 8pm-1am Mon-Sat.* **Main courses** *$$$$.* **Credit** *AmEx.* **Map** *p283 N5.* ⑫ Peruvian–Japanese

Stylish Osaka, with its virtuoso Peruvian–Japanese fusion cuisine, is something of a superstar on the BA dining scene. While there's a range of familiar Japanese dishes, Osaka takes flight with a set of fusion creations featuring eclectic innovations like duck confit-stuffed samosas. Don't miss the chance

to sample a few of the unusual South America-meets-Far East starters, which are big enough to share, or the exotic cocktails – try the Thai Chi (a blend of saké, orange, cranberry and cinnamon). But if you're pinching the pennies, this one's not for you.

★ Las Pizarras
Thames 2296, y Charcas (4775 0625). Subte D, Plaza Italia/bus 15, 29, 34, 36, 55, 152. **Open** *from 8pm Tue-Sun.* **Main courses** *$$$.* **Credit** *AmEx, MC, V.* **Map** *p283 M6.* ⑬ Argentinian (modern)

If Las Pizarras's quirky decor doesn't draw you in, the constantly changing selection of gastronomic delights on its oversized blackboards (*pizarras*) might. This stylish but laid-back restaurant has no menu, just a list of creative concoctions made from whatever owner and chef, Rodrigo Castilla (ex chef *tournant* to Gary Rhodes), has bought fresh from the market that day. Expect simple Mediterranean classics (think fried squid with aïoli), and Argentinian favourites with a sophisticated twist, such as *bife de chorizo* in rosemary jus with roasted vegetables and *croquetas de humita. Photo p125.*

Aldo's Vinoteca y Restorán. *See p113.*

Río Café

*Honduras 4772, entre Malabia y Armenia,
Palermo Soho (4832 2318, www.riocafe.com.ar).
Bus 15, 34, 39, 55, 57, 106, 110, 140, 141,
151, 168.* **Open** 11am-4am Tue-Sat; 11am-7pm
Sun. **Main courses** $$$. **Credit** AmEx, MC, V.
Map p283 M5.  Argentinian (modern)

This resto-bar's interior is all sumptuous brown
leather, armchairs and floor-to-ceiling mirrors: think
sultry 1940s saloon updated for the young and chic.
At the bar the menu is, for the most part, adventur-
ous but sophisticated, and twists on classic cocktails
include the Cherry Collins and a Tangerine Mary.
Top DJs make Río Café the place to be on
Wednesday nights, but BA's beautiful also like to
hang out in the leafy patio come the weekend. Food-
wise, fragrant is the word, and fish and seafood are
refreshingly well represented.

Sipan

*Uriarte 1648, entre Honduras y El Salvador,
Palermo Soho (4833 9383, www.sipan.com.ar).
Bus 39, 55, 168.* **Open** noon-4pm, 8pm-1am
daily. **Main courses** $$$$. **Credit** AmEx, MC,
V. **Map** p283 M5.  Peruvian

Punchy passionfruit pisco sours are reason enough
to head over to the second Sipan in the city, located
in the trendy Palermitano Hotel (*see p99*). Cool decor
– including psychedelic Peruvian posters of vintage
adverts – an open kitchen, breezy terrace seating
and impeccable service are four more reasons. But
you're likely to forget all that once your beautifully
presented food arrives. Favourites include the thinly
sliced octopus in black olive cream and, of course,
the classic tangy ceviche.
Other location Paraguay 624, Microcentro
(4315 0763).

Social Paraíso

*Honduras 5182, entre Thames y Uriarte,
Palermo Soho (4831 4556). Bus 39, 55.* **Open**
12.30-4pm, 8pm-1am Tue-Sat; noon-4pm Sun.
Main courses $$$. **Credit** AmEx, V.
Map p283 M5.  Argentinian (modern)

Youngsters and seniors, new world and old, all mix
together in this sober but attractive, high-ceilinged
bistro that helped pioneer the Palermo Soho gourmet
explosion. Chef-owner Federico Simoes was raised on
Syrian-Lebanese cuisine, and his changing menu is
quite creative. The *bife de chorizo* (rump steak) is
excellent here, as is the tasty mushroom skillet.

★ Sudestada

*Guatemala 5602, y Fitz Roy, Palermo Hollywood
(4776 3777). Subte D, Palermo/bus 15, 55,
111.* **Open** noon-3.30pm, 8.30pm-midnight Mon-
Thur; noon-3.30pm, 8.30pm-1am Fri-Sat. **Main
courses** *Lunch* $$. *Dinner* $$$. **Credit** AmEx,
MC, V. **Map** p283 N6.  South-east Asian

Anyone who has ever walked into a restaurant, taken
in the culinary sights, and thought, I'll have what

Unik. *See p138.*

they're all having, will experience a sense of déjà vu
at Sudestada. This compact, minimalist eaterie
specialises in South-east Asian cuisine, with an
emphasis on Thai. Main dishes can get quite spicy by
local standards, but foreign palates will eagerly
devour the sophisticated items like the lamb curry, or
the charcoal-grilled pork in a homemade barbecue
sauce. If you're on a budget, the lunch menu, which
includes a starter, a main course and a beverage, is a
real steal.

★ Tegui

*Costa Rica 5852, entre Carranza y Ravignani,
Palermo Hollywood (5291 3333). Bus 34, 55,
108.* **Open** noon-3.30pm, 8.30pm-midnight Tue-
Sat. **Main courses** $$$$. **Credit** AmEx, MC, V.
Map p283 O5.  Argentinian (modern)

This swanky hideout is tucked discreetly behind a
(deliberately) graffitied wall and unassuming black
door. Ring the bell and saunter into this sophisticated home-turned-restaurant, which dazzles with
its contemporary decor, accented by all things black
and white. The open-plan kitchen set towards the
back of the restaurant allows diners to peer in on the
catering process, and the VIP room, which borders

CONSUME

the kitchen, presents guests with an opportunity for an exclusive dining experience. In the evening, you can opt for the eight-course menu.

Tô

Costa Rica 6000, y Arévalo, Palermo Hollywood (4772 8569, www.torestaurant.com). Bus 39, 55, 93, 111, 161. **Open** noon-3.30pm, 8pm-1am Mon-Fri; 8pm-1am Sat. **Main courses** $$$$. **Credit** AmEx, MC, V. **Map** p283 O5. French–Japanese

Tô presents Buenos Aires's first-and-only conveyer belt sushi service, with a Gallic twist. Owner Toufic Reda directs a brawny team of sushi *shokunins*, chefs and mixologists that functions like a well-oiled machine, in a slick lofted space with plenty of Asian *onda*. Grab a counter stool for on-demand Cali rolls and salmon sashimi while you choose from a long list of mains, including pork dumplings, prosciutto rolls and seafood tempura; the *bento* box easily feeds two.

Unik

Soler 5132, entre Godoy Cruz y Oro, Palermo Soho (4772 2230, www.unik.pro). Bus 34, 36, 39, 55, 108, 111. **Open** 8.30pm-midnight Mon; 12.30-3pm, 8.30pm-midnight Tue-Sat. **Main courses** $$$$. **Credit** AmEx, MC, V. **Map** p283 N6. International

With hotshot international chefs and an interior put together by architectural whiz Marcelo Joulia, Unik hit Buenos Aires's gastronomic scene with a bang. The menu is graced with dishes such as sole carpaccio and slow-cooked roast lamb with cumin-flavoured quinoa, while the service is efficient. The decor perfectly showcases the eclecticism of Joulia's work – a long, bright red banquette sits under an array of retro lamps, with a huge green neon light plucked from a Parisian nightclub illuminating the patio. All this glitz and glam may come with an international price tag, but all in all, it's a very pretty picture and safely puts Unik among Palermo's most beautiful restaurants. *Photo p137.*

LAS CAÑITAS

Campobravo

Báez 292, y Arévalo, Las Cañitas (4514 5820, www.campobravo.com.ar). Bus 15, 29, 55, 118, 160. **Open** noon-3pm daily. **Main courses** $$$. **Credit** AmEx, DC, MC. **Map** p287 O9. Argentinian (traditional)

A complimentary glass of champagne offered up to waiting diners is not the only thing luring crowds back to Campobravo. Rather, its decade-long residency on a buzzing Las Cañitas corner can be put down to a simple formula: succulent cuts of meat, homemade pastas and flavourful stir-fries at prices ideal for belt tighteners and portions suited to buckle loosening. Chill-out tunes and candlelit tables set the scene for the urban sophisticate, while gauchos on a day trip will appreciate the wood and wrought-iron interior and sizzling parrilla soundtrack. **Other location** Honduras 5600, Palermo Hollywood (4576 5460).

Novecento

Báez 199, y Argüibel (4778 1900, www.bistro novecento.com). Bus 5, 29, 59, 60, 64. **Open** from 8.30am Mon-Fri; noon-4pm, from 8pm Sat, Sun. **Main courses** *Lunch* $$. *Dinner* $$$. **Credit** AmEx, DC, MC, V. **Map** p287 O9. Argentinian (modern)

The flagship restaurant of a chain that has branches in Manhattan, Miami and Punta del Este, Novecento is a thriving, self-styled bistro that is bustling, smart and intimate enough for a candlelit smooch, all at the same time. The menu is modern Argentinian, with dishes like great peppered steaks or booze-soaked sweetbreads. Novecento's main strength lies in the simplicity of the menu, which transcends parrilla fare without being too exotic. Pastas here are also highly recommended.

Cumaná. *See p123.*

Cocina Sunae. See p141.

WEST OF THE CENTRE

Bi Won

*Junín 548, entre Lavalle y Tucumán,
Once (4372 1146). Subte B, Pasteur or D,
Facultad de Medicina/bus 29, 101, 106, 109.*
Open noon-3pm, 7pm-midnight Mon-Fri;
7pm-midnight Sat. **Main courses** $$$.
No credit cards. Map p285 H9. **73** Korean
Don't be put off by the ice-cream freezers that greet
you as you enter, or the chintzy wallpaper and dark-
wood panelling: the place might have had a style
bypass, but a glance at the customers should reassure
you that the food here is authentic. The *mandu guk*
is a huge bowl of broth with meat- and vegetable-filled
dumplings, while the *sengson chigue* is a spicy
seafood stew made to share. If you like your eating
experiences interactive, go for the *bul gogui*, sweet-
tasting macerated meat with a tabletop grill.

La Cocina Discreta

*Address provided when you reserve, Villa
Crespo (4772 3803, mobile 15 6571 1002,
www.lacocinadiscreta.com). Subte B, Malabia/*
bus 15, 71, 106, 109, 110, 141. **Open** from
9.30pm Thur-Sat. **Set menu** $$$$. **No credit
cards.** Puerta Cerrada: Argentinian
Tucked away in Villa Crespo, La Cocina Discreta
offers a gourmet dining experience combined with
art and good music. Owners Alejandro and Rosana
welcome up to 18 guests for a set meal – consisting
of an aperitif, a choice of two starters, three mains
and two desserts – that can include such dishes as
beef medallion with Bordelaise sauce accompanied
by stuffed potato and peppers in malbec.

★ La Esperanza de los Ascurra

*Aguirre 526, entre Malabia y Scalabrini Ortiz,
Villa Crespo (2058 8313, www.esperanza
ascurra.com.ar). Subte B, Malabia/bus 15, 24,
55, 110, 168.* **Open** noon-midnight Tue-Sat.
Tapas $. **Credit** AmEx, MC, V. **Map** p283 M4.
74 Spanish
This Spanish-style tapas bar is as poetic as its name.
Paintings hang on a washing line and are for sale;
while recycled tables and colourful chairs, each dec-
orated by a different artist, give the place a
bohemian vibe. After a shopping stint at the nearby

Villa Crespo outlets, duck in for a miniature *cañita* (draft beer) and tapas at the long bar, or make a meal of it and order raciones to share. We love the *gambas al ajillo* (garlic prawns), *boquerones* (whitebait) and *jamón serrano* (the real deal, imported from Spain). No, scrap that, we love everything.

★$ Sarkis

Thames 1101, entre Jufre y Lerma, Villa Crespo (4772 4911). Bus 34, 55, 106, 109. **Open** noon-3pm, 8pm-1am daily. **Main courses $$. No credit cards. Map** p283 M4. ⓯ Middle Eastern
Good things come to those who wait, and you're guaranteed good things – and a wait – at perennially popular Sarkis. Don't be afraid to ask the staff for recommendations; when the food is as consistently good as it is here, you're unlikely to get a dud. The decor leaves much to be desired, but something keeps pulling the punters back; it might be the Monday-night belly dancer, or the fortune teller who reads your future from the dregs of your *café oriental*, but we're putting our cash on the *comida*.

Urondo Bar

Beauchef 1204, y Estrada, Parque Chacabuco (4922 9671, www.urondobar.com.ar). Subte E, Moreno/bus 25, 126, 135. **Open** 8pm-1am Tue-Sat. **Main courses $$. No credit cards.** Argentinian (modern)
Named after Francisco 'Paco' Urondo, a radical poet who became one of Argentina's 'disappeared', this spot is run by his grandson Sebastián and nephew Javier. The latter mans the kitchen, turning out dishes that are a fusion of Argentinian and intense South east Asian influences. Start with the *copetín*, a mixed platter of cheeses, meat and vegetables, each prepared in a way you'd never expect.

BELGRANO & COLEGIALES

Cocina Sunae

Address provided when you reserve, Colegiales (mobile 15 4870 5506, www.cocinasunae.com). Subte B, Tronador/bus 21, 140. **Open** from 9pm Thur-Sat. **Four-course set menu $$$$. No credit cards.** Puerta Cerrada: South-east Asian
Christina Sunae Wiseman prepares a dazzling and ever-changing array of spicy, traditional East Asian cuisine, serving up Thai, Korean, Vietnamese and Phillippine dishes. Start with the house cocktail, a Ginger Kamikaze, then move on to a choice of main dishes like a red Thai curry with chicken, bamboo shoots, grapes and cherry tomatoes; or prawns in a spicy sweet-and-sour sauce with avocado, steamed rice, red onion, grapefruit, mint and coriander. *Photo p139.*

$ Don Chicho

Plaza 1411, y Zarraga, Colegiales (4556 1463). Subte B, Tronador/bus 21, 76, 87, 93, 127, 140.

Open 8.30pm-1am Mon-Thur; 12.30-3.30pm, 8.30pm-1am Fri, Sat; 12.30-3.30pm Sun. **Main courses $. No credit cards.** Italian
Let your eyes drift past the fading façade and the paint-peeling walls to rest on two flour-covered worktables just inside Don Chicho's entrance, and the cooks shuttling between them and the kitchen, cutting and hand-forming every order of pasta *al momento*. An array of home-made antipasti lines the dilapidated bar; there's no menu; and don't ask the waiter to recite all 29 items the kitchen offers – simply take a recommendation off the board out front or whatever the staff suggests as the pick of the day, then dig into some of the freshest and best-made traditional Italian antipasti and pasta in the city. The tables are packed with locals, so expect some heads to turn when you walk in the door.

Lotus Neo Thai

Arribeños 2265, entre Olazabal y Mendoza, Belgrano (4783 7993, www.restaurantelotus. com.ar). Bus 15, 29, 42, 44, 55, 60, 63, 64, 65, 130. **Open** noon-3.30pm Tues-Sun; from 9pm daily. **Main courses $$$$. Credit** AmEx, MC, V. **Map** p288 S9. ⓰ Thai
Relish classic Thai curries among the psychedelic painted flowers climbing the walls; or head for the candlelit terrace to eat amid real plants, flowers and bamboo. Consider the elegant Lotus cocktail as a starting point with vodka and passionfruit, sugar and ice, it's a delicious riff on the solid-gold caipirinha formula; then go for the popular *kaeng pehd ped yang* – roasted duck and pineapple in a red curry sauce.

El Pobre Luis

Arribeños 2393, y Blanco Encalada, Belgrano (4780 5847). Bus 15, 29, 42, 44, 55, 60, 64, 113, 118, 130. **Open** from 8pm Mon-Sat. **Main courses $$$. Credit** AmEx, MC, V. **Map** p288 S9. ⓱ Argentinian (traditional)
Football and dining legend Diego Maradona cites this as one of his favourite BA restaurants; the shirt of 'El Diez' hangs on one of the walls. But it's meat, not memorabilia, that makes the parrilla and the steaks here definitely part of the premier league. Ever-present owner Luis Acuña is Uruguayan, so you'll find novelties from across the water like *pamplona de cerdo* (pork flank stuffed with cheese and peppers) on the menu. Offal-lovers will rhapsodise over the *mollejas* (sweetbreads). No reservations are taken, so get there early or be prepared to queue.

Pura Tierra

3 de Febrero 1167, entre Federico Lacroze y Teodoro García, Belgrano (4899 2007, www.puratierra.com.ar). Subte D, Olleros/bus 41, 42, 68, 152, 161. **Open** 8pm-12.30am Mon-Sat. **Main courses $$$$. Credit** AmEx, MC, V. **Map** p288 Q8. ⓲ Argentinian (modern)

CONSUME

CONSUME

As its name – 'pure earth'– suggests, the focus here is on fresh produce and clever use of the restaurant's adobe-mud oven to produce the perfect balance of colour, taste and texture. Starters and desserts are the highlights – kick off with *mollejas* (sweetbreads) with caramelised red onions, drizzled with a syrup of sugarcane honey, lime and thyme, before turning your attention to the wonderfully tender rabbit, seasoned with fennel, lemon and almonds and accompanied with sweet potatoes and a tomato and garlic confit. Two tables on the pavement outside are perfect for an intimate dinner.

▶ *The place is also home to the famous pastelería Puro Cacao.*

Sucre

Sucre 676, entre Avenida Figueroa Alcorta y Castañeda, Belgrano (4782 9082, www.sucre restaurant.com.ar). Train to Scalabrini Ortiz/ bus 37, 130. **Open** noon-4pm, 8pm-midnight daily. **Main courses** $$$$. **Credit** AmEx, V. **Map** p288 R10. Argentinian (modern)

If you can swing a ringside seat at dramatic, high-ceilinged Sucre beside the wide open kitchen, then do. There's a spectacle in store, watching the chefs do their thing in perfect harmony. But first, perch on a stool by the long, elegant bar and ask the chirpy barmen to mix you up a concoction such as the Jack Martin (apple martini, bourbon, lime and

sugar) before sitting down to eat. The exemplary staff is only too happy to talk you through the wines, of which there are 350 labels. As for the food, it's an international fusion. Meats are cooked with a local firewood on the parrilla, giving them a special, smoky flavour; and the tenderest lamb risotto is to-die-for, as are the outstanding pasta dishes. With celebrity chef Fernando Trocca in charge, you're in safe hands, whatever you choose.

SAN ISIDRO

O'Farrell

Avenida del Libertador 15274 (4742 4869, www.ofarrellrestaurant.com). Train from Retiro to San Isidro. **Open** 8pm-midnight Mon-Sat. Closed lunch Jan, Feb. **Main courses** $$$$. **Credit** AmEx, V. Argentinian (traditional)

It takes a special restaurant to be deemed exclusive in a neighbourhood as affluent as San Isidro, but O'Farrell is very special indeed and is regularly cited by food critics as one of the best eateries in the whole of the country. Despite his Irish roots, Hubert O'Farrell has developed a menu that nods more towards Carcassonne than Cork, with star dishes including a delicious magret in a garlic sauce, and haunch of lamb in a porcini reduction. The menu changes with the seasons, but freshness and quality is guaranteed.

El Mercado. *See p121.*

Cafés, Bars & Pubs

While away days and nights with coffees and cocktails.

Porteños are creatures of the night and are good at – and look good at – partying hard. Amazingly, it's not copious amounts of alcohol that fuel long nights out. Generally speaking, Argentinians are not big drinkers and so public drunkenness is a no-no. Perhaps their ability to stay up past sunrise is partly down to the gallons of coffee they guzzle. The caffeine-to-go habit has yet to take hold in BA, and *porteños* love nothing more than to while away a few hours in a café. Many cafés, especially old-school establishments with dickie-bowed waiters, stay open until late and also serve alcohol, meaning the line between a café and a bar is often blurred.

Those looking for night-time bustle will need patience and a modicum of self-restraint until around 1am, when most bars really get kicking. Buzzing Palermo is booze central, but you'll be able to find a drinking hole to suit your taste anywhere in the city, from British pubs to elegant cocktail lounges to bars that serve up eclectic cultural menus with their bottles of Quilmes beer.

DRINKING IN BUENOS AIRES

As documented in Rodolfo Reich's book *Mixology in Argentina*, Buenos Aires has experienced the second coming of cocktail culture in recent years. Between the 1930s and 1960s, BA's bartenders travelled the world, bringing back awards and generally being mooted as some of the best. Meanwhile, in Argentina they became TV stars and hung out with presidents and tango legends. Inevitably the fall came during the dictatorship and it has taken until the last few years for the culture to recover. Barmen and women are becoming celebrities, as discerning drinkers follow their favourites from bar to bar. It's an ever altering scene, but in bars such as **878** (*see p153*), **Gran Bar Danzón** (*see p148*) and **Isabel** (*see p151*) or hotels including **Hotel Madero** (*see p91*), the **Alvear Palace** (*see p93*) and **Home Hotel** (*see p97*), a perfectly mixed cocktail is pretty much guaranteed. Restaurants such as the

❶ Green numbers given in this chapter correspond to the location of each café, bar or pub on the street maps. *See pp279-288.*

THE BEST
CAFFEINE KICKS

Cortado
A shot of espresso topped with a 'cut' of hot milk.

Café con leche
A white coffee.

Doble
Any way you like it, but double the dose.

Lágrima
A 'teardrop' of espresso with plenty of warm milk.

En jarrito
Any way you like it, served in a small, elongated glass.

Cappuccino
In Buenos Aires, a cappuccino is generally served in a tall glass and is served with whipped cream and grated chocolate.

swish **Tegui** (*see p137*) and popular **Green Bamboo** (*see p134*) serve up excellent mixes that fuse the kitchen's culinary leanings with a hefty whack of alcohol.

Whether it's down to history, atmosphere or just a national need for a caffeine fix, many of the city's cafés are true classics, integral to the capital's cultural and social life. And it's little wonder, given BA's strong Italian heritage.

A cup of coffee is usually accompanied by *medialunas* (croissants) or an *alfajor* (two biscuits sandwiched together with *dulce de leche*). A sweet speciality for winter is a *submarino*, a frothy glass of hot milk with a bar of chocolate submerged in it. For an early morning sugar rush, try one accompanied by *churros* (cigar-shaped doughnut-like delicacies), often filled with the ubiquitous *dulce de leche*.

THE CENTRE

★ Café Tortoni

Avenida de Mayo 829, entre Esmeralda y Suipacha (4342 4328, www.cafetortoni.com.ar). Subte A, Piedras/bus 64, 86. **Open** 8.30am-1am daily. **Credit** AmEx, MC, V. **Map** 285 F10. ❶
Since opening in 1858, Argentina's oldest café has played host to the depths of BA's bohemia, the heights of its literati, and the full political spectrum. Today, it's teeming with camera-wielding tourists, but don't be put off – the Tortoni is a must. Beyond the wooden tables and marble floor, a salon hosts tango shows, while in the back, pool tables await. Order a draught *cidra* – more like champagne than cider – and breathe in the history.

La Cigale

1st Floor, 25 de Mayo 597, entre Lavalle y Tucumán (4893 2332). Subte B, LN Alem/bus 93, 152. **Open** from 6pm Mon-Fri; from 10pm Sat. **Credit** AmEx, MC, V. **Map** p285 F11. ❷
Now located in a Microcentro *petit hotel*, La Cigale is not a classic French café, but a forerunner among late-night drinking dens. The spot is popular with French expats and music-loving tourists and locals. There's a happy hour every night but the big deal here's the music: La Cigale has an impressive roster of DJs spinning anything from kitsch Rat Pack classics to electropop and darkwave. Tuesday nights – known as Noche Francesa – are very popular.

★ Dadá

San Martín 941, entre Marcelo T de Alvear y Paraguay (4314 4787, www.dadabistro. blogspot.com). Subte C, San Martín/bus 61, 130, 152. **Open** noon-3am Mon-Sat. **Credit** AmEx, MC, V. **Map** p285 G12.❸
Dadá is cited again and again by locals as their favourite meeting spot. This tiny, cheerful space is home to a lovely bar and one of the city's most frequently recommended restaurants. Owner Paulo and

his family weave their magic, managing to both charm and serve clients with a menu that's as colourful and imaginative as the furnishings that adorn the place. The menu regularly changes, but it's the classics like the *lomo Dadá*, the *ojo de bife* (rib-eye steak) and the delicious houmous and guacamole dips that continue to stand out. Chilled lagers, good cocktails and a fine wine list complete a very pretty picture.

Florida Garden

Florida 899, y Paraguay (4312 7902). Subte C, San Martín/bus 93, 130, 152. **Open** 6.30am-midnight Mon-Fri; 6.30am-11pm Sat, Sun. **Credit** AmEx, V. **Map** p285 G11. ❹
A leader in literary and artistic avant-gardism back in the 1960s – prominent local artists have been gathering here on Saturday mornings ever since – today this buzzy, two-tiered café and lunch spot is more geared towards businessmen than culture vultures. But if you can see past the suits, the copper staircase leading to the mezzanine is a standout feature of the place, and the glass bar containing mouth-watering cakes and pastries is a visual feast not to be missed.

Kilkenny

Marcelo T de Alvear 399, y Reconquista (4312 7291, www.thekilkenny.com.ar). Subte C, San Martín/bus 26, 93, 152. **Open** from 5.30pm Mon-Fri; from 8pm Sat, Sun. **Credit** AmEx, DC, MC, V. **Map** p285 G12. ❺
BA's Irish pubs are no longer prime movers of the city's drinking scene, yet the popularity of the Kilkenny is impressive. The ultimate after-office hangout, the welcoming pub attracts droves of thirsty thirtysomethings from the surrounding office blocks for some light drinking and heavy flirting. By Saturday it's all-out mayhem as the tourist set joins in with the alcohol-fuelled game of sardines.

SAN TELMO

Bar Plaza Dorrego

Defensa 1098, y Humberto Primo (4361 0141). Bus 9, 10, 29, 126. **Open** 8am-1am Sun-Thur; 8am-4am Fri, Sat. **No credit cards.** **Map** p284 D9. ❻
With outdoor seating on atmospheric Plaza Dorrego, this century-old watering hole embodies the *tanguero* spirit of San Telmo. Inside are dusty bottles and black-and-white images of Carlos Gardel, and a tango soundtrack crackles away. It's an ideal spot from which to watch the Sunday market goings-on; or, on a warm evening, to drain a frosty *chopp* (small glass of draught beer) while dismembering handfuls of complimentary monkey nuts.

Las del Barco

Bolívar 684, entre México y Chile (4331 3004). Bus 44, 28, 29, 111, 152. **Open** 5pm-5am Tue-Sun. **No credit cards.** **Map** p285 E10. ❼

Frank's. *See p151.*

A deliberately ramshackle stop on the San Telmo haul, Las Del Barco is one of the city's most down-to-earth bars, complete with an assortment of flea market furniture, multicoloured lighting, kids' art and a varied menu featuring guacamole and nachos. But most of the bohemian locals and foreigners that frequent this bar are here for the cheap, all-night bar deals and late closing hour. Mercifully unpretentious, the staff is friendly, and the music a mix of everything from reggae to radical indie.

Doppelgänger

Juan de Garay 500, y Bolívar (4300 0201, www.doppelganger.com.ar). Subte C, San Juan/bus 10, 17, 39. **Open** from 7pm Tue-Sat. **Credit** AmEx, MC, V. **Map** p284 D9. ❽
At this chic, Weimar Republic-style martini bar, the menu celebrates classic gin, vodka and vermouth cocktails with distinctive South American elements, including native herbs and local distillations such as Pisco and Cynar. Try a Blue Krishna, which combines cardamom-infused vodka with Cointreau, Angostura bitters, orange peel and a splash of soda, and as you imbibe, you can graze on tapas-style fare. Happy hours run from 7pm to 9pm Tuesday to Friday.

El Federal

Carlos Calvo 599, y Perú (4300 4313, www.barelfederal.com.ar). Bus 10, 20, 29, 86. **Open** 8.30am-2am Mon-Thur; 8am-4am Fri, Sat; 8am-1am Sun. **Credit** AmEx, MC, V. **Map** p284 D9. ❾
Built in 1864, El Federal is officially listed as one of BA's most historic bars. It's also one of the best kept;

check out the magnificent cash registers. It's pretty original too; bar staff work from a lowered floor while the bar itself is thigh high. There's a standard offering of beers and spirits and a long menu of sandwiches and other snacks. The faded yellow lamps hanging overhead and the old advertising posters capture that elusive spirit of a bygone era.
▶ *The crew from El Federal are also behind the successful La Poesía; see p147.*

★ Gibraltar

Perú 895, y Estados Unidos (4362 5310). Bus 10, 29, 86. **Open** noon-3am daily. **Credit** AmEx, MC, V. **Map** p284 D9. ❿
A pub – a real British pub – might sound like a bit of a gimmick in BA. Gibraltar, a stand-out joint on anyone's terms, is anything but. This highly popular watering hole serves well-priced beer in pint glasses, genuinely spicy curries and an exhaustive collection of whiskies. The beef-and-ale pie or heavenly fish and chips hit the spot too. The place is packed to the gills most nights, especially from Wednesday to Saturday; get there early if you want to find a perch.

Krakow

Venezuela 474, entre Defensa y Bolívar (4343 3916, www.krakow-cafe.com.ar). Bus 2, 29, 45, 86, 195. **Open** 5pm-3am daily. **Credit** AmEx, MC, V. **Map** p285 E10. ⓫
The menu of this Polish-owned pub boasts an impressive range of reasonably-priced beers and vodkas. As you get merry, you can watch sports on the big screen, play Jenga or Nintendo and eat hearty

878

8

2004   2012

Rated Nº 25 in World's 50 Best Bars 2011
by Drinks International
Best Bar in Argentina by Bar&Drinks

THAMES 878_BSAS_ARG_(5411)47731098 _TODOS LOS DÍAS DESDE LAS 20
WWW.878BAR.COM.AR _INFO@878BAR.COM.AR_ **E** @878bar

Melting Moments

BA can scoop it out with the best of them.

Thanks to happy cows munching away on pampas grass, a sweet tooth woven into the nation's genetic fabric and a dedication to using the finest, freshest ingredients, Argentinian ice-cream is among the best in the world.

This dairy love has a rich and creamy history in the capital: since Italian immigrants introduced the gelato-making tradition in the late 19th century, ice-cream parlours such as **El Vesuvio** (Avenida Corrientes 1181) – the oldest operating *heladería* in the country, scooping up since 1902 – have been patronised by the likes of former tango legends Carlos Gardel and Astor Piazzolla, not to mention thousands of punters pouring out of nearby theatres on sticky summer nights.

Perhaps surprisingly in this body-conscious city, there are now more than 2,000 ice-cream parlours in Buenos Aires and like many things, the frozen delight can be delivered to your door. Most quality *heladerías* whip up their creations on-site, dishing out in excess of 60 flavours, with an entire category devoted to variations on *dulce de leche*, each option more decadent than the last.

Chains that are vying for top position are **Persicco** (www.persicco.com), **Un' Altra Volta** (www.unaltra volta.com.ar) and the perennially popular **Freddo** (www.freddo.com.ar).

Less well-known but also ranking high in the quality stakes is **Jauja** (www.heladosjauja.com), which specialises in ice-cream made with Patagonian fruits, while boutique parlour **Nonna Bianca** (Estados Unidos 425) is a mother-and-daughter operation that has more than 80 ice-cream flavours, including *cerveza*, made with beer and peanuts. The only way to discover your favourite is to try them all

CONSUME

European dishes including Polish sausage, which is served flaming. Arrive early if you want to bag a sofa, but think twice before attempting a drinking contest with vodka-enthusiast co-owner Tadeusz.

★ La Poesía
Chile 502, y Bolívar (4300 7340). Bus 29, 45, 86. **Open** 8am-2am Mon-Thur, Sun; 8am-4am Fri, Sat. **No credit cards**. **Map** p285 E10. ⑫
This cosy, dimly lit café-bar gathers a large, eclectic clutch of regulars who visit for coffee and a chat, for the huge menu – containing everything from snacks and decent burgers to full-blown meals – the generally pleasant ambience and the artisan beers. It's a San Telmo classic, and the former owner who ran the joint when it was a buzzing literary café back in the day, is regularly seen at its tables now.

La Puerta Roja
Chacabuco 733, entre Independencia y Chile, (4362 5649, www.lapuertaroja.com.ar). Subte E, Belgrano/bus 39, 60, 152. **Open** 6pm-5am daily. **No credit cards. Map** p285 E9. ⑬

La Puerta Roja (The Red Door, which is all that marks the spot) is a classic, no-nonsense bar. The space is large, the music eclectic, and there isn't a cocktail umbrella in sight. Low prices attract the youngsters, backpackers and resident foreigners who pack the place out till late. There's a pool table with plenty of space to swing a cue, and food has been designed to be cheap, tasty and filling: try the shish kebabs with rice and houmous. Happy hours are 6pm to 10pm.

PUERTO MADERO

Library Lounge
Faena Hotel + Universe, Martha Salotti 445, Dique 2, Madero Este (4010 9000, www.faena experience.com). Subte B, LN Alem/bus 2, 130, 152. **Open** 8am-3am daily. **Credit** AmEx, DC, MC, V. **Map** p284 D11. ⑭
One of the city's hands-down sexiest bars, the Library Lounge at Faena Hotel + Universe (*see p91*) has the air of a gentlemen's club mixed with something far, far more fashionable, epitomised by the effortlessly meshed classic and jokily postmodern decor. DJ sets start from 8pm Wednesdays to Saturdays, with live music from 11.30pm.

CONSUME

RECOLETA

Florencio

Francisco de Vittoria 2363, entre Guido y Agote (4807 6477). Bus 10, 37, 60, 102, 110. **Open** 9am-8pm Mon, Tue, Thur, Sat; 9am-midnight Wed, Fri. **No credit cards. Map** p286 J11. ⑮

Among the affluent buildings in an exclusive Recoleta street is a diminutive patisserie with superlative pastries and cakes. Sink your teeth into a cheesecake made by sometime TV celebrity chef María Laura. Should you be able to draw yourself away from the sweet counter, the sandwiches in home-made ciabatta are superb options. Dinner is served on Wednesday and Friday evenings.

★ Gran Bar Danzón

Libertad 1161, entre Avenida Santa Fe y Arenales (4811 1108, www.granbardanzon.com.ar). Bus 39, 102, 152. **Open** from 7pm Mon-Fri; from 8pm Sat, Sun. **Credit** AmEx, DC, MC, V. **Map** p285 H11. ⑯

Although Gran Bar Danzón's contemporary, cosmopolitan menu is one of the best in the city, cocktail quaffers will sup up the ingenious creations and wine aficionados will be scrambling to gawp at the vast wine list. There's a welcoming, lounge-like ambience to this cool, loft-style space – replete with low sofas and glowing candles – which is complemented by DJ sessions.

★ Milion

Paraná 1048, entre Marcelo T de Alvear y Santa Fe (4815 9925, www.milion.com.ar). Bus 29, 39, 102, 152. **Open** noon-2am Mon-Wed; noon-3am Thur; noon-4am Fri; 7pm-4am Sat; 7pm-2am Sun. **Credit** AmEx, V. **Map** p286 I10. ⑰

Almost certainly the most beautiful bar in BA, Milion has been going strong for over ten years and is still outshining the competiton. Proceed straight through to the garden as you enter, and take the elegant stone staircase to the bar. It's the cocktails rather than the food that are the stars of the show here, but if you're hungry then try bagging a table on the stunning terrace under the stars.

★ The Shamrock

Rodríguez Peña 1220, entre Arenales y Juncal (4812 3584). Subte D, Callao/bus 37, 39, 101, 124, 152. **Open** from 6pm Mon-Fri; from 8pm Sat. **Credit** AmEx, MC, V. **Map** p286 I10. ⑲

Loud music, long happy hours and drinks at excellent prices: what more could you possibly want from a bar? In a great location, this Irish bar is very much a Buenos Aires classic, and a faithful stalwart of a reliably good pub. Things heat up as the night wears on until, when the time is ripe, you part the heavy velvet drapes and head downstairs to check out the Basement Club (*see p214*), with excellent DJs from Thursday to Saturday.

PALERMO

Antares

Armenia 1447, entre Cabrera y Gorriti (4833 9611, www.cervezaantares.com). Bus 15, 55, 151, 168. **Open** 9pm-2.30am Mon-Thur; 9pm-5am Fri, Sat. **Credit** AmEx, DC, MC, V. **Map** p283 M5. ⑲

Real ale-lovers rejoice: Antares's mission is to introduce customers to the delights of its various brews, which include Scotch ale, honey beer and cream stout. The bar attracts all sorts, from beer connoisseurs who will hold their porter up to the light, to sharply dressed lager louts who don't care where their drink came from. The food is mostly hearty Bavarian fare, but also includes tapas and *picadas* (selections of cheeses and cold cuts).

Caracas.

Bangalore Pub & Curry House
Humboldt 1416, y Niceto Vega (4779 2621).
Bus 93, 151, 168. **Open** 5pm-3am daily.
No credit cards. Map p283 N4. ⑳
Think warm woods, soft chairs and a convivial atmosphere and you've some idea what this classic colonial-style establishment has to offer. Bangalore is BA's best-loved pub and curry house and performs both functions with aplomb. Downstairs offers comfy seating and jugs of gin and tonic, while the upstairs dining area is an intimate hideaway in which to sample the selection of curries that melt in the mouth. If you can't decide what to order, stay in the bar and ask for the good-value Indian platter, which comes with mini taster dishes.

Bartola
Nicaragua 5935, entre Arévalo y Ravignani (4777 6183, www.bartolaba.com.ar). Subte D, Ministro Carranza/bus 39, 41, 60, 67, 93, 108, 111, 152. **Open** 9.30am-9pm Tue-Fri; 10am-9pm Sat, Sun. **No credit cards. Map** p283 O5. ㉑
Doing a roaring trade with Palermo-ites who brunch, the festive vibe hits the moment you walk in: rollicking Johnny Cash and Latin tunes crank out of the speakers, while pink benches, voluminous bouquets, colourful bunting, kitsch wall art and friendly staff are an instant mood-lifter. Relax in the cute courtyard with a glass of homemade lemonade and a slice of the heavenly *dulce de leche*-laced *chocotorta*. Or arrive with an appetite and knock it dead with a juicy hamburger with caramelised onion or a thin-crust pizza laden with generous rolls of jamón crudo.
► *The newer branch on Gurruchaga 1795 in Palermo Soho is just as cool-kitsch and popular.*

Caracas
Guatemala 4802, y Borges (4776 8704, www.caracasbar.com.ar). Subte D, Plaza Italia/bus 34, 39, 55, 161. **Open** 7pm-4am Mon-Sat. **Credit** MC, V. **Map** p283 M6. ㉒
On a leafy corner a few blocks from the main Palermo hub of Plaza Serrano, this two-storey building makes for a great bar, especially in the summer, when the large roof terrace comes into its own. The bar's DJ plays a good mix of electro, hip hop and Latino sounds. Delicious *arepas* (cornmeal-based patties popular in Colombia and Venezuela) and imported rums ensure a clientele of trendy South American students and other foreigners, who pile in for the cheerful, happy-go-lucky atmosphere.

Carnal
Niceto Vega 5511, y Humboldt (4772 7582, www.carnalbar.com.ar). Bus 39, 93, 184. **Open** from 7pm Tue-Fri; from 9pm Sat. **Credit** AmEx, MC, V. **Map** p283 N4. ㉓
The vibe at this Palermo Hollywood staple is friendlier than at many trendy bars in the area and the place is bustling with young, party-loving porteños. Alfresco drinking is the main story at Carnal, so arm

Las Violetas. *See p154.*

yourself with a cocktail (the frozen mojito's a winner) and head upstairs to the leafy roof terrace to mingle to your heart's content under the big Palermo sky.

Congo
Honduras 5329, entre Godoy Cruz y Atacalco (4833 5857). Bus 34, 55, 166. **Open** 8pm-4am Wed-Sat. **No credit cards. Map** p283 N5. ㉔
For all the laid-back charm of its cosy, brown and beige leather-clad interior, the true magic of Congo resides in its gorgeous, spot-lit summer garden, which ranks among the city's best outdoor drinking spaces. There's no better place to enjoy an icy Bossa Nova (rum, brandy, Galliano, passion fruit and honey) as BA's sticky summer reaches boiling point. Located steps away from some of Palermo's best clubs, this is a perfect spot for a cocktail or three before hitting BA's dancefloors.

★ Ferona Club Social
Humboldt 1445, y Cabrera (mobile 15 6722 6784, English spoken). Bus 39, 108, 111, 151, 168. **Open** *Restaurant* 9.30pm-midnight Wed-Sat. *Bar* midnight-4am Wed-Sat. **Credit** AmEx, MC, V. **Map** 283 N4. ㉕
Set in a gorgeous house, complete with winding staircase and rooftop terrace, BA's place to see and be seen (and just simply have fun) is as attractive as the people that frequent it. The secret formula? Excellent music (a blues, soul, funk and rock mix that gets people dancing till the early morning); tasteful decor, including vintage radios and a collection of paintings; and easily the best caipiroskas in the city. Be prepared to queue at weekends.
► *Chef Fona cooks up an excellent five-course dinner menu (call to reserve).*

CONSUME

I ♥ **Coffee**
I ♥ **Lemonade**
I ♥ **Sandwiches**
I ♥ **Mark's.**

El Salvador 4701
Capital Federal - Argentina
Tel.: (011) 48 32 62 44
www.markspalermo.com

Frank's
*Arévalo 1445, y Cabrera (4777 6541,
www.franks-bar.com). Bus 39, 93, 108, 111,
140, 151, 168.* **Open** 9.30pm-4am Wed-Sat.
Credit AmEx, V. **Map** p282 O4. ㉖
With one of the strangest entrance policies (you have
to first enter a phone booth and a secret code), a boutique stocking erotic accessories, and decor akin to
a private gentlemen's club, this speakeasy is destined to impress. Split over two floors, the striking
bar serves up traditional and signature cocktails like
the vermouth-based Gregorio. Money seems to have
been no object, from the booths and menus covered
in soft leather to the carpeted floor and thick wall-
paper and a bar that stocks Cristal champagne. So
get your glad rags on, make a reservation and ask
for the code to ensure you get in. *Photo p145.*

Home Hotel
*Honduras 5860, entre Carranza y Ravignani,
(4778 1008, www.homebuenosaires.com). Bus
39, 93, 111.* **Open** 8am-midnight daily. **Credit**
AmEx, MC, V. **Map** p283 O5. ㉗
Apart from running a great hotel, those clever folk
at Home have also managed to draw a fair crowd to
their lovely cocktail bar. It has more vodkas than a
Russian Tsar and serves up scrumptious tapas. The
real draw is the garden, perfect for lounging about
before a big night out. Sample one of the signature
cocktails, like a refreshing cucumber Bellini or the
'sweet and spicy Scotch', which contains honey and
jalapeño-infused whisky and cinnamon syrup. For
a review of the hotel, *see p97.*

Isabel
*Uriarte 1664, entre Honduras y El Salvador
(4834 6969, www.isabelbar.com). Bus 34, 55,
166.* **Open** 9pm-4am Tue-Sat. **Credit** AmEx,
MC, V. **Map** p283 M5. ㉘
Musicians, actors and model types sip gimlets and
mai tais in this sexy bar's dramatic interior, and do
a sterling job of looking like they're each starring in
their own perfume ad. Quality trumps quantity on
the sushi menu – and out back, a fire-lit patio adds
to the sensual experience. Try not to get lost in the
stunning hall-of-mirrors bathroom. Cocktails don't
come cheap but are absolutely worth it.

Magdalena's Party
*Thames 1795, y Costa Rica (4833 9127,
www.magdalenasparty.com). Bus 34, 39, 55.*
Open 8pm-1am Tue; 8pm-3am Wed, Thur; 8pm-
4am Fri; noon-5pm, 8pm-5am Sat; noon-5pm,
8pm-midnight Sun. **No credit cards.**
Map p283 M5. ㉙
Magdalena's Party's eye-catching blue exterior and
laid-back California vibe and fare attracts a varied
clientele; on any given night expect a mix of locals,
expats and backpackers. The generous portions
and reasonable prices of fresh salads, burritos and
American-style brunch keep customers hooked. Be

sure to ask about the weekly events, which range
from beer and wine tastings to tasty taco nights.

Mark's Deli & Coffee House
*El Salvador 4701, y Armenia (4832 6244,
www.markspalermo.com). Bus 15, 39, 55.*
Open 8.30am-9.30pm Mon-Sat; 10.30am-9pm
Sun. **No credit cards. Map** p283 M5. ㉚
A longtime favourite in Palermo, Mark's is mod-
elled on hip New York delis, and does it just right.
Order a *licuado* (like a smoothie) or an icy lemonade
and sink your teeth into a large smoked-salmon
sandwich; or munch on giant chocolate-chip cook-
ies while watching the fashion identicats (mostly
young, female and towards the top end of the
beauty spectrum). You may also wish to observe
the massed ranks of MacBook-owning foreigners,
each busy writing the great South American novel,
or, more likely, tuning in to the free Wi-Fi and wil-
ing away their time mucking about on Facebook.
'Look! I'm in Buenos Aires!'

Mundo Bizarro
*Serrano 1222, entre Niceto Vega y Córdoba
(4773 1967, www.mundobizarrobar.com). Bus
15, 55, 168.* **Open** from 8pm daily. **No credit
cards. Map** p283 M4. ㉛
An institution since 1997, Mundo Bizarro has
changed its location, but it can't change its spots as
one of the city's all-time hedonistic, rocking hotspots.
Artwork hung on the blood-red walls gives the place
a retro cocktail lounge vibe with a rockabilly touch,
and the place really gets going after 1am. The great,
extensive cocktail menu includes classics as well as
unmissable house creations. *Photo p153.*

Omm
*Honduras 5656, entre Bonpland y Fitz Roy
(4774 4224, www.ommbuenosaires.com.ar).
Bus 39, 93, 111.* **Open** 6pm-5am daily.
Credit V. **Map** p283 N5. ㉜
Omm's the word. Compact and simple, this small,
low-key café-bar is easy to miss on Palermo's über-
trendy *calle* Honduras; but for those in search of an
unpretentious place for a drink, it's a treat to discover.
The drinks are made with love and tons of muddled
fruit – try a mojito – and the food is delicious and reasonably priced. The good-looking, friendly staff
caters to a relaxed, thirtysomething crowd. Inside,
dim lighting and good tunes provide for an intimate
date setting – you'll need to lean in close to talk; outside, the pavement seating is open all year, with heat
lamps cranked up on colder nights.

★ Oui Oui
*Nicaragua 6068, entre Arévalo y Dorrego
(4778 9614). Bus 39, 152.* **Open** 8am-8pm
Tue-Fri; 10am-8pm Sat, Sun. **No credit cards.**
Map p283 O5. ㉝
Packed and bustling in the best possible way, this
gorgeous French-style café is one of the nicest

CONSUME

INSIDE TRACK FERNET

This powerful, bitter liquor – at around 41 per cent alcohol it's seriously strong stuff – contains various herbs and spices, including myrrh, cinnamon, cardamom and saffron. Fernet has its roots in 19th-century Europe, but where exactly it was first made, and by whom, is heavily debated. What is known, though, is that Italian immigrants brought bottles of the stuff with them to Argentina, where locals started mixing it with cola to create the questionable, frothy beverage that is wildly popular in both BA and across the country today.

places we know for breakfast, lunch, tea or any of the other possible daytime repasts. Croissants, baguettes, salads, vichyssoise and *pan au chocolat* are all spelt out on blackboards in the jolly, pastel-painted interior; and despite the cake-stands, scones and floral prints, there's nothing twee about this place. Get there early-ish on Sundays, or be prepared to queue.

▶ *If you can't get a seat, try sister establishment Almacén Oui Oui on the opposite corner.*

Porota

Gorriti 5881, entre Carranza y Ravignani (4770 9234, www.lawebdeporota.com.ar). Bus 39, 93, 111. **Open** 9.30am-7pm Mon-Fri; 11am-6.30pm Sat. **No credit cards. Map** p283 O5. ⓸

In Porota, Miren Algañaras prepares delicious fare according to her grandmother's recipes, including an outstanding selection of moist cakes and muffins. There are sandwiches, soups and hot lunches too, but it's the sweet stuff this place excels at, in an atmosphere reminiscent of childhood birthday parties, from the miniscule truffles in coloured paper cuffs to the frothy glass of Nesquik.

Post St Bar

Thames 1885, entre Costa Rica y Nicaragua (mobile 15 6543 9648, www.poststreetbar.com). Subte D, Plaza Italia/bus 39, 55. **Open** from 7pm Mon; from 5pm Tue-Sat. **No credit cards. Map** p283 M5. ⓹

It's not exactly glamorous, but if you fancy a down-to-earth spot for a beer or two, this original space is a good bet. It's hard not to be wowed by the graffiti mania that the bar is famous for: some of BA's best graffiti and stencil artists have dressed up the downstairs walls and upstairs terrace, which – rather dizzyingly – rock over 1,800 stencils.

▶ *Do check out the cool, cutting-edge street art gallery Hollywood in Cambodia located at the back and on the first floor (see p197).*

Soria

Gorriti 5151, entre Thames y Uriarte (4832 1745). Bus 39, 55, 108, 140, 151, 168. **Open** from 9pm Tue-Sat. **No credit cards. Map** p283 N5. ⓸

Slick new joints surface with such frequency in Palermo that carving a niche in the brimming bar scene is quite the challenge. But Soria has a winning combination of haven-like garden setting, mood lighting, on-the-beat music and friendly staff who ensure this unpretentious watering hole feels as laid-back as your hipster friend's backyard. Thursday nights are particularly busy as up-and-coming DJs spin their stuff for a crowd of dapper twentysomethings.

Sugar

Costa Rica 4619, y Armenia (mobile 15 6894 2002). Bus 34, 39, 55, 111, 161. **Open** 7pm-5am Mon-Thur; noon-5am Fri-Sun. **No credit cards. Map** p283 M5. ⓷

Head to expat haunt Sugar for guaranteed good times and a dose of sweet familiarity in the shape of rock'n'pop classics accompanied by budget-friendly drinks. Get stuck in to this wildly popular bar's 300-minute happy hour, which attracts a mixed crowd of Argentinians and foreigners: national beers and spirits are available at inflation-busting prices from 7pm.

▶ *On Tuesdays claim your free-entry flyer for Kika (see p215) before continuing on into the night.*

Unicorn Huset

Honduras 5730, entre Bonpland y Carranza (www.unicornhuset.com). Bus 39, 93, 111. **Open** from 9pm Tue-Sun. **Credit cards** AmEx, MC, V. **Map** p283 N/O5. ⓸

Despite there being dozens of crowded bars in the area, the legendary Unicorn Huset, which lies behind unmarked doors, is the one punters are prepared to queue for. With monochrome walls, intimate seating and a spacious deck up top, Unicorn Huset fills to capacity each weekend with easy-on-the-eye twenty- and thirtysomethings who check each other (and themselves) out while sipping cocktails. As the night turns into morning, the dancefloor heaves with party people having a good time. Every Friday, the bar hosts Avalon, an electronic party that attracts Argentinians and expats mainly from the glamorous worlds of fashion, music and advertising.

Voltaire

Carranza 1946, y Voltaire (4777 4132). Bus 21, 93, 111. **Open** 9am-8pm Tue-Fri; 9.30am-8pm Sat, Sun. **No credit cards. Map** p283 O5. ⓸

This cosy country kitchen, located on the corner of its pretty namesake street, serves up simple, tasty and reasonably priced nosh for breakfast and lunch. The staff are attentive and the fresh pumpkin salad with poached egg and sun-dried tomatoes might just be one of the best light meals in the city. Ask for a table

CONSUME

Mundo Bizarro. *See p151.*

CONSUME

outside and watch Palermo's hipsters parade by as you sip a freshly squeezed juice. For as Voltaire himself once wrote, 'Nothing would be more tiresome than eating and drinking if God had not made them a pleasure as well as a necessity.' *Photo p154*

Wherever Bar

Santa María de Oro 2476, y Santa Fe (4777 8029). Subte D, Palermo/bus 111, 152. **Open** from 10am Mon, Tue; from 10am Wed-Fri; from 9pm Sat. **Credit** AmEx, V. **Map** p283 N6. ⓵
This pub is an oasis of calm in the early evening, and just the spot for a post-shopping pick-me-up. Weeknight drink promotions sweeten the temptation to stay and watch the buzz build as the night wears on; while the tapas menu should keep you going till it feels like time for another whiskey. The bar has an affinity with the spirit, offering a 140-bottle selection.

LAS CAÑITAS

Natural Deli

Gorostiaga 1776, y Arce (4514 1776, www.natural-deli.com). Bus 29, 60, 118. **Open** 8am-midnight Mon-Sat; 9am-midnight Sun. **Credit** AmEx, MC, V. ⓵
Las Cañitas locals struggle to find a seat here these days, as punters come from all over town for the sandwiches, salads and tarts made with fresh, wholesome ingredients. Try the Warm Superfood salad, complete with quinoa, beetroot, broccoli and

goat's cheese – both delicious and virtuous. There are artisan beers and iced tea, and the fresh juices can be jazzed up with ginseng, wheatgrass or echinacea for a healthy kick.

Van Koning

Báez 325, entre Arévalo y Chenaut (4772 9909, www.vankoning.com). Bus 15, 55, 141. **Open** 7pm-5am daily. **Credit** AmEx, MC, V. **Map** p287 O9. ⓵
If the flashier Las Cañitas bars don't appeal, duck into this dimly-lit, exceptionally cosy and atmospheric pub for a pint from its own microbrewery, Otro Mundo. There's also alfresco seating and happy hour specials on beer from 7pm to 9pm.

VILLA CRESPO Y ALMAGRO

878

Thames 878, entre Loyola y Aguirre, Villa Crespo (4773 1098). Bus 15, 55, 106, 140. **Open** from 8pm daily. **No credit cards**. **Map** p283 M4. ⓵
Often cited by local barmen as their favourite cocktail bar, 878 still retains its legendary status as one of the city's top drinking holes. Ring the bell at the unmarked door, and you'll be shown in to a slick, low-lit space with comfortable couches and clear reminders of the venue's early days as a carpentry workshop – and as a one-time speakeasy. It's no longer as *clandestino* as it used to be; in fact, it has become a bit of a classic.

Voltaire. *See p152.*

CONSUME

Los Billares
Avenida Corrientes 5436, entre Gurruchaga y Acevedo, Villa Crespo (4855 3956). Subte B, Malabia/bus 109, 110, 112. **Open** 24hrs daily. **No credit cards. Map** p283 M3. ④
Formerly called Café San Bernardo and still affectionately known by that name, this venue is a strangely cool world where the lines between café, bar and shabby school gymnasium blur. Old-man's haunt by day, youthful ping-pong enthusiasts' hangout by night, the bar offers fun and games that last round the billiard ball-inspired clock. If the table tennis competition is proving tough, scoff peanuts and drink beer over a game of dominoes.

Lo de Roberto
Bulnes 331, y Perón, Almagro. Subte B, Medrano/bus 151, 160, 168. **Open** 6pm-3.30am Tue-Sat. **No credit cards. Map** p282 J4. ④
Step back in time to the Buenos Aires of yesteryear in this historic tango bar. It's the former watering hole of Carlos Gardel, but the star here nowadays is octogenarian Osvaldo Peredo, a tango singer who is enjoying a renaissance among a devoted crowd of young people. A bullet hole in the front window, an ancient manual cash register and shelves lined with dusty booze bottles provide the perfect backdrop for Peredo's crude, *lunfardo*-laced tangos that are lapped up by university students post-midnight on Tuesdays and Thursdays. Other equally impassioned crooners perform on the other nights (free, but a hat is passed around for tips).

Malvón
Serrano 789, y Aguirre, Villa Crespo (3971 2108, www.malvonba.com.ar). Subte B, Malabia/bus 19, 34, 55, 106. **Open** 9am-8pm Tue-Fri; 10am-8pm Sat, Sun. **Credit** AmEx, MC. **Map** p283 M4. ④
In up-and-coming Villa Crespo, this café-cum-bakeshop is the perfect refuge for an afternoon coffee or a spot of brunch in the leafy patio out back. Choose from hot pastrami sandwiches, bagels, *tostados*, croque-monsieurs and sweet nibbles like the delicious chocolate cake. The brunches available on weekends include scrambled eggs with smoked salmon and a fluffy omelette with brie and spinach. Bread-lovers can take home delicious focaccia, sourdough and pumpernickel loaves from the bakery.

Las Violetas
Rivadavia 3899, y Medrano, Almagro (4958 7387, www.lasvioletas.com). Bus 105, 151, 160. **Open** 6am-1am Mon-Thur; 6am Fri-1am Sun. **Credit** AmEx, MC, V. **Map** p282 J3. ④
Step back in time at this huge art nouveau café, which has been in business since 1884. It is one of BA's most famous historic cafés, and the bustling atmosphere and delectable assortment of cakes keeps the trade flooding in. Soaring ceilings, exquisite stained-glass windows and pristine white-jacketed waiters converge for an extra-special café spot. Expect queues on weekends. *Photo p149.*

BELGRANO

Tea Connection
Echeverría 2102, y Arcos (4784 5545, www.teaconnection.com.ar). Subte D, Juramento/bus 15, 29, 60, 64, 113, 152. **Open** 8am-midnight daily. **Credit** AmEx, MC, V. **Map** p288 R8. ④
You can't go wrong with any of the numerous infusions or antioxidant-packed *licuados* (smoothies) at this modern, minimalist teahouse, which has branches dotted across the capital. Devour fresh salads, sandwiches, soups and sweet treats, or linger over a late breakfast of scrambled eggs or scones with homemade jam.
Other locations Cerviño 3550, Palermo (4802 0573); Uriburu 1597, Recoleta (4805 0616); Montevideo 1655, Recoleta (5199 0363); Arenales 2102, Barrio Norte (4823 9254).

INSIDE TRACK WINE O'CLOCK

To swirl, sniff and sip with the experts, book a tasting session with **Anuva Wines** (www.anuvawines.com) or walk, talk and drink around Palermo with the **Time Out Wine Tour** (www.winetourtimeoutba.com.ar).

Shops & Services

Designer threads, gaucho gear and boutique wines – bag a piece of BA.

Porteños are a stylish bunch, and if you've stepped off the plane with a neon bumbag hitched to your cargo pants, you'll soon feel the need to sartorially assimilate.

Imported brands sell at premium prices, so when in Argentina, opt for Argentina's own. From local design to fine wine, you'll find lots to squeeze into your suitcase. The myriad boutiques of Palermo are the obvious place to max out your credit card, and for those lamenting the fact prices are not the bargain they once were, San Telmo's independent clothing stores are a more affordable place to snap up the next big thing.

Don't miss BA's markets either: from quality leather to that gaucho costume you've always wanted, you're sure to find something unique to take home.

SHOPPING TIPS

When you spend AR$70 or more on locally-made goods in a shop, ask, *'tienen Tax Free?'* Most stores that participate in this Global Refund system will display a sticker in the window. Along with your receipt, you will be given a refund cheque to fill in (have your passport number handy). Before passing through airport security on your way out of the country, present the cheques for stamping at the counter indicated, where you will be reimbursed the 21 per cent sales tax.

General

SHOPPING CENTRES

Abasto de Buenos Aires
Avenida Corrientes 3247, entre Agüero y Anchorena, Abasto (4959 3400/ www.abasto-shopping.com.ar). Subte B, Carlos Gardel/bus 24, 26, 124, 146, 168. **Open** 10am-10pm daily. **Credit** varies. **Map** p282 J5.
This spectacular building – formerly a market – in an old tango district houses more than 200 shops. It's a magnet for hordes of teens, and most of the main Argentinian chains are represented, along with some international names like Zara. The complex also has a large food court and a cinema.
▶ *For another massive centre, try Dot Baires (Vedia 3626, Saavedra, www.dotshopping.com.ar).*

Alto Palermo
Avenida Santa Fe 3253, entre Bulnes y Coronel Díaz, Palermo (5777 8000, www.altopalermo. com.ar). Subte D, Bulnes/bus 12, 39, 64, 152. **Open** 10am-10pm daily. **Credit** varies. **Map** p286 K9.
The ever-popular Alto Palermo contains most of the Argentinian favourites like Ayres and Rapsodia (*see p163*). Those prone to claustrophobia can escape the crowds inside and hide out on Starbucks' terrace.

Galerías Pacífico
Florida 737, entre Viamonte y Avenida Córdoba, Microcentro (5555 5100, www. galeriaspacifico.com.ar). Subte B, Florida/ bus 6, 93, 130, 152. **Open** *Shops* 10am-9pm Mon-Sat; noon-9pm Sun. *Restaurants* 10am-10.30pm daily. **Credit** varies. **Map** p285 G11.
This shopping centre is housed in a beautiful building decorated with frescoes by five Argentinian muralists. You'll find famous names such as Lacoste here, along with jewellers Swarovski and plenty of local retail stars. *Photo p157.*

Paseo Alcorta
Salguero 3172, y Figueroa Alcorta, Palermo (5777 6500, www.paseoalcorta.com.ar). Bus 67, 130. **Open** 10am-10pm daily. **Credit** varies. **Map** p286 L11.
The upmarket Paseo Alcorta contains a huge Carrefour hypermarket as well as plenty of clothing shops, including a branch of local designer Martín Churba's Tramando (*see p160*).

Galerías Pacífico. See p155.

Patio Bullrich

Avenida del Libertador 750, entre Montevideo
y Libertad, Recoleta (4814 7400, www.shopping
bullrich.com.ar). Bus 67, 92, 130. **Open** *Shops*
10am-9pm daily. Restaurants 10am-midnight
daily. **Credit** *varies.* **Map** *p286 I12.*
This, the most luxurious of all BA's shopping centres, was once the city's meat auction house. It's
home to many local and international high-end
stores including Trosman (*see p161*) and Carolina
Herrera, as well as an excellent delicatessen, Valenti.

MARKETS

Makeshift market stalls selling everything
from clothing to handmade candles populate
the streets around Palermo's Plaza Serrano
(aka Plazoleta Cortázar) and Plaza Armenia
(aka Plaza Palermo Viejo) at weekends,
offering an alternative to the area's hip
boutiques. For antiques markets, *see p178*.

Feria Plaza Francia

Plaza Francia y Plaza Alvear, Avenida del
Libertador y Avenida Pueyrredón, Recoleta
(www.feriaplazafrancia.com). Bus 17, 92, 110.
Open *11am-8pm Sat, Sun.* **No credit cards.**
Map *p286 J11.*
Handcrafted kitchen utensils, leather bags, maté
gourds, jewellery and paintings – you name it, you
can buy it at this top-quality weekend arts and crafts
fair located close to Recoleta's famous cemetery.
▶ *For more leather goods, as well as gauchos, visit*
the rural-style fair Feria de Mataderos (see p80).

Specialist

BOOKS & MAGAZINES

Avenida Corrientes is home to stores selling
both new and used books. Elsewhere, including
in the city's shopping centres, look out for
well-stocked chains **Cúspide** and **Yenny**.

English language

KEL Ediciones

Marcelo T de Alvear 1369, entre Uruguay
y Talcahuano, Barrio Norte (4814 3788,
www.kelediciones.com). Bus 39, 102,
111, 152. **Open** *9am-7pm Mon-Fri; 9.30am-*
1.30pm Sat. **Credit** AmEx, MC, V.
Map p285 H10.
KEL stocks English-language fiction, non-fiction,
travel books and teaching materials.
Other location Conde 1990, Belgrano (4555 4005).

Walrus Books

Estados Unidos 617, entre Perú y Chacabuco,
San Telmo (4300 7135, www.walrus-
books.com.ar). Subte C, Independencia/bus 29,
130, 152. **Open** *noon-8pm Tue-Sun.* **Credit**
AmEx, DC, MC, V. **Map** p285 E9.
With over 5,000 titles in this shop's eclectic range of
used but good quality English books, you're guaranteed to find something of interest.

General

★ Ateneo Grand Splendid

Avenida Santa Fe 1860, entre Avenida Callao y
Riobamba, Barrio Norte (4811 6104). Subte D,
Callao/bus 39, 152. **Open** *10am-10pm Mon-*
Thur; 10am-midnight Fri, Sat.
Credit AmEx, DC, MC, V. **Map** p286 I10.
Located in a lavish former theatre, El Ateneo is,
without a doubt, the city's most attractive bookshop.
Bag a chair and browse book after book or have a
drink in the on-stage café.
▶ *The Microcentro branch at Florida 340, though*
not as striking inside, is just as well stocked.

Dain Usina Cultural

Nicaragua 4899, y Thames, Palermo Soho
(4778 3554, www.dainusinacultural.com).
Subte D, Plaza Italia/bus 34, 55. **Open** *9am-9pm*
Tue-Sat; 10am-9pm Sun. **Credit** AmEx, MC, V.
Map p283 N5.
This luminous corner locale stocks a good range
of hardback design and travel tomes, with a small
selection in English, and its book launches and free
live music draw in a sedate crowd most evenings.
When you've had your fill of culture, retreat
upstairs to the rooftop terrace and sip mojitos on
the daybeds. *Photo p158.*

CONSUME

Dain Usina Cultural. See p157.

Fedro San Telmo

Carlos Calvo 578, entre Bolívar y Perú, San Telmo (4300 7551, www.fedrosantelmo.com.ar). Bus 24, 29, 152. **Open** noon-9pm Tue-Sat; 3-8pm Sun. **Credit** AmEx, MC, V. **Map** p284 D9.

This excellent shop, two blocks from Plaza Dorrego, stocks new books including titles in English. Nip through to the back for music CDs, childrens' books and more. Note that the Wi-Fi and coffee are on the house.

Libros del Pasaje

Thames 1762, y Pasaje Russel, Palermo Soho (4833 6637, www.librosdelpasaje.com.ar). Bus 34, 39, 55, 140, 151, 168. **Open** 10am-10pm Mon-Sat; 3-10pm Sun. **Credit** AmEx, MC, V. **Map** p283 N5.

The walls of this shop are crammed with books ranging from English literature to Argentinian art and design. The fabulous coffee-table books and quirky little souvenir editions make great gifts, and there's a very pleasant café at the back of the store which has a reasonable daily lunch special.

CHILDREN
Fashion

Félix Niños

El Salvador 4742, entre Armenia y Gurruchaga, Palermo Soho (4833 3313, www.felixba.com.ar). Bus 34, 55, 166. **Open** 11am-8pm Mon-Sat; 2.30-7.30pm Sun. **Credit** AmEx, MC, V. **Map** p287 M7.

Menswear store Félix (*see p165*), known for kitting out hip *hombres*, also makes togs for trendy sprogs. Taking a leaf from big brother's book, fashion-savvy

youngsters can play at being cool with colourful hoodies, bright corduroy trousers and polo shirts that are perfect for preppy pre-teens. Hip little sisters are also catered for.
Other location Paseo Alcorta shopping centre, Palermo (5777 6593).

Mimo & Co.

El Salvador 4721, entre Armenia y Gurruchaga, Palermo Soho (4511 5180, www.mimo.com.ar). Bus 15, 34, 36, 39, 55, 57, 106, 110, 140, 141, 151, 160, 168. **Open** 11am-8pm Mon-Sat; 2-8pm Sun. **Credit** AmEx, MC, V. **Map** p287 M7.

Mimo has been bringing its practical and modern clothing to boys and girls for more than two decades, with products that include garments, footwear and accessories for newly-borns to 12-year-olds.
Other locations throughout the city.

ELECTRONICS & PHOTOGRAPHY

For professional colour photo processing try **Kinefot** (Talcahuano 244 & 250, Tribunales, 4372 5091, www.kinefot.com), which provides a wide range of services. For Canon cameras, visit **Cosentino** (Roque Sáenz Peña 738, 4328 9120, www.opticacosentino.com.ar).

General

Frávega

2nd Floor, Abasto de Buenos Aires shopping centre, Avenida Corrientes 3247, entre Agüero y Anchorena, Abasto (4865 0907, www.fravega.com.ar). Subte B, Carlos Gardel/bus 24, 26, 29, 115, 118, 124, 132, 168, 180, 188, 194. **Open** 10am-10pm daily. **Credit** AmEx, MC, V. **Map** p282 J5.

Located in the Abasto shopping centre, this is a branch of a huge, well-established chain that sells all manner of electrodomestic products including MP3 players and laptops.
Other locations throughout the city.

Specialist

Local pay-as-you-go SIM cards can be bought in the numerous mobile phone shops around the city. There is one on every few blocks. Service providers include **Movistar** (www.movistar.com.ar), **Claro** (www.claro.com.ar) and **Personal** (www.personal.com.ar).

For computer repairs, try **Funziona** (4th Floor, office D, Avenida Callao 420, Microcentro, 5272 0300, www.funziona.com.ar). For problems with Apple Macs, try **One Click Store** (Paraguay 445, Microcentro, 4315 1919, www.oneclickstore.com.ar).

FASHION

While international fashion houses have a presence in the city, imported luxury brands sell at premium prices. Thankfully there's a vibrant fashion scene in Argentina, with young designers selling their garments in the city's multi-brand boutiques. A number of the more established designers mentioned below, like Jessica Trosman and Martin Churba, have earned themselves recognition overseas.

Designer

Agostina Bianchi

Thames 1733, entre El Salvador y Pasaje Russel, Palermo Soho (4833 9357, www. agostinabianchi.com.ar). Bus 34, 55, 166. **Open** noon-8.30pm Mon-Sat. **Credit** AmEx, MC, V. **Map** p283 M5.

Following the triumphant success of her luxury knitwear abroad, Agostina Bianchi decided to set up shop at home in Buenos Aires. Displayed in her elegant boutique is a range of flattering confections made with sumptuously soft yarns including merino wool and mohair, and featuring interesting touches such as metallic-coloured threads.

▶ *Bianchi's handmade creations are also available at the boutique in the Faena Hotel (see p95).*

Benedit Bis

Unit 25, Galeria Promenade, Avenida Alvear 1883, Recoleta (4802 8951, www.beneditbis.com.ar). Bus 34, 140, 151. **Open** 11am-7.30pm Mon-Fri; 11am-2pm Sat. **Credit** AmEx, MC, V. **Map** p286 J11.

Rosa Benedit makes clothes for elegant and uninhibited women. Her folk-chic style garments include multicoloured patchwork dresses, blouses and camisoles in playful combinations of fabrics and patterns.

Cora Groppo

El Salvador 4696, y Armenia, Palermo Soho (4833 7474, www.coragroppo.com). Bus 15, 39, 55, 151, 168. **Open** 10.30am-8pm Mon-Sat; 2-7pm Sun. **Credit** AmEx, MC, V. **Map** p283 M5.

Cora Groppo's creations are known for their flowing forms, and the designer's love of layering and textual details such as ruching and piping is always evident in her collections. Groppo's fine knits in muted tones make excellent wardrobe basics.

Other location Uruguay 1296, Recoleta (4815 8516).

Cubreme

Godoy Cruz 1720, entre Honduras y Gorriti, Palermo Soho (4832 5176, www.cubreme.com). Bus 34, 39, 55, 151. **Open** 12.30-7.30pm Mon-Sat. **Credit** AmEx, MC, V. **Map** p283 N5.

Fashion designer Alejandra Gottelli sources organic wool from Patagonian sheep and llamas

Where to Shop

BA's best shopping areas in brief.

SAN TELMO

If you're looking for antiques or vintage items, head straight to San Telmo. Don't miss the Sunday **Feria San Pedro Telmo** (*see p178*), when the surrounding streets are also filled with what looks like the contents of your great-aunt's attic. But it's not all old tango records and faded frocks – this area is full of cool boutiques and design stores as well.

THE CENTRE

On *calle* Florida, the city's only fully pedestrianised street, you can find plenty of leather goods and tourist tat. Avenida Corrientes, between Cerrito and Avenida Callao, is home to numerous bookstores.

LA BOCA

Don't come here looking for elegance and refinement, but do peruse **Caminito** (*see p56*) for that oversized maté gourd, borderline pornographic tango poster or obligatory Boca Juniors jersey.

RECOLETA AND BARRIO NORTE

Designer stores sit among French palaces in one of the world's most exclusive shopping zones. Try **Buenos Aires Design** (*see p179*) for chic homewares and furniture, or **Feria Plaza Francia** (*see left*) at weekends for quality craft items.

PALERMO AND VILLA CRESPO

Without a doubt the trendiest fashion boutiques in the city are found in Palermo, especially in the streets around Plaza Serrano. Independent designers peddle their creations in and around this plaza on weekends. There are numerous discount outlets on the ten or so blocks of Avenida Córdoba on either side of Scalabrini Ortiz, and in nearby Villa Crespo around *calles* Agüirre, Malabia and Gurruchaga. For discount leather stores, visit *calle* Murillo between Scalabrini Ortiz and Thames.

ONCE AND ABASTO

Wholesalers and discount stores abound in Once; search for a bargain on the street or head to mega mall **Abasto de Buenos Aires** (*see p155*) for chain stores. Look out for speciality food shops too: Once is traditionally a Jewish barrio, while Abasto has excellent Peruvian nosh.

from San Luis, as well as chemical-free cotton from Chaco. The yarns are woven into the softest of fabrics and hand-tailored into classic yet contemporary winter coats, silk-blend scarves and slip dresses in earthy, neutral tones.

Juana de Arco

El Salvador 4762, entre Gurruchaga y Armenia, Palermo Soho (4833 1621, www.juanadearco.net). Bus 15, 34, 39, 57, 151. **Open** 10.30am-8pm Mon-Fri; 11am-8pm Sat; 1-8pm Sun. **Credit** AmEx, MC, V. **Map** p283 M5.

Designer Mariana Cortés's signature pieces are distinctive, multicoloured patchwork confections that incorporate traditional South American textile arts such as *ñandutí*, a Paraguayan lacemaking technique. Underwear is another speciality here: treat yourself to some multicoloured bras or organic cotton knickers.

Other location Juncal 1239, Recoleta (4811 3353).

María Cher

El Salvador 4724, entre Armenia y Gurruchaga, Palermo Soho (4832 3336, www.maria-cher. com.ar). Bus 34, 55, 57. **Open** 10am-8pm Mon-Fri; 10am-9pm Sat; 2-7.30pm Sun. **Credit** AmEx, DC, MC, V. **Map** p283 M5.

Argentinian María Cherñajovsky's womenswear combines feminine pieces like silk-mix tunics and modern minidresses with trousers and jackets clearly influenced by menswear. Black and white are mainstays of Cherñajovsky's collections, though striking shades and colourful prints are introduced each season.

Other locations throughout the city.

Mariana Dappiano

Gurruchaga 1755, entre Costa Rica y El Salvador, Palermo Soho (4833 4731, www.marianadappiano.com). Bus 34, 55, 161. **Open** 11am-8pm Mon-Sat; 2-7pm Sun. **Credit** AmEx, MC, V. **Map** p283 M5.

Rather than following current trends, designer Mariana Dappiano remains faithful to her own distinctive aesthetic, producing clothing for women with a strong sense of personal style and an appreciation for quality and originality. Dappiano's collections are dominated by unstructured forms with details like asymmetrical sleeves, by the juxtaposition of striking colours and by the designer's own unique textiles.

Mon Lorie

Gurruchaga 1739, entre Costa Rica y El Salvador, Palermo Soho (4831 5296/ www.monlorie.com.ar). Bus 34, 55, 161. **Open** 11am-8pm Mon-Sat; 2-8pm Sun. **Credit** AmEx, MC, V. **Map** p283 M5.

Mon Lorie's vintage-inspired pieces are for women who know where they've come from as much as where they're going. Two-toned wide-leg trousers,

baby-doll shift dresses, lurex crop tops and satin maxi skirts reference everyone from *Annie Hall*-era Diane Keaton to Marlene Dietrich's old-Hollywood glamour along with Twiggy's cutesy boldness. Shimmering fabrics are frequently paired with daring clashes of colour, but the result is always polished, timeless and utterly feminine.

Nadine Zlotogora

El Salvador 4638, entre Malabia y Armenia, Palermo Soho (4831 4203, www.nadinez.com). Bus 15, 39, 55. **Open** 11am-8pm Mon-Sat. **Credit** AmEx, MC, V. **Map** p283 M5.

Zlotogora's idiosyncratic styling is an artful blend of fantasy and romance. Her ethereal, other-worldly clothes are distinctively feminine with satin, macramé and embroidered pieces that are individually dyed to ensure uniqueness.

★ Pesqueira

Gurruchaga 1750, y Pasaje Russel, Palermo Soho (4833 7218, www.pesqueiratm.com). Bus 15, 34, 39, 55, 110. **Open** 11am-8pm Mon-Sat; 3-8pm Sun. **Credit** AmEx, MC, V. **Map** p283 M5.

Innocent insouciance reigns at designer Valeria Pesqueira's Palermo store. The pretty womenswear collections, full of sweet, feminine garments that are both classic and modern, are designed for the young at heart. The printed laptop bags and canvas totes are indispensable for any modern ingénue.

Sofía Forbes Jeans

Libertad 986, y Marcelo T de Alvear, Recoleta (4811 6791, www.sofiaforbesjeansparis.com). Subte D, Tribunales/bus 5, 102, 152. **Open** 10am-2pm, 4-7pm Mon-Fri; 10.30am-1.30pm Sat by appointment only. **Credit** AmEx, MC, V. **Map** p285 H11.

What Sofía Forbes doesn't know about jeans is not worth knowing, her fans would argue. The combination of her Argentinian eye for detail, her French flair for fashion and some Italian fine craftsmanship make for a small but perfectly formed collection. Using the softest denims, all beautifully cut, she has created four styles designed to suit a range of body shapes, each with its own individual finishing touches. She also sells a selection of heels, bags and jewellery.

Tramando

Rodríguez Peña 1973, entre Posadas y Avenida Alvear, Recoleta (4811 0465, www.tramando.com). Bus 17, 61, 67, 92, 93. **Open** 10.30am-8.30pm Mon-Fri; 11am-7pm Sat. **Credit** AmEx, DC, MC, V. **Map** p286 I11.

Innovative designer Martín Churba and his crew employ wacky weaving, abstract prints and fabrics with rubbery finishes in their womenswear, which fuses artistry and eccentricity. Unusual homewares are also produced by this creative team.

CONSUME

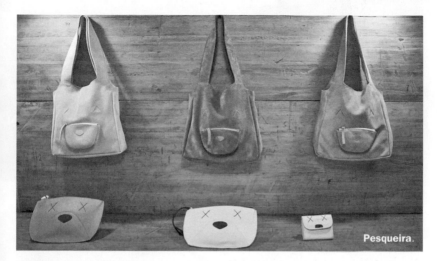

Pesqueira.

Trosman

Paseo Alcorta shopping centre, Salguero 3172,
y Avenida Figueroa Alcorta, Palermo (5777
6595, www.trosman.com.ar). Bus 67, 102,
130. **Open** 10am-10pm daily. **Credit** AmEx,
DC, MC, V. **Map** p286 L11.

Jessica Trosman produces original womenswear for
adventurous spirits. Her enveloping, asymmetrical
garments, which often feature textural embellish-
ment, have been celebrated at home and abroad.
If you want to play it safe in well-fitting basics, her
stores have been cited as some of the city's best for
finding that perfect pair of jeans.

Other location Patio Bullrich shopping centre,
Recoleta (4814 7414).

Vestite y Andate

Nicaragua 4604, entre Gurruchaga y Armenia,
Palermo Soho (4115 6430, www.vestiteyandate.
net). Bus 15, 39, 160. **Credit** AmEx, MC, V.
Map p287 M8.

Luxury fabrics and graphic prints are the hallmarks
of the chic statement pieces dreamed up by Agustina
Bengolea and Clara Campagnola. Frocks made from
shimmery velvet and the softest of suede, silk tops
that drape just so and colourful knits that effortlessly flatter the female form are embellished by
pops of chiffon, mesh and lurex.

Vevû

El Salvador 4663, entre Malabia y Armenia,
Palermo Soho (4833 3360, www.vevu.com).
Bus 15, 110, 151. **Open** 11am-8.30pm Mon-Sat.
Credit AmEx, DC, MC, V. **Map** p287 M8.

Vevû's ultra-feminine collection ranges from demure
pastel blouses and 1950s-style strapless dresses to
classic black and white numbers. Designer Sandra

Delelis takes high fashion trends and reworks them
into everyday, wearable pieces designed to accommodate even the most voluptuous of curves.

Other location Avenida Las Heras 3896,
Palermo (4807 8094).

General

Amores Trash Couture

Ángel Carranza 1979, entre Costa Rica y
Nicaragua, Palermo Hollywood (4775 3601,
www.amorestrashcouture.com.ar). Bus 39, 111,
161. **Open** 11am-7pm Mon-Fri; 1-7pm Sat.
Credit AmEx, MC, V. **Map** p283 O5.

Fans of 1980s fashion should be sure to call in at
this space for party dresses and sexy separates
such as lace or spandex leggings, particularly influenced by BA's 1980s trash fashion moment. These
threads are certainly attention-grabbing but somehow classier than *Desperately Seeking Susan*-era
Madonna, and they're perfect for the dancefloor.
Head upstairs to check out the selection of vintage
clothing and accessories. *Photo p164.*

Other location Pasaje Santa Rosa 4909, Palermo
Soho (5294 7043).

Ay Not Dead

Gurruchaga 1637, entre Pasaje Santa Rosa
y Honduras, Palermo Soho (4833 2999,
www.aynotdead.com.ar). Bus 34, 55, 57.
Open 11am-8.30pm Mon-Sat; 2-8pm Sun.
Credit AmEx, MC, V. **Map** p283 M5.

Anglophile sisters Noel and Angie honed their craft
at London's Central Saint Martin's College, and do
a steady trade in skinny jeans and leather jackets
for the young, self-conscious hipster. The aesthetic
is wedged somewhere between rock-star chic and
understated streetwear, and splashes of lurex,

CONSUME

WW
ROSSICARUS
CO

DISTINCTION APPEARS
WHEN SENSUALITY MEETS ELEGANCE

Argentina

velvet and tough embellishments grace pieces which move seamlessly between day and night. **Other locations** throughout the city.

Chocolate
Honduras 4928, entre Serrano y Gurruchaga, Palermo Soho (4833 3553, www.chocolate argentina.com.ar). Bus 15, 39, 141, 151, 168. **Open** 10am-9pm daily. **Credit** AmEx, DC, MC, V. **Map** p283 M5.

This popular store offers stylish essentials such as Peruvian pima cotton tops, pretty voile blouses in flattering colours and comfortable separates, as well as options for special occasions and high quality, on-trend accessories.
Other locations Avenida Santa Fe 1430, Recoleta (4816 0153); Migueletes 987, Las Cañitas (4776 7301).

DAM
Honduras 4775, entre Malabia y Armenia, Palermo Soho (4833 3935, www.damboutique. com.ar). Bus 39, 55, 168. **Open** 11.30am-8.30pm Mon-Sat; 3.30-8.30pm Sun. **Credit** AmEx, MC, V. **Map** p283 M5.

For some 15 years, this boutique, established by designer Carola Besasso, has been providing those eager for originality with bright, quirky clothing. The antithesis of mass-produced, most of the garments sold here are handmade from fabric offcuts, meaning skirts, dresses and tops come in a plethora of prints and colours.

Desiderata
Esquina Avenida Santa Fe y Avenida Callao, Barrio Norte (4816 5361, www.desiderata. com.ar). Subte D, Callao/bus 10, 17, 140, 152. **Open** 9.30am-8.30pm Mon-Sat. **Credit** AmEx, DC, MC, V. **Map** p286 I10.

This store is good for wardrobe staples, bridging the gap between high street and remote designer. Desiderata garments are comfortable, contemporary and on-trend, but with a twist. Loose, lightweight knits are typical offerings, and the focus is always on good quality fabrics, with wool and silk mixes generally winning over synthetics, and prices reflect this. **Other locations** throughout the city.

Lupe
El Salvador 4657, entre Armenia y Malabia, Palermo Soho (4833 9205, www.lupeba.com.ar). Bus 39, 55, 151. **Open** 11am-8pm Mon-Sat; 3-8pm Sun. **Credit** AmEx, DC, MC, V. **Map** p283 M5.

Pay a visit to this well-known Palermo store for a local take on understated femininity with a touch of rock chic. The bright, spacious outlet is the ideal place to pick up pretty daywear in fabrics like washed silk and pure wool. Current trends are referenced in Lupe's collections, though the emphasis is on combining good quality with cosmopolitan charm.

Paula Cahen D'Anvers
Alto Palermo shopping centre, Avenida Santa Fe 3253, entre Coronel Díaz y Bulnes, Palermo (5777 8227, www.paulacahendanvers.com.ar). Subte D, Bulnes/bus 12, 15, 39, 64, 152. **Open** 10am-10pm daily. **Credit** AmEx, DC, MC, V. **Map** p286 K9.

This brand does classic comfort rather than avant-garde adventurism, with preppy separates that play it safe. The easy-to-match colours, flattering fits and oh-so-soft fabrics have won this women's clothing line a place in many a wardrobe, though prices may make you pause before purchasing.
Other locations throughout the city.

★ Las Pepas
Avenida Santa Fe 1631, entre Montevideo y Rodríguez Peña, Recoleta (4811 7887, www.laspepas.com.ar). Bus 10, 37, 39, 152. **Open** 10am-9pm Mon-Fri; 10am-8pm Sat. **Credit** AmEx, DC, MC, V. **Map** p286 I10.

An eclectic array of garments graces the rails at pop ular Las Pepas, though one mainstay of the brand's collections is the range of leather outerwear and accessories. The large selection of leather jackets includes classic blousons and belted trenches, as well as pretty, feminine styles in sumptuously soft suede. Bags range from classic holdalls to dainty clutches, and footwear is also available.
Other locations Alto Palermo shopping centre, Barrio Norte (5777 8001); Gurruchaga 1573, Palermo Soho (4833 0601).

Rapsodia
Honduras 4872, entre Gurruchaga y Armenia, Palermo Soho (4831 6333, www.rapsodia. com.ar). Bus 15, 57, 93. **Open** 10am-9pm daily. **Credit** AmEx, DC, MC, V. **Map** p283 M5.

This popular local brand takes international trends and gives them a bohemian twist, mixing shabby chic with sophisticated hippie. Sumptuous velvets, delicate gauzy materials and the softest pima cotton are some of the fabrics used in Rapsodia collections, which feature plenty of patterns and embellishments, from lace trims to embroidery and sequins.
Other locations throughout the city.

Vitamina
El Salvador 4757, entre Gurruchaga y Armenia, Palermo Soho (4897 2180, www.vitamina.com.ar). Bus 15, 55, 168. **Open** 10am-8.30pm Mon-Sat; noon-8.30pm Sun. **Credit** AmEx, MC, V. **Map** p283 M5.

Silk tops, buttery smooth leather jackets and T-shirts in the softest of yarns: Vitamina's clothes are luxuriously touchy-feely. Designer Silvia Ortiz has cornered the market for the sophisticated girly girl, and her elegant pieces are dreamy enough to float away in.
Other locations throughout the city.

Amores Trash Couture. *See p161.*

Multi-brand boutiques

Diversa
Humberto 1° 580, entre Bolívar y Perú, San Telmo (4362 1262, www.tiendadiversa.com.ar). Bus 10, 22, 29, 126. **Open** 11am-2pm, 3-8pm daily. **Credit** AmEx, MC, V. **Map** p284 D9.
Diversa is all about talking points with a touch of quirkiness, and houses a variety of unique items created by more than 80 Argentinian artists and designers. The range includes womenswear, childrenswear, jewellery, accessories, leather bags and wallets.

Moebius
Defensa 1356, entre Cochabamba y Avenida Juan de Garay, San Telmo (4361 2893). Bus 10, 24, 93. **Open** 1.30-8pm Mon; 11am-8pm Tue-Fri; 11.30am-8pm Sun. **Credit** AmEx, DC, MC, V. **Map** p284 D9.
This boutique stocks cutting-edge pieces by more than 20 up-and-coming local designers. Dreamy woollen jumpers by the Moebius label rub shoulders with sculptural 1950s-inspired dresses by Natacha Morale, while floral dresses, reversible tops and men's loafers keep things casual. Well-priced accessories include wacky laptop cases, leather handbags, one-off broaches and chunky resin necklaces.

Puntos en el Espacio
Perú 979, entre Estados Unidos y Carlos Calvo, San Telmo (4307 1742, www.puntosenelespacio.com.ar). Bus 10, 22, 29, 126. **Open** 11am-8pm daily. **Credit** AmEx, DC, MC, V. **Map** p284 D9.
Visit this ample, well-laid out space for a selection of clothing for hip guys and girls, plus pretty underwear, bags, accessories, footwear and decorative household items from dozens of talented young designers.
Other location Independencia 402, San Telmo (4307 5665).

Menswear specialists

Balthazar
Don Anselmo Aieta 1087, Plaza Dorrego, San Telmo (4362 4926, www.balthazarshop.com). Bus 10, 29, 195. **Open** 11am-8pm Tue-Sat; 11am-7pm Sun. **Credit** AmEx, MC, V. **Map** p284 D9.
The Balthazar store in San Telmo is a stunning shrine to masculinity: browse striking shirts in high-quality Italian fabrics and classic alpaca wool scarves while admiring the motorbike mounted on a snooker table, and the titillating yet tasteful images and animal skulls adorning the walls.
Other location Gorriti 5131, Palermo Soho (4834 6235).

Bensimon
Honduras 4876, entre Armenia y Gurruchaga, Palermo Soho (4833 6857, www.bensimon.com.ar) Bus 15. **Open** 11am-8.30pm Mon-Sat; 2-8.30pm Sun. **Credit** AmEx, DC, MC, V. **Map** p283 M5.
Bensimon's sophisticated take on casual cool is ideal for metrosexual types looking for toned down but trendy gear. Slim-fitting trousers and T-shirts, lightweight knits and skimpy leather jackets are ideal for lean-bodied twentysomethings keen to attain an unfussy, informal look.
Other locations throughout the city.

Bolivia
Gurruchaga 1581, entre Gorriti y Honduras, Palermo Soho (4832 6284, www.boliviaonline.com.ar). Bus 39, 55, 151. **Open** 11am-8pm Mon-Sat; 3-8pm Sun. **Credit** AmEx, MC ,V. **Map** p283 M5.
If you're the type to carry a man bag, have a gander at the garments at Bolivia. Floral print shirts and shockingly bright knitwear are a far cry from macho menswear; and don't be fooled by the dark pinstripe suits – they may look tame on the outside, but the leopard print linings are anything but subtle.
Other location Thames y Nicaragua, Palermo Soho (4832 6409).

Bowen
Gurruchaga 1548, y Pasaje Soria, Palermo Soho (4831 1710, www.bowenlondon.com.ar). Bus 15, 55, 140, 151. **Open** 11am-8pm Mon-Sat; 2-8pm Sun. **Credit** AmEx, MC, V. **Map** p283 M5.

Soft cotton T-shirts, thick leather belts, ripped jeans and clunky boots make this a good spot to pick up some classy urban casualwear, with a rock 'n' roll edge. The quality of materials used by this chain is also tip-top.
Other locations Abasto shopping centre, Abasto (4959 3629); Alto Palermo shopping centre, Palermo (5777 8254); Paseo Alcorta shopping centre, Palermo (5777 6580).

El Burgués
Gurruchaga 1743, entre Costa Rica y El Salvador, Palermo Soho (4834 6880, www.elburgues.com). Bus 34, 55, 161. **Open** 11am-8pm Mon-Sat; 2-8pm Sun. **Credit** AmEx, MC, V. **Map** p283 M5.
Model-like staff can help you choose from good quality shirts, knitwear, sharp short macs and skinny jeans. The El Burgués chap wouldn't dream of ruining the line of his trousers with an overstuffed pocket, and to avoid such a fashion crime there's a manbag here to suit everyone. Soft leathers hang beside rainbows of fine cotton shirts, and natty blazers have playful contrasting-coloured elbow patches.

Etiqueta Negra
Honduras 4850, entre Gurruchaga y Armenia, Palermo Soho (4831 3291, www.etiqueta negra.us). Bus 151. **Open** 10am-8.30pm Mon-Sat; 2-8pm Sun. **Credit** AmEx, DC, MC, V. **Map** 283 I12.
Etiqueta Negra oozes elegance. Cultivate effortless chic with slick suits and Italian cotton shirts, or buy yourself a bit of old-school cool with the brand's subtly worn-in jeans, timeless T-shirts, cashmere-mix knitwear and buttery soft leather jackets. There is also a compact range of clothing for women.
Other locations throughout the city.

Félix
Gurruchaga 1670, entre El Salvador y Pasaje Santa Rosa, Palermo Soho (4832 2994, www.felixba.com.ar). Bus 15, 110, 160. **Open** 11am-8pm Mon-Sat; 2.30-8pm Sun. **Credit** AmEx, MC, V. **Map** p283 M5.
Modern dandies will love Félix's natty clothing, which has drawn comparisons with English designer Paul Smith's menswear. Founded by Martin Egozcue in 2002, Félix has established a following among hip types happy to spend time and cash cultivating an image of effortless cool. If you've dreamed of being snapped by street style spotter The Sartorialist, hotfoot it to this store.
Other location Factory outlet at Godoy Cruz 1645, Palermo Soho (4833 1444).

Hermanos Estebecorena
El Salvador 5960, entre Ravignani y Arévalo, Palermo Hollywood (4772 2145, 93, 111. **Open** 11am-8pm Mon-Sat. **Credit** AmEx, DC, MC, V. **Map** p283 O5.

Practical types with an eye for design will appreciate the ingenious details of HE's functional, modern menswear. Hidden pockets and adjustable cuffs are just some of the features of these garments, and the range of accessories is full of equally clever elements. Go for comfortable, casual cool with multi purpose trousers and stylish leather jackets, or choose from smart jackets and jumpers in various weights.

Key Biscayne
Armenia 1735, entre Costa Rica y El Salvador, Palermo Soho (48332104, www.keybiscayne. com.ar). Bus 15, 34, 39, 55, 57, 106, 110, 141, 151, 168. **Open** 11am-9pm Mon-Sat; 1-8pm Sun. **Credit** AmEx, MC, V. **Map** p283 M5.
This Argentinian menswear chain is aimed squarely at the anti-corporate metrosexual. Comfy hooded cardigans, tank tops and polo shirts come in earthy browns, greys and greens, while T-shirts and sleeveless vests are bright and beach-ready. For the urban gaucho there's a wide range of leather jackets.
Other locations throughout the city.

Penguin
Gurruchaga 1650, entre Honduras y Pasaje Santa Rosa, Palermo Soho (4831 7272, www.originalpenguin.com). Bus 15, 55, 57. **Open** 10am-8pm Mon-Sat; 11am-8.30pm Sun. **Credit** AmEx, MC, V. **Map** p283 M5.
This classic US brand, established in 1955, brings its iconic polo shirts and other fine quality garments to Palermo. Knitted sweaters, short-sleeve shirts, hoodies and hip accessories, including belts, watches and sunglasses, are all available.
Other location Paseo Alcorta shopping centre, Palermo (4808 9710).

Used & vintage

El Buen Orden
Defensa 894, entre Independencia y Estados Unidos, San Telmo (mobile 15 5936 2820, www.elbuenorden.com.ar). Bus 10, 22, 29. **Open** 11am-6pm daily. **No credit cards**. **Map** p284 D10.
Strategically located a block from Plaza Dorrego, El Buen Orden is more than your average vintage shop. New treasures appear daily as stock is constantly rotated, and the store is home to everything from clothing and handbags to period-piece jewellery, hats and eyewear, all with surprisingly accessible prices.

Galería 5ta Avenida
Avenida Santa Fe 1270, entre Libertad y Talcahuano, Recoleta (4816 0451). Bus 10, 39, 59, 152. **Open** 10am-8pm Mon-Sat. **Credit** varies. **Map** p285 H11.
This arcade is lined with used clothing shops and boasts bargains for those prepared to rummage. For vintage eyewear, pay a visit to Óptica Nahuel at store number 38 (4811 2837).

▶ *Nearby, Juan Pérez (Marcelo T de Alvear 1441, 4815 8442, www.vestitenjuanperez. blogspot.com) stocks second-hand and vintage gear and is well worth a look.*

★ Gil Antigüedades

Humberto 1° 412, y Defensa, San Telmo (4361 5019, www.gilantiguedades.com.ar). Bus 10, 29, 126, 152. **Open** 11am-1pm, 3-7pm Tue-Sat; 11am-7pm Sun. **Credit** AmEx, DC, MC, V. **Map** p284 D9.

This excellent shop has attracted fashion superstars like John Galliano and Carolina Herrera, who have turned up to browse owners María Inés and Héctor Horacio's collection of over 6,000 pieces of exquisite period clothing, jewellery, footwear and accessories. Upstairs there are plenty of trunks, figurines and other antiques to peruse.

FASHION ACCESSORIES

Cleaning & repairs

For shoe repairs, visit **Fix Shoe** in Recoleta (Vicente López 1668, 4811 0226), where most jobs can be completed in one day.

There are launderettes on almost every block, some with dry-cleaning services. A popular chain is **Lava Ya**. Try Esmeralda 577 (4322 1768, www.laundryargentina.com.ar) in Microcentro. In Palermo Hollywood, the **Laundry Company** (El Salvador 5537, www.laundrycompany.com.ar) is particularly reliable with delicates.

Clothing hire

Last-minute wedding to attend and you haven't packed your handy tux? Not to worry, suit hire and sale is available at **London Tie** (Florida 795, 5555 5202, www.londontie.com), which offers a fitting service. English is spoken.

Eyewear

Carla Di Sí

Gurruchaga 1677, entre El Salvador y Honduras, Palermo Soho (4832 1655, www.carladisi.com.ar). Bus 15, 39, 110, 140, 151, 168. **Open** 11am-8pm Mon-Sat; 3.30-7.30pm Sun. **Credit** AmEx, MC, V. **Map** p283 M5.

Local eyewear designer Carla Di Sí has her own classy and sassy line, with an emphasis on handmade cat-eye frames. Vintage fans will also love her selection of secondhand frames dating from the 1950s to the 1980s. Sourced by Carla's optician grandfather, they include everything from Wayfarer frames to tortoiseshell styles – perfect for playing the sexy librarian.

Infinit Boutique

Thames 1602, y Honduras, Palermo Soho (4831 7070, www.infinitnit.la). Bus 39, 55. **Open** 11am-8pm Mon-Sat; 3-7pm Sun. **Credit** AmEx, MC, V. **Map** p283 M5.

Stock at this cool eyewear emporium includes tortoiseshell frames that are reminiscent of Woody Allen's specs, cat's eye frames with metallic detailing in the corners, and sleek sunglasses in a variety of shapes and colours.

General

★ Autoría BsAs

Suipacha 1025, entre Avenida Santa Fe y Marcelo T de Alvear, Retiro (5252 2474, www.autoriabsas.com.ar). Subte C, San Martín/ bus 10, 132. **Open** 9.30am-8pm Mon-Fri; 10am-6pm Sat. **Credit** AmEx, MC, V. **Map** p285 G11.

Autoría hits the nail on the head with its tasteful fusion of art and design. Browse through carefully selected garments from fashion designers like Benedit Bis and Vero Ivaldi, bags and accessories from the likes of Neumática and Perfectos Dragones, and jewellery from Juana Maraña and Marina Massone.

▶ *Don't miss the in-store gallery, which includes works from recognised artists as well as novices.*

Jewellery

925nueveveinticinco

Honduras 4808, y Armenia, Palermo Soho (4833 5343, www.nueveveinticinco.com.ar). Bus 15, 55, 151. **Open** 11am-8pm Mon-Sat; 1.30-7pm Sun. **Credit** AmEx, DC, MC, V. **Map** p283 M5.

Designer Mario Paluch works with silver, gold, wood and semi-precious stones like malachite, amber and rhodochrosite to create unique, eye-catching designs. Choose from huge chunky rings combining silver and ebony from the 'Madera' line or the colourful, mosaic-like examples in the 'Gaudi' range.

Gabriela Horvat

Honduras 5238, entre Godoy Cruz y Uriarte, Palermo Soho (4833 5423, www.gabriela horvat.com). Bus 34, 39, 55. **Open** 11am-7pm Mon-Sat. **Credit** AmEx, MC, V. **Map** p283 M5.

Covetous objets d'art in their own right, Horvat's jewellery spans clean-cut rings to elaborately fashioned wool necklaces, cocooned in silver spirals and adorned with precious stones. The one-of-a-kind pieces are guaranteed to inject a touch of cocktail-party glamour into any outfit, while the classic range is demure enough to complement elegant day attire.

Manu Lizarralde

Gorriti 5078, entre Thames y Serrano, Palermo Soho (4832 6252, www.manulizarralde.com). Bus 55, 151, 168. **Open** 11am-7pm Mon-Sat. **Credit** AmEx, MC, V. **Map** p283 M5.

CONSUME

The unique gems in Manu Lizarralde's glowing showroom are selected for their purity and encased in beautiful settings. The result is a range of contemporary but timeless jewellery that fuses elegance and originality with old-fashioned craftsmanship. **Other location** San Martín 1107, Retiro (4314 4379).

Marcelo Toledo
Humberto 1º 462, entre Bolívar y Defensa, San Telmo (4362 0841, www.marcelotoledo.net). Subte C, San Juan/bus 17, 59, 100, 126. **Open** 10.30am-5.30pm Mon-Fri, Sun. **Credit** AmEx. **Map** p284 D9.

One of the most respected jewellers in BA is one of the favourites of the King of Spain and has also made pieces for Prince Charles and his mum. Toledo's 'Evita' collection featured more than 120 items including earrings, brooches and necklaces in silver and gold with precious stones, many of them replicas of pieces found in Eva Perón's wardrobe.

Plata Nativa
Unit 41, Galería del Sol, Florida 860, entre Avenida Córdoba y Paraguay, Microcentro (4312 1398, www.platanativa.com). Subte C, San Martín/bus 6, 26, 93, 152. **Open** 10am-7.30pm Mon-Fri; 10am-2pm Sat. **Credit** AmEx, MC, V. **Map** p285 G11.

This is a treasure trove of indigenous and Latin American art, antique silver and ethnic accessories. The store's clients include the Rolling Stones, fashion designer Marc Jacobs, Shakira and Pedro Almodóvar, who have all been wowed by Marta Campana's mind-boggling collection.

Made in Argentina
What to fill your suitcase with, and where to find it.

You've lived and breathed *porteño* culture, digested half a cow and your weight's worth in pizza, and even picked up some cool *lunfardo* phrases. How to take some of that magic home with you? Leather footwear and wine are solid choices, but here are a few other inspiring ideas for Argentinian mementos.

PENGUIN JUG
During the 1930s, it was usual to serve table wine in penguin shaped pitchers. These quaint ceramic carafes are still used for house wines in traditional neighbourhood restaurants. Bag yourself a hand-painted *pingüino* at **Pehache** (*see p179*) or buy an original (cheaper) version at a *ferretería* (hardware store).

ALFAJORES
For a sweet reminder of your stay, stock up on some *alfajores*, the sugary two- or three-tier layers of maize biscuit

and gooey *dulce de leche* (a near mandatory Argentinian confectionary component). Household name **Havanna** (www.havanna.com.ar, locations throughout the city) sells some of the best – along with the equally addictive chocolate-covered *conitos* – and the presentation boxes make ideal gifts.

POLO SHIRT
Get into the spirit of one of the country's top sports even if only by dressing the part. **La Martina** (*see p180*) has a range of good-quality cotton polo shirts as well as leather boots, bags and jackets. Note that in polo, players' positions are indicated by the numbers one to four. Four is the captain and usually the best player on the team – something to bear in mind when selecting your shirt.

CONSUME

Silver Shop

Jorge Luis Borges 1948, entre Nicaragua y Soler, Palermo Soho (4774 3313, www.thesilver shop.com.ar). Subte D, Plaza Italia/bus 34, 55. **Open** 11am-8pm Mon-Sat; 2-8pm Sun. **Credit** AmEx, MC, V. **Map** p283 M5.

This boutique is the labour of love of Argentinian Claudina Bonansea and Brit David Sturmer, a sculptor and a former ballet dancer-turned jeweller respectively. The exquisite jewels are inspired as much by art nouveau and ancient motifs as by local flora and fauna.

Leather goods

The area on and around *calle* Florida has become the main leather zone; be prepared to contend with an overly zealous sales approach. Or check out *calle* Murillo in Villa Crespo for leather wholesalers; *see p157* **Where to Shop**.

Casa Lopez

Marcelo T de Alvear 640/658, entre Florida y Maipú, Retiro (4311 3044, www.casalopez. com.ar). Subte C, San Martín/bus 10, 17, 59, 70, 101. **Open** 9am-8pm Mon-Fri; 9.30am-7pm Sat; 10am-6pm Sun. **Credit** AmEx, DC, MC, V. **Map** p285 G11.

Coats, jackets, bags and luggage come in mostly classic, traditional styles at this shop, and the quality is top notch. Native leathers such as those from *carpincho* (a large rodent) and *yacaré* (a South American caiman) are used in a number of products. **Other locations** Galerías Pacífico shopping centre, Microcentro (5555 5241); Patio Bullrich shopping centre, Recoleta (4814 7477).

GAUCHO KNIFE SET

Live out your *Rawhide* fantasies and purchase a gaucho knife set for some macho kudos. There are four main types of knife: the *facón* and *daga* are recognised as fighting weapons, while the *cuchilla* and *puña* are multipurpose tools. You can find them at the gaucho fair **Feria de Mataderos** (*see p80*) as well as in upmarket gift shop **Arandú** (*see p175*). Remember to avoid startling airport staff by stowing knives in your hold luggage.

SIPHON BOTTLES

Vintage glass siphon bottles make wonderful objets d'art displayed on your shelf at home. Dating from pre-1940s Argentina, they were once filled with carbonated water and delivered to people's homes, much like milk was in bygone days. Sure, these antique bottles are now purely ornamental (don't expect them to perform their original function) and not the lightest of souvenirs to schlep home, but they come in brilliant shades of red, blue and green, complete with elaborate etchings. Check the neck for the date of issue. For the best range, rummage around the antique stores on Plaza Dorrego at Sunday's **Feria San Pedro Telmo** (*see p178*).

MATÉ GOURD

Argentinians love maté, a herbal drink that's deeply entrenched in the national culture and lifestyle. Emulate those cool locals, just try not scrunch up your nose: maté tends to be drunk *amargo* (bitter). There are strict maté making rules and any foreigner that attempts the fine art of pouring hot water on to dried leaves is likely to be told they're doing it wrong. The day an Argentinian tells you your maté is *rico* (delicious) is a cause for celebration.

Maté gourds are widely available and are typically made from a dried-out squash, wood or metal; find traditional examples at **Feria Plaza Francia** (*see p157*). For contemporary versions, try the glass or ceramic matés from **Nobrand** (*see p179*) or the silicon Mate Mateo (www.matemateo.com), available from **Autoría** (*see p167*).

COFFEE TABLE BOOK

If you haven't quite managed to capture the stunning Buenos Aires cityscape with your own camera, invest in one of the glossy coffee-table books sold at **Ateneo Grand Splendid** (*see p158*), **Libros del Pasaje** (*see p158*), **Dain Usina Cultural** (*see p158*) or **Fedro San Telmo** (*see p158*), and inspire envy in the folks back home.

CONSUME

Hide and Seek

Our round-up of the city's best leather stores.

If the questionable leather merchandise on *calle* Florida (floral-print bumbag, anyone?) makes you wonder how this noble material could form such an important part of the Argentinian economy and identity, rest easy: there are plenty of local designers and artisans who believe a bovine's backside is destined for better things.

FOOTWEAR

European immigration to 19th-century Argentina helped establish a strong tradition of shoemaking that is still in evidence today. Bootmakers for polo players and princes, **Casa Fagliano** (Tambo Nuevo 1449, Hurlingham, 4665 0128, www.fagliano.com.ar) has been creating polo and riding boots and elegant lace-up shoes using old-school production methods for over a century. At **Comme Il Faut** (*see p173*), the high-quality heels designed for tango dancers also have a following off the dancefloor. But if it's pure footwear frivolity you're after, the retro-inspired women's shoes at **Mishka** (*see p174*) are sartorial shorthand for effortless cool.

HOUSEHOLD & DECORATIVE ITEMS

Buenos Aires may be a modern metropolis, but there are still plenty of *talabarterías* (traditional leather goods shops) crammed with gaucho and equestrian accoutrements such as *boleadoras* (a hunting tool), leather matés, stirrups, saddles and riding crops. Try **Arandú** (*see p175*) for upmarket items, or the **Feria de Mataderos** (*see p80*) for more economical options. For cow hides, visit leather wholesalers **Nueva Casa Antonio** (Avenida Boedo 1411, Boedo, 4921 2227, www.nuevacasaantonio. com.ar) to avoid paying the premium prices charged in the city's more touristy neighbourhoods. If space in your suitcase is limited, **L&R Handcraft** (Montevideo 1691, Recoleta, 4814 4010, www. lrhandcraft.com) stocks beautifully crafted leather-bound notebooks and photo albums.

ACCESSORIES

For inanimate arm candy, luxury brand **Peter Kent** (*see p171*) has chic leather handbags in appealing colours. **Humawaca**'s (*see p171*) innovative and eye-catching products include totes, purses, weekend bags and even a briefcase that can charge phones, iPads and digital cameras; while classic handbags, belts, gloves – as well as riding equipment – in leather, suede and snakeskin form part of the range at **Rossi & Caruso** (*see p171*).

JACKETS

Investing in a locally-made leather jacket doesn't have to mean choosing between boring black and brown. **Murillo 666** (Murillo 666, 4856 4501, www.murillo666.com.ar) in Villa Crespo's leather district has an extensive selection of outerwear for men and women (as well as bags, accessories and sofas), though it's worth comparing prices and products in the surrounding stores. For some serious style, the biker and bomber jackets in sumptuously soft lamb's leather at **Doma** (*see p171*) come in an array of colours and there are also cool *camperas* (jackets) for men; or try the form-fitting feminine styles at womenswear shop **Las Pepas** (*see p163*).

TOP TIPS

Attention to detail in construction – double stitching at stress points, the same number of stitches per inch, internal pockets, durable lining and hardware, no loose threads or glue streaks – suggests high-quality leather has been used. Look out for the distinctive pitted leather of the *carpincho* (capybara), a semiaquatic rodent, used in everything from jackets to *alpargatas* (espadrilles). Be wary of items labelled *cuero ecológico* (ecological leather). Usually, this is a composite of leather fibres and latex or synthetic resin. At worst it's pure plastic. If the price seems too good to be true, it probably is.

CONSUME

Doma

*El Salvador 4693, y Armenia, Palermo Soho
(4831 6852, www.doma-leather.com). Bus 15,
34, 39, 55, 110, 140, 151, 160, 168.* **Open**
10am-8pm Mon-Fri; 11am-8pm Sat; 1.30-8pm
Sun. **Credit** AmEx, MC, V. **Map** p283 M5.

If Kate Moss or Sienna Miller were in town and looking for a leather jacket, Doma is where they'd go to
find it. Forget shapeless old-school classics – this
brand is all about keeping up with the latest trends on
the street and has reinvented the biker jacket to make
it sexier than ever. Jackets comes in a range of colours,
from classic *dulce de leche* and charcoal to electric blue.
Much of the top-quality stock is made from velvety
soft sheep's leather. Pick up a vintage-style bag or a
pair of suede heels to complete the boho-chic look.
Other locations throughout the city.

Humawaca

*El Salvador 4692, y Armenia, Palermo Soho
(4832 2662, www.humawaca.com). Bus 55, 151,
168.* **Open** 11am-8pm Mon-Sat; 2-7pm Sun.
Credit AmEx, DC, MC, V. **Map** p283 M5.

At Humawaca, top-quality local leather is used to
create original bags, wallets and more in cool colour
combinations and quirky shapes. Function is just as
important as form: a chic leather and suede iPod
shoulder bag allows the user to manage his or her
music via controls on the bag's strap, fusing modern
technology with Humawaca's signature style.
Other location Posadas 1380, Recoleta
(4811 5995).

Milla

*Armenia 1532, entre Gorriti y Honduras, Palermo
Soho (4831 4447, www.millastore.com.ar). Bus
15, 39, 55.* **Open** 11am-8pm Mon-Sat; 2-8pm Sun.
Credit AmEx, MC, V. **Map** p283 M5.

Twin brother designers Diego and Sebastián
Smolkin have done the Argentinian leather industry
proud by creating quality jackets, bags, belts and
accessories. But what makes this collection shine are
the vibrant colours – turquoises, yellows and reds
which, along with punky extras such as studs and
zippers, give the leather staples a cool individuality.

Peter Kent

*Arenales 1210, y Libertad, Recoleta (4815 6581,
www.peterkent.com.ar). Bus 10, 17, 39, 60, 152.*
Open 10am-8pm Mon-Fri; 10am-2pm Sat.
Credit AmEx, MC, V. **Map** p286 I12.

Founded in 1972, Peter Kent is one of the city's best
luxury brands. Season after season the high-quality
bags, both practical and stylish, will accompany any
outfit, but you won't be able to resist splashing out
on new shades and styles. For a smaller slice of
designer luxury, snap up a purse, wallet, laptop bag
or passport holder.
Other locations Avenida Alvear 1820, Recoleta
(4804 7264); Paseo Alcorta shopping centre,
Palermo (4806 5442).

INSIDE TRACK
GRAND GALERÍAS

In the early 20th century, BA was quick to
copy the designs of monumental European
commercial centres. **Galerías Pacífico**
(*see p155*) is the oldest of these arcades
still standing (it's a copy of the Bon Marché
in Paris, which was finished in 1889), while
Pasaje Roverano (Avenida de Mayo 560)
and Milan-inspired **Galería Güemes**
(Florida 165) followed shortly after.

Prüne

*Florida 963, entre Paraguay y Marcelo
T de Alvear, Microcentro (4893 2641,
www.prune.com.ar). Subte C, San Martín/
bus 70, 91, 106.* **Open** 10am-8pm Mon-Sat;
11am-6pm Sun. **Credit** AmEx, MC, V.
Map p285 G11.

Well-established Argentinian brand Prüne is a popular destination for bag fans, and its selection of
styles ranges from handy holdalls to sparkly purses.
Studs, chains, animal prints and textured leathers
feature frequently in the collections, which also
include wallets, belts, footwear, jackets and coats.
Other locations throughout the city.

Rossi & Caruso

*Posadas 1387, entre Rodríguez Peña y
Montevideo, Recoleta (4811 1965,
www.rossicaruso.com). Bus 17, 60, 61, 62,
67, 92, 93, 100, 102, 110, 124, 130, 152.*
Open 9.30am-8pm Mon-Fri; 10am-6pm Sat.
Credit AmEx, DC, MC, V. **Map** p286 I11.

Rossi & Caruso has been fashioning leather goods
for more than six decades. It produces classic, elegant handbags, travel bags, men's and women's
leather jackets, wallets, footwear and notebooks, as
well as saddles and riding crops.
Other locations Recoleta Mall, store 212, Junín
y Uriburu, Recoleta (4806 1935); Galerías Pacifico
shopping centre, Microcentro (5555 5308).

Santesteban

*Galería Promenade, Avenida Alvear 1883,
entre Avenida Callao y Ayacucho (4800 1174,
www.santesteban.net). Bus 17, 67, 92, 93.*
Open 10am-8pm Mon-Fri; 10am-6pm Sat.
Credit AmEx, DC, MC, V. **Map** p286 I11.

If luxury and limited editions are your thing, this
shop should be at the top of your list. Beautifully
crafted handbags and women's footwear are offered
at Verónica Santesteban's store in the exclusive
Galería Promenade shopping arcade. The impressive range of exotic materials includes stingray and
crocodile skin, supple leather and the softest of furs,
with horn and precious stones used in detailing;
every piece is handmade by skilled artisans.

CONSUME

CONSUME

Pehache. *See p179.*

Comme Il Faut

Lingerie & swimwear

Coco Marie

Armenia 1764, entre El Salvador y Costa Rica, Palermo Soho (4832 3449, www.lovecoco marie.com). Bus 15, 39, 140, 160. **Open** 11am-8pm daily. **Credit** MC, V. **Map** p283 M5.
American designer Emily Weston set up shop in Palermo in 2010, with her fabulous collection of Brazilian-inspired bikinis on sale all year round. Finally, girls, here's a shop that makes us actually enjoy trying on swimwear. No more squirming in the changing room and feeling uncomfortable in your own (semi-naked) skin. These quality textiles are silky soft and make you feel – and look – damn fine. Patterns range from tropical and fun to classic and stylish. Billowy summer dresses and nightwear are also available and the French-style café out back offers a world of calm after the buzz of a Palermo shopping spree.

Luggage

Karpatos

Avenida Córdoba 834, entre Suipacha y Esmeralda, Microcentro (4328 3008, www.karpatos.com.ar). Subte C, San Martín/ bus 5, 111, 152. **Open** 9am-8pm Mon-Fri; 9.30am-2pm Sat. **Credit** AmEx, MC, V. **Map** p285 G11.
All your luggage needs can be easily met at this chain of stores. Karpatos's own products are sturdy and hardwearing. Padlocks are also stocked. **Other location** throughout the city.

Shoes

28 Sport

Gurruchaga 1481, entre Cabrera y Gorriti, Palermo Soho (4833 4287, www.28sport.com). Bus 93, 142. **Open** 11.30am-7pm Mon-Sat. **Credit** AmEx, MC, V. **Map** p283 M5.

Hand stitching, leather lining and reinforced toes are hallmarks of a well-made shoe and hark back to an era when footwear was made with durability in mind. And that's exactly the ethos of this Argentinian company, which bases its unisex designs on original sports footwear from the 1930s to the 1950s. The shoes are actually moulded from original hockey, hiking, climbing, football, boxing and bowling shoes. Unlike other brands with such a strong focus on quality and tradition, 28 Sport's products are decidedly unstuffy, and, better still, they are produced in limited editions. Get your hands on one of the extra-special pairs made only once, in just one size.

★ Comme Il Faut

Apartament M, Rue des Artisans, Arenales 1239, entre Libertad y Talcahuano, Recoleta (4815 5690) Bus 39, 111, 152. **Open** 11am-7pm Mon-Fri; 11am-3pm Sat. **Credit** MC, V. **Map** p285 H11.
Comme Il Faut offers beautifully made tango shoes for milongas and more. The technical part of the design makes the footwear ideal for even the most demanding dancer, and the aesthetic element ensures that these stunning shoes are coveted by both *tangueras* and footwear fans.

INSIDE TRACK
WAX ON, WAX OFF

We're not in Rio, but Buenos Aires inherited the love of smooth skin and multiplied it by ten. Legs, bikini line, armpits, face, back, and yes, even arse – in Argentina, the wax goes on, and on. Useful phrases include '*hasta ahí no mas*' ('thus far and no further') and '*no quiero que me hagas el culo, gracias*' (I don't want you to do my arse, thanks all the same').

CONSUME

Jackie Smith

Gurruchaga 1660, entre Honduras y El Salvador, Palermo Soho (4115 6820, www.jackiesmith. com). Bus 15, 55, 140, 168. **Open** 11am-8.30pm Mon-Sat; 1-7pm Sun. **Credit** AmEx, MC, V. **Map** p283 M5.

Plastic at the ready, ladies: these classic and feminine leather bags and shoes are too tempting to leave behind. The Bellini range with its glossy, black peep-toe heels and glamorous tote in Italian leather with a snakeskin effect is ideal for a Park Avenue princess. Timeless purses, shoulder bags, pumps and smart boots are great staples given a twist with textured leather and modern colour options.

Josefina Ferroni

Armenia 1687, entre Honduras y El Salvador, Palermo Soho (4831 4033, www.josefinaferroni. com.ar). Bus 39, 55. **Open** 11am-8pm Mon-Sat. **Credit** AmEx, DC, MC, V. **Map** p283 M5.

Ferroni's immaculately handcrafted boots and sophisticated shoes make her the queen of stylish footwear. Her irresistible designs come in lush colours and are made in limited editions.

★ Lucila Iotti

Malabia 2212, entre Paraguay y Charcas, Palermo Soho (4833 0206, www.lucilaiotti.com). Subte D, Scalabrini Ortiz/bus 29, 39, 152. **Open** 2-8pm Mon-Fri. **Credit** AmEx, MC, V. **Map** p283 M6.

This designer from a shoemaking family impressed *Sex and the City* stylist Patricia Field with her footwear, which includes dizzyingly high heels that combine colours and textures to stunning effect.

★ Mishka

El Salvador 4673, entre Malabia y Armenia, Palermo Soho (4833 6566, www.mishkashoes.com.ar). Bus 15, 57, 110. **Open** 10.30am-8.30pm Mon-Sat; 3-8pm Sun. **Credit** AmEx, MC, V. **Map** p283 M5.

Trends are given a retro slant at Mishka with footwear that appeals to everyone from teens and thirtysomethings to a more mature customer. With the design team's knack for combining femininity, comfort and quirkiness, this is the perfect place to pick up original, high-quality footwear.

Other locations Guido 1539, Recoleta (4816 4816); Patio Bullrich shopping centre, Recoleta (4814 7493); Paseo Alcorta shopping centre, Palermo (5777 6540).

Terán

Thames 1855, entre Costa Rica y Nicaragua, Palermo Soho (4831 7264, www.teranonline.com). Bus 34, 55, 93. **Open** noon-8.30pm daily. **Credit** AmEx, MC, V. **Map** p283 M5.

Expert artisans craft Gonzalo Terán's designs from top class materials including vegetable-tanned

---

INSIDE TRACK
FERIAS AMERICANAS

The local terminology for thrift store or second-hand shop, *ferias americanas* are found all over the city. Rummage through the mounds of bizarre cast-offs in the hope of unearthing that golden bargain item: persistence pays off.

---

leather and the softest suede. At the store Gonzalo himself is on hand to help you select anything from comfortable suede moccasins or rustic leather sandals to white patent lace-ups or lustrous Derby styles that will complement an elegant suit perfectly.

FOOD & DRINK

Drinks

0800-VINO

Anchorena 695, entre Lavalle y Zelaya, Abasto (4966 2500, www.0800-vino.com). Subte B, Carlos Gardel/bus 24, 26, 99, 124. **Open** 10am-6pm Mon-Fri. **Credit** AmEx, MC, V. **Map** p282 J5.

Friendly sommelier Nigel Tollerman offers a delivery service (orders in the city area are delivered within an hour), as well as hugely popular tailored tasting sessions that can include *picadas* (selections of cheeses and cold cuts) and wines that you won't be able to try anywhere else in town. For out-of-hours deliveries, Nigel can be reached on 15 5771 0259.

Lo de Joaquín Alberdi

Jorge Luis Borges 1772, entre El Salvador y Costa Rica, Palermo Soho (4832 5329, www.lodejoaquinalberdi.com). Bus 34, 55, 39, 140. **Open** 11am-9.30pm Mon-Sat; noon-9.30pm Sun. **Credit** AmEx, MC, V. **Map** p283 M5.

Step inside this attractive old house and let yourself be guided by the enthusiastic, well-informed staff through the wide range of wines. Boutique bodegas are especially well represented here – some of the names to look out for include Achaval Ferrer and De Angeles. Enquire about tasting sessions.

Siete Spirits

Nicaragua 5924, entre Arévalo y Ravignani, Palermo Hollywood (0800 777 47487/ www.sietespirits.com). Subte D/Ministro Carranza/bus 39, 93, 152, 168. **Open** noon-8pm Tue-Fri; noon-9pm Sat. **Credit** AmEx, MC, V. **Map** p283 O5.

Wines from all over the New World are stocked floor-to-ceiling in this snug little shop, but the speciality is Argentinian *tinto* (red) produced in small bodegas, from Patagonia to Salta and everywhere in between. If wine isn't your area of expertise, the knowledgeable, friendly staff will point you in the right direction, and discounts when you buy six or more bottles might have you upping your baggage allowance. If you want to try before you buy, the shop holds free weekly tastings on Thursdays between 6.30pm and 8.30pm.

General

Disco (Rodriguez Peña 1430, Recoleta) and **Coto** (Honduras 3862, Palermo) are some of the most common supermarkets, with branches in each barrio. They usually stay open until 10pm. Carrefour and the discount supermarket Dia are also easily found. There are minimarts on nearly every block in central areas.

Delis are becoming more common: an established city-wide chain with cold meats (*fiambres*) and cheeses is **Al Queso, Queso** at Uruguay 1276, Recoleta (4811 7113).

GIFTS & SOUVENIRS

Arandú
Ayacucho 1924, entre Avenida Alvear y Quintana (4800 1575, www.arandu.com.ar). Bus 10, 17, 59, 110, 124. **Open** 9.30am-8.30pm Tue-Sat; 10am-8pm Sun, Mon. **Credit** AmEx, MC, V. **Map** p286 J11.
Under Arandú's roof you'll find all you need to kit yourself out as a hard-bitten gaucho: the saddle, the riding boots, and, of course, the trusty maté gourd. It's a spot-on place for special, excellent quality gifts like beautifully engraved knives.
Other locations Talcahuano 949, Tribunales (4816 1281); Paraguay 1259, Tribunales (4816 3689).

Arte Étnico Argentino
El Salvador 4656, entre Armenia y Malabia, Palermo Soho (4832 0516, www.arteetnicoargentino.com). Bus 34, 55, 161. **Open** 11am-7pm Mon-Fri; 11am-2pm Sat. **Credit** AmEx, MC, V. **Map** p283 M5.
Beyond the pretty courtyard of this shop are a couple of rooms – one full of beautiful, bright textiles; the other full of an assortment of painted wardrobes, lovely leather and carob wood tables, colourful saint boxes made from recycled wood, and chairs hanging from the ceiling. The pieces, a mix of antiques and new designs, are all handmade by the Quichua-Santiagueño peoples of the relatively unvisited Santiago del Estero, in northern Argentina.

Elementos Argentinos
Gurruchaga 1881, entre Nicaragua y Costa Rica, Palermo Soho (4832 6229, www.elementosargentinos.com.ar). Bus 39, 93, 111, 161. **Open** 11am-7pm Mon-Sat. **Credit** AmEx, DC, MC, V. **Map** p283 M5.

This Palermo store with English-speaking staff stocks a selection of unique objects and attractive textile art. Handmade by craftspeople from the northern provinces of Argentina, the pieces range from blankets and cushions to toys and furniture. The traditional textiles sold here are made from sheep, alpaca and llama wool.

Pasión Argentina
Ground floor A, Scalabrini Ortiz 2330, entre Güemes y Charcas, Palermo Soho (4832 7993, www.pasion-argentina.com.ar). Subte D, Scalabrini Ortiz/bus 39, 111. **Open** 2-6pm Mon-Fri. **Credit** AmEx, MC, V. **Map** p286 L9.
Pasión Argentina was one of the first fair-trade companies in the country, and it remains one of the best. Launched after training women from Argentina's northern provinces in ethical, small-scale manufacturing, it now works with more than 50 families. Look out for the well-priced sling-style leather bags, smart totes and suede clutches in great colours. *Photo p179.*

Pueblo Indio
Defensa 869, entre Estados Unidos y Giuffra, San Telmo (4362 3860, www.puebloindio.com.ar). Bus 10, 22, 195. **Open** 10am-7pm daily. **Credit** AmEx, MC, V. **Map** p284 D10.
Pueblo Indio's handcrafted art makes for perfect gifts and one-of-a-kind memorabilia from your trip to BA. This little shop in the heart of San Telmo is full of affordable and tasteful home accoutrements, from leather tapestry to papier-mâché mosaic boxes and picture frames, all with an indigenous flavour.

Siete Spirits.

Autoría BsAs. *See p167.*

Shops & Services

HEALTH & BEAUTY
Hairdressers

Cerini
Marcelo T de Alvear 1471, entre Paraná y Uruguay, Recoleta (4813 3594, www. cerini.net). Bus 39, 102, 111, 152. **Open** 8am-10pm Mon-Sat. **Credit** AmEx, MC, V. **Map** p285 H10.
Cerini is a super-modern and incessantly bustling salon that offers good service. Colouring, roll-brush drying, trims, manicures and pedicures are done by professional stylists.

Javier Luna
1st Floor, Godoy Cruz 3212, entre J F Segui y Avenida del Libertador, Palermo (4772 5498, www.javierluna.com.ar). Bus 10, 34, 67. **Open** 10am-8pm Tue-Sat. **Credit** AmEx, V. **Map** p287 N10.
Javier Luna's chic salon, with its white leather couches and velvet curtains, is made for gals who know they're worth it. Luna's international career has taken him from BA to Paris, Milan, London and Berlin, and has seen him working his hairdressing magic on Cindy Crawford and Naomi Campbell.

Roho
Malabia 1931, entre Nicaragua y Soler, Palermo Soho (4833 7227, www.roho.com.ar). Bus 15, 34, 55, 57. **Open** 10am-9pm Tue-Fri; 10am-8pm Sat. **Credit** AmEx, MC, V. **Map** p283 M5.
Roho's Oscar Fernández is known for having tousled the tresses of local rock god Gustavo Cerati. The Palermo branch of this salon looks more like a club than a hairdresser's, with its fluorescent-lit interior and thumping soundtrack revealed once the heavy black door is opened.
Other location República de Indonesia 66, Caballito (4901 3292).

Opticians

If you need a prescription for glasses or contact lenses, you'll need to visit an eye doctor. Once you have the prescription, **Pförtner** (Avenida Pueyrredón 1706, Recoleta, 4827 8600, www. pfortner.com) distribute lenses and glasses. For hip eyewear try **Carla Di Sí** (*see p167*).

Pharmacies

FarmaCity
Florida 474, entre Avenida Corrientes y Lavalle, Microcentro (4322 6559, www.farmacity.com). Subte B, Florida/bus 10, 59, 111. **Open** 24hrs daily. **Credit** AmEx, DC, MC, V. **Map** p285 F11.
This mega-chain has plenty of well-stocked stores across the city. Most are open 24 hours and offer delivery services. Remember that some prescriptions cannot be fulfilled outside your home country.
Other locations throughout the city.

Spas & salons

Home Spa
Honduras 5860, entre Carranza y Ravignani, Palermo Hollywood (4778 1008, www.home buenosaires.com). Bus 39, 93, 111. **Open** 9am-8.30pm Mon-Fri; noon-8.30pm Sat. **Credit** AmEx, MC, V. **Map** p283 O5.
The spa at Home Hotel (*see p101*) is the perfect place to get pampered after a hard day's shopping. Open to guests and non-guests, the spa offers a range of treatments including Thai Shiatsu and hot-stone massages, and body treatments and facials using organic products. Enquire about the Jet Lag Recovery package, which includes a calming hydrotherapy bath followed by a glorious massage; then head to the hotel bar to unwind further.

Markus Day Spa
Ground floor, Avenida Callao 1046, entre Avenida Santa Fe y Marcelo T de Alvear, Barrio Norte (4811 0058, www.markus formen.com). Subte D, Callao/bus 10, 12, 152. **Open** 10.30am-10.30pm Mon-Sat; 10.30am-9pm Sun. **Credit** AmEx, MC, V. **Map** p286 I10.
Latin America's first integral spa exclusively for men, Markus has friendly staff and killer services, including a three-hour pampering package, Adore Me. There are also skin treatments, manicures, Botox, and a decent barbers'. You'll leave feeling a different man.

Queenies
Fitz Roy 1889, y Costa Rica, Palermo Hollywood (4899 0746, www.queeniesbuenosaires.com). Bus 34, 39, 57, 93, 108, 111, 166. **Open** 2-7.30pm Mon; 10.30am-7.30pm Tue-Sat. **Credit** AmEx, MC, V. **Map** p287 N8.
This luxurious nail parlour has pampering and quality down to a science – and selection galore. Come on girls, you don't have to sacrifice your favourite Chanel or OPI hue just because you're far from home. Pop in for an animal-print manicure or a classic French.

Spa Castelar
Avenida de Mayo 1152, entre Salta y Lima, Congreso (4381 4037, www.castelarhotel. com.ar). Bus 10, 39, 152. **Open** *Men* 10am-9pm Mon-Fri; 8am-7.30pm Sat. *Women* noon-9pm Mon-Fri; 11am-7.30pm Sat. **Credit** AmEx, MC, V. **Map** p285 F10.
A great value spa in the centre of the city, the Spa Castelar is open to non-guests and is divided into male and female sectors. Relax in the saunas or Turkish and Finnish baths, or try a stress-releasing and reasonably priced massage.

CONSUME

Shops & Services

Tattoos & piercings

Galería Bond Street
*Avenida Santa Fe 1670, entre Montevideo y
Rodríguez Peña, Recoleta. Subte D, Callao/bus
37, 39, 111, 152.* **Open** 11am-8pm Mon-Sat.
Credit varies. **Map** p286 I10.
A favourite with wannabe rebels, emo kids and
trendy twentysomethings, this grungy arcade is
home to everything from hip trainers and urban
wear to bondage gear. Lucky Seven and American
Tattoo, a favourite of Diego Maradona, are just two
of the many body art and piercing parlours.

HOUSE & HOME

Antiques

San Telmo – particularly *calle* Defensa
between *avenidas* Independencia and
San Juan – has the biggest concentration of
antiques dealers in the city. Plaza Dorrego is
the site of a large and popular antiques fair
on Sundays *(see below)*. **Gil Antigüedades**
(see p167) specialises in period clothing and
also stocks antiques.

Feria San Pedro Telmo
*Plaza Dorrego, y Defensa entre Avenida
Belgrano y Avenida San Juan, San Telmo
(www.feriadesantelmo.com). Bus 9, 10, 29,
195.* **Open** 10am-5pm Sun. **No credit cards**.
Map p284 D9.
Stroll down *calle* Defensa and its surrounding
streets on a Sunday, soak up the atmosphere, be
impressed by the busking talent and check out the
stalls selling antiques, handmade jewellery, tango

memorabilia, paintings, vintage clothing, leather
accessories and a host of other items.
▶ *At Defensa 961 is the covered Mercado de San
Telmo. Open from Tuesday to Sunday, it's a good
place for antiques as well as food items.*

Guevara Art Gallery
*Defensa 982, entre Carlos Calvo y Estados
Unidos, San Telmo (4362 7718, www.guevara
gallery.com). Bus 24, 29, 126, 130, 152.* **Open**
2-8pm Mon-Fri; 11am-6pm Sun. **Credit** AmEx,
MC, V. **Map** p284 D10.
The motherlode for lovers of art deco and art nouveau, this gallery has around 2,000 collector's items
from 1850 to 1930, including WMF German
tablewear and Daum and Lalique pieces.

HB Antigüedades
*Defensa 1016, entre Humberto Primo y
Carlos Calvo, San Telmo (4361 3325,
www.hbantiques.com). Bus 24, 29, 152.*
Open 10am-7pm Mon-Fri; 10am-5pm Sun.
Credit AmEx, MC, V. **Map** p284 D9.
Stepping into this vast antiques emporium is like
walking into a slightly over-furnished palace. It's
worth a look if only to take in the imposing centre-
piece, a pink Italian chandelier.

El Mercado de las Pulgas
*Avenida Dorrego, entre Avenida Álvarez
Thomas y Martínez, Colegiales (5382 6234).
Bus 140, 161, 168.* **Open** 10am-8pm Tue-Sun.
Credit varies. **Map** p287 O7.
This cluttered flea market focuses on antique
furniture and household items. Packed with atmos-
phere, it's a good alternative for vintage fans tired
of San Telmo.

Cualquier Verdura.

General

For one-stop designer shopping for the home, head to **Buenos Aires Design** (Avenida Pueyrredón y Avenida del Libertador, 5777 6000, www.designrecoleta.com.ar). Located next to the **Centro Cultural Recoleta** (*see p61*), the mall has numerous upmarket interior design shops as well as restaurants and cafés.

Coucou

Cap. Gral. Ramón Freire 1302, y Virrey Arredondo, Colegiales (4554 8776, www.mi coucoublogspot.com.ar). Bus 65, 140, 151, 168, 184. **Open** 11-7pm Mon-Sat. **Credit** AmEx, MC, V.

This shop is the place for chic presents. There are sweet home decor items like printed cushions, wall decals and Lola Goldstein's irresistibly cute ceramics; plus cool printed bags from the likes of VoulezVous and interesting accessories like hand-embroidered brooches and Soledad Kussrow's bird silhouette earrings.

★ Cualquier Verdura

Humberto 1° 517, entre Bolívar y Perú, San Telmo (4300 2474, www.cualquierverdura.com.ar). Bus 4, 9, 10, 17, 22, 24, 28, 29, 33, 45, 53, 86, 93, 126, 129. **Open** noon-8pm Thur-Sun. **Credit** AmEx, MC, V. **Map** p284 D9.

Like some fantastic white elephant stall, this unique shop unites the curious, the quirky and the downright kitsch. The differently coloured price tags are not randomly assigned, but indicate whether the product is new, locally made or a vintage find. There's even a category for pieces the owners are reluctant to see leave.

L'ago

Defensa 919 and Defensa 970, entre Estados Unidos y Carlos Calvo, San Telmo (4362 3641, www.lagosantelmo.com). Bus 24, 29, 152. **Open** 10am-8pm daily. **Credit** AmEx, MC, V. **Map** p284 D10.

L'ago's exquisite window displays, which brighten up both sides of *calle* Defensa, are enough to stop you in your tracks. Once inside, you can lose yourself willingly in a world of eclectorama, from original vintage furniture and lighting fixtures to creative toys and art and design by the cream of Argentinian artists and product designers.

Nobrand

Gorriti 5876, entre Carranza y Ravignani, Palermo Hollywood (4776 7288, www.nobrand.com.ar). Bus 93, 111, 161. **Open** noon-8pm Tue-Sun. **Credit** AmEx, MC, V. **Map** p283 O5.

This spacious locale isn't your typical souvenir shop: here you'll find a series of witty products featuring Argentinian icons like Che Guevara, Maradona, maté and *dulce de leche*. The T-shirts and the glass

Elementos Argentinos. *See p175.*

matés make for stylish, modern gifts or mementos, as does the book featuring the 75 local icons that form the core of the Nobrand project.

★ Pehache

Gurruchaga 1418, entre Cabrera y Gorriti, Palermo Soho (4832 4022, www.pehache.com). Bus 15, 34, 39, 55, 106, 140. 151, 168, **Open** 11am-8pm Mon-Sat. **Credit** AmEx, DC, MC, V. **Map** p283 M5.

Set in a renovated house in the heart of Palermo, Pehache (as in PH, which stands for *propriedad horizontal*) is one of those concept stores that even shopping phobes could spend hours in. Everything is for sale, including the chairs in the changing room and the paintings on the walls. All objects are by local designers and range from hand-painted penguin-shaped jugs to a stand-alone bath. *Photo p172.*

Specialist

Papelera Palermo

Cabrera 5227, entre Uriarte y Godoy Cruz, Palermo Soho (4833 3081, www.papelera palermo.com.ar). Bus 34, 39, 55, 108, 111, 140, 151, 166, 168. **Open** 10am-8pm Mon-Fri; 11am-8pm Sat. **Credit** AmEx, DC, MC, V. **Map** p283 M5.

With handmade paper in all shapes, sizes and textures, this super stationer is a joy to behold. An impressive array of design and art books is further inspiration to take up a craft, and if you do, Papelera offers workshops including bookbinding, printing, origami, caligraphy, paper making, drawing and painting, all at reasonable prices.

CONSUME

CONSUME

Sabater Hermanos

Gurruchaga 1821, entre Costa Rica y Nicaragua, Palermo Soho (4833 3004, www.shnos.com.ar). Bus 39, 55, 151. **Open** 10am-8pm Mon-Sat; 1-7pm Sun. **No credit cards. Map** p283 M5.
Run by the third generation of Sabater family soap makers, this funky shop/workshop is a soap version of a pick 'n' mix counter. Select from a huge range of smells and shapes, including plenty of whimsical options and coloured flakes, petals and hearts.

Wussmann

Rodríguez Peña 1399, y Juncal, Recoleta (4811 2444, www.wussmann.com). Bus 10, 37, 101, 124. **Open** 10.30am-2pm, 3-8pm Mon-Fri; 11am-2pm Sat. **Credit** AmEx, V. **Map** p286 I10.
Dedicated to providing *porteños* with the perfect paper, this exclusive stationer stocks beautiful leather journals, albums and handcrafted paper with ancient prints. Bookbinding and restoration services are also available.

MUSIC & ENTERTAINMENT

CDs, records & DVDs

Zivals

Avenida Callao 395, y Avenida Corrientes, Congreso (5128 7500, www.zivals.com). Subte B, Callao/bus 12, 24, 37, 60. **Open** 9.30am-9.30pm Mon-Sat. **Credit** AmEx, DC, MC, V. **Map** p285 H9.
The large selection of music at Zivals includes all genres, but classical, jazz, folk, tango and hard-to-find independent local recordings are a speciality.
Other location Serrano 1445, Palermo Soho (4833 7948).

Musical instruments

For all types of musical instruments, including native *bandoneones* and *charangos*, head downtown to *calle* Talcahuano, especially between Avenida Rivadavia and Avenida Corrientes. **Daiam** (Talcahuano 139, 4374 6510, www.daiammusica.com.ar) has a large selection.

SPORTS & FITNESS

La Martina

Paraguay 661, entre Florida y Maipú, Retiro (4576 7998, www.lamartina.com). Subte C, San Martin/bus 7, 10, 17, 152. **Open** 10am-8pm Mon-Fri; 10am-2pm Sat. **Credit** AmEx, DC, MC, V. **Map** p285 G11.
La Martina's flagship store feels like a polo museum, but it also has a collection of branded polo clothing and equipment, perfect for sporty types, preppy dressers or souvenir hunters.
Other locations throughout the city.

Wildlife

Hipólito Yrigoyen 1133, entre Salta y Lima, Congreso (4381 1040). Subte A, Lima/bus 29, 59, 86. **Open** 10am-8pm Mon-Fri; 10am-1pm Sat. **Credit** AmEx, DC, MC, V. **Map** p285 F9.
You can find camping, outdoor and extreme sports gear here, both brand new and second-hand. There's equipment for climbers, anglers, parachutists and more, and the store's expert staff are well equipped to guide you in all your purchases – and to fill you in on where to practise these outdoor pursuits.

TICKETS

Many music and sports venues, and especially clubs, are unlikely to accept credit cards at the door, so take cash. You can buy tickets in advance using major credit cards through **Ticketek** (5237 7200, www.ticketek.com.ar).

TRAVELLERS' NEEDS

Shipping goods to the UK, US and Europe can be a problem: **Correo Argentina** is not very reliable. For details of couriers, *see p256*. For computer repairs *see p159*. For luggage, *see p173*.
Below is a list of recommended travel agents and tour operators. Reliable concierge companies offering high-end services include **PlanBA** (4776 8267, www.planba.com), **Landing Pad BA** (www.landingpadba.com) and **BA Cultural Concierge** (www.ba culturalconcierge.com). For city tours *see p42* **Terrific Tours**.

Say Hueque

Office 1, 6th floor, Viamonte 749, entre Esmeralda y Maipú, Microcentro (5199 2517/ www.sayhueque.com). Subte C, Lavalle/bus 10, 17, 23, 24, 26, 45, 50, 59, 67, 70, 75, 99, 100, 101, 106, 108, 109, 111, 115. **Open** 10am-6.30pm Mon-Fri; 10am-1pm Sat. **Credit** AmEx, MC, V. **Map** p285 G11.
Say Hueque offers a range of trips for discerning travellers looking for chic accommodation and interesting, unique tours around Argentina and Chile.

Tangol

Unit 31, Ground floor, Florida 971, entre Paraguay y Marcelo T de Alvear, Microcentro (4363 6000/www.tangol.com). Subte C, San Martin/bus 10, 17, 20, 22, 23, 26, 28, 33, 45. **Open** 10am-7pm Mon-Fri. **Credit** AmEx, MC, V. **Map** p285 G11.
This innovative and highly professional travel and tour agency offers a variety of activities both in Buenos Aires and the rest of the country. These include city tours, football excursions, estancia visits and trips to Patagonia, Iguazú, Salta and Jujuy.
Other location Defensa 831, San Telmo.

Arts & Entertainment

Centro Cultural Borges. *See p45.*

Calendar

Whether it's food or fashion, there's always an excuse for a fiesta.

A packed cultural agenda combines with a Latin party spirit in Buenos Aires, meaning there's always something to celebrate in the Argentinian capital, from the **Exposición Rural** (*see p185*), when the cows come to town, to the annual gay pride parade (*see p183*). Details of events dedicated to film (*see p189*), art (*see p192*), music (*see p205*), performing arts (*see p218*) and tango (*see p229*) are given in their respective chapters.

The bilingual city government tourist website www.bue.gov.ar is a great starting point for information on local cultural events. Other useful resources include the hip www.whatsupbuenosaires.com, www.wipe.com.ar, www.argentinaindependent.com, Time Out BA's Facebook page and newspapers (*Página 12* on Thursdays, *Clarín* on Fridays, and the English-language *Buenos Aires Herald*).

SPRING

Expotrastiendas
Venue varies (www.expotrastiendas.com.ar).
Date early Sept.
Galleries and private collectors gather to showcase works by more than 500 artists, of all ages, working in a wide range of media, at this art fair, which attracts a large public attendance.

Feria Vinos y Bodegas
Predio La Rural, Avenida Santa Fe 4201, y Sarmiento, Palermo (4777 5500, www.expovinosybodegas.com.ar). Subte D, Plaza Italia/bus 10, 29, 39, 60, 152. **Map** p287 M9.
Date mid Sept.
Vineyards from around Argentina exhibit at this, the country's biggest wine fair, aimed at popularising home-grown brands. Grape connoisseurs can enjoy four glorious days of wine-swilling with over 1,000 different labels to sample, in addition to specialist tastings, seminars and master chef demonstrations on what dishes to best accompany your *vino* with.

Festival Internacional de Teatro Buenos Aires
Teatro San Martín and other venues (www.festivaldeteatroba.gov.ar).
Date every 2 years; next Sept 2013.
Going strong for over a decade, Buenos Aires's major contemporary performing arts festival is held every two years and promises audiences an impressive fortnight of Argentinian and international theatre, dance and performances.

Maratón de Buenos Aires
Throughout the city (www.maratondebuenos aires.com). **Date** Oct.
International and local runners flock to the capital to compete in this annual marathon. There is also a half marathon, which is usually held in September.

THE BEST ANNUAL EVENTS

Abierto Argentino de Polo
Champagne, cigars, celebrities...oh, and the world's best polo players battling it out on the Palermo polo field. *See p184.*

Festival y Mundial de Tango
Prepare to be dazzled and danced off your feet at this thrilling city-wide celebration of all things tango. *See p185.*

Feria de Vinos y Bodegas
Drink your way through Argentina's finest full-bodied reds and floral whites at this wine-lover's paradise. *See left.*

ARTS & ENTERTAINMENT

Marcha del Orgullo Gay

Plaza de Mayo (www.marchadelorgullo.org.ar).
Subte A, Plaza de Mayo or D, Catedral or E,
Bolívar/bus 24, 64, 86, 152. **Map** p285 E11.
Date early Nov.

BA's ever growing Gay Pride March gathers gays, lesbians, transexuals and heteros for a fun-filled parade through the city centre, followed by some serious partying in the city's nightclubs. It might not be as big as its Sydney or San Francisco counterparts, but it's definitely colourful. The fun continues in mid-to-late November when same-sex dancing is celebrated at the week-long **Festival Internacional de Tango Queer** (www.festivaltangoqueer.com.ar).

Creamfields

Venue varies (www.creamfieldsba.com).
Date Nov.

This one-day dance music festival has a relationship with rain similar to Glastonbury, but a bit of mud doesn't deter 60,000 party-loving dance fans from stepping out for 15 hours of non-stop raving when local and international DJs hit the decks. Check the website or Facebook page (www.facebook.com/creamfieldsba) for confirmation of dates and venues.

Día de la Tradición

Feria de Mataderos, Lisandro de la Torre y
Avenida de Los Corrales, Mataderos (www.
feriademataderos.com.ar). Bus 55, 80, 92,
126, 180. Also San Antonio de Areco, BA
province (www.sanantoniodeareco.com).
Date 10 Nov.

The town of San Antonio de Areco (*see p241*), 113km (70 miles) north-west of the capital is the place to be for this, the annual gaucho day, which is celebrated

INSIDE TRACK NAME THE DAY

In Argentina, important historical figures are commemorated with a *feriado* (public holiday), usually on the anniversary of their death. But dedicating days to humble workers or even inanimate objects and abstract ideas is also popular. Below are just a handful of days on which you can celebrate *something*:
7 April Día del Acoplado y Semirremolque (Trailer and Breakdown Trucks Day)
8 May Día Nacional de la Prevención Sísmica (National Day for the Prevention of Earthquakes)
20 July Día del Amigo (Friend's Day)
12 August Día del Jabonero (Day of the Soap Maker)

on the birthday of José Hernández, creator of the epic poem *Martín Fierro*. Regional food and music and displays of horsemanship are guaranteed. Visiting BA's Feria de Mataderos (*see p80*) on the weekend closest to this date is also recommended.

Gran Premio Nacional

Hipódromo Argentino de Palermo, Avenida del
Libertador 4101, y Dorrego, Palermo (4778
2880/www.palermo.com.ar). Bus 10, 36, 160.
Map p287 O10. **Date** mid Nov.

First run in 1884, Argentina's top annual horse race attracts both knowledgeable punters and social climbers. In recent years it's become a day-long event with plenty of track-side entertainment and celebrity

La Noche de los Museos. *See p184.*

ARTS & ENTERTAINMENT

Ciudad Emergente

Buenos Aires's international jazz festival sees artists from Europe and all over the Americas descend on the city to perform in various clubs, theatres and public spaces around town. Complementary activities include conferences and public interviews; and a massive jam session is held every night during the festival's duration.

SUMMER

Chinese New Year
Arribeños 2000-2200, Belgrano (Chinese Embassy 4547 8100, www.mibelgrano.com. ar/barriochino.htm). Bus 15, 29, 55, 60, 64.
Map p288 S9. **Date** Jan/Feb.
This day-long festival is an explosion of colour and clamour in Belgrano's tiny Chinatown, known locally as Barrio Chino. Local restaurants set up stalls on the streets and in the adjacent park (Barrancas de Belgrano) and dole out delicious dim sum to hungry festival-goers.

Aires Buenos Aires
Held at various locations throughout the city (www.airesbuenosaires.gob.ar). **Date** Jan-mid Feb.
The city government provides over 300 free events to help cope with the sticky summer heat, from rock concerts to outdoor tango milongas.

Carnaval
Throughout the city (www.buenosaires.gov.ar).
Date Feb.
Don't expect Rio – in Buenos Aires festivities are on a much smaller, but still enthusiastic scale, with groups of *murga* drummers performing in plazas and a parade down Avenida de Mayo. The best carnivals in the region are in the Uruguayan capital, Montevideo (*see p249*), or Gualeguaychú (pronounced Gwal-ay-gwah-CHOO) in Argentina's Entre Rios province.

Abierto de Tenis de Buenos Aires (Copa Claro)
Buenos Aires Lawn Tenis Club, Olleros 1510, y Libertador, Palermo (4772 0983, www.copaclaro.com). Bus 29, 59, 60.
Map p288 Q9. **Date** Feb.
Argentina's Tennis Open gives locals the rare opportunity to watch their own players slug it out on the city's premier clay courts.

Buenos Aires Fashion Week
Predio La Rural, Avenida Santa Fe 4201, y Sarmiento, Palermo (www.bafweek.com.ar). Subte D, Plaza Italia/bus 10, 29, 39, 60, 152.
Map p287 M9. **Date** Feb & Aug.
The latest trends from local designers grace the catwalk during Buenos Aires's twice-yearly fashion week; the winter collection is presented in February, the summer one in August. Pay AR$30 and get an introduction to Argentinian labels at the numerous

spotting. Dress appropriately – hats are not essential for ladies, but gentlemen should note that the jumper draped louchely over the shoulders is a must.

★ Campeonato Argentino Abierto de Polo
Campo Argentino de Polo, Avenida del Libertador y Dorrego, Palermo (Asociación Argentina de Polo 4777 6444, www.aapolo.com). Bus 10, 55, 64, 160. **Map** p287 O9. **Date** mid Nov-mid Dec.
Argentina has long been polo's spritual home, and has produced the world's top stars both on four legs and two. Held at Palermo's magnificent Campo Argentino de Polo, which can accommodate 30,000 spectators, the Argentinian Polo Open is without a doubt the sport's annual highlight.

La Noche de los Museos
Various venues (4313 4082, www.lanochede losmuseos.gob.ar). **Date** mid Nov.
A not-to-be-missed night on the town that sees the city's museums, galleries and cultural centres open their doors for free until the small hours. Live music, guided tours and dozens of special events attract crowds of all ages. *Photo p183.*

Festival Internacional Buenos Aires Jazz
Various venues (0800 333 7848/www. buenosairesjazz.gov.ar). **Date** late Nov.

showrooms. BAF Week, as it's known, is a very accessible way to find out what's going on with local fashion and to get a seat at a catwalk show.

AUTUMN

★ Buenos Aires Festival Internacional de Cine Independiente (BAFICI)

Hoyts Abasto & other venues (www.bafici.gov.ar). **Date** mid April.

This independent film festival is a hugely popular showcase for international non-Hollywood films and the work of local directors. It attracts big-name film-makers and high-profile actors usually seen only at the likes of the Cannes or Berlin film festivals, and is your best bet to check out flicks that wouldn't otherwise make it to BA.

▶ *For alternative film festivals featuring blood, gore and more, see p189.*

Feria Internacional del Libro

Predio La Rural, Avenida Santa Fe 4201, y Avenida Sarmiento, Palermo (www.el-libro. org.ar). Subte D, Plaza Italia/bus 10, 39, 60, 152. **Map** p287 M9. **Date** mid Apr-May.

The annual BA Book Fair is a monster three weeks of readings, book signings and debates, some of which are in English. Geared much more towards readers than publishers, the fair attracts bookworms as well as authors from all over the globe.

★ ArteBA

Predio La Rural, Avenida Santa Fe 4201, y Avenida Sarmiento, Palermo (www.arteba. com). Subte D, Plaza Italia/bus 10, 39, 60, 152. **Map** p287 M9. **Date** mid to late May.

National and international galleries, specialist publishers, artists and collectors (not to mention paying punters) descend on this week-long contemporary art fair, which has evolved into one of the best-attended and most-hyped cultural events in Latin America and provides a great opportunity to spot up-and-coming talent.

Aniversario de la Revolución de Mayo

Plaza de Mayo (Museo del Cabildo 4342 6729). Subte A, Plaza de Mayo or D, Catedral or E, Bolívar/bus 29, 64, 86, 152. **Map** p285 E11. **Date** 25 May.

The humble celebration of the 1810 revolution begins at midnight the day before, when people gather in front of the Cabildo for a lusty rendition of the (lengthy) national anthem. At 8pm on the 25th, crowds mass again for another patriotic singalong.

WINTER

★ Ciudad Emergente

Centro Cultural Recoleta, Junín 1930, Recoleta (www.ciudademergente.gob.ar). Bus 17, 62, 92, 93, 110. **Map** p286 J11. **Date** early June.

INSIDE TRACK MUSICAL METROPOLIS

BA is home to a host of hot music festivals. Besides **Creamfields** (*see p183*), keep an eye out for **Personal Fest** (www.personalfest.com.ar), **Pepsi Music** (www.pepsimundo.com) and **Quilmes Rock** (www.quilmes.com.ar).

Fresh local talent shines at this music festival with an indie vibe. There is also a focus on fashion, film and dance as well as digital and street art. The festival is a great chance to see up-and-coming bands, as well as more established acts; and even better, entrance is free.

Día de la Independencia

Across Argentina. **Date** 9 July.

Although the main events are held in freedom's birthplace in the north-western city of Tucumán, cafés along Avenida de Mayo serve up traditional hot chocolate with *churros* (deep-fried, doughnut-like delicacies) on this day and a solemn mass at the cathedral is attended by the president, who is forced to sit through a tongue-lashing homily delivered by the city's archbishop.

Exposición Rural

Predio La Rural, Avenida Santa Fe 4201, y Sarmiento, Palermo (www.exposicionrural.com. ar). Subte D, Plaza Italia/bus 10, 39, 60, 152. **Map** p287 M9. **Date** late July-early Aug.

The Exposición de Ganadería, Agricultura e Industria Internacional – known as the Exposición Rural – is the nation's supremely important two-week farm fair. Lambs, rams, pigs and other farm animals get a look-in, but it's the bulls who enjoy the most respect. The best events are the macho gaucho stunts, and this is the time of year when BA's *peñas* (folklore music venues; *see p211*) fill with genuine foot-stamping Argentinian cowboys.

★ Festival y Mundial de Tango

Various venues (0800 333 7848/www. tangobuenosaires.gob.ar). **Date** mid Aug.

This is the big one: it's the city's – and therefore the world's – most important tango festival, and includes over two weeks of concerts, shows, classes, exhibitions and milongas. It also includes the World Tango Championships with prequalifying stages, strict rules and an eagle-eyed jury (Simon Cowell has nothing on these guys) just a few of the hurdles awaiting those couples battling it out to be the world's best tango dancers. The prize money is small but the prestige is priceless, and those with two left feet can marvel at the leg flicking athleticism and passionate clinches on stage.

Children

Big fun for small people..

Far from being seen and not heard, Buenos Aires is a city where children are adored. With kids welcomed and well catered to in many restaurants, dining out isn't destined to mean 5pm feeds and mum and dad missing out on BA's gastronomic delights. There are a number of other evening activities for kids to enjoy too, such as night-time visits to the zoo; and witnessing even the tiniest of tots happily slurping ice-cream in the city's *heladerías* well after conventional bedtimes is a regular sight.

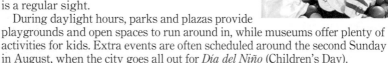

During daylight hours, parks and plazas provide playgrounds and open spaces to run around in, while museums offer plenty of activities for kids. Extra events are often scheduled around the second Sunday in August, when the city goes all out for *Día del Niño* (Children's Day).

PRACTICALITIES

Pushing a buggy along Buenos Aires's streets can be something of a challenge, with uneven pavements resembling obstacle courses. But, believe it or not, BA can be a child-friendly metropolis. *Porteños* are generally very receptive to children; doors are opened and bus seats readily relinquished for mum and child.

Early bedtimes appear unheard of, and you'll frequently see kids accompanying their parents to dinner well into the night. Most restaurants are more than happy to cater to children. At **Cumaná** (*see p123*) and **Las Cabras** (*see p130*) kids can draw on the paper tablecloths with crayons; and not far from Parque Las Heras, *parrilla* **La Payuca** (Arenales 3443, 4825 5959, www.lapayuca.com) has a supervised playarea complete with a ball pool. In Palermo, **Cante Prí** (Charcas 5216, 4777 7236, www.cantepri.com), which opens at weekends, is a bar designed specifically for children, and offers *meriendas* (afternoon snacks), shows, activities and a play space.

Although the larger chain hotels are usually better equipped for children's needs, apart-hotels make family holidays that much easier as they offer kitchenettes and extra beds. **Art Suites** (*see p107*) is a reliable option.

If you're at a loss for where to go to keep the kids busy, a good starting point is **Revista Planetario** (www.revistaplanetario.com.ar). The user-friendly website lists up-to-date information on children's events. Outdoor activities are organised by the city government during the summer, with many aimed at children. See www.bue.gov.ar for information.

OUTDOORS

Green spaces aren't as uncommon as you might think, and most parks have been revamped to attract families. **Parque Tres de Febrero** has a lake where paddle and rowing boats can be rented by the hour. Rollerblades and bicycles with child seats are also available for hire. Close by, the **Jardín Japonés** (*see p68*) has hide-and-seek-style gardens as well as mesmerising koi lurking in the pond.

Puerto Madero's **Reserva Ecológica** (*see p78*) is also a good option for fresh air. Made up of 865 acres of land, it is home to mammals, many species of birds, reptiles and butterflies. Free guided tours are given on Saturdays and Sundays at 9.30am and 4pm (Nov-March) and 10.30am and 3.30pm (April-Oct).

If you can manage a long bus ride or shelling out the taxi fare, **Feria de Mataderos** (*see p80*) is a lively weekend gaucho fair where you can watch traditional folk dancing, listen to live music and witness real gauchos displaying their horsemanship. But perhaps the most curious day out is a trip to **Tierra Santa** (*see p78*), a religious theme park where the story of Jesus is re-created in a laser light show.

For swimming pools and ideas for sporty kids, *see pp223-228* **Sport & Fitness**.

Jardín Zoológico de Buenos Aires
Avenidas Las Heras y Sarmiento, Palermo (4011 9900/www.zoobuenosaires.com.ar). Subte D, Plaza Italia/bus 15, 36, 37, 60, 152. **Open** 10am-6pm Tue-Sun. **Admission** AR$25-$40; free under-12s, reductions. **Credit** V. **Map** p287 M9.
All types of creatures are housed at BA's zoo, which features buildings that mimic the architecture of the animals' native countries. Note that this is a popular destination at weekends and can get extremely busy. *Photo p188.*

INDOORS

La Calle de los Títeres
Centro Cultural del Sur, Avenida Caseros 1750, y Baigorri, Constitución (4306 0301). Bus 6, 9, 25, 28. **Open** *Mar-Dec* puppet shows 3.30pm, 5pm Sat, Sun. **Map** p282 E7.
Free puppet shows and puppet-making classes keep kids engaged and occupied in the picturesque patio of this old mansion, where your child has a chance to interact with local youngsters.

Museo Argentino de Ciencias Naturales Bernardino Rivadavia
Avenida Ángel Gallardo 470, entre Warnes y Marechal, Caballito (4982 4494, www.macn.gov.ar). Subte B, Ángel Gallardo/bus 15, 55, 65, 105. **Open** 2-7pm daily. **Admission** AR$5; free under-6s. **No credit cards. Map** p282 L3.
This natural history museum is thrilling for kids who love dinosaurs. The star skeleton belongs to a carnotaurus – the 'bad guy' in Disney's *Dinosaur* movie. The museum also offers occasional workshops in topics such as palaeontology geared towards children.

★ Museo de los Niños
Level 2, Abasto de Buenos Aires, Corrientes 3247, entre Agüero y Anchorena, Abasto (4861 2325, www.museoabasto.org.ar). Subte B, Carlos Gardel/bus 24, 26, 124, 146, 168. **Open** 1-8pm Tue-Sun. **Admission** *Tue-Fri* AR$50 under-18s; AR$20 adults. *Sat, Sun & holidays* AR$55 under-18s; AR$20 adults. Free under-2s. **Credit** AmEx, DC, MC, V. **Map** p282 J5.
Housed in a large shopping mall, this play centre for active minds encourages kids to develop skills to

Museo Participativo de Ciencias.

impress and outdo grown-ups by trying out life in the worlds of builders, bankers, doctors or one of any number of other professions.
▶ *The centre also has a 12-screen cinema (see p190).*

Museo Participativo de Ciencias
1st Floor, Centro Cultural Recoleta, Junín 1930, y Quintana, Recoleta (4806 3456, www.mpc.org.ar). Bus 10, 17, 60, 92, 110. **Open** *Jan, Feb* 3.30-7.30pm Tue-Sun. *Mar-Dec* 10am-5pm Mon-Fri; 3.30-7.30pm Sat, Sun & holidays. **Admission** AR$25; free under-4s. **No credit cards. Map** p286 J11.
'Prohibido no tocar' (it's forbidden not to touch) is the appealing motto of this science museum in the Recoleta Cultural Centre, where children can investigate the mysteries of physics and have fun at the same time. Older kids can wander around the interesting exhibitions held at this great cultural space.

Planetario de la Ciudad de Buenos Aires Galileo Galilei
Parque Tres de Febrero, Belisario Roldán y Avenida Sarmiento, Palermo (4771 9393, www.planetario.gov.ar). Subte D, Plaza Italia/bus 37, 67, 152, 160. **Open** *Museum* 10.30am-6pm Mon-Fri; 1-7.30pm Sat, Sun. *Shows* 3pm, 4.30pm, 6pm Sat, Sun. **Admission** *Museum* free. *Shows* AR$20; free under-5s, reductions. **No credit cards. Map** p287 M11.
Although the talks here are given in Spanish, kids will be fascinated with the solar system spectacle; and for added appeal this planetarium is in the

INSIDE TRACK SCREEN TIME

BA's cinemas often screen the original versions of children's films. Try the **Atlas**, **Cinemark** or **Hoyts** chains (*see p190*), and look for showings that are *subtitulada* (subtitled) rather than *doblada* (dubbed).

ARTS & ENTERTAINMENT

shape of a spaceship. On Saturday and Sunday nights, weather conditions permitting, the public can test out telescopes for free.

OUTSIDE BUENOS AIRES

Outside the Capital Federal, estancias (*see p243*) are an excellent way to tire out children with healthy outdoor fun. **Tigre** (*see p236*) is another good option: a short train ride can get you to a Jurassic-looking world of streams and swampy islands that can be explored by boat. See our **Escapes & Excursions** section (*pp235-252*) for more inspiration.

La Granja Chocolatada
Panamericana km48, entre El Memorial y el Sheraton Hotel, Pilar (0230 4644118, www. granja-chocolatada.com). Bus 57 Atlántida Pilar Express from Plaza Italia. **Open** 11.30am-5.30pm Sat, Sun & holidays. **Admission** AR$45. **No credit cards.**
The visit is entirely in Spanish, but if you're up to the trip (about an hour from BA), this farm hosts activities designed so that kids can experience the countryside in a thoroughly enjoyable way. Bread-making, animal petting and games are all included in the visit.

Parque de la Costa
Vivanco 1509, y Mitre, Tigre (4002 6000, www.parquedelacosta.com.ar). Tren de la Costa to Delta/bus 60. **Open** *Mar-Dec* 11am-7pm Fri-Sun; *Jan, Feb* 11am-8pm Tue-Sun. **Admission** AR$30-$100; free under-3s. **Credit** AmEx, DC, MC, V.

Next to the Delta train station in Tigre is a substantially sized amusement park (to find it just follow the screams of excitement). Rides, roller coasters, themed restaurants and a lake show should be enough to keep everyone happy during an action-packed day.

★ Parque Temaikén
Ruta Provincial 25, km 1, Escobar (03484 436900/www.temaiken.com.ar). Bus 60 from Plaza Italia. **Open** *Dec-Feb* 10am-7pm Tue-Sun. *Mar-Nov* 10am-6pm Tue-Sun. **Admission** AR$85; AR$66 reductions; free under 2s; Tue half price. **Credit** AmEx, DC, MC, V.
This wonderful wildlife park is just 30 minutes from downtown Buenos Aires. Among the land mammals that roam its vast expanses are white tigers and pumas. In the aquarium, sharks, stingrays and other fish swim around in an overhead tank.

Tren de la Costa
Avenida Maipú 2305, Olivos (4002 6000). From Retiro, Ramal 2 train on Mitre line to Olivos/bus 59, 60, 71, 152. **Open** 6.50am-8.30pm Mon-Fri; 8am-9.30pm Sat, Sun. **Return ticket** AR$40 non-residents; AR$20 residents; free under-3s. **Credit** V, MC.
On this 25-minute train ride from Olivos to Tigre, you can get on and off at stations along the route, where there are cinemas, restaurants and shops. San Isidro station has the most options, including an arts fair on Saturdays and Sundays from 10am to 9pm (www.artesanos-sanisidro.com.ar). Pack some sandwiches for a picnic or better yet, swimming costumes, and splash about at Perú Beach (*see p228*) where there's kayaking and windsurfing.

Jardín Zoológico de Buenos Aires. *See p187.*

Film

See the big picture in this city of avid filmgoers.

Buenos Aires has a thriving film scene, with venues ranging from shopping centre multiplexes to bijou microcinemas. Plenty of independent cinemas show foreign art-house as well as home-grown fare. Everyone else can munch popcorn in front of the latest Hollywood blockbusters, most of which are screened with subtitles.

The highlight of the annual film calendar is the **Buenos Aires Festival Internacional de Cine Independiente** (BAFICI), which pulls in a quarter of a million cinephiles every April with its multifarious programme of independent local and international flicks. Directors frequently shoot in and around BA, so you've a fair chance of seeing something being filmed as you walk the city's streets.

FESTIVALS

For proof of the *porteño* passion for cinema, look no further than the booming **Buenos Aires Festival Internacional de Cine Independiente**, known as BAFICI (*see p185*), which takes place in April. For ten days of cinematic frenzy, the Hoyts Abasto multiplex and other city centre venues show around 400 films from the most diverse reaches of the indie scene around the world. There's a fierce official competition and screenings of bizarre cinema. Not to be outdone, the coastal city of Mar del Plata throws its own annual bash in November or December, the **Festival Internacional de Cine de Mar del Plata** (www.mardel platafilmfest.com). As well as showcasing a variety of international flicks, the festival focuses on new movements in Latin American cinema, and takes a look at the particular issues facing local directors and screenwriters in a series of talks by industry insiders from all over the continent.

Alternative festivals include **Cine Francés** (http://cine-frances.com) held in March, the human rights-focused **Festival Internacional de Cine de Derechos Humanos** (www. imd.org.ar/festival) in late May, and the **Green Film Fest** (www.greenfilmfest.com.ar), held in late August. Fans of independent horror films should keep an eye out for the **Buenos Aires Rojo Sangre** festival (http://rojosangre.quinta dimension.com), held, appropriately enough, in late October.

CINEMAS

Rather rundown downtown cinemas are located on Avenida Corrientes and *calle* Lavalle. These days, new multiplexes in the suburbs attract most of the audiences: the Hoyts complex at the **Dot Baires** (www.dotshopping.com.ar) shopping centre in Saavedra is a popular option and includes two 'premium class' theatres, where you can sit back in enormous, comfortable seats and order gourmet food and drink throughout the screening; while the **IMAX Theatre Showcase** (Esteban Echeverría 3750, Vicente López, 4756 7887, www.todoshowcase.com) can be found in the Norcenter complex close to massive shopping mall **Unicenter** (*see p82*). Smaller cinemas are fading at an alarming rate, but a number of cultural centres host regular *ciclos* (series) of specialist and art-house flicks. In the summer, open-air screenings are held at places like the Rosedal in Palermo (*see p68*).

INFORMATION, TIMINGS AND TICKETS

Nearly all films are shown in their original version with Spanish subtitles. Children's films are the only exception, and are generally dubbed into Spanish, but even original versions of these are shown at selected venues. Some cinemas have late-night showings (*trasnoches*) beginning around 1am, usually on weekends only. Tickets cost less from Mondays to Wednesdays and during the day.

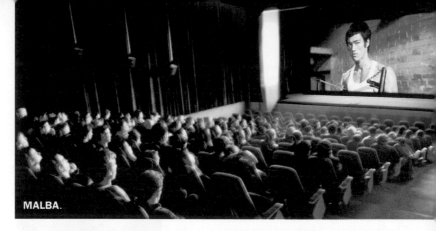

MALBA.

Check the *Espectáculos* sections of local papers or www.cinesargentinos.com.ar for cinema listings. The *Buenos Aires Herald* has English-language listings. The website www.cinenacional.com is a superb Spanish-language resource on Argentinian cinema. Argentina has four different rating categories: ATP (suitable for all ages); SAM13 (under-13s only if accompanied by an adult); SAM16 (no under-16s); and SAM18 (no under-18s).

★ Espacio INCAA KM 0 – Gaumont Rivadavia
Avenida Rivadavia 1635, entre Rodríguez Peña y Montevideo, Congreso (4382 0003, http://espacios.incaa.gov.ar). Subte A, Congreso/ bus 12, 37, 102, 151. **Open** 12.30pm-midnight daily. **Tickets** AR\$8; AR\$4-\$6 reductions. **No credit cards. Map** p285 G9.
This charming and cheap three-screen cinema is supported by INCAA (the National Film Board). It's an ideal venue for catching showings of new Argentinian releases (with no English subtitles).

Lorca
Avenida Corrientes 1428, entre Paraná y Uruguay, Tribunales (4371 5017). Subte B, Uruguay/bus 24, 26, 102. **Open** 1.30-11pm daily. **Tickets** AR\$22 Mon-Wed; AR\$30 Thur-Sun. **No credit cards. Map** p285 G10.
One of Avenida Corrientes's traditional cinemas, Lorca is one of BA's best options for independent film, and shows an excellent selection of local and foreign non-mainstream movies on its two screens.

Multiplexes

Arteplex
Diagonal Norte 1150/56, Microcentro (4382 7934, www.cinesarteplex.com). Subte D, 9 de Julio/bus 10, 17, 140. **Open** from 1pm daily. **Tickets** AR\$35 Thur-Sun; AR\$25 Mon-Wed; AR\$25 reductions. **No credit cards. Map** p285 G10.

Arteplex screens local films and some of Hollywood's more inventive offerings.
Other location Cuenca 3035, Villa del Parque (4505 8074).

Atlas Patio Bullrich
Avenida del Libertador 750, entre Montevideo y Libertad, Recoleta (4814 7447, www.atlascines. com.ar). Bus 67, 92, 102. **Open** from noon daily. **Tickets** AR\$38 Thur-Tue; AR\$28 Wed. **Credit** AmEx, MC, V. **Map** p286 I12.
After you've stocked up on imported designer gear at the city's most exclusive mall, take a break to watch the latest Hollywood blockbusters. If it's well known enough, the occasional locally made flick also gets a chance to impress audiences here.

Cinemark 8
Alicia Moreau de Justo 1920, y San Juan, Puerto Madero (0800 222 2463, www.cinemark.com.ar). Bus 4, 64, 130, 152. **Open** from noon daily. **Tickets** AR\$38 after 4pm; AR\$27 Mon-Wed, before 4pm Thur-Sun, under-12s and over-65s, reductions, under-2s free. **Credit** AmEx, MC, V. **Map** p284 D10.
This modern complex down in the docklands has eight screens and a restaurant. It shows a mixture of Hollywood and Latin American new releases. Another branch, with ten screens, is conveniently located near the Alto Palermo shopping centre.
Other locations Beruti 3399, Palermo (0800 222 2463) and throughout the city.

★ Hoyts Abasto Buenos Aires
Abasto de Buenos Aires shopping centre, Avenida Corrientes 3247, entre Agüero y Anchorena, Abasto (0810 1224 6987, www.hoyts.com.ar). Subte B, Carlos Gardel/bus 24, 26, 124, 146, 168. **Open** from 10am daily. **Tickets** AR\$38; AR\$28 reductions; AR\$19 Wed. **Credit** AmEx, MC, V. **Map** p286 J8.
One of the best of the multiplexes, Hoyts Abasto has something of a split personality. During most of the year it shows Hollywood movies, but every April it

mutates into an art-house venue during BA's excellent BAFICI independent film festival (*see p185*).
Other location Dot Baires Shopping, Vedia 3626, Saavedra (0810 1224 6987).

Repertory & art-house venues

With ticket prices rising at conventional cinemas, a number of alternative venues and cultural centres give film-lovers the chance to catch a flick on the cheap and generally in quirky surroundings. The **MALBA** (*see p69*) hosts excellent cinema events: new indie releases, retrospectives with restored 35mm prints and lectures by actors and filmmakers. The **Teatro Nacional Cervantes** (*see p219*) is noteworthy for its cycle of classic Argentinian cinema, shown free on Wednesdays and Thursdays at 5pm. **Club Cultural Matienzo** (Matienzo 2424, Colegiales, www.clubculturalmatienzo.blogspot. com.ar) shows independent Argentinian films every Wednesday at 9pm (AR$10); in summer the screenings are on the terrace. If you're homesick for some British humour, try the **British Arts Centre** (*see p48*), which screens movies focused on British culture. Classic sitcoms such as *Fawlty Towers* and *Blackadder* are sometimes shown. Opening and screening times can vary, so make sure to call ahead or check websites beforehand.

Alianza Francesa de Buenos Aires
Avenida Córdoba 946, entre Suipacha y Carlos Pellegrini, Microcentro (4322 0068, www. alianzafrancesa.org.ar). Subte C, Lavalle/bus 59, 99, 106. **Open** Varies by month; call ahead. **Tickets** free. **Map** p285 G11.
The respected French-language institution doubles up as a prestigious cultural centre, offering riveting cycles of international cinema in its refined and comfortable auditorium.

Buenos Aires Mon Amour
Reserve online, location given on booking. (mobile 15 5507 2733, www.cineclubmonamour. com). Bus 10, 17, 29, 152. **Open** from 7pm Thur-Sun. **Tickets** AR$25.
This back-room 38-seater shows independent films and is run as a non-profit venture by a pair of local film-lovers. Discussions follow screenings, and film courses and workshops are also offered. The owners also operate a microcinema with a concurrent programme at the hotel Elevage (Maipú 960, Retiro, www.elevage.com.ar).

Centro Cultural Ricardo Rojas
Avenida Corrientes 2038, entre Junín y Ayacucho, Once (4954 5521, www.rojas.uba.ar). Subte B, Callao/bus 24, 26, 60, 124. **Tickets** free. **No credit cards. Map** p285 H9.

This lively cultural centre shows interesting cycles of art-house and experimental films in its large theatre and, best of all, entrance is free. Numerous film-related courses are also offered at the centre.

Cine Club Eco
2nd Floor, Avenida Corrientes 4940, entre Lavalleja y Julián Álvarez, Almagro (4854 4126). Subte B, Malabia/bus 36, 92. **Open** 8pm Sat; 7pm Sun; call ahead. **Tickets** AR$30. **No credit cards. Map** p282 L3.
If Bergman and Polanski retrospectives get your pulse racing, get your arty self down to Cine Club Eco. More obscure films are often shown, and the entrance price includes an invitation to a short post-screening coffee to discuss the movie. Now that's what we call a bargain.
▶ *For a post-film cocktail, stroll ten blocks to cool Villa Crespo bar 878; see p153.*

Sala Leopoldo Lugones
10th Floor, Avenida Corrientes 1530, entre Paraná y Montevideo, Tribunales (4371 0111, www.teatrosanmartin.com.ar). Subte B, Uruguay/bus 24, 26, 60, 102. **Tickets** AR$15. **No credit cards. Map** p285 G9.
Named after the Argentinian poet and cultural icon Leopoldo Lugones, this cinema is located within the San Martín theatre complex, and mostly screens leftfield and hard-to-find art-house movies from all over the world, as well as many national affairs. This is the place to check out first if you're into unconventional films and documentaries.

INSIDE TRACK
OSCAR WINNERS

Argentina has twice found Oscar glory with the golden statuette for Best Foreign Language Film. The first occasion was in 1985, for Luis Puenzo's drama *La historia oficial* (The Official Story), set during the dark years of Argentina's brutal military dictatorship. The film tells the story of a middle-class woman forced to face up to the fact that her adopted daughter had been taken from a couple held in detention. It was to be another 25 years before Argentina had its second Oscar win, and there was much jubilation in 2010 when thriller *El secreto de sus ojos* (The Secret In Their Eyes, *see p266*), set in the paranoid pre-dictatorship 1970s, was victorious. The win propelled the country's cinematic dream team, actor Ricardo Darín and director Juan José Campanella, into the international spotlight.

ARTS & ENTERTAINMENT

Galleries

It's always a fine time for art in Buenos Aires.

Buenos Aires may not be on the major art exhibition circuit, but what it lacks in geographical proximity or economic nous, it more than makes up for in ingenuity.

The 2001 economic crash ushered in an era of activism and DIY creativity, taking art beyond the realm of the stuffy gallery. More than a decade on, the creative juices of the city's artists continue to bubble over with an energy that's both chaotic and contagious: blink-and-you-miss-it spaces continue to spring up in private living rooms and abandoned factories, and the street art scene is booming.

Argentinian and international masters have their place in BA too, and must-see major institutions include **MALBA** (*see p69*) and **Fundación Proa** (*see p56*). Cultural centres like the **Centro Cultural Borges** (*see p45*) and **Centro Cultural Recoleta** (*see p61*) also often have excellent exhibitions of art and photography.

GALLERIES

Highbrow galleries tend to be clustered in and around Retiro and Recoleta, with Palermo and San Telmo – traditionally home to more experimental art – now competing with the established art zones. Many of BA's best major non-commercial galleries and art museums, such as **MALBA** (*see p69*), the **Museo Nacional de Bellas Artes** (*see p65*) and the **Museo Nacional de Arte Decorativo** (*see p65*), are also located in these neighbourhoods. Other spots include La Boca's **Fundación Proa** (*see p56*), San Telmo's **MAMbA** (*see p52*), Puerto Madero's **Colección de Arte Amalia Lacroze de Fortabat** (*see p77*) and the **Faena Arts Centre** (*see p78*).

Events to keep an eye out for include the annual **La Noche de los Museos** (Night of the Museums) as well as the regular **Gallery Nights** (www.gallery-nights.com.ar) programme, when dozens of neighbourhood galleries open their doors (not to mention bottles of bubbly) to the public. Also on the agenda are the art fairs **Expo Trastiendas** (*see p182*) and **ArteBA** (*see p185*). The latter is the city's major contemporary art fair and has evolved into one of the best-attended cultural events in Latin America, attracting more than 100,000 buyers and enthusiasts.

For an introduction to the local art scene, **BA Local** (www.balocal.com) offers tailored tours to traditional and contemporary art galleries, and on the **Artists' Atelier Tour** (www.arttour.com.ar) you can visit artists at work in their own spaces. Or for a street-side insider's look at the innovative graffiti scene, take a tour of side streets, tunnels and artists' studios with **Graffitimundo** (www.graffitimundo.com).

For up-to-date information on artists, galleries and other exhibition spaces, check the well-organised www.mapadelasartes.com.

Centre

Arroyo

Arroyo 830, entre Suipacha y Esmeralda, Retiro (4325 0947/www.galarroyo.com). Subte C, San Martín/bus 17, 59, 67, 92. **Open** 11am-8pm Mon-Fri. **No credit cards**. **Map** p285 H12. Located close to Plaza San Martín, Arroyo's real strong point is its monthly auctions. The gallery offers a wide range of relatively affordable works by renowned local and international artists.

Galería Alberto Sendrós

Pasaje Tres Sargentos 359, entre San Martín y Reconquista, Retiro (4312 0995, www.alberto sendros.com). Bus 28, 106, 129, 130, 152. **Open** 2-8pm Mon-Fri. **No credit cards**. **Map** p285 G11.

Alberto Sendrós provides a dose of young, wacky energy in the bustling Retiro neighbourhood. The quirky nature of the exhibitions makes the space sometimes resemble an archaeological excavation site or a mad scientist's laboratory. The thoughtfully curated gallery promotes emerging artists, who work in various media.

Ignacio Liprandi Arte Contemporáneo
Level 3, Avenida de Mayo 1480, entre Uruguay y Paraná, Congreso (4381 0679, www. ignacioliprandi.com). Subte A Sáenz Peña/bus 2, 5, 6, 7, 86, 129, 151, 168. **Open** 11am-8pm Mon-Fri. **No credit cards. Map** p285 F9.
Argentinian collector Ignacio Liprandi has his finger firmly on the pulse of cutting-edge local and Latin American conceptual art, plucking stars from the likes of London's Tate Modern and New York's MoMA to show in his third-floor gallery with head-on views of the Congreso building. Rotating exhibitions have a multimedia bent, showcasing some of the most talked-about – and controversial – artists on the circuit.

★ Ruth Benzacar
Florida 1000, y Marcelo T de Alvear, Retiro (4313 8480, www.ruthbenzacar.com). Subte C, San Martín/bus 10, 17, 132, 152. **Open** 11.30am-8pm Mon-Fri. Closed Feb. **No credit cards. Map** p285 G11.

Founded in 1965 by Ruth Benzacar and now run by her daughter Orly, this is one of the most highly regarded art galleries in town and is a regular fixture at the annual Art Basel and Art Basel Miami Beach fairs. Though the bulk of the gallery's work happens elsewhere these days, an afternoon spent trawling around the *calle* Florida basement space is a surefire way to take in some of the best art currently being produced in BA.

South of the Centre

713 Arte Contemporáneo
Defensa 713, entre Chile e Independencia, San Telmo (1362 7331, www.arte713.com). **Open** 2-8pm Mon-Fri; 2-6pm Sat. **Credit** AmEx, V. **Map** p285 E10.
Collage, photography, installation, video and painting: gallery directors Julia Grosso and Martín Cortés are open to any medium, as long as the result is experimental. Their strong roster of Argentinian and Brazilian artists has seen the gallery shine at both ArteBA and Mexico's Zona Maco art fairs.

Popa
Lamadrid 882, entre Garibaldi y Carlos F Melo, La Boca (4302 7244, www.galeriapopa.com.ar). Bus 24, 29, 64, 70. **Open** 2-8pm Thur-Sat, or by appointment. **No credit cards. Map** p285 E10.

Tec at **Gachi Prieto**. See p195.

A hedonistic, sexually ambiguous energy pervades this gallery just beyond the Caminito tourist strip. Director Marcelo Bosco likes his art out, loud and proud, and the mixed-media works run the gamut from the sublime to the shocking. Exhibition openings here are schmoozy affairs, with the eccentric crowd draping artistically over vintage chairs in the garden, sipping on cocktails.

Zavaleta Lab

Venezuela 571, entre Bolívar y Perú, San Telmo (4342 9293, www.zavaletalab.com). Bus 9, 10, 24, 29, 86. **Open** 11am-8pm Mon-Fri. **No credit cards. Map** p285 E10.

When art impresario Hernán Zavaleta put down roots on *calle* Venezuela, he bridged the gap between the area's flashy, contemporary hotspots and their downright dusty older counterparts, projecting the neighbourhood into the ranks of the bona fide art districts in the process. The sheer size of the back room (downstairs and open for browsing) ensures a consistent turnout of solid exhibitions by both up-and-comers and local art darlings, among them Mariano Ferrante.

North of the Centre

Bacano

Armenia 1544, entre Honduras y Gorriti, Palermo Soho (4831 3564, www.bacano.com.ar). Bus 39, 55, 111. **Open** 10am-8pm Mon-Fri; 11am-6pm Sat. **Credit** AmEx, MC, V. **Map** p283 M5.

This hip art and design gallery is located within an attractive 19th-century house in Palermo. Handsome wood furniture and recycled objects, alongside contemporary art created by well-known painters and sculptors on the BA scene, are offered.

★ Braga Menéndez Arte Contemporáneo

Humboldt 1574, entre Cabrera y Gorriti, Palermo Hollywood (4775 5577, www.galeriabm.com). Bus 93, 140. **Open** 1-8pm Tue-Sat. Closed Jan, Feb. **No credit cards. Map** p283 N5.

Proudly independent, this slick Palermo space houses contemporary works by artists who, in the words of founder Florencia Braga Menéndez, are 'from way down south'. Uniting the core group of artists is a scornful contempt for the phony modishness that trend-defining tags such as 'Latin American art' are often freighted with.

★ Daniel Abate

Pasaje Bollini 2170, entre French y Peña, Recoleta (4804 8247, www.danielabategaleria. com.ar). Bus 10, 21, 37. **Open** 11am-5pm Mon-Fri. Closed Jan. **Credit** AmEx. **Map** p286 K10.

A repeated winner of the coveted best exhibitor prize at the prestigious ArteBA fair, this surprisingly compact gallery – situated in a house along a lovely lane in Recoleta – is considered one of the best nurseries

for young and original Argentinian artistic talent in a variety of media. Dashing owner Daniel Abate has, among his many other feats, taught Buenos Aires that contemporary art can be red-carpet glam.

Daniel Maman Fine Arts

Avenida del Libertador 2475, entre Bulnes y Ruggieri, Palermo (4804 3700, www.daniel maman.com). Bus 10, 37, 59, 60, 102. **Open** 11.30am-8pm Mon-Fri; 11.30am-2pm Sat. **No credit cards. Map** p286 L10.

New work rubs shoulders with pieces by renowned Argentinian stars including Xul Solar, Guillermo Kuitca and Antonio Berni at Daniel Maman, whose openings always attract a chic and good-looking crowd. The gallery's uncanny flair for selecting talented and charismatic artists means its influential shows always make the headlines, and more often than not kick-start successful careers.

Elsi del Río

Humboldt 1510, entre Cabrera y Gorriti, Palermo Hollywood (4899 0171, www.elsidelrio.com.ar). Bus 108, 140, 151. **Open** 2-8pm Tue-Fri; 11am-3pm Sat. **No credit cards. Map** p287 L10.

This spirited contemporary space is smack bang in the nucleus of Palermo's trendy art scene. The cast of characters under director Fernando Entin include portrait photographer Gaby Messina and collage artist José Luis Anzizar. *Photo p199.*

Gachi Prieto

Uriarte 1976, entre Soler y Nicaragua, Palermo Soho (4774 6961, www.gachiprietogallery.com). Bus 34, 39, 55. **Open** 1-8pm Tue-Fri; noon-6pm Sat. Closed Jan. **Credit** AmEx. **Map** p287 M8.

This was one of the first galleries in Argentina to show street art in a commercial setting, and boundary-busting director Gachi Prieto continues to keep the art scene guessing with her roll call of 24 (mostly local) names, many of whom are setting tongues wagging on the international circuit. The graffitied car parked outside sets the decidedly unstuffy tone, and you can expect to find everything from erotic pop art to socially incisive photography. *Photo p193.*

ARTS & ENTERTAINMENT

EXPLORE FROM THE INSIDE OUT
Time Out Guides written by local experts

Covering 50 destinations, our city guides are
written from a unique insider's perspective by
teams of local writers.

visit timeout.com/shop

Galería Foster Catena

1st Floor, Honduras 4882, entre Armenia y
Gurruchaga, Palermo Soho (4833 9499,
www.fostercatena.com). Bus 39, 55. **Open**
1-7.30pm Tue-Sat. **No credit cards.**
Map p287 M7.
As director of one of BA's few photography-centric
spaces, curator Guadalupe Chirotarrab is committed
to promoting talented snappers, of which the country boasts not a few. The hip upstairs space sits on
a much-transited Palermo block and attracts a
sophisticated, see-and-be-seen crowd.

Galería Isabel Anchorena

Libertad 1389, entre Juncal y Arroyo,
Recoleta (4811 5335,
www.galeriaisabelanchorena.sion.com). Bus 39,
152. **Open** 11am-8pm Mon-Fri; 11am-3pm Sat.
Credit AmEx. **Map** p285 H11.
For a glimpse of the more traditional side of BA's
art output, visit Isabel Anchorena. The superbly
curated Recoleta gallery displays the two- and three-
dimensional works of over 30 artists, including
Miguel Darienzo and Eduardo Gualdoni. The gallery
has made strong showings at events like the
monster San Pablo Arte and ArteBA fairs.

Hollywood in Cambodia

1st floor, Thames 1885, entre Costa Rica
y Nicaragua, Palermo Soho(no phone,
www.hollywoodincambodia.com.ar). Bus
39, 93, 130, 152. **Open** 5-9pm Thur-Sun.
No credit cards. Map p287 M8.
The graffiti craze has officially taken Buenos Aires
by storm, and you may even have started to
recognise the styles plastered all over the city.
Now you can put a name to the image at this
gallery, run by a 'collective of collectives' comprising some of BA graffiti's big names like
Bs.As.Stencil, Run Don't Walk and Doma, among
others. Entering the gallery requires passing
through the graffiti-festooned Post St bar: grab a
bottle of beer and some glasses and head up to
the heavily tagged terrace.
► *For a little schooling, take a graffiti walking*
tour with Graffitimundo (see p42).

Mar Dulce

Uriarte 1490, entre Gorriti y Cabrera,
Palermo Soho (mobile 15 5319 3597,
www.galeriamardulce.blogspot.com).
Bus 93, 168. **Open** 3-8pm Tue-Sat.
No credit cards. Map p287 M7.

ARTS & ENTERTAINMENT

Antonio Seguí at **Rubbers**. *See p199.*

Xul Solar

Artistic visionary Xul Solar was master of his own rarefied universe.

Polyglot, astrologer, inventor, musician, university dropout and eternal student, Xul Solar (1887-1963) may be best known as an artist, but perhaps his own description of himself as a 'utopian by profession' is most accurate.

Solar's singular body of work is testament to his insatiable intellectual curiosity and apparent belief that everything – from the Kabbalistic Tree of Life to his wife's piano – could be improved upon.

Born in Buenos Aires as Oscar Agustín Alejandro Schulz Solari, the man Jorge Luis Borges dubbed 'one of the most remarkable events of our age' at one point dithered about his career path. Abandoning a degree in architecture, he devoted himself for a time to music, all the while dabbling in painting. A period spent in Europe, where he crossed paths with Picasso, Modigliani and fellow Argentinian artist Emilio Pettoruti, helped shift his primary focus to art.

Music, however, would remain an important influence on Solar's work. Paintings like *Coral Bach* and *Cinco Melodías* have led to the artist being described as a 'visual musician', and that piano was transformed into a three-row, multicoloured keyboard designed to play a scale devised by Solar. It can still be seen at his former home, now the Museo Xul Solar (*see p67*).

Those years in Europe also fuelled Solar's fervour for learning. In Stuttgart,

he attended talks by anthroposophist Rudolf Steiner; in Paris, he spoke extensively with occultist Aleister Crowley; and the impressive collection of books he amassed on his travels included titles on theosophy, philosophy, mysticism and magic. Back in BA he began to associate with the Martín Fierro group, a literary circle that included Borges, and attended meetings on astrology. This vast universe of learning was distilled into the small-scale watercolours and temperas that were Solar's preferred media, meaning that everything from Christian crosses to astrological references and alchemical symbols comprised his arsenal of iconography.

When he wasn't painting, Solar was busy proposing a duodecimal numeral system, developing a new form of musical notation, reworking the game of chess and inventing languages. He hoped that one of these languages, a mix of Spanish and Portuguese called Neocriollo, would unite Latin America; and that Panlengua (Panlanguage), with its numerical and astrological roots and lack of grammar, would aid understanding between all people on Earth. These languages, like so many of Solar's academic explorations, also found their way into his paintings.

In the epilogue to his 1960 work on creativity, *El Hacedor*, Borges wrote: 'A man sets out to draw the world.' With his idealism, intellect and very particular vision, Xul Solar redrew it entirely.

Pareja.

ARTS & ENTERTAINMENT

Liniers at **Elsi del Río**. *See p195.*

Cosy Mar Dulce exhibits works in small and medium formats by contemporary and classic artists from the River Plate region, including father-and-son printmakers Raoul and Ral Veroni and master painter Tulio de Sagastizábal. More like a stylish friend's apartment than a typical art gallery, the space has an intimate atmosphere where genuinely engaging shows are held.

Mite

Unit 30, 1st Floor, Avenida Santa Fe 2729, entre Laprida y Anchorena, Barrio Norte (4822 9433, www.mitegaleria.com.ar). Subte D, Agüero/bus 12, 39, 64, 152. **Open** 2-8pm Tue-Sat. **No credit cards. Map** p286 J9.

Mite is one of a handful of galleries inside Galería Patio del Liceo, Barrio Norte's exciting art hub. Exhibition openings at any one of the galleries often coincide with parties being held at other spaces in the building, with the cool crowd spilling out of the *galerías* into the shared patio spaces. Mite has a rotating cast of work by a dozen contemporary artists, from photographer Julia Corsaro's hazy prints to Ariel Mora's incandescent postmodernist installations. Seize the chance, too, to drop by the contemporary art and design bookstore Purr Libros, which is located on the ground floor.

Nora Fisch

Ground floor, Güemes 2967, entre Gallo y Agüero, Barrio Norte (4824 5743, www.norafisch.com). Bus 29, 64, 68, 152. **Open** 3-8pm Tue-Fri. **No credit cards. Map** p286 K9.

Leave reality at the door and enter into a world that resembles a David Lynch set. Mixed media installations that lie at the extreme end of the conceptual scale is how New York-educated owner Nora Fisch likes to deck out her space. Get lost in mesmerising prints or ruminate over minimalist sculptures as starkly hypnotic as a lone door handle on a wall.

Praxis

Arenales 1311, y Talcahuano, Recoleta (4812 6254, www.praxis-art.com). Bus 10, 152. **Open** 10.30am-8pm Mon-Fri; 10.30am-2pm Sat. **Credit** AmEx, DC, MC, V. **Map** p285 H11.

Recoleta-based Praxis is one of the few Argentinian galleries with international reach, with spaces in New York and Miami as well as Buenos Aires. As a result, it's one of the driving forces in promoting Argentinian art abroad.

Rubbers

Avenida Alvear 1595, y Montevideo, Recoleta (4816 1864, www.rubbers.com.ar). Bus 17, 61, 67, 92, 93. **Open** 11am-8pm Mon-Fri; 11am-1.30pm Sat. **No credit cards. Map** p286 I11.

As you might imagine from the gallery that hosted Andy Warhol's first Latin American exhibition back in 1966, only the most upmarket names in art make it into museum-like Rubbers. A diverse range of works includes Carlos Gallardo's photography and pieces from Xul Solar (*see left*), the quirky artist-inventor whose work gave this gallery clout during its infancy in the late 1950s. *Photo p197.*

WEST OF THE CENTRE

Wallrod

Carlos Calvo 3619, entre Boedo y Colombres (3534 3603, www.wallrod.com.ar). Subte E, Boedo/bus 20, 53, 128. **Open** 3-9pm Thur-Sat. **No credit cards.**

This unique gallery is well off the tourist circuit, but its location close to an atmospheric stretch of restaurant- and bar-dotted Avenida Boedo is perfect for those in search of something different from the world of contemporary sculpture, photography, painting and video art. Soak up some alternative culture at the beautiful historic house on Saturday nights from 9pm when it hosts theatre performances, or pop in outside gallery hours for tango, theatre, photography and life drawing classes.

ARTS & ENTERTAINMENT

Gay & Lesbian

In gay-friendly BA, it's better out than in.

As a party capital, an eye-candy destination and an open-minded city for gay and lesbian visitors, Buenos Aires beats its Latin American competitors hands-down. From lusty late nights to the intimate embrace of gay tango, it's little wonder the international queer crowd is flocking here to party with pretty *porteños*.

The city's gay pride parade (*see p183*), which takes place in November, attracts thousands to support diversity and indulge in some seriously hedonistic celebrating. And there's much to celebrate: in 2010, Argentina became the first country in Latin America to legalise same-sex marriage, giving a further boost to gay tourism. To help you slip into the scene, the **Out & About Gay Pub Crawl** (*see below*) is a great way to meet both locals and travellers.

THE CITY'S GAY SCENE

Gay tourism in Buenos Aires is an accepted and successful trade, and visitors can choose from several travel agencies devoted to serving gay tourists, including **Tije Travel** (www.tije.com), **Thennat Travel** (www.thennat.com), **BA Gay Travel** (www.bagaytravel.com) and **Hadrianus Gay Travel** (www.hadrianus.com.ar).

Porteños – no matter what their sexual preference – are night owls. Nightlife is *the* life. To test your stamina, head to popular club **Human** (*see p202*) or go bar-hopping with the fun and fabulous crew at **Out & About Gay Pub Crawl** (www.outandaboutpub crawl.com). For something more intimate, try a tango lesson at gay-friendly *milongas* **Tango Queer** (*see p232*) or **La Marshall** (*see p232*), or pull all your moves at November's **International Queer Tango Festival** (www.festivaltangoqueer.com.ar).

Safety & Information

Look out for the excellent free listings guides **Circuitos Cortos BsAs Gay** (www.circuitoscortos.com.ar), **GMAPS** (www.gaymaps.org) and **The Ronda** (www.theronda.com.ar) in shops, bars and hotels. **AG Magazine** (www.ag magazine.info) is an excellent online source of local and international LGBT news and goings-on.

When going out, always take condoms with you, as very few venues supply them. Male prostitutes (*taxi boys*, as they're known in Buenos Aires) continue to be an unavoidable – and illegal – fact of nightlife. So if you're not leaving alone, choose your post-club escort with caution. When in doubt, ask: a few hours of passion could cost you a few hundred pesos, or worse, a trip to the police station as the perpetrator or victim of a crime. Further information about safety and health can be found through the organisations listed below. Basic English is often spoken by their staff.

Resources

As well as the gay and lesbian organisations listed here, **Lugar Gay de Buenos Aires** (*see p201*) is another useful source of information.

Casa Brandon

Luís María Drago 236, entre Lavalleja y Julián Álvarez, Villa Crespo (4858 0610, www.brandon gayday.com.ar). Subte B, Malabia/bus 15, 55, 65, 127. **Open** from 8pm Wed-Sun. **Map** p282 L3. Where's a girl to go when she wants to have fun? Try this four-level house, named after Brandon Teena, the trans-man played by Hilary Swank in *Boys Don't Cry* – it's a community centre, gallery, resto-bar, lounge and performance space rolled into one. Come for information on gay, lesbian and transgender life in BA, for sapphic socialising at the bar (boys also welcome) or just to take in the scenery.

Comunidad Homosexual Argentina (CHA)

Tomás Liberti 1080, y Irala, La Boca (4361 6382, www.cha.org.ar). Bus 10, 24, 39, 70, 93. **Open** call to arrange a visit. **Map** p284 B9.
This is Argentina's oldest and most politically influential queer organisation. Visit for advice, information and a library of books, films, newsreels and press clippings. It also offers free legal advice for those who have suffered discrimination.

La Fulana

Apartment 2C, Avenida Corrientes 1785, y Culluo, Tribunales (mobile 15 6548 9542, www.lafulana.org.ar). Subte B, Callao/bus 12, 24, 26, 29, 168. **Open** 8-10pm Thur. **Map** p285 H9.
The most useful community centre for lesbians and bisexual women in Argentina, La Fulana provides health and human rights information and hosts weekly discussion groups. Poetry, essays and interviews with gay rights activists are published on the centre's superb (but Spanish only) website.

Sociedad de Integración Gay-Lésbica Argentina (SIGLA)

Pasaje del Progreso 949, y Salas, Parque Chacabuco (4922 3351, www.sigla.org.ar). Subte E, Emilio Mitre/bus 26, 86. **Open** 4-9pm Wed; 4-10pm Sat.
Founded in 1992, SIGLA is one of the oldest sexual minority organisations recognised by the government. The centre provides legal advice, health information, workshops and recreational activities for gays and lesbians. Check the website for listings of upcoming parties and events, from film screenings to gay and lesbian discussion groups.

Where to stay

While many of the city's hotels are gay-friendly, they often lack contact with the community. For longer stays get in touch with **Friendly Apartments** (www.friendlyapartments.com), which offers rentals in Recoleta. Otherwise, try a gay-owned guesthouse like **Bayres B&B** (Avenida Córdoba 5842, Palermo, 4772 3877, www.bayresbnb.com, US$75 double) or one of the options listed below. If you're not kicking off your party shoes alone, you can also opt for one of BA's *telos* – short-stay love motels (*see p92*) where you can spend a few hours getting to know your new, ahem, acquaintance better. Look for the signs that say *'albergue transitorio'*.

Axel Buenos Aires

Venezuela 649, entre Chacabuco y Perú, San Telmo (4136 9393, www.axelhotels.com). Subte E, Belgrano/bus 2, 10, 26, 29. **Rates** US$145 double. **Credit** AmEx, MC, V. **Map** p285 E10.

There's nothing particularly Argentinian about South America's first all-gay luxury hotel, but the Axel offers comfortable, stylish rooms with the latest technological accessories. Start your evening at the Sky Bar, the site of a grand swimming pool whose transparent bottom is visible from the lobby. The hotel's Sunday night pool party, held year-round from 5pm to 10pm, and open to the public, should also be high on your social agenda.

Lugar Gay de Buenos Aires

Defensa 1120, entre Humberto 1 y San Juan, San Telmo (4300 4747, www.lugargay.com.ar). Bus 24, 29, 126. **Rates** US$25 shared room; US$50-$90 double. **Credit** AmEx, V. **Map** p284 D9.
Bringing a touch of Key West to the heart of picturesque San Telmo, Lugar Gay is a racy men-only B&B where the host isn't shy of greeting guests with a big Argentinian man-kiss. The cheeky atmosphere further manifests itself in the decor and amenities, which include a G-stringed mannequin at reception and a jacuzzi and video salon.

Palermo Viejo Bed & Breakfast

Niceto Vega 4629, entre Malabia y Scalabrini Ortiz, Palermo Soho (4773 6012, www.palermoviejobb.com). Bus 39, 55, 168. **Rates** US$75 single; US$85 double. **No credit cards. Map** p283 M4.
This petite, excellently located bed and breakfast used to be a factory, and with its handful of uniquely decorated rooms it has bags of arty character.

ARTS & ENTERTAINMENT

There's Wi-Fi, air-conditioning and cable TV all available at your fingertips, as well as a courtyard that's ideal for sitting out in on a pleasant evening with a glass of wine or two.

OUT & ABOUT

Evening action doesn't get started until well into the night. Midnight is considered premature and clubs don't always fill until 3am, so take your time preening yourself before prowling the scene. Pad your pockets with enough cash to cover entry charges as well as pricey cocktails.

The gay bar and club scene in Buenos Aires ranges from the comfortably chaste to the outright lubricious. To track down the most happening spot, check out www.gay-ba.com, www.whatsupbuenosaires.com or www.wipe.com.ar.

Bars, nightclubs & club nights

Amerika

Gascón 1040, entre Rocamora y Estado de Israel, Villa Crespo (4865 4416, www.ameri-k.com.ar). Subte B, Medrano/bus 24, 55, 168. **Open** from 1am Thur-Sun. **Admission** AR$50-$90. **No credit cards. Map** p282 K5.

BA's biggest gay disco regularly draws thousands of boozed-up, party-hungry punters of increasingly mixed and flexible sexual orientations, including a good-times straight crowd. There are two dancefloors, with four bars and ultra-flirtatious bartenders – sorry, guys: they're mainly straight. Add to that regular live shows (check the website for details), strippers, all-you-can-drink nights on Fridays and Saturdays for AR$90, and a very packed darkroom. Hold on to your valuables!

Bach Bar

Cabrera 4390, y Julián Álvarez, Palermo (mobile 15 5184 0137, www.bach-bar.com.ar). Bus 39, 151, 168. **Open** from 11pm Wed-Sun. **Admission** AR$30-$35. **No credit cards. Map** p282 L5.

There are no frills at this charming lesbian bar in Palermo. The one-drink cover charge guarantees a blast in what must be the friendliest dyke joint in town. Don't miss karaoke on Sundays, and on Wednesdays and Thursdays there are live performances, such as stripper shows. Ooh la la.

Contramano

Rodríguez Peña 1082, y Santa Fe, Recoleta (4811 0494, www.contramano.com). Bus 12, 39, 152. **Open** midnight-6am Fri, Sat; 11pm-5am Sun. **Admission** AR$30-$60. **No credit cards. Map** p286 I10.

Remember the 1980s? Well, the crowd here – some of it original in more ways than one – is living proof

that the gay hustler bar theme never really died. The cover charge gets you a couple of drinks and the chance to cruise and dance to the pop, disco and electro. Be aware, though, that many of the twenty somethings are looking for a 'visa daddy'.

★ Fiesta Plop!

Fridays at Teatro Vorterix, Federico Lacroze 3455, entre Delgado y Álvarez Thomas, Colegiales. Bus 39, 93. **Open** from 12.30am. **Admission** AR$25. **No credit cards. Map** p283 P4.

Ready to party with BA's electric youth? What started as an underground party has grown up with its uber-young revellers who now range from barely out of their teen wonder years to late twenties and beyond. Fill up on cheap booze, cheap music (cumbia and the best of Britney and Lady Gaga) and cheap thrills.

Fiesta Puerca

Saturdays at Teatro Vorterix, Federico Lacroze 3455, entre Delgado y Álvarez Thomas, Colegiales (4555 4671). Bus 19, 39. **Open** from 12.30am. **Admission** AR$30. **No credit cards. Map** p283 P4.

Like its sister party, Fiesta Plop (*see above*), Puerca brings out a crowd of young, all-out partygoers looking to get down to cumbia, reggaeton and pop remixes. The electrifying atmosphere is further charged by a team of barely clothed dancers – male and female – who take to the stage to slather each other in mud. The night's called *puerca* (sow) for a reason: don't stand too close to the action or you'll get splattered.

Glam

Cabrera 3046, entre Laprida y Agüero, Barrio Norte (4963 2521, www.glambsas.com.ar). Bus 29, 109, 111. **Open** from midnight Thur, Sat; Fri fornightly. **Admission** AR$50. **No credit cards. Map** p286 J8.

Glam packs them in on Thursdays and Saturdays (entry is free with a pass from Sitges; *see 203*), with expats, tourists (you'll hear as much English as Spanish) and *porteños* of all ages rounding out the crowd. The boogie area in the back features 1980s pop and Latin beats, and the incredibly hot playroom behind the back bar is just a short climb up a stairway to heaven.

▶ *Fortnightly Fridays at Glam are lesbian nights.*

★ Human

Mandarine, Punta Carrasco, Avenida Costanera Norte, y Avenida Sarmiento, Costanera Norte (mobile 15 5478 5478, www.humanclub. com.ar). Bus 37, 45, 160. **Open** from 12.30am. **Admission** AR$40 (before 2.30am), AR$50 (after 2.30am). **No credit cards. Map** p287 M12.

This Saturday night event at Mandarine comes closer than most to recreating the New York City

Human.

gay club experience. Human attracts the best cross-section of the Buenos Aires gay scene, from post-adolescents to model beauties and thirtysomething professionals, with both locals and tourists in the mix. There are two dancefloors (one for techno, another for pop), a VIP area, several lounge areas and multiple bars. They combine to create a nightlife experience that is most definitely not to be missed.

Fiesta Dorothy
Alsina, Alsina 940, Monserrat (mobile 15 3430 2711,www.fiestadorothy.com). Bus 17, 56, 59, 64, 67, 70. **Open** from 12.30am. **Admission** AR$40-$70. **No credit cards**. **Map** p285 F10.
Put on by the Rheo Group, the city's gay event powerhouse, the night draws some of the best-looking guys and gals BA has to offer, from pill-popping *musculocas* dancing shirtless on the main floor downstairs to young model wannabes. DJs spin electronic and pop remixes and three-storey high video screens put you in the mood to dance it out with 2,000 partygoers.

Sitges
Avenida Córdoba 4119, entre Palestina y Pringles, Palermo (4861 3763, www.sitgesonline. om.ar). Bus 92, 140, 168. **Open** from 11pm Wed-Sun. **Admission** AR$35-$58. **No credit cards**. **Map** p282 L4.
This is one of BA's few options for gays and lesbians who've tossed out their dancing shoes. The drinks are no bargain, but getting hammered isn't exactly the point here, unless it's Friday (when a AR$58 wristband at the door gets you as much

beer and liquor – local brands only – as you can handle). Some nights, drag comedy, musical numbers and strippers liven up the mood, and there's karaoke on Sundays too.
▶ *Pick up a pass for Glam (see p202) at Sitges to entitle you to discounted entry at the club.*

The Sub
Avenida Córdoba 543, entre Florida y San Martín, Microcentro (www.thesub.com.ar). Subte C, San Martín/bus 7, 20, 55, 62, 130. **Open** from 12.30am Fri, Sat. **Admission** AR$60. **No credit cards**. **Map** p285 G11.
This downtown disco enjoys a sizeable following of anti-fashion, shun-the-establishment gay boys who prefer their play nights to be unpretentious and set to an irresistible pop beat. The big night here is Friday's basement bash Fiesta Oliver (www.fiestaoliver.com), which includes an open bar with the AR$60 admission.

Gyms, saunas & darkrooms

Buenos Aires A Full
Viamonte 1770, entre Callao y Rodríguez Peña, Tribunales (4371 7263, www.afullspa. com.ar). Subte D, Callao/bus 12, 29, 37, 60. **Open** noon-midnight Mon-Thur; 24hrs Fri-Sun. **Admission** AR$60. **No credit cards**. **Map** p285 H10.
This centrally located spa, which is equipped with saunas, a jacuzzi, a sunbed and massage services, attracts a relatively young clientele. The biggest crowds are found here at the weekends and after work during the week.

Time Out Buenos Aires **203**

ARTS & ENTERTAINMENT

Caribbean

Uriburu 1012, entre Marcelo T de Alvear y Santa Fe, Barrio Norte (4829 2164). Subte B, Pueyrredón/bus 39, 152. **Open** 7am-11pm Mon-Fri; 9am-8pm Sat. **Admission** AR$140 monthly; AR$30 daily. **Credit** MC, V. **Map** p286 I9.

This is a great gym with a good range of free weights and machines, and some cardio workouts too. But the real draw is the guys. The place is packed from 6pm to 9pm on weekdays.

Energy Spa

Bravard 1105, y Ángel Gallardo, Almagro (4854 5625). Bus 55, 92. **Open** 11.30am-11.30pm daily. **Admission** AR$45. **No credit cards**. **Map** p282 L3.

A good option close to Parque Centenario, Energy Spa has a bar, a gym, a swimming pool, relaxation rooms, jacuzzis, massage services and even a VIP area complete with a TV lounge.

Homo Sapiens

Gascón 956, entre Guardia Vieja y Rocamora, Almagro (4862 6519). Subte B, Medrano/ bus 24, 92, 99, 160. **Open** noon-midnight daily. **Admission** AR$40. **No credit cards**. **Map** p282 K4.

Handily located just a block away from Amerika (*see p202*), this complex has private cabins, wet and dry saunas and a smoking terrace.

Tom's

Basement, Viamonte 638, entre Maipú y Florida, Microcentro (4322 4404, www.tomsbuenos aires.com). Subte B, Florida/bus 12, 37, 60. **Open** 1pm-7am Mon-Fri; 24hrs Sat, Sun. **Admission** AR$30. **No credit cards**. **Map** p285 G11.

There's something for everyone (well, perhaps not your Aunt Mabel) at this underground sex club. Its central location means you'll find married men on a break from work during the week, and post-disco guys swinging by for one last stand at the weekends.

Zoom

Uriburu 1018, y Marcelo T de Alvear, Barrio Norte (4827 4828, www.zoombuenosaires.com). Subte D, Pueyrredón/bus 39, 152. **Open** 24hrs; closed 8am-3pm Wed. **Admission** AR$35-$50. **No credit cards**. **Map** p286 I9.

Conveniently located next to one of the gayest gyms in town (Caribbean; *see left*), this Barrio Norte sex club offers every nook and cranny you can dream of and draws a good mix of customers. Bring your own condoms and lube – none are provided.

Fabulous Weddings.

Music

Sound advice for moving to the beat in the capital.

Increasingly, the sound Argentina is exporting is digital: the dirty beats of *cumbia villera*, the mournful melodies of the tango, and even traditional *folclórico* from northern Argentina are receiving the kinds of electronic makeovers that shake dancefloors from Bogotá to Berlin. But good old rock'n'roll still has pride of place in the hearts of *porteños*, and the last decade has seen the development of a new movement of excellent, home-grown independent rock. Traditional folkloric music too is garnering a devoted following among young urbanites who crave a bit of *campo* sounds (*see peñas, p211*).

In the world of classical music, Buenos Aires is a destination for many international acts, who perform at the magnificent **Teatro Colón** (*see below*).

ARTS & ENTERTAINMENT

Classical & Opera

High up on your BA bucket list – up there with eating steak, watching football and dancing tango – should be attending an opera, concert or ballet at the magnificent **Teatro Colón** (*see right*). Classical music can be found elsewhere in the city, including the **Teatro Coliseo** (Marcelo T de Alvear 1125, Tribunales, 4814 3056, www.fundacioncoliseum.com.ar), La Boca's **Usina del Arte** (*see p57*), the **Museo Isaac Fernández Blanco** (*see p48*), the **Teatro San Martín** (*see p220*) and **Teatro Margarita Xirgú** (*see right*). The **Teatro Nacional Cervantes** (*see p219*) has intermittent free contemporary orchestral concerts, and the **Auditorio de Belgrano** (Virrey Loreto 2348, Belgrano, 4783 1783) holds free classical concerts on Friday evenings. The **Centro Cultural Recoleta** (*see p61*) hosts occasional classical concerts as do other cultural centres in the city. Modest, unsubsidised institutions like **La Scala de San Telmo** (Pasaje Giuffra 371, San Telmo, 4362 1187, www.lascala.com.ar) are awash with talented performers. A large part of BA's classical music scene is in the capable hands of private professional and amateur groups, including the **Mozarteum Argentino** (www.mozarteumargentino.org) and **Festivales Musicales** (www.festivalesmusicales.org.ar).

Fans of opera can enjoy performances by BA Lírica (www.balirica.org.ar) at the **Teatro Avenida** (*see p222*) where *zarzuela* – lyrical

opera – is a house speciality; the venue also hosts classical music evenings. Interest in opera extends beyond BA's aristocracy, and performances also take place at more intimate, unusual venues like **La Casa de la Opera** (Manuel Samperio 969, Barracas, 4307 7055, www.lacasadelaopera.com.ar).

For a calendar of concerts, it's worth taking a look at www.musicaclasicaargentina.com (Spanish only).

Teatro Colón

Cerrito 628, entre Viamonte y Tucumán, Tribunales (4378 7100, www.teatrocolon. org.ar). Subte D, Tribunales/bus 29, 39, 59. **Open** *Box office* 10am-8pm Mon-Sat; 10am-5pm Sun. *Tours* 9am-5.30pm daily. **Tickets** from AR$40. *Tours* AR$110. **Credit** AmEx, MC, V. **Map** p285 G10.
Unquestionably BA's greatest cultural monument, the seven-storey Teatro Colón boasts an ornate interior, powerful acoustics and a 2,500-seat capacity (there's standing room for an additional 500). As well as regular performances by the BA Philharmonic Orchestra, it stages superb ballets and operas. If you can't catch a concert, take a guided tour.

Teatro Margarita Xirgú

Chacabuco 875, y Estados Unidos, San Telmo (4300 8817, www.margaritaxirgu.com). Bus 10, 17, 29, 59, 156. **Box office** 2pm-start of show Tue-Sun. **Tickets** AR$70-$120. **No credit cards.** **Map** p285 E9.

Time Out Buenos Aires **205**

Alvy Singer and Tomi Lebrero at Café Vinilo.
See p208.

This stunning example of Catalonian architecture, named after the Spanish actress who made her way from Europe to Buenos Aires in 1914 and starred in Lorca's *La Casa de Bernarda Alba* in 1945, is a treat for your eyes as well as ears, boasting a carefully preserved interior and superb acoustics.

Rock, Folk & Jazz

BA has well and truly established itself on the international concert circuit with well-known acts like Bjork and Foo Fighters performing in recent years. Latin American acts also enjoy massive popularity and Spanish performers are particularly respected. But whatever gig you go to, the enthusiastic crowd will be loud, appreciative and more than likely dancing in their seats and singing along to every word.

ROCK OUT

Most people think tango when they think Buenos Aires, but, as you'll soon glean from the preponderance of power chords blaring out

---

INSIDE TRACK WHAT'S ON

For gig listings, check out www.vueno sairez.com (in Spanish), Ticketek (www.ticketek.com.ar), www.whatsup buenosaires.com, Time Out Buenos Aires's Facebook page, and the BA section of www.songkick.com.

---

from stereo systems, it seems that Argentina prefers to rock. Brazilians and Mexicans may disagree, but locals claim that Latin American rock was born in BA.

Home-grown *rock nacional* enjoys massive popularity, with artists like Charly Garcia (*see p209*) Kevin Johansen, Alfonso Barbieri (*photo p210*), and bands like Onda Vaga, Divididos and Babasónicos just some of the acts currently doing the rounds in the capital.

Argentina's *rock nacional* has had a tough trajectory. After gaining a toehold in the early 1970s, many rockers, labelled subversive by the military dictatorship, were censored or forced to leave the country in the 1970s and early 1980s. During the Falklands/Malvinas War, English-language music was banned, giving local talent the exposure it needed, and with the return of democracy the scene took off, aided by Rock & Pop (95.9FM) radio station. Tours by the likes of Virus and Soda Stereo caused mass hysteria wherever the bands played.

Despite this love of Argentinian rock, most local hipsters still consider the Rolling Stones to be the definitive band. Fans of all ages, known as *rolingas*, continue to sport that lips logo on their T-shirts. Stones-inspired local bands include La 25, Ratones Paranoicos, Intoxicados, Jóvenes Pordioseros and Viejas Locas. An opposing fan group is (almost) as passionate about *Los* Beatles.

ALTERNATIVE SOUNDS

Once the soundtrack of the city's shantytowns, cumbia now commands fans from across the social strata, and along with tango and traditional folk tunes, has been given the electro treatment. The record label ZZK Records (www.zzkrecords.com) is taking digital cumbia to the world stage, with acts like Chancha Via Circuito and DJ Villa Diamante. Digital folklore artist Tremor is also on its roster, pairing synth loops with Andean flutes and *bombo legüero* (drum) samples.

Despite the digital hybrid boom, most young *porteños* still prefer rock. An exciting deviation from the standard rock format are innovative groups such as the lively Me Darás Mil Hijos and Orquesta de Salón, led by the irresistible chain-smoking Pablo Dacal.

Punk and metal are still popular in BA (check out Whitesnake copyists Rata Blanca), and ska and reggae nights are advertised around San Telmo. Rockabilly and swing have small but devoted followings, and seven-piece swing band Orquesta Inestable play regularly around town.

Despite its macho reputation, BA boasts an impressive range of female singer-songwriters. Keep an eye out for Juana Molina's enthralling shows. Hip hop, dancehall, reggae and cumbia are the genres traversed by the feisty Miss Bolivia, whose fearless live shows have made her a hot ticket. All-girl punk trio Las Kellies (*photo p208*) have garnered plenty of attention in Europe for their riot grrrl sound and fun lyrics (they sing in seven languages).

The waif-like folk singer Flopa's strong and definitive sound is heard in both her solo work and her collaboration Flopa-Mínima, and indie-folk singer Sol Pereyra continues to win fans across Latin America. The growing popularity of traditional folkloric sounds among young *porteños* is being spearheaded by gutsy singer-songwriters like Sofia Viola, who peppers her songs with plenty of humour. Soema Montenegro, Paloma del Cerro and La Yegros create tantalising fusions of folklore, electronic and Latin beats, as do the vibrant male-female duo Tonolec.

ALL THAT JAZZ

A growing jazz and blues scene is emerging in Buenos Aires and there are free and inexpensive recitals to be found throughout the city. Inspired by New York jazz clubs, **Thelonius Club** (*see p210*) combines the comforts of a very well-stocked bar with an impressive programme of live jazz. **Teatro IFT** (Boulogne Sur Mer 549, Once, 4961 9562, www.teatroift.org.ar) boasts varied live performances every weekend, including occasional jazz shows. A head-nodding crowd flocks to the nightly recitals at the cosy **Jazz & Pop** (Paraná 340, Tribunales, 4372 2302,

www.jazzypopclub.com.ar), while San Telmo's **Café Rivas** (*see p117*) and Boedo's boho **Pan y Arte** (Boedo 880, 4932 4299, www.pan yarte.com.ar) are intimate spots to enjoy weekly jazz recitals over a glass of red wine. In Barrio Norte, **Clásica y Moderna** (Avenida Callao 892, 4812 8707, www.clasicaymoderna.com) hosts regular evening jazz and blues performances. For other major jazz venues, *see p209*.

The city government organises an international festival, **Buenos Aires Jazz** (*see p184*), which takes place annually. In neighbouring Uruguay, the **Festival Internacional de Jazz de Punta del Este** (www.festival.com.uy) is a first-class spectacle.

GIGS AND FESTIVALS

Buenos Aires boasts a huge number of live music venues. As with so many city spaces, they are often multifunctional – a place listed under 'Jazz' might have a tango class on Tuesday, a folk night on Thursday and a mime performance on Friday. In this chapter we list places that have at least two shows a month; call ahead in January and February since some places put their agenda on ice over the summer.

Many venues, especially clubs, are unlikely to accept credit cards. However, you can buy tickets using major credit cards at Ticketek (5237 7200, www.ticketek.com.ar).

Festivals include mobile phone company-sponsored **Personal Fest** (www.personalfest.com.ar), which has seen groups like The Strokes and Calle 13 take to the stage, as well as some of the most important local bands. Other corporate sponsored festivals to look out for include **Pepsi Music** (www.pepsimundo.com) and **Quilmes Rock** (www.quilmes.com.ar). The city government often subsidises free outdoor concerts in places like Palermo's **Parque Tres de Febrero** (*see p67*); check www.buenosaires.gov.ar for upcoming events.

ROCK & FOLK VENUES
Major venues

When international names hit the capital, their shows tend to sell out quickly. The biggest acts regale the masses at **River Plate Stadium** (Avenida Figueroa Alcorta 7597, Núñez, 4789 1200), **Estadio Obras** (Avenida del Libertador 7395, Núñez, www.estadioobras.com.ar), **GEBA Jorge Newberry** (Marcelino Freyre 3831, Palermo, 4777 8400), **Luna Park** (*see p208*), and **Estadio Único** (www.estadiolp.gba.gov.ar), outside the capital in the city of La Plata. Occasional concerts are also held at **Teatro Opera Citi** (*see p220*).

ARTS & ENTERTAINMENT

Groove

Avenida Santa Fe 4389, entre Darregueyra y Uriarte, Palermo (4776 6440, www.palermo groove.com). Subte D, Palermo/bus 10, 29, 60. **Open** *Shows* Varies. *Club* from midnight Fri, Sat. **Box office** 10am-8pm Mon-Sat. **Tickets** varies. **Credit** AmEx, MC, V. **Map** p287 M9.

This 1700-capacity live venue-cum-nightclub is wildly popular with a younger crowd thanks to its eclectic line-up of local and international rock, reggae and electronic acts. Local heroes Las Pelotas, as well as LCD Soundsystem and Echo & the Bunnymen, have worked the crowd here.

Luna Park

Avenida Madero 420, entre Avenida Corrientes y Lavalle, Microcentro (information 5279 5279, tickets 5353 0606, www.lunapark.com.ar). Subte B, LN Alem/bus 26, 93, 99, 152. **Box office** 10am-7pm Mon-Fri; noon-7pm Sat; varies Sun. **Tickets** varies. **Credit** AmEx, DC, MC, V. **Map** p285 F11.

Duran Duran, Roxette and local heroes Bersuit Vergarabat are among the stars to have graced the stage of this boxing stadium, where Maradona famously tied the knot in 1989 in front of thousands of fans. The 15,000-capacity indoor venue attracts enthusiastic audiences, but there are some negative aspects: thick columns can block views from the upper levels and the sound system has been known to make top acts sound like shambling amateurs.

Teatro Gran Rex

Avenida Corrientes 857, entre Suipacha y Esmeralda, Microcentro (4322 8000). Subte B, Carlos Pellegrini or C, Diagonal Norte or D, 9 de Julio/bus 10, 17, 24, 29. **Box office** 10am-9pm daily. **Tickets** varies. **Credit** V. **Map** p285 F10.

The Gran Rex is ideal for artists who require the rapt attention of a comfortably seated audience. Sell-out past performers include Regina Spektor, Bob Dylan and local electrotango masters Bajofondo. The venue holds 3,500 punters, who can choose between the stalls (*platea*), the mezzanine (*super pullman*) or the dress circle (*pullman* – cheaper seats, worse sound and a pretty distant view). The theatre is also a venue for musicals and visiting ballet companies, and has its own car park and coffee shop.

La Trastienda Club

Balcarce 460, entre Belgrano y Venezuela, San Telmo (4342 7650, www.latrastienda.com). Subte A, Plaza de Mayo or D, Catedral, or E, Bolivar/bus 24, 29, 126, 130. **Box office** 10am-8pm Mon-Fri; varies Sat, Sun. **Tickets** varies. **Credit** AmEx, MC, V. **Map** p285 E10.

In the ruins of an old mansion dating from 1895, the Trastienda holds 400 people seated at small tables, or about 700 fans standing. A mecca for serious musicians and discerning fans, it attracts cutting-edge local bands, established Latin American talent and international acts like Yo La Tengo.

Smaller venues

Some of Buenos Aires' most enjoyable gigs take place on the smallest of stages. **Niceto Club** (*see p216*) is the place to catch international indie bands, while nightclub **Crobar** (*see p214*) occasionally has weeknight gigs by acts like Cut Copy and D12. The excellent **Ciudad Cultural Konex** (*see p221*) in Abasto hosts Monday's popular improvisational percussion night La Bomba de Tiempo as well as concerts from the likes of local lads Onda Vaga. Downtown's **Ultra** (San Martín 678, 4312 5605, www.ultrapop-ar.blogspot.com) is indie gig central, and you can also catch occasional bands at **La Cigale** (*see p144*). In Palermo, the atmospheric **Café Vinilo** (Gorriti 3780, 4866 6510, *photo p206*), **NoAvestruz** (*see p221*) and **La Oreja Negra** (Uriarte 1271, 2053 3263, www.cluborejanegra.blogspot.com.ar) all

Las Kellies. See p207.

INSIDE TRACK
CHARLY GARCÍA

Blessed with perfect pitch and an obvious unconcern for heights (the singer famously jumped from the ninth floor balcony of a Mendoza hotel), Charly García is the Argentinian rock star. Politicians aside, he is also one of two Argentinians – Maradona is the other – who does what he wants, when he wants. His musical career spans four decades and is coloured by headline-making incidents and addiction. Rehabilitation has left García looking less emaciated, but the bespectacled maestro with the bicolour moustache still manages to resemble a drug-addled secondary school science teacher. Never one to pass up a publicity opportunity, he marked his 60th birthday in 2011 by embarking on an Americas-wide tour and releasing a live box set, appropriately titled 60x60. His classic tracks include 'Los Dinosaurios'; 'Seminare'; 'Yendo de la Cama al Living'; 'No Soy Un Extraño'.

have varied live music programmes, while the eclectic acts who play at Colegiales's **Club Cultural Matienzo** (Matienzo 2424, www.clubculturalmatienzo.blogspot.com.ar) frequently defy genre. In Barracas, catch singer-songwriters and up-and-coming bands at **Plasma** (Piedras 1856, 4307 9171, www.sitioplasma.com.ar).

ND/Ateneo
Paraguay 918, y Suipacha, Retiro (4328 2888, www.ndateneo.com.ar). Subte C, San Martín/bus 10, 59, 109, 152. **Box office** noon-8pm Mon-Sat. Closed Jan. **Tickets** AR$80-$150. **Credit** MC, V. **Map** p285 G11.
This traditional theatre is a key venue for all musical genres, from folklore and tango to rock and jazz. There are concerts most evenings, mainly by talented Argentinian performers or other Latin American artists, as well as occasional theatre performances.

Salón Pueyrredón
Avenida Sante Fe 4560, entre Godoy Cruz y Oro, Palermo Soho (www.salonpueyrredon.blogspot.com). Subte D, Palermo/bus 15, 29, 39. **Open** 9pm-5am Thur; 9pm-6am Fri, Sat. **Tickets** AR$20-$50. **No credit cards. Map** p287 N9.
Dark, noisy and poorly painted, Salón Pueyrredón is the closest thing Buenos Aires has to a classic punk club, for people who don't actually like to be spat on. While the jerky strains of punk can often be heard, it's also a major testing ground for local rock and pop

outfits, and, most nights, ironed jeans and designer T-shirts outnumber mohawks and studded dog-collars. When the live music's over, DJs spin a mix of punk, new wave and mod tunes. The punk spirit is perhaps most notable at the bar, where heavy-handed bartenders fling out cheap, lethal drinks.

Samsung Studio
Pasaje 5 de Julio 444, entre Belgrano y Venezuela, San Telmo (4342 5159, www.samsungstudio.com.ar). Subte A, Plaza de Mayo or E, Belgrano/bus 2, 152, 33. **Open** varies. **Tickets** varies. **Credit** AmEx, MC, V. **Map** p285 F10
Stripped-down Samsung Studio is dedicated to rock, indie and more. Sponsored by the eponymous electronics company and the brainchild of Popart, one of Argentina's biggest live music production companies, the venue has seen artists like Laura Marling and Simian Mobile Disco take to the stage.
▶ *M Buenos Aires (see p121), a sophisticated bar and Japanese-Peruvian fusion restaurant, is housed within the same building.*

Vorterix Teatro
Federico Lacroze 3455, y Álvarez Thomas, Colegiales (www.elteatroonline.com.ar). Bus 19, 39, 112, 168. **Open** varies. **Tickets** AR$50-$300. **No credit cards. Map** p283 P4.
An unpretentious, decidedly long hair and leathers rock joint, this spectacular old theatre is the place to catch national acts like Él Mató a un Policía Motorizado. There are no fancy cocktails served here, just beer and basic spirits. But great acoustics combine with a good atmosphere to make a night here a decent outing.

JAZZ VENUES
Boris
Gorriti 5568, y Fitz Roy, Palermo Hollywood (4777 0012, www.borisclub.com.ar). Bus 34, 39, 93, 108, 111, 140, 151, 168. **Open** from 10pm Tue-Sat; from 9pm Sun. **Tickets** AR$50-$150. **Credit** AmEx, MC, V. **Map** p287 N7.
The decor says it all: grand piano, velvet-backed stage, viewing balcony and moody coloured lighting. With live shows six nights a week, Boris has got the substance to back up the style. The cocktail list is also a major draw: try house special Boris – a delightful twist on the G&T with the genius addition of rosehip jam.

Notorious
Avenida Callao 966, entre Marcelo T de Alvear y Paraguay, Barrio Norte (4813 6888, www.notorious.com.ar). Subte D, Callao/bus 12, 39, 60, 111. **Open** 8.30am-1am Mon-Fri; 10am-3am Sat; 5pm-1am Sun. **Tickets** AR$60-$100. **Credit** AmEx, MC, V. **Map** p286 I10.
Notorious has daily shows by respected local jazz musicians such as Adrián Iaies, as well as occasional

ARTS & ENTERTAINMENT

Alfonso Barbieri and Kevin Johansen.
See p206.

new folk and world music acts. The tables are close to the stage, so you can catch every groan and moan during the improvs – but reserve ahead to be as near to the front as possible.

Thelonious Club
Salguero 1884, entre Güemes y Charcas, Palermo (4829 1562, www.thelonious.com.ar). Subte D, Bulnes/bus 29, 39, 111, 152. **Open** from 9pm Wed-Sat. **Tickets** AR$20-$70. **No credit cards.** **Map** p286 L9.
Inspired by the sultry vibe of New York jazz clubs, the Thelonious Club successfully combines the comforts of a bar with an impressive programme of live modern jazz and DJs. Order from an ample cocktail menu at the mammoth 13 metre-long bar, or make yourself at home in a cosy cushioned booth. If you want to hear good local jazz, this is the place to come.

OTHER VENUES
Hotels, pubs & bars

Whether you want to cry into your beer to the melancholy strains of tango, or twirl a cocktail stick to a bossanova beat, BA has plenty of suitable venues. **The Library Lounge** at the very fancy **Faena Hotel + Universe** (*see p91*) is a beautiful venue with pricey sauce. In San Telmo, **Tabaco** (Estados Unidos 265, 4232 9794) is a grungy little club populated by rocker types, and **Bar Guebara** (Humberto Primo 463) is another good bet for live music on certain nights. Chic bar and restaurant **Milión** (*see p148*) in Barrio Norte uses part of its lovely mansion to provide an intimate setting for live music and DJ sets. In Palermo, **Makena** (Fitz Roy 1519,

4772 8281, www.makenacantinaclub.com.ar) serves a mean cocktail and a varied line-up of bands, while indie-cool **El Quetzal** (Guatemala 4516, www.elquetzalcasacultural. blogspot.com) has live music most nights and a great outdoor patio. Swing bands, tango orchestras and sedate piano recitals are on the weekly menu at Almagro's **Sr Duncan** (Avenida Rivadavia 3832, 4958 3633), a bar hidden inside a century-old mansion. Down the road, anything goes at **El Club del Arte** (Medrano 484), while bands rock out in the basement of student-favourite **Imaginario Cultural** (Bulnes 901, Almagro).

Peñas

Experience the typical folk sounds and taste the regional cuisine of Argentina's interior provinces at a *peña*. Traditional music is always played with great passion in these venues. For the lowdown on this scene, *see p211*.

Los Cardones
Jorge Luis Borges 2180, entre Paraguay y Guatemala, Palermo Soho (4777 1112, www.cardones.com.ar). Subte D, Plaza Italia/bus 34, 55. **Open** 9pm-5am, Wed-Sat. **Tickets** AR$10-$35. **Credit** MC, V. **Map** p283 M6.
An energetic *peña* all year round, this spot becomes particularly popular at the end of July, when the young gauchos descend on Buenos Aires for the Exposición Rural (*see p185*) country fair. You can also grab a guitar yourself after the scheduled performances and join in the fun.
▶ *Folk-dancing lessons are held here on Friday from 7.30pm to 9pm.*

La Paila

Costa Rica 4848, entre Thames y Jorge Luis Borges, Palermo Soho (4878 2688, www.lapaila-restaurante.com.ar). Subte D, Plaza Italia/bus 34, 55. **Open** 7pm-2am Tue-Fri; 12.30pm-3am Sat, Sun. **Tickets** AR$25-$40. **Credit** AmEx, MC, V. **Map** p283 M5.

Rustic decor and colourful textiles from the north of Argentina kit out this spacious *peña*, which delivers an equally gastronomical and musical experience. Exotic meats such as yacaré and llama accompany wines from Jujuy, Salta and Catamarca. When things get lively, the tables are moved away for dancing.

La Peña del Colorado

Güemes 3657, entre Vidt y Salguero, Palermo (4822 1038, www.delcolorado.com.ar). Subte D, Bulnes/bus 15, 29, 39, 160. **Open** noon-2am Mon-Thur, Sun; noon-5am Fri, Sat. **Tickets** AR$25-$35. **Credit** AmEx, DC, MC, V. **Map** p286 L9.

This friendly *peña* is popular with students, and offers good acts and tasty *criollo*-style food. There is usually an impressive number of performers on any given evening and, once the troubadours have finished, guitars are passed around for you to make your own music well into the night.

A little bit of country

Folkloric music has a strong voice in the city's peñas.

Forget the beardy weirdy sensibility of folk clubs back home: in Argentina, *folclore* (pronounced folk-lo-ray) nights are wine-sloshing, foot-stomping, twirling and twisting shindigs, known as *peñas*. In Buenos Aires, they serve as portals to the vast Argentina that exists outside the capital. As well as being a meeting place for rural souls marooned in the city, *peñas* are increasingly popular among young *porteños*.

Lively carnival tunes from the Andean north-west, such as *chacarera* and *zamba*, steamy accordion-led *chamamé* from the north-east and provincial pampas, as well as guitar-plucking gaucho laments of the *milonga* can all be heard at *peñas* around BA. *Folclore* sounds spring from pre-Columbian sources and from the *criollo* syncretism of colonial and indigenous peoples. Thus, European violins and guitars are played alongside the woodwind *quena*, the percussive *caja* (box) and the mandolin-like *charango* (often made from an armadillo shell), which all hail from the Argentinian north, Bolivia, Peru and Chile.

Peñas come in two guises: the more sedate version takes place in a restaurant setting where the highlight is the post-show *guitarreada*, a musical free-for-all where anyone can pick up an instrument and start an informal sing-along around the table. (Don't be surprised if you are asked to play a couple of folk tunes from home yourself – and no, Oasis and Led Zeppelin covers don't count). The most popular restaurant peñas are clustered around Palermo, namely **Los Cardones**, **La Peña del Colorado** and **La Paila** (*see p210-211*), all of which have an intimate, friendly atmosphere that will transport you light years away from the barrio's pouting

hipsters. Restaurant *peñas* are also the perfect opportunity to sample Argentina's fine regional cuisine. Besides the staple empanadas are tasty *tamales* and *humitas* (stuffed corn-meal dough pasties steamed in husks) and a warming stew of meat, corn and whatever is lying around, called *locro*. Argentina's national drink, maté, a herbal tea served in a gourd, may well also be passed around early on in the evening.

For those with more stamina, *peña bailables* are all-night dancing affairs where you're guaranteed a happy hoedown, and most certainly a hangover. Occasionally, there are real life knife-sporting gauchos who, unlike their British Morris-dancing counterparts, successfully manage to jig about with a handkerchief and retain their I-can-kill-a-cow-with-my-bare-hands mystique. If you are lucky enough to hit one of the monthly parties organised by **Los Cumpas** (Solís 485, Congreso, 4825 3656, www.loscumpas.net), brace yourself for a night of Fernet-and-coke fuelled fun. Also held monthly, **La Residenta** (Bacacay 1600, Caballito, www.laresidenta.com.ar) has become a word-of-mouth phenomenon, and a dance class warms up the crowd before the guitar strumming and dizzy dancing begins. In summer, the monthly open-air **De La Ribera** (Díaz de Solís 2289, www.webfolklore.com.ar/laribera) has a magical riverside setting, making the trek out to Olivos well worthwhile.

For a daytime open-air alternative, the weekly **Feria de Mataderos** (*see p80*), held in the capital's western limits, is a top spot for watching locals dance to live folkloric music.

To find out what's on take a look at www.folkloreclub.com.ar.

ARTS & ENTERTAINMENT

Nightlife

Dance the night – and half the next day – away in BA's clubland.

Getting the most from BA's *boliches* (nightclubs) involves post-midnight starts, dancing till *la madrugada* (dawn) and marvelling over how the typical Argentinian clubber stays shine, frizz and sweat-free until sunrise. Along with a disco nap before you hit the town, you might want to guzzle Speed, the energy drink preferred by locals.

Buenos Aires's reputation as one of South America's hottest club destinations ensures regular visits from international DJs to clubs like **Alsina** (*see p213*) and **Pacha** (*see p217*), while wild nights at classic favourite **Club 69** (*see p216*) are a hit with the hordes of travelling party people.

From upscale venues such as **Jet** (*see p215*) to regular mash-up fiesta **Zizek Club** (*see below*), the variety of late-night parties guarantees good times.

THE LOCAL SCENE

When planning a night out, pace yourself and be prepared to travel. BA venues are basically split between downtown and Palermo and the Costanera Norte riverfront club strip, so carry the number of a radio taxi company (*see p255*). Clubs don't open until at least midnight and get lively late (after 3am), although last entrance is at 4am and licencing laws prohibit clubs from serving booze from 5am to 9am.

Notable club nights with staying power include **State**, held monthly on Fridays at **Alsina** (*see p213*); electronic cumbia bash **Zizek Club** (www.zzkrecords.com), held bimonthly at **Niceto Club** (*see p216*); the weekly extravaganza **Club 69**, held on Thursdays, also at Niceto Club; and the raucous roving **Fiesta Bubamara** (www.fiestas-bubamara.com.ar), which sees live bands fuse surreal gypsy tango with Balkan beats. Steadfast gay nights include **Human** (*see p202*), and **Fiesta Plop!** (*see p202*).

Dress codes are not very strictly enforced, though the porteño addiction to fashion means clubbers are often dressed to kill. In general, a friendly vibe prevails around town, partly thanks to the low alcohol consumption levels. Turning up to a venue blind drunk or looking for trouble will almost certainly guarantee that you don't get past the door.

During the Argentinian summer (January and February), many of the city's bigger clubs move their operations to the coastal resort of Punta del Este in Uruguay. You should still pack your dancing shoes, however, since this gives smaller, underground venues in BA the chance to flex their decks. But check the status of all the clubs listed here before rolling up, especially during the post-Christmas dash for the dunes.

Prices & information

Admission prices to smaller venues range from AR$20 to AR$60 (women usually pay less than men and sometimes get in for free), with larger clubs sometimes charging AR$100 and beyond, depending on who's in the booth. Check clubs' websites: you can often email ahead to put yourself on a guestlist, though this usually has little impact on skipping queues and is more to do with securing a discounted admission for arriving early.

INSIDE TRACK NIGHT GUIDERS

If the thought of navigating BA's nocturnal hotspots alone fails to appeal, contract the services of the savvy folk at **Night Aires** (4150 8820, www.night-aires.com), who will custom-design your night and take care of tickets, VIP passes and transport.

Credit cards are usually not accepted – don't hit the town without cash in small bills. A drink is often included with the cost of entrance: look out for '*con consumición*' or '*con trago*'.

For information about the latest happenings on the club scene, check out www.buenos aliens.com, www.whatsupbuenosaires.com or www.vuenosairez.com.

Note that while all the clubs listed below are active and recommended at time of going to press, it's possible that by the time you read this, some may be history. Check online or call up before venturing forth.

VENUES

★Alsina

Adolfo Alsina 940, entre Bernardo de Irigoyen y Tacuarí, Monserrat (4331 3231, www.statebsas.com.ar). Bus 10, 17, 59, 64, 86. **Open** midnight-7am monthly on Fri; 7.30pm-2.30am Sun. **Admission** varies. **Credit** MC, V. **Map** p285 F10.
State, a night at the cathedral-like Alsina is the talk of electro partyland these days, thanks to the hi-fi sound and consistently strong line-up of international names (Sven Väth, Loco Dice, Richie Hawtin, James Zabiela and Calvin Harris to name a few), which ensures that the 2000-head capacity is nor-

mally reached early on in the night. State takes place once a month on Fridays – check the website to find out when the next one will be. Sunday's Club One attracts an experienced party-hard crowd and is pumping by 10pm.

Asia de Cuba

Pierina Dialessi 750, y Macacha Güemes, Puerto Madero Este (4894 1328, www.asiadecuba. com.ar). Bus 2, 130, 152. **Open** *Dinner* 9pm daily. *Club* 1-6am Wed-Sat. **Admission** AR$120. **Credit** AmEx, MC, V. **Map** p285 E12.
Wednesday Glamour Nights are the main event at chichí Asia de Cuba in Puerto Madero, when a fashionable crowd descends around 10pm and stays late. This swish waterfront resto-club packs in executives, models and tourists from the swanky hotels nearby for the sushi, decent (if pricey) drinks and deep house. Dress to impress and get ready to splash out.

Bahrein

Lavalle 343, entre Reconquista y 25 de Mayo, Microcentro (4315 2403, www.bahreinba.com). Subte B, LN Alem/bus 6, 10, 22, 28, 93, 126, 129, 152. **Open** midnight-7pm Thur-Sun. **Admission** AR$50-$70. **Credit** AmEx, DC, MC, V. **Map** p285 F11.
Swish Bahrein is party central for electro-heads, with the basement of this grand former bank

ARTS & ENTERTAINMENT

Zizek Club at Niceto Club. *See p217.*

pumping out all manner of house, techno and electronic beats four nights a week. Saturdays usually plays host to an international DJ when the attendees flit between the glam 'Funky Room' (only open at weekends) and the basement, where the energy is concentrated.

Basement Club

The Shamrock, Rodríguez Peña 1220, entre Juncal y Arenales, Recoleta (4812 3584). Bus 37, 39, 124, 152. **Open** 7pm-6am Thur, Fri; 11pm-6am Sat. **Admission** AR$20-$40. **Credit** AmEx, MC, V. **Map** p286 I10.

This spot is the product of some serious nightlife know-how, and some of the city's top turntable talent is brought in as part of an ever-changing, hand-picked roster focusing on electronica and deep house. It's one of the few clubs that gets busy early, especially on Thursdays. The place is usually rocking with a mix of locals, tourists and some of the hardiest clubbers from the BA night scene.

▶ *Start the night upstairs in the popular Irish pub the Shamrock (see p148).*

Boutique

Perú 535, entre México y Venezuela, Monserrat (4331 6164, www.boutiqueba.com). Subte E, Belgrano/bus 10, 17, 22, 24, 29, 45, 152, 195. **Open** 7pm-2am Wed. **Admission** AR$25. **No credit cards. Map** p285 E10.

An after-office institution (Buenos Aires lingo for after-work parties), Boutique, formally known as Museum, has been drawing a faithful following of *porteños* in office attire, as well as tourists to it's Wednesday night slot for years. It's the setting that gives Boutique its edge: a cavernous three-storey industrial building designed by Gustave Eiffel (of Parisian tower fame), with a huge dancefloor to boot. The party starts early by BA standards and descends into a meat market by the early hours, ending at 2am, just in time for the office workers to get a few hours' kip. Free entry and happy hour drinks fuel the fun until 10pm. The music served up is of the safe '80s and '90s pop variety with a dash of cumbia and reggaeton for good measure.

Club Aráoz

Aráoz 2424, entre Güemes y Avenida Santa Fe, Palermo (4832 9751, www.clubaraoz.com.ar). Subte D, Scalabrini Ortíz/bus 36, 39, 106, 152. **Open** midnight-6am Thur-Sat. **Admission** AR$30-$45. **No credit cards. Map** 282 L6.

Hip hoppers take note: Thursday night at Club Aráoz means Buenos Aires' chief urban beats party, Lost. Breakdancers bust a move early in the night to the delight of the mostly foreign crowd on the packed dancefloor; the tiered upper levels fill up shortly thereafter and getting your hands on a drink becomes more and more a mission. Weekends are devoted to the joys of pure commercial dance, rock and Latin sounds. You can get in free before 2.30am.

Club Severino

Hipólito Yrigoyen 851, entre Piedras y Tacuarí, Monserrat (15 5763 7257, www.clubseverino.com.ar). Subte A, Piedras/bus 17, 59, 67, 91. **Open** 11.30pm-6am Mon. **Admission** AR$40-$50. **No credit cards. Map** p285 F10.

While the rest of Buenos Aires is slumbering Monday nights away, the city's carefree party crowd is dancing at Club Severino. The evening features rock, pop and hip-hop hits as well as electro beats spun by a line-up of some of the city's top DJs. Check the website for themed parties as well as live rock and hip-hop acts. Arrive before 1am for free entry. Around a thousand punters make this their party of choice in Monday's post-Bomba de Tiempo timeslot, and for good reason.

Cocoliche

Avenida Rivadavia 878, entre Suipacha y Esmeralda, Microcentro (4331 6413, www.cocoliche.net). Subte A, Piedras/bus 10, 17, 24, 28, 29, 39, 64, 100, 126. **Open** 11pm-7am Fri, Sat. **Admission** AR$40. **No credit cards. Map** p285 F10.

Underground, über-cool Cocoliche is a favourite with young local punters and party-hardy foreigners who take their electro seriously. Minimal house and drum 'n' bass pound the good-natured crowd to a trance-like pulp in the crammed basement while happy boozers line the street-level bar. The rotating programme often features the beatmaster owners in the box and draws in a good crowd.

THE BEST CLUB NIGHTS

Hype at Kika
Let your hair down on Tuesdays to hip hop, electro and drum 'n' bass. *See p216.*

Club 69 at Niceto Club
Thursday's debauched Club 69 is an unmissable classic. *See p216.*

MSTRPLN at Crobar
Join the hipster brigade on Friday for the line-up of bands, then hit the dancefloor to electro beats and indie tunes. *See right.*

Club One at Alsina
House beats make Sunday's fun-loving crowd forget it's back to work in the morning. *See p213.*

Club 69 at Niceto Club. *See p217.*

Crobar

Av. Cnel. Marcelino E. Freyre, y Avenida Infanta Isabel, Palermo (4778 1500, www.crobar.com). **Bus** 10, 34, 36. **Open** from 1am Fri, Sat. **Admission** varies. **Credit** AmEx, V. **Map** p287 N10.

Friday-night crowds hoof it to this superclub for the thumping debauchery of MSTRPLN (pronounced 'masterplan'), which brings in international and local bands, a first-rate crew of DJs mixing indie and electronic tunes as well as a rollicking bunch of global party people of the over-25 variety. A network of balconies, walkways and tiered VIP areas are cantilevered over Crobar's sometimes suffocating main dancefloor, which can get crowded on popular nights. Dress is flirty and sporty; and come with money to spare to cover the hefty entrance fee and pricey sauce. Saturday nights go off to Latin sounds.

Gong

Avenida Córdoba 634, entre Florida y Maipú, Retiro (4322 0680). **Bus** 22, 93, 126, 152. **Open** from 11.30pm Thur-Sat. **Admission** AR$30. **No credit cards**. **Map** p285 G11.

Gong has long been on the radar as a hangout for local teens: the central location, cheap booze and no-frills beats certainly make for some good times but perhaps not the night out of your wildest dreams. However, thanks to the fab underground party Dengue Dancing, this boliche buzzes on Thursday nights with fun-loving gay kids. House music takes over on Fridays, while Saturdays attract a thirty something crowd who relive their youth to rock music from the '70s and beyond.

★ Jet

Avenida Rafael Obligado 4801, Costanera Norte (4782 5599, www.jet.com.ar). **Bus** 45, 152, 160. **Open** from 10pm Thur-Sat. **Admission** varies. **Credit** AmEx, MC, V. **Map** p286 K12.

Night owls who enjoy permanent three-day weekends – including some of the poshest BA clubbers around – migrate week after week to Jet. Thursday night here is easily among the best club nights in the capital, attracting easy-on-the-eye locals and foreigners who come for a generous dose of electro fun that really gets going around 3am. Cocktails and tapas in a chilled-out lounge-bar setting get things started; as the night continues, the joint starts to resemble a tightly packed meat market. Friday – usually an indie night for a slightly younger crowd – is also popular, and Jet's the place to be seen on Saturday nights, when the restaurant opens and house beats pump on late into the night. But a word of warning girls and boys: dress to impress as Jet has one of the strictest door policies in BA.

Kika

Honduras 5339, entre Juan B Justo y Godoy Cruz, Palermo Soho (4137 5311, www.kikaclub.com.ar). Bus 34, 39, 55. **Open** from 12.30am Tue-Sat. **Admission** AR$40-$60. **No credit cards.** **Map** p283 N5.

Kika is one of the hottest nightclubs in BA, and Tuesday is Kika's weeknight to shine. Dubbed Hype, the event attracts a mix of in-the-know foreigners and party-hard locals who come to dance to

hip hop, electro, drum 'n' bass and dubstep. The partying continues on Wednesdays, as many *porteños* regularly choose to end their after-office evenings at the club, thanks to its big electro night. Come the weekend, DJs reel in large crowds who dance to *cachengue* and house beats.

Liv

Juan B Justo 1658, entre Gorriti y Cabrera, Palermo Soho (mobile 15 6222 9387). Bus 93, 140, 151, 168. **Open** midnight-6am Thur-Sat. **Admission** AR$50-$60. **No credit cards.** **Map** p283 N5.

If you like your nights out to be full-body experiences – light on conversation and heavy on music and people-watching – then Liv's Friday event, Together, should be just your thing. Pulsating tech house syncs with your heartbeat while deep red

Hype at Kika.

lighting casts the evening in naughty hues. Mingle with upper-crust twentysomething *porteños* out to see and be seen; bust your stuff on the dancefloor overhung with disco balls or make eyes at that hottie at the bar. On Thursdays the musical smörgåsbord broadens, serving a little bit of everything that you fancy, while on Saturdays, a more Latin beat keeps the younger crowd heaving.

★ Niceto Club

Niceto Vega 5510, entre Humboldt y Fitz Roy, Palermo Hollywood (4779 9396, www.niceto club.com). Bus 39, 93, 151, 168. **Open** from 9pm Thur-Sat. **Admission** AR$40. **No credit cards. Map** p283 N4.

One of the most sure-fire spots in town to get down, Niceto powers on with a packed roster in each of its two rooms. Now well into its second decade on the party scene, Thursday's glittering freak magnet Club 69 is an absolute must – the pumping crowd made up mainly of in-the-know foreigners rings in the weekend early with a full-on, jaw-dropping show of strippers, breakdancers and majestic drag queens bopping in time with the eclectic electro beats. Friday's Invasión *fiesta* draws in fun-loving throngs for live indie bands followed by electronica, pop and rock, while Saturday sees a rotating line-up of acts and DJs. *Photos p213, p215.*

★Pacha

Avenida Costanera Rafael Obligado, y La Pampa, Costanera Norte (4788 4280, www.pachabuenosaires.com). Bus 37, 160. **Open** from 1am Sat. **Admission** AR$50-$120. **Credit** V. **Map** p288 R11.

Riding on the stellar reputation of the global brand, Pacha remains a go-to destination for top-notch partying on Saturday nights, which feature international names from the DJ stratosphere, including Fat Boy Slim, Seb Fontaine and Marco Carola. The chandeliered main floor forms a sweaty pit of party-hard dance fiends, while those pretty and rich enough to go VIP have more chill-out options, including a sizeable upstairs terrace and a downstairs open-air seating and dancing area.

Podestá

Armenia 1740, entre Costa Rica y El Salvador, Palermo Soho (4832 2776, www.podestafotos. com). Bus 15, 34, 39, 55, 151, 160, 168. **Open** 10pm-3am Thur; 11pm-6am Fri, Sat. **Admission** AR$40-$50. **No credit cards. Map** p283 M5.

In the heart of Palermo Soho, this unpretentious two-floor club brings a refreshing change to the Buenos Aires clubbing scene. Attracting mainly laid-back, local folk, here it's not about who's wearing what but instead just about having a blooming good time. A generous happy hour (11pm-1am) and other drink promotions get punters merry, while DJs spin rock, house and popular remixes of old-school classics.

Roxy

Niceto Vega 5542, entre Fitz Roy y Humboldt, Palermo Hollywood (4777 0997, www.theroxy bar.com.ar). Bus 39, 140, 151, 168. **Open** from 9.30pm Thur; from 11pm Fri, Sat. **Admission** AR$30. **No credit cards. Map** p282 N4.

With a killer weekend line-up featuring two smash-hit club nights for the young and the restless, The Roxy is on top of its game. The spacious lounge area is perfect for relaxing into a cushy couch, knocking back a couple of cocktails and keeping an eye on the stage happenings (usually too-hip-to-care bands and VJs) before stepping out to boogie. Drop in for Friday's Roxtar rock fiesta or Saturday's Sympathy for the Party featuring live music then DJs afterwards. If you're partial to folk and indie sounds, hit Thursday's Underclub.

Tequila

Avenida Rafael Obligado 6211, y La Pampa, Costanera Norte (4781 6555). Bus 33, 34, 37, 45, 160. **Open** from midnight Thur-Sat. **Admission** AR$150. **No credit cards. Map** p288 R11.

This glitterati magnet is posh like Puerto Madero's Asia de Cuba (*see p213*) but with a distinct club feel (read: better house beats). Pad your pockets with plenty of *dinero* in order to properly enjoy the tasty brew, and expect to rub elbows with the international polo set or touring rock stars. Dress to impress. Credit cards are accepted at the bar but not at the door.

You Know My Name

Marcelo T de Alvear 1540, entre Montevideo y Paraná, Tribunales (4811 4730, www.youknowmyname.com.ar). Bus 39, 152. **Open** 7pm-3am Thur; 10pm-5am Fri, Sat. **Admission** AR$40 after 2am. Free Thur. **No credit cards. Map** p285 H10.

More pumped-up lounge than rocking club, You Know My Name (formerly called El Living) attracts a crowd of indie-hipsters and rockers. Quaff a cocktail on the couches under a row of TV monitors while the VJ (that's right, no DJs here) rotates quirky music videos – think early 1990s Eurotrash electronica, tunes from Madonna's *True Blue* era and contemporary pop. Arrive early for the decent set dinner menu.

INSIDE TRACK SEXY TIMES

For the polyamorous, BA boasts one of the largest swingers centres in South America. The seven-floor Anchorena SW Club (Anchorena 1121, Barrio Norte, 4961 8548, www.anchorenasw.com) has a club, pool, restaurant, bar and hotel and hosts an annual 'marathon'.

ARTS & ENTERTAINMENT

Performing Arts

Eclectic and experimental theatre thrills the porteño public.

Prestigious or vulgar, elitist or mass-market, theatre is what Buenos Aires breathes. On any given night you might be able to catch a big-budget Broadway-style musical, a no-budget production by a local playwright or an aerial interpretation of Shakespeare.

Don't worry if Spanish isn't your strong point: in local performance art, body language is key. It's not uncommon to catch shows that abandon dialogue altogether in favour of wild movement and pounding soundtracks.

Tickets in larger theatres can be pricey, but there are plenty of venues where you can catch mesmerising, passionate performances for just a handful of pesos.

Theatre

Wandering along Avenida Corrientes, the 'street that never sleeps' and the traditional centre of BA theatre, you can find glam porteño productions of foreign shows; or sample the *Revista Porteña* cabaret revue shows that have to be seen to be (dis)believed, where scantily-clad showgirls, ageing and surgically enhanced ex-vedettes and sarcastic comedians vie for stage time.

Off-Corrientes and off-off Corrientes venues can mean anything from modest playhouses in Abasto (the traditional centre of the city's alternative theatre scene) to improvised performance spaces – from plazas to living rooms – in San Telmo, Villa Crespo or Palermo.

Buenos Aires' taste in comedy is blunt and not always completely intellectual: slapstick routines based on mime are hugely popular, and are generally universally hilarious, even if you don't speak Spanish.

Thanks to the award-winning efforts of companies **De La Guarda**, **Fuerzabruta** and **Ojalá**, whose successful spectacles combine acrobatics with theatre, water and dangling on wires, all sorts of sensory effects are now often integral features of performances. Another great choice for non-Spanish speakers are the 'blind theatre' experiences offered by **Teatro Ciego** (*see p221*) and **AviTantes** (www.avitantes.com.ar), where the audience is blindfolded and shows are heavy on music and light on dialogue.

FESTIVALS

Although usually of the highest quality in terms of performance, theatre and dance festivals can be a bit disorganised. The most important is the **Festival Internacional de Teatro Buenos Aires** (*see p182*), which next swings through town in September 2013 and showcases local and international actors, dancers and musicians. In late March, keep an eye out for **Ciudanza** (www.ciudanza.gob.ar), a celebration of dance using parks, plazas and other public spaces as stages. At the **Festival Cambalache** (www.festivalcambalache.com.ar, *photo p222*), held each December, tango is fused with theatre and alternative dance forms. Helping to keep alive the traumatic memory of Argentina's 'Dirty War' is the sober and moving **Teatro por la Identidad** (Theatre for Identity, www.teatroxlaidentidad.net). This festival, which usually takes place in August, broaches the issue of the identity of children abducted from their 'disappeared' parents.

INFORMATION AND TICKETS

You can buy tickets at each venue's *boletería* (box office), often with cash only, or through **Ticketek** (5237 7200, www.ticketek.com.ar) or **TuEntrada** (www.tuentrada.com) for major productions or venues. These ticket agencies accept credit cards and booking fees apply, or you can pay in cash at ticket offices around town. Discounted tickets for plays, musicals, and films are available from **Cartelera Baires**

(Unit 24, Avenida Corrientes 1382, www. cartelerabaires.com) and from **Cartelera Lavalle** (Lavalle 742, 4322 1559, www.123info. com.ar). You can reserve by phone, but must pay in cash when you collect the tickets.

MAJOR VENUES

There are two main theatre centres funded by the national government. The attractive **Teatro Nacional Cervantes** (*see right*), and the **Complejo Teatral de Buenos Aires,** comprised of five separate venues including La Boca's picturesque **Teatro de la Ribera**. The flagship is the **Teatro San Martín** (*see p220*) on Avenida Corrientes. You can buy tickets in person, or at www.teatrosanmartin.com.ar.

Well worth checking out are the cultural centres, such as the **Ricardo Rojas** (*see p191*), **Ciudad Cultural Konex** (*see p221*), **Centro Cultural Recoleta** (*see p61*) and **Centro Cultural Borges** (*see p45*), which host wide-ranging programmes and often run performing arts workshops. Also on Avenida Corrientes are the **Teatro Opera Citi** (*see p220*) and the **Gran Rex** (*see p208*), used for concerts.

Multiteatro

Avenida Corrientes 1283, entre Talcahuano y Libertad, Tribunales (4382 9140, www.multi teatro.com.ar). Subte B, Uruguay/bus 26, 60, 102. **Box office** 10am-8pm daily. **Tickets** AR$130-$150. **Credit** AmEx, DC, MC, V. **Map** p285 G10.
In its three smallish auditoriums, Multiteatro stages regular provocative one person shows as well as local adaptations of contemporary classics. Well-known actress Cecilia Roth has been known to tread the boards here. Tickets can be bought online.

Teatro Astral

Avenida Corrientes 1639, entre Montevideo y Rodríguez Peña, Tribunales (4374 5707, www.teatroastral.com.ar). Subte B, Callao/ bus 12, 24, 37, 60. **Box office** 10am-10pm daily. **Tickets** AR$150-$230. **Credit** MC, V. **Map** p285 G9.
Argentina's most famous feather-clad showgirls have swayed their hips on the stage of the Astral, the main revue theatre on Corrientes, but Spanish-language shows for children are held here too.
▶ *Try another Corrientes classic: pizzeria Guerrín is just three blocks away at Corrientes 1368.*

Teatro Liceo

Avenida Rivadavia 1499, y Paraná, Congreso (4381 5745, www.multiteatro.com.ar). Subte A, Sáenz Peña/bus 39, 60, 102, 168. **Box office** 10am-8pm Mon, Tue; 10am-start of first show Wed-Sun. **Tickets** AR$120-$160. **Credit** AmEx, MC, V. **Map** p285 G9.
Part of the same theatre group as Multiteatro (*see left*), this 700-seater, 140-year-old venue is the oldest in the city and is still going strong. It focuses largely on Spanish-language productions.

★ Teatro Nacional Cervantes

Libertad 815, y Avenida Córdoba, Tribunales (4816 4224, www.teatrocervantes.gov.ar). Subte D, Tribunales/bus 29, 39, 109. **Box office** 10am-9pm Wed-Sun. Closed Jan. **Tickets** AR$30 Thur; AR$40 Fri-Sun. **No credit cards. Map** p285 G10.
The packed programme at the Cervantes includes Latin American and Spanish theatre and dance, as well as free film screenings of mainly Argentinian classics on Wednesdays and Thursdays. The building is a work of art in its own right. *Photo p220.*

ARTS & ENTERTAINMENT

Ojalá.

Teatro Nacional Cervantes. See p219.

Teatro Opera Citi
Avenida Corrientes 860, entre Suipacha y Esmeralda, Microcentro (4326 1335, www.operaciti-teatro.com.ar). Subte B, Carlos Pellegrini or C, Diagonal Norte or D, 9 de Julio/bus 10, 17, 24, 29, 70. **Box office** 10am-8pm daily. **Shows** varies. **Tickets** AR$50-$220. **Credit** AmEx, DC, MC, V. **Map** p285 F10.
This is one of BA's classic auditoriums. Since its opening in 1872 it has hosted concerts from the likes of tango star Hugo del Carril as well as international greats such as Louis Armstrong. These days, it's the place to find Broadway musicals such as *Beauty and the Beast*, as well as occasional concerts.

Teatro del Pueblo
Avenida Roque Sáenz Peña 943, entre Carlos Pellegrini y Suipacha, Microcentro (4326 3606, www.teatrodelpueblo.org.ar). Subte B, Carlos Pellegrini or C, Diagonal Norte or D, 9 de Julio/bus 17, 24, 59. **Box office** 4-8pm Wed-Thur; 5-9pm Fri-Sun. **Shows** varies. **Tickets** AR$60. **No credit cards. Map** p285 G10.
Founded in 1930, this was one of the very first independent theatres in Latin America. Dedicated to bringing national theatre to the public, it only stages works by Argentinian playwrights, and organises a busy programme of acting workshops and courses.

★ Teatro San Martín
Avenida Corrientes 1530, entre Paraná y Montevideo, Tribunales (0800 333 5254, www.teatrosanmartin.com.ar). Subte B, Uruguay/bus 24, 26, 60, 102. **Box office** 10am-10pm daily. **Shows** Wed-Sun. **Tickets** AR$30-$120; half-price Wed. **Credit** AmEx, MC, V. **Map** p285 G9.
Renowned for the quality and eclecticism of its programmes which range from cast-iron classics to avant-garde experiments – the Teatro San Martín incorporates three auditoriums with a combined capacity of 1,700, in a building that is a serious testament to 1970s design.

ALTERNATIVE VENUES

For listings of independent theatre, see www.alternativateatral.com (in Spanish only). Many performance spaces are small, so it's best to reserve by phone, then pay in cash on arrival.

Actors Studio
Avenida Díaz Vélez 3842, entre Medrano y Jerónimo Salguero, Almagro (4958 8268, www.actors-studio.org). Subte A, Castro Barros/bus 19, 128, 180. **Box office** 5-8pm Mon, Tue, Thur-Fri; 5-9pm Sat, Sun. **Tickets** AR$40. **No credit cards. Map** p285 J4.
Alongside a varied programme that features new versions of classics and a diverse selection of original works, this studio also runs acting classes and intensive workshops.

Belisario Club de Cultura
Avenida Corrientes 1624, entre Rodríguez Peña y Montevideo, Tribunales (4373 3465). Subte B, Callao/bus 24, 26, 60, 102. **Box office** 7-11pm Fri, Sat; 6-8pm Sun. **Shows** 9.30pm, 11.30pm Fri, Sat; 8pm Sun. **Tickets** AR$45-$55. **No credit cards. Map** p285 G9.
A small but interesting venue, the Belisario Club de Cultura is home to some of the best experimental theatre around in the city, including performances with circus-influenced antics, and improvisation shows where the actors take their cue from audience requests.

El Camarín de las Musas

Mario Bravo 960, entre Tucumán y Avenida
Córdoba, Abasto (4862 0655, www.elcamarin
delasmusas.com.ar). Subte B, Medrano/bus 26,
128. **Box office** from 8.30pm Thur; from 8pm
Fri; from 7.30pm Sat. **Tickets** AR$50-$80.
No credit cards. Map p286 K8.
This is a sophisticated, multi-purpose venue that
gets rave reviews for its highbrow productions. You
can enjoy a reasonably priced meal or a drink in the
arty restaurant before moving to the stripped-down
space to watch a show.

La Carbonera

Balcarce 998, y Estados Unidos, San Telmo
(4362 2651). Bus 20, 64, 86, 195. **Box office**
varies. **Tickets** AR$25-$50. **No credit cards.**
Map p284 D10.
Contemporary dance, theatre and experimental performances all take place in this edgy backstreet
space tucked within an old colonial house in
San Telmo.

★ Ciudad Cultural Konex

Avenida Sarmiento 3131, entre Jean Jaurès
y Anchorena, Abasto (4864 3200, www.
ciudadculturalkonex.org). Subte B, Carlos
Gardel/bus 26, 111, 180. **Box office** 5-10pm
daily. **Tickets** AR$35-$80. **Credit** AmEx,
MC, V. **Map** p282 I5.
This trendy complex, based in a former factory in
the Abasto neighbourhood, provides a gritty industrial backdrop to a wide array of original events,
pulling in a young, bohemian (and often dread-
locked) crowd of locals and in-the-know visitors.
▶ *Popular percussion ensemble La Bomba de*
Tiempo performs here every Monday night.

Espacio Callejón

Humahuaca 3759, entre Bulnes y Mario Bravo,
Abasto (4862 1167, http://espaciocallejon.blogspot.
com). Subte B, Medrano/bus 92, 151, 168. **Box**
office opens 1hr before shows; and 7.30-10.30pm
Wed-Sun. **Tickets** AR$30-$60. **No credit cards.**
Map p286 J7.
One of the best places in BA for gutsy and unusual
new productions, this quirky theatre also offers
evening classes in clowning and theatre.

NoAvestruz

Humboldt 1857, entre Costa Rica y El Salvador,
Palermo (4777 6956, www.noavestruz.com.ar).
Bus 21, 111, 161, 166. **Box office** 5-8.30pm
Tue-Sun. **Tickets** from AR$30. **No credit**
cards. Map p287 N7.
This intimate multispace offers dance and
theatre performances, short courses, shows for
children and concerts embracing classical, world
music, tango and contemporary folk. There's
also a bar. Reserve tickets by calling the number
listed above after 6pm.

Teatro Ciego

Zelaya 3006, entre Jean Jaurès y Anchorena,
Abasto (6379 8596/www.teatrociego.org). Subte
B Carlos Gardel/bus 24, 140, 168. **Box office**
from 3.30pm Mon; from 5pm Tue-Thur; from 6pm
Fri; from 3pm Sat; from 4pm Sun. **Tickets**
AR$40-$80. **Credit** AmEx, MC, V. **Map** p282 J6.
For those looking for a sensory rather than cerebral
experience, the 'blind theatre' offers dinners, performances and tango classes in pitch darkness. Shows
are often music-based (ideal for non-Spanish speakers) and the audience is blindfolded.

Timbre 4

Avenida Boedo 640, entre México e
Independencia, Boedo (4932 4395/, www.timbre4.
com). Bus 126, 128, 160. **Box office** from 5pm
Wed-Sun. **Shows** 7-11pm Thur-Sun. **Tickets**
AR$30-$70. **Credit** AmEx, MC, V.
The likes of Francis Ford Coppola and Gael García
Bernal have been known to drop by to catch the lat-
est provocative, experimental show crafted under
cult director Claudio Tolcachir.

Dance

Although tango (*see pp229-234*) tends to
dominate the dance scene in Buenos Aires,
there's a strong classical tradition dating
back to the 1920s, when South America's first
academic ballet company was founded in the
Teatro Colón. The world of tutus and pointe
shoes remained the reserve of the elite until
Julio Bocca arrived in 1985 and brought ballet
to the masses, staging hugely successful
performances in non-conventional arenas
such as the Boca Juniors football stadium.
His choreography to Astor Piazzolla's tango
music was equally audacious. In 1990,
Bocca founded the **Ballet Argentino**
(www.granballetargentino.com), and in 2007
he danced for the last time in a star-studded
outdoor show that blocked off Avenida 9 de
Julio. Nowadays, Argentinian ballet dancers
such as Paloma Herrera, Iñaki Urlezaga and
Hernán Cornejo have become, in their field,
as famous as football stars. Another world-
renowned, home-grown company to look
out for is Maximiliano Guerra's **Ballet del**
Mercosur. And keep an eye open for the
avant-garde company **Tangokinesis**
(www.tangokinesis.com), known for its
absurdist take on tango.
   Traditional styles of dance, such as the foot-
stomping *zamba* and *chacarera*, both from the
north-western province of Salta, can be seen
and practised at *peñas* (folk music venues; *see*
p210). *Murgas*, neighbourhood groups that
combine energetic, semi-tribal dance moves
with a steady drum beat, perform in plazas

and parks around the city, especially during the carnival season in February. Catch the cheerful drumming troupe that gathers on Sunday afternoons at Parque Lezama before winding noisily through San Telmo's streets.

VENUES

The **Centro Cultural Borges** (*see p45*) organises a diverse programme of flamenco, ballet and postmodern tango. Ballet performances are also staged at the magnificent **Teatro Colón** (*see p205*).

For modern dance, a good option is **El Portón de Sánchez** (*see below*) and the **Teatro Presidente Alvear** (Avenida Corrientes 1659, 4374 1425, www.complejoteatral.gob.ar). Alternative spaces include the tiny Congreso-area **Teatro del Sur** (Venezuela 2255, 4941 1951, www.teatrodelsur.blogspot.com) and San Telmo's **La Carbonera** (*see p221*). Flamenco fans should try the **Teatro Astral** (*see p219*) or **Teatro Avenida** (Avenida de Mayo 1222, Congreso, 4381 0662). The Compañía de Danza Contemporánea is based, along with the Ballet Folklórico Nacional, at the **Centro Nacional de la Música y la Danza** (México 564, 4361 1672), in a splendid old building that was the national library back in the day.

El Portón de Sánchez

Sánchez de Bustamante 1034, entre Avenida Córdoba y San Luis, Abasto (4863 2848, http://portondesanchez.blogspot.com). Bus 29, 106, 140. **Box office** 9am-9pm Mon-Fri; 1hr before the show Sat, Sun. **Tickets** AR$40-$50. **No credit cards. Map** p286 J8.

This venue is a dance studio by day and offers a contemporary, dance-heavy programme featuring celebrated avant-garde troupes, plus plays that fall at the pricier, polished end of the indie spectrum.

DANCE SCHOOLS

Dance classes are popular, and there are plenty on offer. If your Spanish is up to it, the cultural centres like the **Centro Cultural Ricardo Rojas** (*see p191*) and **Centro Cultural Borges** (*see p45*) are the most accessible. As well as its regular tango programme, **La Viruta** (*see p283*) offers classes in rock'n'roll and salsa. **Swingin' Buenos Aires** (www.swinginbuenosaires.com.ar) runs swing classes for all levels at venues around the city. **Tedancari** (Avenida Corrientes 4534, Almagro, 4504 4115, www.tedancari.com) instructors teach dance styles from Afro-Cuban to rumba. For modern and classical dance, check out the schools run by **Noemí Coelho** and **Rodolfo Olguín** (www.coelholguin.com.ar). If you're tempted to follow in the footsteps of De La Guarda and get airborne, you can learn a few trapeze tricks at **Brenda Angiel**'s school (Bartolomé Mitre 4272, Almagro, 4983 6980, www.danzaerea.com.ar) or at **Circo del Aire** (Chacabuco 629, San Telmo, 4362 9556, www.circodelaire.blogspot.com). Or sign up for an aerial combat course in English at **Cuerda Producciones** (Iguazú 451, Parque Patricios, mobile 15 6381 6796, www.cuerdaproducciones.com). Details about tango classes and schools are included in the **Tango** section (*see p229*).

Cambalache Festival. *See p218.*

Sport & Fitness

BA is kicking (and punching, and trotting, and tackling).

Whether nationally or at local level, football is what many Argentinians eat, sleep and breathe, and since the government bought the exclusive rights to televise matches, it has become a controversial political marketing machine. But although football is king, Argentina has produced big names in many other sports. Luciana Aymar is the world's best hockey player, Adolfo Cambiaso is the world's best polo player and in Juan Martín del Potro, Argentina has a genuine chance of producing the world's top tennis player. Rugby, too, occasionally makes the headlines: national team Los Pumas is consistently ranked in the top ten by the International Rugby Board.

SPECTATOR SPORTS

Basketball

Along with Brazil, Argentina has one of the strongest South American basketball teams: it's won the South American Championships 12 times. Home-grown talent has produced NBA stars like Carlos Delfino (Milwaukee Bucks) and Emanuel 'Manu' Ginóbili (San Antonio Spurs). It's worth trying to catch a local league game; the best teams to watch are Boca Juniors, who play in La Boca at **Estadio Luis Conde** (Arzobispo Espinoza 600, 4309 4748, www.bocajuniors.com.ar) and Obras Sanitarias, whose home is in Núñez at the **Club Atlético Obras Sanitarias de la Nación** (Avenida del Libertador 7395, 4702 4655, www.clubosn.com.ar). The national league (La Liga Nacional de Básquetbol) runs from October to June.

Boxing

Argentina's glory days in the boxing arena peaked in the mid 1980s, but the sport still draws crowds to **Luna Park** (*see p208*), BA's answer to Madison Square Garden, where the red carpet is rolled out every month or so for the ritual of the Saturday night fight. Smaller matches are sometimes held at the **Federación Argentina de Box** (Castro Barros 75, 4981 8615, www.fabox.com.ar) in Almagro, or in other venues throughout the country.

Football

Many of the top clubs started out in Buenos Aires before moving to the suburbs, and today, more than half of the 20 first division teams are located in and around the city. The league is split into two seasons: *Apertura* (opening) from August to December and *Clausura* (closing) from February to July. Football here tends to be spirited, highly competitive and a source of national pride. The best-known team is **Club Atlético Boca Juniors**, which plays at the **Estadio Alberto J Armando**, more commonly known as 'La Bombonera' – the chocolate box. The so-called *superclásico* fixtures between Boca Juniors and arch-rivals **Club Atlético River Plate** are thought by some to be the greatest 'derbies' in the world. In June 2011, to the shock of fans across the country, River Plate was astonishingly dumped out of the first division, but managed to creep back up a year later.

Other clubs include **Club Atlético Independiente**, with a ground just south of La Boca in the suburb of Avellaneda, and along with **Racing Club** and **San Lorenzo de Almagro**.

For Boca Juniors or River Plate matches, you can get tickets through agencies like **Tangol** (4312 7276, www.tangol.com). Tickets sold at La Bombonera run out fast, and it's not

Striking Out

Brazil and Argentina's football gods are fierce on and off the pitch.

Picture the scene: it's 13 July 2014, and the colossal Maracana stadium in Rio de Janeiro is packed to bursting point with frenzied fans. Football's World Cup final is about to be played and the atmosphere is a heady mix of exhilaration and nervous tension. At last, the two teams stride out on to the pitch to a thunderous roar. One side is dressed in canary yellow and the other wears sky blue and white. It is Brazil versus Argentina – the fiercest rivalry in international football is to be played out on the biggest stage of all.

This scenario may still be a long way from becoming reality, but ever since Brazil was awarded the hosting rights to the 2014 World Cup, it has already played out in the daydreams of millions of Brazilians and Argentinians.

It would be a dream final indeed; one that would tantalise the sporting world and both excite and terrify football-lovers from the two countries involved.

The only thing that pleases an Argentinian as much as the national team winning a football match is Brazil's national team losing a football match. And the sentiment is mutual. It's understandable, then, that when the two teams clash, the winners experience such an intoxicating mix of joy and *schadenfreude* that they can often be seen laughing while simultaneously crying hysterically and generally acting like complete nutters. The losers are plunged into the dark pits of depression, where despair precipitates further despair and there is almost certainly no light at the end of the tunnel.

Unfortunately for Argentina, when it comes to not winning World Cups, they are comfortably ahead of the old enemy. Despite consistently producing absurdly talented players, Argentina has thus far only achieved world champion status on two occasions, in 1978 and 1986. In the second case, the team was inspired by the greatest player of all time (if you are talking to an Argentinian), the street urchin-turned-demigod, Diego Maradona. Brazil

meanwhile, as a result of consistently producing absurdly talented players, has won a record five world titles. Three of those championships were in part down to the sublime skills of Pelé, the greatest player of all time (according to Brazilian lore).

There is simply nothing more entertaining than an overweight, half-crazy Argentinian man in his fifties arguing with a 70-something narcissistic Brazilian. Lucky for us, then, that in the intolerable four-year wait between World Cups, Maradona and Pelé keep everybody amused with unremitting, playful banter-slash-venomous diatribe. These days they can often be found bickering over the comparative greatness of Argentina's multiple World Player of the Year winner, Lionel Messi, and Brazil's emerging *wunderkind*, Neymar.

HIGHLIGHTS INCLUDE
Pelé 'Now everyone is talking about Messi; he is a star. But [to be the best ever] he must first become better than Neymar.'
Maradona 'My God, that is just stupid. Maybe Neymar is the best player in the world, but only if you say that Messi is from a different planet.'
Pelé 'Maradona or Pelé? I reply that all you have to do is look at the facts: how many goals did he score with his right foot or with his head?'
Maradona 'I think Pelé mixed up his medication. He took the morning pill instead of the night pill.'

As the 2014 World Cup draws closer, the heat will gradually be turned up on this already-simmering sporting rivalry. Though Pelé and Maradona already appear to be overcooked, the likes of Neymar, Messi and Co. will have to survive the blast furnace of expectations from their respective nations if they are to achieve the ultimate goal. With the passing of time, however, failure to win the big prize is eventually forgiven. Unless you happen to fail against that rival South American team – in which case it's intolerable.

Sport & Fitness

advisable to walk around La Boca with lots
of money on you. Do stay away from touts
as they often sell fakes. For any other team,
tickets can be bought at the relevant ground
(cash only). Standard prices range from AR$50
to AR$80, rising to AR$200. Go with a local
who knows the territory, or with an organised
tour company – prices start from AR$400 for
a Boca Juniors game and they offer transport
to and from the stadium and guarantee good
seats in the *platea* rather than down in the
more brazen *popular* (terrace) area, where bags
of wee, among other things, have been known
to fly. Don't take valuables, and keep your wits
about you for occasional instances of violence,
mostly restricted to the *popular* areas.

Estadio Alberto J Armando (La Bombonera)

Brandsen 805, y la Vía, La Boca
(4309 4700/www.bocajuniors.com.ar).
Bus 10, 29, 53, 64. **Map** p284 B9.
Watching a game here is a unique experience: come
kick-off, a cacophony of fireworks and abuse greets
both players and refs, and even if you're not a fully
fledged footy fan, it's hard not to be moved by the
spectacle. The *platea baja* in the stands area is your
recommended vantage point. *Popular* tickets will put
you in with the hardcore fans: not a particularly safe
place to be. Neither is the area around the stadium,
so leave valuables at home and avoid walking
around the area unnecessarily.

Estadio Monumental

Avenida Figueroa Alcorta 7597, y Udaondo,
Núñez (4789 1327/www.cariverplate.com.ar).
Bus 12, 29, 42, 107, 130. **Map** p288 T10.
The Monumental – home to Club Atlético River
Plate, eternal rivals of Boca Juniors – was the
setting for the opening and the final of the 1978
World Cup. Spend that extra few pesos on a ticket
for the *platea* and avoid the *popular*, unless knife
fighting and sweaty hooligans are your thing.
Guided tours are given daily between 11am
and 5pm (AR$45).

Horse racing

The year's most important races fall in
November and December, but you can catch
smaller meets all year round. The only grass
track in Argentina, Zona Norte's **Hipódromo
de San Isidro** (Avenida Márquez 504, 4743
4011, www.hipodromosanisidro.com.ar) hosts
races on Wednesdays and at weekends, with
entry at AR$5-$10. Turf's most important
venue, the **Hipódromo Argentino**
(Avenida del Libertador 4101, 4778 2800,
www.palermo.com.ar) in Palermo hosts year-
round meets on Mondays and alternating
Fridays, Saturdays and Sundays. Entrance

is free, and attendance is often sparse. Betting
is on the tote system, and no alcohol can be
purchased at the track.

Motor racing

If you stare at 9 de Julio and Avenida de Mayo
long enough (or any intersection in the city for
that matter) you'd probably think motor racing is
the country's national sport. See the real thing at
**Autódromo de la Ciudad de Buenos Aires
Oscar Gálvez** in Villa Lugano (Avenida Roca
6902, 4604 9100, www.autodromoba.com.ar),
where races are held most Fridays, Saturdays
and Sundays, and there is stock car racing some
Fridays at 8.30pm.

Polo

Polo is played in the spring in BA, with the
season starting in September and running
through to December when the final of the
venerable Argentinian Open is played at the
Campo Argentino de Polo de Palermo
(Avenida del Libertador 4300, 4777 6444,
www.aapolo.com). Tickets for tournaments
are available from Ticketek. For the rest of
the year, the grounds remain relatively quiet,
though chukkas continue to be played
elsewhere, except in winter. Complete beginners
and experienced players can have polo lessons
at several estancias in Buenos Aires province.
For more on polo and polo day options, see
p226 **Horse Play**.

Rugby

The Argentinian rugby season runs from
March to November and is mostly dominated
by two teams from the affluent northern
suburb of San Isidro: **Club Atlético de San
Isidro** (CASI) (Roque Sáenz Peña 499, 4743
4242, www.casi.org.ar) and the **San Isidro
Club** (SIC) (Blanco Encalada 404, 4766 2030,
www.sanisidroclub.com.ar). Argentina's
national team, nicknamed Los Pumas, is
currently ranked best in the Americas.

Tennis

Argentina's obsession with winning the Davis
Cup goes on and on. In the past ten years, they
have reached three finals and countless semi
and quarterfinals. The good news is that Juan
Martín del Potro is back to top form, while
clay court specialist Juan Monaco and former
number three seed David Nalbandian continue
to give del Potro plenty of support. Sadly,
since the retirement of doubles specialist
Paula Suárez, Argentina has struggled to
challenge for major prizes on the women's

ARTS & ENTERTAINMENT

Horsing Around

Pretty ponies and studs in white trousers: what's not to like?

It's easy to dismiss polo as a sport for toffs, but in Argentina, it's far more accessible and it's easy to have a go or just watch from the sidelines (and you don't even have to buy a hat).

The world's oldest team sport, polo found its way from India to Europe in the mid 19th century, and was brought to its spiritual home of Argentina by British ranchers and engineers in 1875. Nowadays, the best players in the world are Argentinian; nine of them currently with a perfect ten handicap. The best ponies are also bred in Argentina: intelligent, agile thoroughbreds. Glance at the team sheets and you might wonder if it's only the horses that are bred to win. Out of the six brothers that make up the Novillo Astrada clan, four saddle up for the prize-winning La Aguada team, then there are six Heguys scattered across the country's other top teams, as well as the Pieres brothers of the Ellerstina team.

At its best, polo can be genuinely thrilling to watch. Once the teams have bullied off, the concept is pretty simple: use the mallets (*tacos*) to hit the ball into the goal, or set up your mount for a crowd pleasing 'pony goal'. There are six chukkas of seven minutes each in a match, with the four players on each team changing horses every chukka (the best without touching the ground). The teams change ends after each goal, which both minimises wind advantage and confuses inattentive newcomers. To watch the best in action – and spot a fair few local celebrities to boot – buy seats to the highly exciting **Argentinian Open**, the climax of the polo season, held at Palermo's magnificent 16,000 capacity **Campo Argentino de Polo** (*see p225*) in November/December. Here, you'll no doubt catch a glimpse of the 'Maradona of Polo' in action (but think Beckham on a horse rather than the not particularly equestrian Diego), Adolfo Cambiaso – a Grand Slam winner too many times to count, captain of champions team La Dolfina, and polo's most swooned over pin-up. After the matches, the surgically-enhanced and the naturally beautiful stay on for much champagne quaffing and networking.

The other two big tournaments making up the coveted Triple Crown are **Tortugas** (mid October at Tortugas Country Club) and **Hurlingham** (early November at Hurlingham). Tickets are available on Ticketek (www.ticketek.com).

If you're keen to rid yourself of elite preconceptions and have a go yourself, the friendly folk at **Guapa Polo** (www.guapapolo.com.ar) offer personalised polo days at a lovely *estancia* just 50 minutes from the city. These include a traditional *asado* (barbecue) and transport – perfect for those in search of authenticity. Outside the city, in Pilar, **Argentina Polo Day** (www.argentinapoloday.com.ar) also has informative polo days all year round, as does the smart **Puesto Viejo Polo Club** (www.puestoviejoestancia.com.ar) in Cañuelas.

scene. Important matches, like the Abierto de Tenis de Buenos Aires (Copa Claro) in February, are played at the **Buenos Aires Lawn Tennis Club** (Olleros 1510, y Avenida del Libertador) in Palermo.

ACTIVE SPORTS & FITNESS

Whether for bowling, horseriding on the plains, having a kick around or hitting the gym solo, BA is perfect for hands-on sports enthusiasts. Some multi-sport venues (*centros deportivos*) with good locations and facilities are **Parque Norte** in Núñez (Avenida Cantilo, y Güiraldes, 4787 1382, www.parquenorte.com) and in Palermo, **Club de Amigos** (Avenida Figueroa Alcorta 3885, 4801 1213, www.clubdeamigos.org.ar), both of which have swimming pools, tennis courts and football pitches.

Cycling

BA's flat streets are ideal for exploring on two wheels, and with the introduction of the city's extensive cycle paths and bike sharing scheme, **Mejor en Bici** (http://mejorenbici. buenosaires.gob.ar), it has become more bike-friendly. Still, great care should be taken and defensive cycling practised. **Critical Mass** rides take place on the first Sunday of each month (check out the Facebook page). **La Bicicleta Naranja** (www.labicicleta naranja.com.ar) offers bike hire in San Telmo at Pasaje Giuffra 308 and Palermo at Nicaragua 4825, and bikes are also available for hire near the entrance to the **Reserva Ecológica** (*see p78*). Take ID for any bike hire. **Biking Buenos Aires** (www.biking buenosaires.com) offers half- and full-day city tours (AR$200-$400) and has teamed up with **Graffitimundo** (*see p142*) for weekend graffiti tours (AR$160) around Palermo and Villa Crespo.

Football

Whether it's joining an impromptu game in the park – just ask to play – or getting a group together and hiring out a pitch, you'll never be far from a good match in Bueno Aires. Look out for the words *cancha de fútbol* (football pitch); there are hundreds of them. One of the bigger, better five-a-side centres in Recoleta is **Catalinas Futbol y Paddle Claudio Marangoni** (Coronel Diaz y French, 4804 0524, www.claudio marangoni.com.ar), which charges around AR$250 for an hour. Or try **Buenos Aires Fútbol Amigos** (mobile 15 3198 1550, www.fcbafa.com), which organises weekly

five-a-side games and *asados* for locals and foreigners of all levels (AR$35).

Golf

Though Buenos Aires has no stand-out golf tournament to speak of – most are played at the seaside city of Mar del Plata – recreational golfers can get their putt on at the **Campo de Golf de la Ciudad de Buenos Aires** (Avenida Tornquist 6397, 4772 7261) in Palermo, which has an 18-hole course. There's also plenty to aim at at the modern driving range, **Driving Norte** (Avenida Cantilo y La Pampa, 4788 5666, www.drivingnorte.com.ar), from a green on an island to the huge net protecting the religious theme park, **Tierra Santa** (*see p78*), located right next door. For the more serious golfer, customised tour service **Sur Golf** (mobile 15 5515 2322, www.surgolf.com) has access to 25 of the best golf courses in Buenos Aires province.

Gyms & spas

Buenos Aires gyms are generally well equipped, though the multi-sport complexes listed above are cheaper. Most larger hotels let non-guests use their facilities for a fee.

Slick, clean and busy, the **Megatlón** (www.megatlon.com) chain has all the latest exercise devices and all manner of interesting-looking hamster wheels. It offers a good range of classes and has branches throughout the city, with rates from AR$145 per day or AR$560 per month. One of the city's most exclusive clubs, **Le Parc Gym & Spa** (San Martín 645, 4311 9191, www.leparc.com) has exercise machines plus a swimming pool, squash courts and even beauty treatments, all bang in the centre of downtown. Rates are AR$100 per day and AR$380 per month.

Horseriding

As well as tasty home-cooked food and charming accommodation, most of the estancias (ranches) in Buenos Aires province offer day and weekend packages, which include as much riding as your backside can stand. Beginners and experienced riders are catered for. One recommended option is **Estancia Los Dos Hermanos** – for this and others, *see p243*. For a more structured approach within the city limits, Palermo's **Club Alemán de Equitación** (Avenida Dorrego 4045, 4778 7060, www.hipico-cae.com.ar) gives riding and show jumping classes. For polo classes and matches, *see p225*.

ARTS & ENTERTAINMENT

Racquet sports

Salguero Tenis (Salguero 3350, 4805 5144) has open-air clay tennis courts as well as squash courts. **Pasco Tenis** (Cochabamba 2258, 4941 0333, www.pascotenis.com.ar) is a small, well-equipped complex with a gym, parking and six quality clay tennis courts for all weather.

Running

Veteran marathoners and iPod-rocking joggers show up at Palermo's **Parque Tres de Febrero**. Hammer your workout on the marked 1,600-metre loop around the lake, or head out on dirt trails that take you along the safe, tree-lined Avenida Figueroa Alcorta. Scores of running groups can be found here too: if you'd like to join, just head for the Rosedal (rose garden) and ask around. The best routes downtown are the flat promenades along **Puerto Madero** or the red-earth tracks in the **Reserva Ecológica** (*see p78*).

Swimming

Swimming and the Río de la Plata ought not to be mentioned in the same sentence – at least not near the city centre, where the water is very polluted. Instead, try the gym chains with pools – **Megatlón** (*see p227*) has several around the city. Belgrano's **Acercar** (José Hernández 1350, 4783 5864, www.natatorioacercar.com.ar) has lap lanes open to the public, while hotel pools are often open to non-guests for a daily or monthly fee. The **Hilton** has a lovely outdoor pool for those who can afford it (www.hilton.com, day use of pool and spa costs AR$350). Multi-sport venues **Parque Norte** and **Club de Amigos** (*see p227*) also have outdoor pools.

Watersports

Most of the aquatic and nautical activities on the Río de la Plata take place in Zona Norte, 45 minutes from downtown Buenos Aires. Popular riverside leisure spot **Perú Beach** (Elcano 794, 4793 8762, www.peru-beach.com.ar) in Acassuso can be reached by the **Tren de la Costa** (*see p188*) and offers kitesurfing, windsurfing, roller hockey and skateboarding, as well as a snack bar.

At **Renosto Náutica y Deportes** in San Fernando (Avenida del Libertador 1999, 4744 6090, www.wake-board.com.ar), you can take lessons in waterskiing and wakeboarding. One-hour kayaking classes are offered by **Puro Remo** (4313 8008, www.puroremo.com.ar) from AR$60; it also offers full-moon rowing trips from September to April.

Buena Onda Yoga.

Yoga & pilates

Buena Onda Yoga (www.buenaonda yoga.com) is an American-run studio that offers group and private classes in English and Spanish at locations across the city, at AR$60 per class.

The cosier **Buenos Aires Life Centre** (www.balifecentre.com) in the heart of Barrio Norte is a friendly studio that also offers both group and private sessions in English given by native speakers, as well as massages and nutritious lunches.

Meanwhile, **Bikram Yoga Buenos Aires** (Avenida Las Heras 3541, Palermo, www.byba.com.ar) is the only bikram studio in the city. Lunchtime sessions are in English.

At pilates studio **La Usina Pilates** (Studio 18, Costa Rica 4684, 4831 2534, www.pilates lausina.blogspot.com) in Palermo Soho, you can take classes using reformers, balls and other equipment.

Tango

Traditionalists and hipsters are embracing this seductive dance.

Largely abandoned by the mid 20th century, the *tanguero* and his genre are presently enjoying a colourful revival. Beyond the gimmicky tourist shows and pouty posers of La Boca and San Telmo, Argentina's most famous cultural export is part of everyday life for many *porteños*, and *milongas*, or tango dancehalls, are the places to discreetly observe locals working their way across packed dancefloors.

Visitors are not restricted to simply watching from the sidelines, of course. The inexperienced can get to grips with the basics at a class before trying out their moves at beginner-friendly venues like **La Catedral** (*see p232*) and **La Viruta** (*see p233*), which are increasingly attracting a young and bohemian crowd.

TANGO IN THE CAPITAL

Tango boasts a set of myths and traditions born out of the iconography of the songs – fedora-wearing men waiting on lamplit corners at night and femme fatales strutting their stuff on the cobbled streets. In barrios vying for the title of the birthplace of tango – La Boca, San Telmo and Abasto – bars and cafés named after tango stars attempt to re-create this look. For total immersion, you can even stay in a tango hotel – check out **Lina's Tango Guesthouse** (Estados Unidos 780, 4361 6817, www.tango guesthouse.com.ar), **Caserón Porteño** (Ciudad de la Paz 344, 4554 6336, www. caseronporteno.com) or **Mansión Dandi Royal** (*see p93*), all of which can arrange lessons and visits to *milongas* and shows.

Carlos Gardel is to tango what Elvis Presley is to rock 'n' roll, so, unsurprisingly, his mug is ubiquitous, smiling down from murals around town. In the sprawling Chacarita cemetery, there's a bronze statue of his body; and there's even a Subte station named after him. Besides the main man, plazas and streets are dedicated to Enrique Santos Discépolo, Homero Manzi and Astor Piazzolla.

If you want to see tango exhibits, there are a few places worth checking out. In Abasto, the **Museo Casa Carlos Gardel** (*see p72*), where the star was born, offers an interesting glimpse of his early years. **Botica del Ángel** (Luis Sáenz Peña 541, Monserrat, 0800 333 8725) is described as a 'living museum' of tango, but

can only be visited via prearranged guided tours. The **Academia Nacional del Tango** houses a World Tango Museum (Rivadavia 830, Congreso, 4345 6967, www.anacdeltango.org.ar, open 2-8pm Mon-Fri) for those who want to delve into the history behind the moves.

After all the tombs and artefacts, you might even feel like dancing. The annual **Festival & Mundial de Tango** (*see p185*) in August is the city's main tango extravaganza, while November heralds the annual **Queer Tango Festival** (*see p183*), part of the city's campaign to become a major gay tourism capital and secure an inflow of pink pounds, pesos and dollars. With its fierce women and camp Gardel lookalikes, tango lends itself to easy queering.

Switch on Solo Tango cable TV channel for 24 hours of tango classics, or tune into radio station 2x4 (www.la2x4.gov.ar, 92.7 FM), which

INSIDE TRACK
TANGO IN THE DARK

Many *tangueras* close their eyes while dancing, in an attempt to shut out the world and focus entirely on the music and their partner. The Teatro Ciego (Blind Theatre, *see p221*) in Abasto takes this concept to whole new levels, offering tango classes for men and women in total darkness. If love is blind, then tango is too.

is dedicated exclusively to tangos past and present. All major record shops have tango sections, but the selections at **Zivals** (*see p180*) and **Casa Piscitelli** (San Martín 450, Microcentro, 4394 1992, www.piscitelli.com) are the most impressive in the city.

For a deeper understanding of tango, get out your *lunfardo* dictionary and have a look at the lyrics. Once you decipher all the slang, the result is both filthy and tragic, nostalgic and sexually charged. The singer, our protagonist, is usually a thug or a mama's boy down on his luck because (A) he was taken to the cleaners by a woman who broke his heart (all women, except for the singer's saintly mother, are tramps), or (B) his plans for robbing, looting and committing all manner of dastardly deeds went horribly awry.

INFORMATION

Navigating your way round the tango scene isn't easy, but there are plenty of free guides with listings of classes and milongas, most with English translations. You can pick them up in *milongas* – for updated schedules, the *Tango Map Guide* is indespensible. Also look out for *El Tangauta*, *La Milonga* and *Diostango*.

WHERE TO DANCE TANGO

Tango tourists are easy to spot at the airport on their way home: pale, hobbling and weighed down by suitcases full of shoes. That's what a fortnight of dancing till dawn at *milongas* (tango nights that at best combine the neighbourliness of a social club with the faded elegance of a 1930s ballroom dance) can do to a person. But you don't have to be a tango fanatic

to enjoy a wobble around the dancefloor; there are plenty of laid-back *milongas* that welcome novices. Most *milongas* have beginner's classes first; check the level for *nivel inicio* or *principiante*. Classes are usually included in the admission price.

A *milonga* traditionally features three musical sets (*tandas*) separated into straight tangos, faster and more playful *milongas* (country songs) and formal waltzes. Note that taking photos and filming are not always popular (that may, or may not, be his wife); besides, you don't want to disturb the intimacy of the dancers.

Don't treat a *milonga* like an ordinary bar or club; and don't drink too much, get rowdy, or get up on the dancefloor to try out a few rusty moves. At more traditional *milongas*, flamboyant footwork and high kicks are frowned upon. If you're learning, head to a place that welcomes beginners; otherwise, sit back and watch the experts.

If you want to leap straight into the BA tango scene without looking, **María Lelia Ivancovich** (www.marialeliadebsas.com.ar) can arrange guided trips to the city's *milongas*.

Traditional milongas

The venues listed in this chapter usually hold classes prior to the *milonga*. They mostly attract an older generation who prefer to dance *al suelo*; that is, feet pegged to the floor and legs discreetly doing tricks.

Seating is carefully organised and you'll be shown to the men's or women's side, or the places for couples and groups. It sounds weird, but it signals who's available to dance. Finding

Rojo Tango. *See p234.*

Tango Timetable

Our pick of the places to get your daily dance in.

Whether you're an experienced *tanguero* or a beginner, our seven-day guide will steer you in the right direction.

MONDAY
Start the week with Parakultural at **Salón Canning** (*see p232*). Beginner's classes from 7pm to 9pm mix locals and foreigners.

TUESDAY
For something different, **La Catedral** (*see p232*) is a cross between an eclectic art space and a funky student loft. A young crowd dances mainly *tango nuevo*.

WEDNESDAY
La Maldita Milonga is a mid-week treat and the fantastic orchestra adds real magic to the bohemian Buenos Ayres Club (*see p232*).

THURSDAY
Experienced dancers shouldn't miss the beautiful dance hall and inspirational *tangueros* at the Niño Bien event at the **Centro Región la Leonesa** (*see below*).

FRIDAY
A young crowd pulls showy *nuevo moves* at the informal Tangocool milonga inside the school hall-like **Villa Malcolm** (*see p233*) .

SATURDAY
La Viruta (*see p233*) attracts dancers from all over the world for classes, shows and *milongas*.

SUNDAY
The alfresco **La Glorieta** milonga (*see p232*) attracts both exhibitionists and voyeurs to this park rotunda.

---

a partner involves a bewildering code of *cabaceos* (nods) and subtle signs, the man leading the way. Basically, girls watch for the eyebrow twitch, the twirly finger, the chin jutting, the no-messing glare or something that resembles a fish impersonation. Once eye contact is made, you move on to the floor; this is a clear case of selection of the fittest and it can be scary.

While the couple waits for the first few bars of music to be over before moving, they locate each other's hands as they make eye contact – anything more obvious is considered amateurish and unrefined. Don't be too alarmed when you're grabbed disturbingly tight – what is 'friendly' here in Buenos Aires might well be considered hilariously inappropriate back home. It's all part of the fun, though.

El Beso
1st Floor, Riobamba 416, entre Corrientes y Lavalle, Once (4953 2794, www.elbesotangoclub. com.ar). Subte B, Callao/bus 37, 60, 124. **Open** *Milonga* varies, check website. *Classes* varies, check website. **Admission** *Milonga* AR$30-$35. **No credit cards. Map** p285 H9.
A bijou setting for night-time dances, this attractive venue is also used by La Academia Tango Milonguero to host classes of a very high standard, which are not suitable for beginners.

Centro Región la Leonesa
Humberto Primo 1462, y San José, Constitución (4304 5595). Subte E, San José/bus 39, 60, 126. **Open** *Milonga* 11pm-4am Thur; 4.30-11pm Sat.

Classes 9-10.30pm Thur; 3-4.30pm Sat. **Admission** AR$30. **No credit cards. Map** p285 E8.
Excellent *milongas* are held at this venue in a superb hall boasting one of the best *pistas* (dancefloors) in town. Reservations are essential for the hugely popular Niño Bien event on Thursday nights, when the crowd of experienced dancers really makes an effort and gets its glad rags on.

Club Gricel
La Rioja 1180, y San Juan, San Cristóbal (4957 7157). Subte E, Urquiza/bus 20, 61, 118, 126. **Open** *Milonga* from 8.30pm Mon, Wed, Thur; from 10.30pm Fri, Sat; from 9pm Sun. *Classes* 7-8.30pm Mon, Tue; 6.30-8.30pm Wed; 8-10pm Fri; 6.30-8.30pm, 8.30-10.30pm Sat; 6.30-9pm Sun. **Admission** *Milonga* AR$35. **No credit cards.** You can't beat the atmosphere of Club Gricel for some serious tango enjoyment. A regular clientele rotates gracefully around the well-sprung dancefloor, showing off their moves under the attractive lighting. Saturdays and Sundays are aimed more at couples.

Confitería Ideal
1st Floor, Suipacha 382, y Corrientes, Microcentro (5265 8078, www.confiteriaideal.com). Subte C, Diagonal Norte/bus 6, 10, 24. **Open** *Milonga* 3-8.30pm Wed-Mon; 9pm-2am Wed-Sat. *Classes* varies, check website. **Admission** AR$25-$40. *Classes* AR$40. **No credit cards. Map** p285 G10.
This busy spot has a full schedule of classes by day and attracts a post-office crowd, but really comes alive on the nights with the *milonga*

La Glorieta.

and orchestra. Particularly good are Thursday's Tangoideal bash and Unitango's Friday night affairs (www.unitango.com).

★ La Glorieta

Barrancas de Belgrano, 11 de Septiembre, entre Sucre y Echeverría, Belgrano (mobile 15 6304 8185). Bus 15, 29, 60. **Open** *Milonga* 6.30-10pm Sat; 6.30-11pm Sun. *Classes* 5-6.30pm Sat, Sun. **Admission** *Milonga* donation. *Classes* AR$35. **No credit cards**. **Map** p288 R8.

Held year-round under a park bandstand, this thoroughly romantic and popular open-air *milonga* attracts dancers of all standards and ages as well as enchanted observers and dog-walkers.

Salón Canning

Scalabrini Ortiz 1331, entre Gorriti y Cabrera, Palermo (4832 6753). Bus 15, 39, 141. **Open** *Milonga* 11pm-4am Mon, Tue, Fri, Sat; 4-11pm Wed; 9pm-3am Thur. *Classes* 7pm, 9pm Mon, Tue, Fri; 8pm, 9.30pm Sat. **Admission** *Milonga* AR$25-$30. **No credit cards**. **Map** p282 L5.

This large, traditional hall hosts a variety of different *milongas*, and dancers are generally of a high standard. Particularly popular are Monday, Tuesday and Friday night's Parakultural events.

Modern milongas

At these relaxed venues anyone can get up and dance no matter what their level, and if there's any kind of code, it's simply to have fun and enjoy yourself. In addition to the places listed below, other popular modern *milongas* for more serious dancers include **DNI** (Bulnes 1011, Almagro, 4866 3663, www.dni-tango.com,

4-7pm Sat), **Divertango** (1st Floor, Yatay 961, Almagro, mobile 15 5782 7417, 10.30pm-3am Thur) and **Milonga 10** (Loyola 828, Villa Crespo, mobile 15 4066 5831, www.milonga10.com, 10pm-3am Tue, 10pm-5am Sat). Gay-friendly *milonga* **La Marshall** (15 5458 3423, www.la marshall.com.ar, *photo p234*) is very welcoming and has no strict rules about who dances with whom; it's held in different locations around town; check the website for details.

★ Buenos Ayres Club

Perú 571, entre Venezuela y México, San Telmo (4560 1514). Bus 10, 22, 29, 86. **Open** *Milonga* 10.30pm-2am Mon, Wed, Sun; 10pm-2am Tue. *Classes* 9pm Mon, Wed, Sun; 8.30pm Tue. **Admission** AR$25. **No credit cards**. **Map** p285 E10.

The great thing about Wednesday night's Maldita Milonga is the fantastic live music from a young outfit called Orquesta Típica El Afronte. The musicians, including a row of *bandoneonistas* stretching and squeezing with passion, a wild pianist and a by turns heartbroken and enraged vocalist, make this an unforgettable experience. There's also a *bendita* (blessed) *milonga* on Mondays to complement Wednesday's *maldita* (damned) one. On Tuesday nights, tango's rigid gender rules are turned on their head at gay-friendly *milonga* Tango Queer (www.tangoqueer.com).

★ La Catedral

Sarmiento 4006, y Medrano, Almagro (mobile 15 5325 1630, www.lacatedralclub.com). Subte B, Medrano/bus 24, 124. **Open** *Milonga* from 11pm daily. *Classes* 8pm-11pm daily. **Admission** AR$30-$40. **No credit cards**. **Map** p282 J4.

The atmosphere at this high-ceilinged bohemian venue is pitched somewhere between post punk/neogoth and old-style circus/music hall. There are good beginner's classes on Tuesdays and folkloric classes on Sundays. The helter-skelter bar and vegetarian restaurant also makes this a popular hangout for non-tango dancers.

Villa Malcolm
Avenida Córdoba 5064, entre Thames y Serrano, Villa Crespo (4772 9796). Bus 55, 110, 140, 168. **Open** *Milonga* after classes Mon, Wed-Fri; 8pm-4am Sat. *Classes* 7-10pm Mon; 9-10.30pm Wed; 9-11pm Thu, Fri. **Admission** AR$35. **No credit cards. Map** p283 M4.
Start with a class then dance into the early hours with the international crowd at this atmospheric old hall with a restaurant and bar. It packs out for Monday night's El Motivo, Wednesday night's Fruto Dulce and Friday night's Tangocool, all informal *milongas*. An older crowd takes over on Saturday evenings for a more traditional flavour.

★ La Viruta
Armenia 1366, entre Niceto Vega y Cabrera, Palermo Soho (4774 357, www.lavirutatango.com). Bus 15, 55, 168. **Open** *Milonga* 11.30pm-3am Wed; 12.30-3am Thur; midnight-6am Fri, Sat; 11.30pm-3am Sun. *Classes* varies, check website. **Admission** AR$30; free after 1.30am Wed, Thur; 4am Fri, Sat; 1am Sun. **No credit cards. Map** p287 M7.
Dancers of all ages come together for tango at this homely Armenian community centre. The *milonga* gets going around 1am after the crowd has had a chance to warm up on the dancefloor with a sprinkling of salsa and even rock'n'roll jiving.

Classes and information

All of the *milongas* listed above have resident teachers, with classes available before the dance begins; and hundreds of couples offer private – though considerably more expensive – classes for all levels. For complete beginners, classes at **La Viruta** (*see above*) and **La Catedral** (*see p232*) are fun and unintimidating. If you prefer a more contemporary style, **DNI** (*see p232*) has a comprehensive schedule of 90-minute classes. It also has a restaurant, shoe shop and regular events. **El Esquinazo** (Gurruchaga 1218, Palermo Soho, 4774 1823) has dynamic instructors and an eclectic programme of classes. The **Escuela Argentina de Tango** (Talcahuano 1052, Recoleta & San Martín 768, Galerías Pacífico shopping centre, Microcentro, 4312 4990, www.eatango.com) has two locations and classes all day every day.
To really master the moves you'll need the footwear. Slippery soled tango shoes are

available in any number of outlets, but our top recommendations are **Comme il Faut** (*see p173*) and **DNI** (*see p232*).

WHERE TO HEAR TANGO

For the wooden-legged, there is, of course, tango music to simply enjoy, glass in hand. **La Trastienda** (*see p208*) and **ND/Ateneo** (*see p209*) are both serious venues for tango music, and passionate and skillful tango musicians can work up as much sweat as their dancing counterparts: look out for *bandoneón*-playing Piazzolla disciple Rodolfo Mederos and virtuoso pianists Pablo Ziegler and Sonia Possetti.
Outside the ever evolving mainstream, there's a more experimental scene led by Daniel Melingo and Latino fusioneers La Chicana. Several young orchestras are committed to keeping the rebel spirit of the original *tangueros* alive. Try catching a performance by the excellent **Orquesta Típica Fernández Fierro**, who play at the Club Atlético Fernández Fierro (Sánchez de Bustamante 764, Abasto, www.caff.com.ar) on Wednesdays as well as some Saturday nights, filling the warehouse-like space with their dramatic, thundering, rock-inspired tango and pulling in an enthusiastic crowd. Check the website for upcoming events.

Centro Cultural Torquato Tasso
Defensa 1575, entre Caseros y Brasil, San Telmo (4307 6506, www.torquatotasso.com.ar). Bus 24, 29, 39, 93, 130. **Open** 10pm-midnight Wed-Sat. *Class* 7-10pm Wed-Sat. **Admission** varies. **No credit cards. Map** p284 C9.
This is a serious tango venue, with respected artists performing from Wednesdays to Saturdays (admission prices vary), including renowned orchestras as well as younger, up-and-coming outfits that stray further from traditional tango. The Sunday tango class attracts all levels.

WHERE TO WATCH TANGO

Tango shows are often rather artificial affairs focused on the tourist peso, but can be an entertaining, if slightly cheesy, introduction to the genre. Most include the option of dinner while you marvel at the manoeuvres on stage, and a live band belts out tango classics. For a large-scale, glitzy spectacle, try **Señor Tango** (Vieytes 1655, Barracas, 4303 0231, www.senortango.com.ar), **Sabor a Tango** (Perón 2535, Once, 4953 8700, ww.sabora tango.com.ar) or **Café de los Angelitos** (Rivadavia 2100, San Cristóbal, 4314 1121, www.cafedelosangelitos.com). The atmosphere of bygone days in a traditional *porteño* neighbourhood is recreated at **Esquina Homero Manzi** (Avenida San Juan 3601, Boedo, 4957 8488, www.esquinahomeromanzi.com.ar).

Splendid old **Café Tortoni** (*see p144*) and **Confitería Ideal** (*see p231*) are on the more affordable side of things and highly atmospheric, as is the **Centro Cultural Borges** (*see p45*), which has a small theatre in which some of BA's best tango shows are held at least twice weekly – consult the website for dates and times.

To catch street tango for the price of a tip dropped into a hat, head for *calle* Florida in the late afternoon or to San Telmo or La Boca on Sundays.

Bar Sur
Estados Unidos 299, y Balcarce, San Telmo (4362 6086, www.bar-sur.com.ar). Bus 29, 93, 130. **Open** 8.30pm-2am daily. *Show* 9pm-2am daily. **Tickets** AR$280; with dinner AR$440. **Credit** AmEx, MC, V. **Map** p284 D10.

La Marshall. *See p232.*

The show here is fairly fancy, but the intimate bar and emphasis on participation make this a fun and friendly little joint. The venue has been featured in films and evokes the Buenos Aires of cobbled streets and sharp-suited men.

Complejo Tango
Avenida Belgrano 2608, y Saavedra, San Cristóbal (4941 1119, www.complejotango. com.ar). Subte H, Venezuela/bus 56, 101, 168. **Open** from 7.30pm daily. *Class* 7.30pm. *Dinner* 8.30pm. *Show* 10pm. **Tickets** AR$350; with class and dinner AR$515. **Credit** Amex, MC, V. **Map** p285 G7.
A huge space deep inside this old house is the venue for a show filled with tango passion, complete with an edgy knife-fight dance by a lone *hombre*, scuffles in a bordello and an all-round dramatic performance. This is one *tanguería* where the dinner is well worthwhile, and don't miss the brilliant class beforehand.

La Esquina de Carlos Gardel
Pasaje Carlos Gardel 3200, y Anchorena, Abasto (4867 6363, www.esquinacarlosgardel.com.ar). Subte B, Carlos Gardel/bus 24, 124, 168. **Open** 8.30pm-midnight daily. **Tickets** AR$455; with dinner AR$630. **Credit** AmEx, MC, V. **Map** p286 J8.
OK, so it's a very touristy show. But the venue is grand, the dancers sexy and showbizzy, and the dinner involves big juicy steaks and blood-red wine.

Rojo Tango
Faena Hotel + Universe, Martha Salotti 445, entre Aime Paine y Juana Manso, Puerto Madero Este (5787 1536, www.rojotango.com). Bus 2, 4, 60, 130, 152. **Open** 8.30pm-midnight daily. *Dinner* 8.30pm. *Show* 10pm. **Tickets** AR$855; with dinner AR$1215. **Credit** AmEx, DC, MC, V. **Map** p284 D11.
From the moment you enter Faena Hotel + Universe, you realise that Rojo Tango is not your average dinner and show. You'll be greeted with a glass of champagne before an excellent three-course meal is served, setting the scene for a sexy and intimate spectacle. The tango show itself doesn't really break any rules, but it's very polished, very flamboyant, very Faena. *Photo p230*.

El Viejo Almacén
Avenida Independencia 300, y Balcarce, San Telmo (4307 6689, www.viejoalmacen.com). Bus 29, 93, 130, 152. **Open** 7pm-midnight daily. *Dinner* 8pm. Show 10pm. **Tickets** from AR$320; *with dinner* from AR$500. **Credit** AmEx, DC, MC, V. **Map** p284 D10.
This charming colonial venue located on an atmospheric San Telmo corner is a tourist favourite. Two singers, a sextet orchestra and four dance couples make up the two-hour show, which is more intimate than many larger productions.

Escapes & Excursions

Punta del Este. *See p248.*

Upriver

Retreat from city life and sail down waterways flanked by lush vegetation.

The town of Tigre is the gateway to the Delta del Paraná – a labyrinth of verdant isles, narrow estuaries and secluded lodgings, as well as the occasional floating general store.

Though experiencing a revival of sorts, Tigre had its heyday in the last quarter of the 19th century, when the Delta served as a refuge for wealthy families during the yellow fever epidemic.

Close enough to the city to justify a day trip yet far away enough to merit a weekend escape, the Delta still boasts colonial charm and a slow, ambling pace. Wander through the town centre of Tigre, which has English-influenced architecture and several interesting museums, restaurants and an amusement park; or take a boat trip down the river to one of the area's many resorts and enjoy an *asado* or a lazy swim.

TIGRE

Less than an hour north of busy BA, this riverside town is the ideal spot for a lazy lunch and a welcome breath of fresh air. Tigre appeals to both locals and foreigners, with its vividly coloured colonial edifices, humid microclimate and blood-orange sunsets that are reminiscent of more tropical zones, and have won the town a somewhat exotic reputation; it's easy to forget, when strolling along palm-lined streets, that this is as much a working community as a day-tripper destination. It's also the gateway to the islands and waterways that make up the **Delta** (*see p238*).

ABOUT THE LISTINGS

Prices in this section are represented by peso signs. For restaurants, $ indicates a range of roughly AR$25-$39 for main courses, $$ is AR$40-$59, $$$ is AR$60-$84 and $$$$ indicates AR$85 and above. For hotels, $ is for budget (US$50-$100/AR$225-$450); $$ indicates moderate (US$100-$200/ AR$450-$900); $$$ represents high-end (US$200-$350/AR$900-$1500); and $$$$ represents deluxe (over US$350/AR$1500 for a double). Hostel prices are quoted in full.

The town retains the charm of a well-kept colonial port, having flourished at the end of the 19th century, when BA's high society used it as a summer playground, hosting extravagant galas and balls. Soon after, though, improved transport and white sands lured the aristocrats south to the beaches of Mar del Plata, and all that remained were magnificent buildings such as the **Buenos Aires Rowing Club**. Over a century later, Tigre is enjoying something of a revival, and around 80,000 visitors now crowd in each weekend.

The **Mercado de Frutos** (Sarmiento y Perú, photo p238) is a thriving daily market where you'll find local honey, handicrafts, wicker furniture, jewellery and food. Head to the **Museo Naval de la Nación** (Paseo Victorica 602, 4749 0608) for an insight into the maritime history of Argentina and an amazing collection of model boats. Housed in a painstakingly restored 1910 belle époque building is Tigre's finest cultural offering: the **Museo de Arte Tigre** (Paseo Victorica 972, 4512 4528, www.mat.gov.ar, closed Mon, Tue). The museum displays Argentinian figurative art from the late 19th and early 20th centuries. At the informative **Museo de la Reconquista** (Padre Castañeda 470, 4512 4496, closed Mon, Tue), find out how General Liniers won Buenos Aires back from the British. Need more thrills? Follow the screams to the **Parque de la Costa** (*see p188*) amusement park for all the fun of the fair, or head to the **Nuevo Trilenium Casino**

(Perú 1385, 4731 7001), where three floors of slot machines twinkle and chime. Big betters can step up to the roulette tables in the VIP room.

Tangol (*see p180*) offers an interesting eight-hour tour of Tigre that includes a visit to the Mercado de Frutos and the Delta. The return trip to BA by boat is a chance to witness unique views of the city.

Where to eat & drink

The **Mercado de Frutos** (*photo p238*) has plenty of food stalls offering quick, cheap snacks and good smoothies. For something more substantial than a waffle or greasy *choripán* (chorizo sandwich), try the excellent **La Terraza** (Paseo Victorica 134, 4731 2916, www.laterrazatigre.com.ar, $$), set further along the main restaurant drag of Paseo Victorica (overwhelmingly parrilla joints). Book in advance to get a table on the terrace. Somewhat more expensive is **Il Novo María Luján de Tigre** (Paseo Victorica 611, y Vito Dumas, 4731 9613, www.ilnovomariadellujan. com, $$$). Located in a grand old colonial house, with a terrace overhanging the Río Luján, it's worth the extra pesos for its lovely setting as much as the tasty homemade pasta.

Where to stay

Built in 1893, the Italian-style **Casona La Ruchi** (Lavalle 557, 4749 2499, www.casonalaruchi.com.ar, $) is a charming little hotel close to the main bridge. Its home-from-home feel is complemented by exquisite rustic decor, a secluded garden containing a swimming pool and a parrilla for those outdoor summer *asados* (barbecues).

Tigre Hostel (Avenida San Martín 190, 4749 4034, www.tigrehostel.com.ar, US$18 dorm, $ double), housed in a restored 1860 posada, has high-ceilinged dorm rooms and doubles, although the latter face the main road and can be noisy. Friendly staff, a huge kitchen, cosy communal areas and the tree filled garden make it a good spot to relax. Breakfast and Wi-Fi are included in the room price. A more upmarket option is the elegant **Villa Julia** (Paseo Victorica 800, 4749 0242, www.villa juliaresort.com.ar, $$). This converted mansion dates from 1913, and is the perfect place to dine, sleep and unwind in style. In summer, you can relax on the lawn among the shady palms or take a dip in the pool, and there's also a library and reading room if it's nippy outside. The restaurant, open to non-guests, serves superb gourmet dinners, reasonably priced lunches and afternoon teas.

For more accommodation options, enquire at the tourist information centre, the **Ente Municipal de Turismo de Tigre** (*see p238*). An alternative is to jump on a river boat and head into the **Delta** (*see p238*). Here, accommodation options tend to be pricier and establishments are often resorts in themselves,

Museo de Arte Tigre.

ESCAPES & EXCURSIONS

Mercado de Frutos. *See p237.*

some providing spa and other pampering services. They also offer a variety of activities such as kayaking and riding.

Getting there

By bus The colectivo 60 from BA (which stops at main hubs like Constitución and Plaza Italia) takes between 1hr 15mins and 1hr 45mins, depending on traffic, and costs AR$2 one-way.
By train Tigre is a 50min train ride from Retiro station (a one-way ticket costs AR$1.35). Trains run every 10mins from 7am to 10pm, and less frequently during the night. For a more scenic route, you can take the Tren de la Costa (*see p188*) from Olivos.

INSIDE TRACK
ARGENTINIAN ALCATRAZ

A tiny but strategically placed land mass technically closer to Uruguay than to Argentina, **Isla Martín García** was established as an Argentinian territory in 1973. Since its discovery in 1516 by Juan Díaz de Solís, the island has served as a penal colony, a naval base and a prison for political leaders like Hipólito Yrigoyen and Juan Perón. Now a nature reserve that's home to over 250 bird species, the populated island can be visited on a trip from Tigre with tour operator **Cacciola** (4749 0931, www.cacciolaviajes.com).

Tourist information

Ente Municipal de Turismo de Tigre
Estación Fluvial de Tigre, Mitre 345 (4512 4497, www.tigre.gov.ar). **Open** 9am-6pm daily.
As well as providing information on Tigre, staff here will be able to advise you on accommodation in the area and the different boats that cruise the Delta.

THE DELTA

On a sunny day, your best bet is to get out on to the Delta rather than hang about in Tigre. This network of waterways and islands extends over approximately 14,000 square kilometres (5,405 square miles) and offers a wealth of recreational and gastronomic possibilities. It is broken into three sections, the first (*primera sección*) being closest to Tigre. Further away, rare flora and fauna are protected in a jungle-like UNESCO Biosphere Reserve.

River excursions

To explore the less travelled waterways, sign up for a boat tour or fishing trip. Prices vary according to the number of passengers and length of the excursion. A good option is **Navegando por el Delta** (4815 8974, www.navegandoporeldelta.com.ar), which organises half-day, full-day or – the speciality – night trips. *Bruma*, a spacious wooden sailing boat piloted by 'Chuck' Serantes, is a stylish way to cruise the waterways, boasting two dining areas (one below deck, one above with barbecue), a solarium and a library.

Where to eat & drink

Ask which boat service is best for getting to each of these riverside restaurants at the **Estación Fluvial de Tigre** (*see p240*). Bohemian hangout **Rio Bar & Bistro** (Arroyo Pajarito y Vinculación, mobile 15 6358 4343, www.riobarbistro.com.ar, $$) is a fun spot for a mojito and a plate of calamares. Colourful **Beixa Flor** (Arroyo Abra Vieja 148, mobile 15 5228 1367, www.beixaflor.com.ar, $$$) has very good homemade food. Top tunes, a huge open stove, private beach and verdant gardens make it a perfect summer stop-off. One of the biggest eateries on the Delta, and popular with families, is the sophisticated **Gato Blanco** (Río Capitán 80, 4728 0390, www.gato-blanco.com, $$$$). There's even a children's playground.

Where to stay

There are some highly atmospheric places to stay at, tucked away amid the verdant vegetation of the Delta. Fifty minutes from

ESCAPES & EXCURSIONS

Chasing Waterfalls

A visit to the dazzling Iguazú Falls is an unmissable mini-escape from BA.

When it comes to destinations to see before you die, the **Cataratas de Iguazú** (*iguazú* meaning 'big water' in Guaraní) should rank near the top of the list. This natural wonder is 23 kilometres (14 miles) of foaming water thundering into a 70-metre (230-foot) deep river canyon. Located in the lush Parque Nacional Iguazú in Misiones province, it borders Brazil and Paraguay, and is just a 90-minute plane ride (or an 18-hour bus trip) from BA.

The falls have both Argentinian and Brazilian sides. If you haven't enough time to hop across the border, don't worry: a visit to the Argentinian side allows you to get up closer to the action. LAN (www.lan.com) offers multiple daily flights (US$450 return) from BA's Jorge Newbery airport to **Puerto Iguazú**, the small town outside the park, while buses leave regularly from Retiro for about AR$550 one way. **Parque Nacional Iguazú** (0800 266 4482, www.iguazuargentina.com, admission AR$130 non-residents) is a short bus ride from Puerto Iguazú.

Once inside the park, the main attraction is the **Garganta del Diablo** (The Devil's Throat), an awe-inspiring 80 metre horseshoe-shaped drop-off that sees about 70 per cent of the Río Iguazú rush over its edge into the depths below. If you're quiet, you might spy some of the fauna that abounds in the park: coatis, capuchin and squirrel monkeys, plenty of lizards, and, only under the cover of darkness, a jaguar or two. When the moon is full, park rangers run night hikes (AR$200-$270); during the day you can get closer to the falls with the Aventura Náutica tour organised by **Iguazú Jungle Explorer** (03757 421696, www.iguazu jungle.com, AR$125) or go on an overland safari with **Explorador Expediciones** (03757 421632, AR$220).

After a full day of falls and jungle flora and fauna, head back to town and refuel at **La Rueda** (Avenida Córdoba 28, 03757 422531, www.larueda1975.com, $$$$) or **Aqva Restaurant** (Avenida Córdoba y Carlos Thays, 03757 422064, www.aqva restaurant.com), where you can try grilled *surubí*, a local river fish. For a good steak with a view of three countries, head to **Bocamora** (Avenida Costanera 20, www.bocamora.com, 03757 420550, $$$), on the edge of town.

While most travellers stay in Puerto Iguazú, the **Sheraton Iguazú** (03757 491800, www.sheraton.com/iguazu, $$$$) is located within the park itself. Just 15 minutes from the park is the **Iguazu Grand** (Ruta 12, km 1640, 03757 498050, www.iguazu grand.com, $$$$), a resort with a casino, spa, pools and tennis courts. In town, the **Hotel Saint George** (Avenida Córdoba 148, 03757 420633, www.hotelsaintgeorge.com, $$) and **Iguazú Jungle Lodge** (Hipólito Irigoyen s/n, 03757 420600, www.iguazu junglelodge.com, $$$) are good options with pools and restaurants; while **Secret Garden Iguazú B&B** (Los Lapachos 623, 03757 423099, www.secretgardeniguazu.com, $$) has three rooms set within lush gardens and a welcoming host who serves complimentary cocktails and hors d'oeuvres.

For those eager to explore the area and its jungle atmosphere a little further (and in style), **Posada Puerto Bemberg** (Fundadores Bemberg, 03757 496500, www.puertobemberg.com, $$$ per person) is an attractive luxury lodge located 30 kilometres (20 miles) from Iguazú's airport, which offers jungle walks, birdwatching, mountain biking and other activities.

ESCAPES & EXCURSIONS

INSIDE TRACK
TIGRE WATER SPORTS

Fancy row, row, rowing a boat? Then get behind the oars with **Sculls** (Paseo Victoria 614, mobile 15 69922235/ www.sculls.com.ar), which offers personalised rowing and kayak classes in English and Spanish. For a complete river day out, **El Dorado Kayak** (Arollo Bordeau s/n, mobile 15 6503 6961/ www.eldoradokayak.com) offers day trips comprising a short boat ride, an *asado* and three hours of kayaking. The company does overnight full-moon trips too. If you're keen to slip into a wetsuit, then **Wake School** (4728 0031/www.wakeschool. com.ar) offers waterskiing classes.

Tigre lies **Bonanza Deltaventura** (Rio Carapachay, 4728 1674, www.deltaventura.com, $$ per person all inclusive). The simple rooms are warmed with a crackling fire on colder nights, and are good value. Bilingual owner Rosana offers action-packed days of riding, kayaking in a nearby lagoon or birdspotting in the marshes. Or you can simply snooze in a hammock until it's time for a scrumptious meal made from local products. Hidden under thick foliage, **La Becasina Delta Lodge** (Arroyo Las Cañas, 4328 2687, www.labecasina.com, $$$ per person all inclusive) – built entirely from wood from its own island – includes 15 luxury cabins, a pool and a self-service cocktail bar. The all-inclusive deal includes food from the gourmet restaurant, booze and the use of all recreational equipment. Another good deal is available at **Rumbo 90° Delta Lodge & Spa** (Canal Del Este, mobile 15 5843 9454, www.rumbo90.com.ar, $$$$ per person all inclusive), a stunning riverside lodge with six suites, natural spa and swimming pool. You can take canoes out on the river, sign up for fishing excursions or explore the forest on marked trails. Further afield, some 140 kilometres north-west of BA by road, **El Vintén** (mobile 15 4972 1888, www.elvinten. com.ar, $$$ per person all inclusive) is a lovely guesthouse overlooking the Baradero River. Use of the pool, riding and fishing excursions, and meals and wine are included in the all-inclusive package.

Getting there

By boat Lanchas colectivas (public river buses) depart regularly from the boat terminal in Tigre, the Estación Fluvial de Tigre (Mitre 345). Three companies serve different sections of the Delta. Ask in the ticket office for the service you need. Prices depend on the journey. A return trip of one or two hours costs between AR$35 and AR$52.

The Delta. *See p238.*

Country

Horses, cowboys and a whole lot of meat.

You may want to explore past the big city's limits, and the world of the gaucho is one of the best escapes from modernity Argentina offers.

If Carlos Gardel is the popular – as well as the homoerotic – icon of Argentina's urban masses, then the gaucho is his country counterpart. Living partly on horseback, partly around the campfire, these criollo cowboys are, from their berets to their boots, the antithesis of European urbanity. They roam around the pampas – Argentina's vast, flat plains that lie just beyond Buenos Aires.

Take a day or, far better, a long weekend away from the city to see gaucho country for yourself, whether you choose to relax on one of the estancias (ranches) dotted around the pampas or wander the streets of a small traditional town such as San Antonio de Areco.

SAN ANTONIO DE ARECO

San Antonio de Areco is at the epicentre of gaucho lore, not simply because walking around the cobbled streets you are as likely to pass a cowboy trotting on horseback as a child pedalling a bicycle, but also because this was the home of author Ricardo Güiraldes and his semi-mythical gaucho hero, Don Segundo Sombra. Around 113 kilometres (70 miles) from Buenos Aires, with a population of 20,000, this popular weekend tourist destination is a mass of one-storey, century-old buildings surrounded by seemingly limitless grassy plains. Perfect for brushing up on half-forgotten riding skills in the company of a few of these genuine Latin cowboys.

Begin your tour with a stroll along the town's main drag, Alsina, to the town's centre and the charming square **Plaza Ruiz de Arellano**. This central plaza is overlooked by the **Iglesia Parroquial**, built in 1728 by the town's original settlers in honour of San Antonio de Padua, thanking him for protecting them from attacks by local tribes. Directly opposite the church, in the centre of the plaza, is a statue of locally born hero Juan Hipólito Vieytes, and a plaque commemorating a visit from former Irish president Mary Robinson and the Sociedad

For price codes, see p236.

Argentino Irlandesa of San Antonio de Areco. It's ironic that, in an area central to the gaucho mystique, an Irish community predating Güiraldes's novel by over a century should have been so pivotal to the evolution of a town so important to Argentinian identity.

One thing that strikes you as you walk through San Antonio de Areco is the separation of town and country, sharply divided by the Areco River that marks a border between the stone streets and the pampas. The easiest way to cross this divide is via **Puente Viejo**, one of the country's first toll bridges and the unofficial symbol of the town. Passing over the bridge to the north of the town, you will arrive at the **Parque Criollo & Museo Gauchesco Ricardo Güiraldes** (Camino al Ricardo Güiraldes, y Camino al Parque, 02326 455839, closed Tue; AR$20, free under-12s). Partly closed for renovations at the time of writing, this small museum re-creates an 18th-century ranch, with each room in a different style. The 90 hectares of green parkland contain a stud farm and the atmospheric **Pulpería La Blanqueada**, a rustic tavern-cum-general store that featured in Güiraldes' writing. The museum, which opened in 1938, is a homage to Güiraldes himself, exhibiting early editions of *Don Segundo Sombra*, photographs of the real-life characters of the book and random curiosities, such as a bed that once belonged to General Rosas. A hundred metres from the museum, on Camino al Ricardo Güiraldes, you can get a real

San Antonio de Areco.

feel for the gaucho lifestyle with horses for hire by the hour. The owners (but probably not the horses) are more than happy to chaperone those who've spent more time in bars than barns.

Tradition is everywhere in San Antonio de Areco and many of the structures remain exactly as they were a century ago, albeit a little worse for wear. One must-see building is the **Los Principios** grocery store, located to the west of the town centre at Bartolomé Mitre 151. The dusty, old dark-wood store is a throwback to 1922, the year it opened, and the present owner, Américo Fernández, has been selling his wares

there for over 60 years. Confectionary of all kinds is weighed out on ancient metal scales and the rolling ladder is still the only way to reach the very highest shelves.

The town is small enough to get around on foot, though most of the locals travel by moped or bicycle (three-hour free hire at the **Dirección de Turismo de la Municipalidad**; *see p244*). If you want to save time or are heading straight to an estancia, your best bet is a car service. **Remis Zerboni** (02326 453288) operates 24 hours a day.

If this quiet town has a high season it's in November, when a buzz of rural activities leads up to the spirited gaucho festivities of the annual **Día de la Tradición** (*see p183*). Exhibitions of the traditional *gato* (cat) dance and performances by folklore bands are coupled with feats of country skills and horsemanship, in a busy programme spread out over two weeks. The celebrations culminate in the Día de la Tradición itself and a procession of gauchos in full regalia, riding horses adorned with silver and gold. If you don't want to miss out on the festivities, book hotel rooms early.

INSIDE TRACK YERBA MATE

Yerba maté is a tropical plant that was used by the Guaraní and Guaycurú peoples long before the arrival of Europeans. Most commonly, its dried stems and leaves are combined with hot water to make an energy-packed infusion, which is served in a vessel called a maté and imbibed through a *bombilla* (metal straw). Maté is a social drink: it's passed around from person to person and filled up with very hot water by the *cebador* (server) before each individual round. It's an aquired taste, and most foreigners find it too bitter, at least at first. Although it's popular in the city, in the *campo* it's an indispensable part of life. You're practically guaranteed to see country folk sitting, chatting, with maté in hand and you may well be invited to take part in the cultural ritual. Some basic rules for consumption: remember not to wipe the *bombilla* when it's your turn to sup and only say *gracias* when you don't want any more.

Where to eat & drink

The pick of the town's restaurants is **Almacén de Ramos Generales** (Zapiola 143, 02326 456376, www.ramosgeneralesareco.com.ar, $$), a popular parrilla serving traditional fare made from locally-sourced ingredients, and decorated in the style of an old general store or *almacén*. For modern dishes in a stylish contemporary setting, try **Zarza** (San Martín 361, 02326 453948, $$). If you're after something a bit more local, head for **Puesto la Lechuza** (Victorino Althaparro 423, 02326 15 405745, main courses $$$$, open Sat, Sun), a covered-terrace restaurant serving traditional country fare with regular

Dude, Where's My Ranch?

Indulge your cowboy fantasies or just escape the city at an estancia.

Dotting the fertile pampas around Buenos Aires are large estancias – ranching estates – founded by 19th century cattle barons who spearheaded Argentina's transformation from post-colonial backwater to economic powerhouse. Many of these country mansions are now open to the public for day visits and weekend stays.

Most estancias offer a *día de campo* (country day) package, which generally includes a hearty *asado*, horse riding and the use of the facilities. Many have pools and open spaces to explore. But the most traditional activity you can indulge in is to do, well, absolutely nothing. Sit back, share a maté, talk off the five kilos of steak you just ate, and enjoy the *buena onda* (good vibes) away from the city's smoggy pretensions.

If it's a day excursion you're after, and you'd like to try your hand at polo, **Guapa Polo** (mobile 15 5111 8214, www.guapapolo.com.ar, US$190 *día de campo*, including transport) offers friendly, personalised service and an authentic taste of country life on a working estancia 50 minutes south of the capital. The day includes a fun polo lesson and match (suitable for people of all riding abilities) with a professional player on wonderfully trained horses, followed by an undo-the-top-button-of-your-jeans *asado*.

The elegant **Puesto Viejo Polo Club** (RN 6 towards La Plata, 5279 6893, www.puestoviejoestancia.com.ar, $$ or US$150 *día de campo*), 70 kilometres from BA, has daily polo matches, rustic-chic rooms and a small but lovely infinity pool.

There's more riding to be had at **Estancia Los Dos Hermanos** (Panamericana, RN 9, km10.5, 4723 2880, www.estancialosdoshermanos.com, $$$ or US$100 *día de campo*), which offers lengthy horseback tours and serves tasty *asados*.

For a gaucho experience on a family-run estancia, **El Ombú** (Ruta 31, Cuartel 6, 02326 492080, in BA 4737 0436, www.estanciaelombu.com, $$ or US$80 *día de campo*) occupies a colonial-style mansion 16 kilometres from San Antonio de Areco (*see p241*). Segundo Ramírez was the real-life inspiration for the main character in *Don Segundo Sombra*, the

book that immortalised gaucho life, and his son Oscar now leads visitors on horse rides and sings folkloric songs at lunch.

For a ritzy retreat, escape to **La Candelaria** (RN 205, km 114.5, 02227 424404, www.estanciacandelaria.com, $$), a fairytale-like French-style château in Lobos, 115 kilometres south-west of BA, that offers everything from airplane rides to gaucho shows.

Families can enjoy a relaxing stay at **La Horqueta** (on Ruta 20 to Ranchos, 4777 0150, www.lahorqueta.com, $$), less than two hours from the capital. Its extensive grounds are best explored on bicycle or horse.

If you're looking to put more distance between yourself and the capital, utter relaxation and fly fishing by the lake is offered at the stylish **La Oriental** (JB Justo 429, Junín, mobile 15 5146 5210, www.estancia-laoriental.com, $$), 250 kilometres north-west of BA. **La Margarita** (Cacharí km 7, Tapalqué, in BA 4951 0638, 02283 420530, www.estanciala margarita.com, $$ or $ self-catering) lies on verdant plains 280 kilometres south of BA; activities range from riding, swimming and cycling to the more hands on milking of cows and feeding of chickens.

ESCAPES & EXCURSIONS

folklore shows. If you're just in need of a drink, **Barril 900** (San Martín 381) is a typical downtown pub, with outdoor seating. The cosy **La Vieja Sodería** (Bolívar 196) serves coffee during the day, and gin and tonics at night.

Where to stay

Boutique lodging **Patio de Moreno** (Moreno 251, 02326 455197, www.patiodemoreno.com, $$$) raises the bar dramatically in this unsophisticated town where the available accommodation is dominated by humble guesthouses. Aimed at the wannabe-gauchos-with-iPhones market, it occupies a former workshop, which has been carefully modernised while maintaining its original charm – dark hardwood floors and high-beamed ceilings frame antique wall clocks, while skylights, a wine bar, and abstract art keep the place firmly grounded in the 21st century. The six spacious rooms are the ultimate in gaucho chic – think jet-black cow hides and fluffy white towels – and the gorgeous garden has a small pool.

Nothing else in San Antonio de Areco quite matches this standard, but two other hotels situated in converted colonial buildings are **Paradores Draghi** (Lavalle 387, 02326 455583, www.paradoresdraghi.com.ar, $$), which also showcases locally made silverware,

Polo in the province of Buenos Aires.

and **Antigua Casona** (Segundo Sombra 495, 02326 456600, www.antiguacasona.com, $). Typical, but not particularly special, country hotels include **Hostal de Areco** (Zapiola 25, 02326 456118, www.hostaldeareco.com.ar, $) and **Hotel Los Abuelos** (Zerboni y Zapiola, 02326 456390, $), which has motel-like rooms with ceiling fans, cable TV and a pool that's just about big enough for a duck under the water. (The fact that the name of this establishment translates as 'Grandparents Hotel' probably tells you most of what you need to know.) Directly opposite, **Hotel San Carlos** (02326 453106, www.hotel-sancarlos.com.ar, $) has smaller rooms and the option of six-person apartments with air-conditioning.

Shopping

You'll be able to pick up a cowboy hat and poncho at any of the gaucho-themed souvenir shops, but, for a unique memento, visit the workshop of esteemed Argentinian jewellery designer **Marina Massone** (General Paz 294, mobile 15 3181 7685, www.marinamassone.com.ar) to see her covetable contemporary pieces; her jewellery is also available at **MALBA** (*see p69*) in Buenos Aires.

For an edible souvenir, the town's **La Olla de Cobre** chocolate factory (Matheu 433, 02326 453105, www.laolladecobre.com.ar) is famous for its delicious *alfajores* (typical Argentinian biscuits filled with *dulce de leche*) and hot chocolate.

Tourist information

Dirección de Turismo de la Municipalidad

Boulevard Zervoni y Arellano (02326 453165/ www.sanantoniodeareco.tur.ar). **Open** 9am-6pm Mon-Fri; 8am-8pm Sat, Sun.
Staff will provide you with brochures and maps pointing out the town's historic sites. They also organise free tours of the town on Saturdays, Sundays and holidays (Spanish only).

Getting there

By road San Antonio de Areco is 1hr 30mins from Buenos Aires on Ruta Nacional 8. A taxi from BA will cost around AR$400. If you're travelling by bus, Chevallier (4000 5255, www.nuevachevallier.com) offers the most frequent daily service, about once an hour, AR$42 one-way, from Retiro bus terminal. The journey takes about 2hrs. Upon arrival in San Antonio, ask at the bus station (located on the edge of town, 15mins walk from the main square) for the departure schedule.

Beach

A seaside city resort and peaceful pine-fringed sands.

A four-hour hop from the capital, the coastal towns nearest to Buenos Aires range from heaving, amenities-heavy hubs to bare-bones beach hamlets.

Mar del Plata screams big business and, during the high season, seriously big beach crowds, while the Costa Verde (Green Coast) – an area that includes popular Pinamar and the bijou resorts of Cariló and Mar de las Pampas – is the summertime playground of the smart set and provides more tranquil, expansive spaces, defined by pine trees that fringe the wide, sandy shores.

During the summer, accommodation prices rise exorbitantly – make sure to book in advance. Some places shut up shop in the sleepy low season, but visitors are rewarded with evenings by log fires after blustery walks along deserted beaches.

MAR DEL PLATA

Mar del Plata is tacky, brash and, throughout the peak summer season, extremely crowded. During school holidays the beaches are bloated with families fleeing the soupy streets of Buenos Aires in mass exodus: you'll be hard pushed to find a place to lay your towel.

The city – 400 kilometres (250 miles) south of Buenos Aires, with a year-round population of 650,000, swelling to over a million in summer – was founded in 1874. Once a refuge for the porteño aristocracy, it's now the Argentinian middle-class tourist destination of choice, with plenty of restaurants, bars and clubs to keep you entertained.

To the south, 20 kilometres (12 miles) beyond the lighthouse, lie the most exclusive beaches: **La Reserva**, **Del Balcón** and **La Caseta**. Continuing south on Ruta 11 brings you to Miramar, with magnificent views, woodland and 20-metre (65-foot) high cliffs running down to the ocean. This is the best spot for surfing; for more information, see www.elsurfero.com.

In Mar del Plata the seafront boardwalk, **La Rambla**, constructed in 1940 by architect Alejandro Bustillo (who also built the casino

For price codes, see p236.

and the San Martín pedestrian area), is the most popular walkway. In the south docks there's a large colony of sea lions (the symbol of Mar del Plata), and you can take a boat trip to view the main beaches from the sea. At night the port fills with people visiting seafood restaurants.

For a blast of Mar del's past, walk through the barrios of Stella Maris, Playa Grande, Los Troncos and Divino Rostro. There you'll find the **Centro Cultural Victoria Ocampo** (Matheu 1851, 0223 4920569, closed Tue). The centre is housed in a mansion that was once home to writer and literary patron **Victoria Ocampo**.

Where to eat & drink

The all-you-can-eat *tenedor libres* tend to be concentrated in the San Martín area and are extremely cheap, sometimes with queues out the door. **Montecatini Alpe** (Belgrano 2350, 0223 4943446, $$) has decent, cheap nosh including fish, pasta and superb *sorrentinos gratinados*. In the port, check out **Chichilo** (Unit 17, Centro Comercial Puerto, 0223 4896317, www.chichilo.com, $$), where the *calamares a la provenzal* (squid in garlic sauce) are highly recommended. But if you only have time to try one seafood restaurant in Mar del Plata, head straight to **Viento en Popa** (Avenida Martínez de Hoz 257, 0223 4890220, $$), which serves simple but exquisite cuisine.

Where to stay

Mar del Plata boasts an enormous variety of accommodation options. Opposite Playa Grande is the five-star Hotel Costa Galana (Boulevard Marítimo Patricio Peralta Ramos 5725, 0223 4105000, www.hotelcostagalana.com, $$$$). For something mid-range, try Hotel Guerrero (Diagonal Juan B Alberdi 2288, 0223 4958851, www.hotelguerrero.com.ar, $$), with a sea-facing location, beautiful views and great, out-of-season promotions. The cheaper Hotel Amsterdam (Boulevard Marítimo Patricio Peralta Ramos 4799, 0223 4515137, www. hotelamsterdam.com.ar, $$) is housed in a 1920s family home and comes with spacious rooms complete with excellent amenities.

Getting there

By air Mar del Plata is served by daily flights from Buenos Aires (55mins). The city airport **Aeropuerto Internacional Ástor Piazzolla** (Ruta 2, km396, 0223 4785811) is 9.5km from the centre.

By road Numerous hourly services make the 5hr trip from BA's Retiro bus station to Mar del Plata's main terminal (Alberti 1600, 0223 4515406). Buses also run from Retiro to Pinamar (5hrs) and other resorts along the coast. Those driving to Mar del Plata from Buenos Aires (4hrs) should take the RN2.

Tourist information

Centro Información Turística
Boulevard Marítimo Patricio Peralta Ramos 2270 (0223 495 1777, www.turismomardel plata.gov.ar). **Open** 8am-8pm daily.

PINAMAR, CARILÓ & OSTENDE

The summertime playground of moneyed porteños, **Pinamar**, located 340 kilometres (211 miles) south of BA, is surrounded by golden dunes and wonderfully fragrant pine forests. It clings to a reputation as the trendiest beach resort in Argentina, so don't expect peace.

A couple of kilometres from Pinamar is the very exclusive resort of **Cariló**. It's a separate and far quieter world of eclectic architecture set among woodland. Eight kilometres (five miles) from Pinamar is **Ostende**, a small resort with one of the best beaches in the area. It was founded at the beginning of the 20th century by a group of homesick Belgians.

Where to eat & drink

In Pinamar, **Sociedad Italiana** (Eneas 200, 02254 4845555, $$$) offers a satisfying slice of Italy with inexpensive, simple pasta. Pinamar is renowned for good fish; local classic **El Viejo Lobo** (Avenida del Mar y Bunge, 02254 483218, $$) also has a good wine list.

Cariló.

Where to stay

In Cariló, the **Hotel Marcin** (Laurel y Albatros, 02254 570888, www.hotelmarcin. com.ar, $$$$) is ideally situated on the beachfront. **Cariló Village** (Carpintero y Divisadero, 02254 470244, www.carilovillage. com, from $$$ all inclusive) has 59 bungalows that can sleep up to eight people.

In the centre of Pinamar is one of the coolest options in the area: **Hotel Las Calas** (Avenida Bunge 560, 02254 405999, www.lascalashotel.com.ar, $$). The fully equipped boutique suites can sleep up to four guests.

In Ostende, the attractive **Viejo Hotel Ostende** (Biarritz y Cairo, 02254 486081, www.hotelostende.com.ar, $) has a programme of live music and art exhibits.

Tourist information

Secretaría de Turismo

Avenida Shaw 18, y Avenida Bunge, Pinamar (02254 491680/www.pinamar.gov.ar). **Open** *Jan, Feb* 8am-9pm daily. *Mar-Dec* 8am-8pm Mon-Fri; 10am-6pm Sat, Sun.

Getting there

By bus Buses for **Pinamar** depart daily from Retiro bus station (AR$172 one-way); companies include Empresa Santa Fe (4314 9393) and Plusmar (4315 3424). The trip takes 5hrs.
By car For **Pinamar**, take Ruta 2 to Dolores, Ruta 63 to Esquina de Croto, Ruta 11 to General Conesa, Ruta 56 to Madariaga, and finally Ruta 74 to Pinamar.

To reach **Cariló** and **Ostende**, it's easiest to take a taxi or a minicab from Pinamar.

MAR DE LAS PAMPAS & MAR AZUL

Emerging out of the thick pine forests bordering the coast, **Mar de las Pampas** is how Pinamar was 25 years ago: quiet and beautiful. Cul-de-sacs and sandy roads limit the speed of passing vehicles and strict building laws keep the pine trees standing, although it's hard to believe that in 1957 there wasn't a tree to be seen – these were planted by developers who bought the land at an auction. It is now also home to willows, acacias and eucalyptus.

The village is neatly split into three zones: commercial, residential and hotel. On the beach, **El Soleado** is where people come to buy refreshments, relax and shelter from the winds.

Mar Azul is even smaller, even quieter and equally paradisiacal. The village is little more than a clutch of sandy roads centred on cabin-style lodgings, a hotel and a supermarket.

Where to eat & drink

In Mar de las Pampas, **Amorinda Tutto Pasta** (Avenida Gerchunoff y El Lucero, 02255 479750, www.amorinda.com.ar, $$$) is a village classic. **Cabaña Huinca** (Querandíes, entre Avenida El Lucero y El Ceibo, 02255 479718, closed weekdays in winter, $$$) serves up culinary treats as well as the owner's homemade beer.

Tiny Mar Azul has far fewer dining options but boasts an excellent sushi restaurant, **Heiwa** (Calle 34, 02255 453674, $$$).

Where to stay

In Mar de las Pampas, metres from the beach, are the cabañas of **Rincón del Duende** (Virazón y Playa, 02255 479866, www.rincondelduende.com, $$$ for four people per day). As well as a fine restaurant, the complex has a pool and a tennis court. The apartments at plush **Miradores del Bosque** (Mercedes Sosa y Hudson, 02255 452792, www.miradoresdelbosque.com) are suitably luxurious and include a spa. Rates are US$2500 per week for two to six people, and are 40 per cent less out of season.

Just off the crossroads in Mar Azul, and 100 metres from the beach, are the cabañas of **Puerto de Palos** (Calle 36, entre Avenida Mar del Plata y Punta del Este, 02255 470311, www.puertodepalosweb.com.ar, $$$$ per cabin). This mini complex of log cabins set in the woods, with a pool, is one of the best value options in the area. For a seafront location, check out the **Rincón del Mar** (Calle 30 y La Playa, 02255 456003, www.rincondelmar.com.ar, $$$).

Tourist information

Avenida El Lucero, y Mercedes Sosa, Mar de las Pampas (02255 470324, www.mardelaspampas.com.ar). **Open** *Dec-Mar* 8am-midnight daily. *Apr-Nov* 10am-6pm daily.

Getting there

Plusmar has regular buses from Buenos Aires to **Villa Gesell** (5hrs, AR$180 one-way), just 10km (6 miles) away from Mar de las Pampas. Mar Azul is 5km (3 miles) further on; take a taxi or use the local bus service that runs from Villa Gesell to Mar de las Pampas and Mar Azul.

Uruguay

Colonial charm and flashy beach resorts lie across the river from BA.

A side trip across the Río de la Plata offers more than just another passport stamp. While Uruguay shares its larger neighbour's penchant for meat, *maté* and the characteristic accent heavily influenced by Italian immigrants, the *onda* (vibe) is perceptibly different as soon as you step off the ferry.

Colonia del Sacramento is an idyllic town with pretty, cobblestone streets; while Montevideo moves at a much slower, friendlier pace than its wild, sometimes spiny sister city, Buenos Aires.

This tiny country also lays claim to South America's hippest beach resorts in Punte del Este and José Ignacio (not to mention its most exclusive, decadent parties), as well as unspoiled countryside that provides the ultimate crowd-free escape.

COLONIA DEL SACRAMENTO

Ah, Colonia del Sacramento. A city by name, a sleepy world of cobbled streets by nature. Its origins as a Portuguese settlement date back to 1680, but now the UNESCO World Heritage Site generally just acts as a soothing antidote to the pacy onslaught of Buenos Aires. For serious downtime, Colonia is ideal.

The charming **Barrio Histórico** (old town) is where most of the sights are found. Stroll along the **Calle de los Suspiros** (Street of Sighs), with its knock-kneed cobbles and typical colonial architecture; take in the view from the working lighthouse, amid the ruins of the 17th-century **Convento de San Francisco**; or enjoy a leisurely amble beside the walls of the old town's fortification.

To fully unwind, it's well worth bedding down for a night or two. Faded paintwork and vintage cars make the city a joy for photographers, and the long coastal road west of town leads to some great beaches and countryside; mopeds, bicycles and even golf carts are widely available for hire. Sunbathers take note: summer temperatures can be relentlessly high.

Finally, near the swish out-of-town Sheraton resort, keep an eye out for one of the oddest

sights in Uruguay; a vast and long-defunct Moorish-style bull ring, now decaying quietly. Horses can still be heard thundering around the neighbouring track.

Where to eat & drink

Colonia has plenty of costly, average places to eat (like Buenos Aires, it can be tough to escape parrilla and pizza) although there are a number of exceptions. In the old town, **El Drugstore** (Portugal 174 y Vascocellos, 00 598 522 5241, $$) provides a colourful variety of tapas, salads and mains in jaunty surroundings; you can even take a table in a vintage car outside. At café **Lentas Maravillas** (Playa Álamo, Rambla de las Américas, 00 598 522 0636, $$), Maggie Molnar opens up her pretty garden and living room for guests to enjoy light meals and five o'clock tea while browsing her bookshelves.

Where to stay

The best lodgings in the old town are at the **Posada Plaza Mayor** (Calle del Comercio 111, 00 598 52 23193, www.posadaplazamayor.com, $$), a historic house on the main square. For a cheap stay, try cheery hostel **El Viajero** (Washington Barbot 164, 00 598 522 2683, www.elviajerocolonia.com, doubles $, US$20 per person dorm). Or head nine kilometres out of town to the rustic-chic **Casa Los Jazmines** (Camino del Caño s/n, 00 598 4520 2799,

For price codes, see p236.

ESCAPES & EXCURSIONS

www.casalosjazmineshotel.com, $$), with an outdoor pool, cosy fireplace and sheep grazing in the surrounding fields. The **Sheraton Colonia Golf & Spa Resort** (Continuación de la Rambla de Las Américas, 00 598 52 29000, www.hotelsheratoncolonia.com, $$$$), six kilometres west of the centre, boasts luxurious amenities and an 18-hole golf course.

Getting there

By boat From its Puerto Madero terminal in BA, **Buquebus** (www.buquebus.com) has three fast crossings per day to Colonia (1hr, from US$100 return) on a comfy hydrofoil, and two slow ferries (3hrs, from US$70 return), both with room for cars. An often cheaper option is **Seacat** (www.seacatcolonia.com), whose small ferries make three crossings daily (1hr, from US$40 return) and leave from the same terminal as Buquebus, or **Colonia Express** (www.coloniaexpress.com), whose hydrofoils also reach Uruguay in an hour (from US$40 return). Colonia Express services leaves from a small terminal at Pedro de Mendoza 330 in La Boca.

Tourist information

Centro de Bienvenida, Interpretación y Turismo del Uruguay
Miguel Ángel Odriozola 434, entre Alberto Méndez y Lavalleja, Colonia (00 598 4522 1072). **Open** 9am-7pm daily.

CARMELO

Some 70 kilometres west of Colonia, the sleepy backwater town of Carmelo is situated where

Colonia del Sacramento.

the River Uruguay broadens to become the River Plate. It's a destination for romantic weekend getaways and relaxing retreats: the golden beaches just a short walk from town are the main draw for visitors.

Between Carmelo and Colonia, on the R21, is **Los Cerros de San Juan** (00 598 481 7200, www.loscerrosdesanjuan.com.uy), the country's oldest bodega. Founded in 1854, it still stores its wines in a century-old stone warehouse.

Nestled in a pine forest outside town on the R21, is the stunning **Four Seasons Carmelo Resort** (in BA 0800 122 0179, 00 598 542 9000, www.fourseasons.com/carmelo, $$$$), Carmelo's budget-busting big draw, with 20 zen-inspired bungalows around a gigantic pool, plus a deluxe spa and golf course.

Eating at **Bodega y Granja Narbona** (Ruta 21, km 267, 00 598 454 04778, www.puertocarmelo.com, $$$$), a 1909 farmhouse 13 kilometres from the centre, is a highlight of any trip to Carmelo. Many of its products are made on-site, from the sharp cheese to the fantastic olive oil.

Tourist information

Dirección de Turismo
Plaza Independencia, 19 de Abril y Roobell. **Open** 9am-6pm daily.

MONTEVIDEO

Montevideo is barely more than a river breeze away from Buenos Aires, but if you're expecting the Uruguayan capital to be a near-mirror image of its trendy neighbour, think again. It's altogether quieter, smaller and less frenetic. Many visitors love it for its slower pace, sandy beaches and measured friendliness; others find it, well, ho-hum.

There's plenty of ebbing grandeur in the **Ciudad Vieja** (old town), where wrought iron balconies and stucco façades lead to pleasant green plazas. The largest civic space, **Plaza Independencia**, is overlooked by the cupola-crazed whimsy of **Palacio Salvo**; built in 1928, this was for decades the highest structure in South America. In the square itself, you can head below the statue of independence hero José Artigas to see his singular final resting place.

The city is home to several notable museums. The **Museo Romántico** (25 de Mayo 428, 00 598 2915 1051, closed Sat, Sun) showcases the impeccably preserved belongings of the local 19th-century elite, and the **Museo Gurvich** (Ituzaingó 1377, 00 598 2915 7826, www.museogurvich.org, closed Sun) displays the eclectic work of painter José Gurvich.

Head into the residential suburbs for a change of scenery; follow the coastal path and you'll eventually be rewarded by miles of city-front beaches. The city's youth hostels are the best option for bike hire.

Montevideo is one of the spiritual homes of international football, and for anyone who has ever harboured dreams of goal-scoring glory, a trip to the **Estadio Centenario** (Avenida Américo Ricaldoni s/n, 00 598 2 487 2059, http://estadiocentenario.com.uy), which hosted the first World Cup Final in 1930, is more or less obligatory.

If you're in town for the weekend, don't miss the **Feria Tristán Narvaja** (Tristán Narvaja y 18 de Julio). Every Sunday, from 9am to 2pm, Tristán Narvaja street is packed with antique dealers touting all manner of curious trinkets and furniture.

Never considered Uruguay as a wine-producing country? Visit wineries around Montevideo and further afield on the **Wine Roads** tour (www.uruguaywinetours.com), a route set up by a group of local wine-growers.

Where to eat & drink

For the most atmospheric lunch in town, head to the **Mercado del Puerto**. It's possible to take a lively ringside seat at most of the gut-busting indoor parrillas, or for special occasions try **El Palenque** (Pérez Castellano 1579, 00 598 2 915 4704, www.elpalenque.com.uy, $$$$), which pulls in international celebrities and local politicians. Come hungry. For upmarket but still relaxed dining, there's a bar and restaurant scene surrounding the one-block pedestrianised street Bacacay in the city's old town.

Where to stay

Posada al Sur (Pérez Castellano 1424, 00 598 2 916 5287, www.posadaalsur.com.uy, $) is a comfortable and reasonably priced option with a strong sustainable tourism philosophy.

The imaginatively refurbished **Plaza Fuerte Hotel** (Bartolomé Mitre 1361, 00 598 2 915 6651, www.plazafuerte.com, $$) includes all the original details of the stunning building that is home to the hotel, but also features thoroughly modern components. Chain hotel **NH Columbia** (Rambla Gran Bretaña 473, 00 598 2 916 0001, www.nh-hoteles.es, $$) is in a modernist building boasting attractive rooms and river views. For a boutique experience, book yourself into **Esplendor Montevideo** (Soriano 868, 00 598 2900 1900, www.esplendormontevideo.com, $$), set in a beautiful Florentine-style building.

Getting there

By air Aerolíneas Argentinas (www.aerolineas.com.ar) and **Sol Líneas Aéreas** (www.sol.com.ar) fly several times a day from BA to Montevideo (40mins). Flights depart from BA's Aeropuerto Jorge Newbery (*see p254*) and arrive at Montevideo's Carrasco airport (00 598 2 604 0329), 10km (6 miles) from the centre of the city.

By boat From its Puerto Madero terminal (Avenida Córdoba y Madero, www.buquebus.com) in BA, **Buquebus** has at least two fast boats a day direct to Montevideo (3hrs, from US$80 one-way).

Tourist information

Centro de Información Turística
Explanada Palacio Municipal, Avenida 18 de Julio, y Ejido (00 598 2 1950 1830).
Open 9.30am-5.30pm daily.

PUNTA DEL ESTE

Brazen, cool and shamelessly obsessed with aesthetics, this glamorous resort is one of the world's most exclusive. Concrete and crowded, the **Punta del Este** of today has come a long way from the time when 1950s starlets such as Rita Hayworth graced its shores. But it remains a staggeringly expensive luxury destination for American and European tourists, as well as Argentinian and Brazilian regulars, all lured by its combination of fashionable beaches, superb restaurants and chichi clubs where you can greet the dawn dancing away, cocktail in hand.

The demographic features a fascinating cast of millionaire yacht owners, 18-year-old models with their 49-year-old beaus, surgeons and plastic surgeons, successful and disgraced former footballers, and teenage surfers with their families. But it's this dynamic clash of cultures that gives Punta its unique, indefinable charm, creating a magic that transcends the ephemeral summer season.

As you travel north out of the peninsula, the white sands empty and the high-rises are replaced by mansions. After about ten kilometres you hit Punta's most happening

INSIDE TRACK
HAND IN THE SAND

La Mano (the hand), as the iconic sculpture surging out of the sand at Parada 4 beach is popularly called, is the work of Chilean artist Mario Irarrázabal. He completed the piece in just under a week, winning first prize in the first International Meeting of Modern Sculpture held in Punta del Este.

Punta del Este.

patch: **La Barra**. The town has mushroomed from scarcely a village to the summer residence of the international fashion set, who've fled the uncouth masses crowding into Punta. In January it's the throbbing heart of the area's scene; it's also the gastronomic capital of the area, and the best place to take in an exhibition at one of the many galleries, or simply frolic on the beautiful beaches – **Bikini beach** is the focal point for the catwalk show of sunbathers. But the indisputable draw here is the nightlife: peak rush hour is 3am.

Where to eat & drink

Remember that during the busy summer months, restaurant reservations are a must everywhere. For sublime fish and seafood with Mediterranean flourishes, try the upmarket **Lo de Charlie** (Calle 12 no.819, y Calle 9, 00 598 4244 4183, $$$). **Patxi** (Dodera 944, Maldonado, 00 598 42 238393, $$$$) lures in diners with its delicious Basque seafood dishes and well-stocked wine cellar.

Substance over style is the order of the day at **El Viejo Marino** (Calle 11 no.739, 00 598 4244 3565, www.viejomarino.com, $$$). Ignore the tacky decor and the over-fussy service and focus instead on the huge portions and wonderfully fresh seafood. The large platter of diced *chipirones* (baby squid) and fried onions is an absolute must. And no visit to Uruguay is complete without a trip to **La Pasiva** (Gorlero y Calle 28, 00 598 4244 1843, $); the *panchos* (hotdogs), bathed in mustard, make the perfect cheap snack.

For a strong tonic, head to **Moby Dick Bar** (Rambla General Artigas 650, 00 598 4244 1240, www.mobydick.com.uy, $$$). Wiling away the afternoons in this popular sailors' haunt are captains of incredible yachts, rugby players on tour, and a multitude of monied American and British tourists.

In La Barra, an established bistro in the centre is the local branch of **Novecento** (Ruta 10, esquina Las Sirenas, 00 598 42 772363, www.novecento.com, $$$$), the preferred meeting place of the young and wealthy. A cheaper and more relaxed option off the main strip is **Rex** (Ruta 10, 00 598 42 771504, $$), where tasty *chivitos* and refreshing *licuados* (fruit smoothies) are served.

In Manantiales, overlooking model-packed Bikini beach, **Cactus y Pescados** (00 598 42 774782, $$$$) is perfect for a late, post-beach lunch. The snug and charming **O'Farrell** (Calle Punta del Este, almost Ruta 10, 00 598 42 774331, $$$$) is one of the highlights of the local restaurant scene: think juniper berry-seasoned veal carpaccio, and for dessert, lemongrass and ginger crème brûlée.

Where to stay

Lodging in Punta is expensive, but becomes considerably cheaper if you buy a package through ferry operator **Buquebus** (*see p249*). **Conrad Resort & Casino** (Parada 4, Playa Mansa, 00 598 42 472065, www.conrad.com.uy, $$$$), best known for its bikini fashion shows and cavernous casino, became the peninsula's first five-star hotel on opening its doors in 1997. Run by a family of inveterate travellers, boutique art-hotel **Las Cumbres** (Ruta 12, km 3.5, Laguna del Sauce, 00 598 42 578689, www.cumbres.com.uy, $$$) is a visual feast

ESCAPES & EXCURSIONS

containing a fascinating collection of objets d'art from around the world. The eclectic interior design features high-tech gadgets and plasma TV screens as well as cosy fireplaces.

For a relaxed, informal stay in La Barra, **Hotel La Bluette** (Ruta 10, Parada 49, 00 598 42 770947, www.hotellabluette.com, $$$$) is a delightfully decorated guesthouse. Impromptu summer *asados* and roaring fires in winter pull guests together for wine and spirited chat. At the peak of high season, most of La Barra stops in at **Le Club** (Avenida de los Cangrejos y Calle del Mar, 00 598 42 772082, www. leclubposada.com, $$$) for a sunset cocktail. This chic hotel-cum-bar-cum-restaurant dedicates itself to the fine art of good living.

JOSÉ IGNACIO

Leave behind the high-rise towers of Punta del Este to visit the seemingly sleepy fishing village of José Ignacio. Just 40 kilometres (25 miles) north-west of Punta, José Ignacio is a small, stubby peninsula of tidy, single-storey houses with thatched roofs. A slight hill makes sure the ocean is omnipresent for the lucky 300 or so inhabitants.

But don't let its apparent sleepiness fool you. Those quaint thatched roofs have sheltered many a model, photographer, tycoon and ageing pop-star. Residents and visitors have included Naomi Campbell, Gisele Bündchen, Mario Testino, Ralph Lauren, Michael Eisner, Martin Amis and Simon Le Bon. Owing to the march of big names in high season (Christmas to January), mere mortals may have to wait for a table at José Ignacio's famous beachside fish shack **Parador La Huella** (*see below*).

First, to find your bearings, head to the lighthouse. On a rocky promontory jutting out to sea, the 130-year-old, iconic **Faro de José Ignacio** is one of the only structures on the peninsula that's over two storeys tall. You really can't miss it. Climb up any time between 10am and sunset to get the lie of the land.

From the lighthouse, facing the water, Playa Brava (a beach with rougher surf) is on your left and Playa Mansa (the gentler one) on your right. Playa Mansa, next to **Laguna José Ignacio**, is a top fishing spot. Playa Brava, heading out towards the kitesurfers' favoured Laguna Garzón, is the best place to eat fish.

Where to eat & drink

On the Brava beach, don't miss **Parador La Huella** (Los Cisnes y la playa, 00 598 448 62279, www.paradorlahuella.com, $$$$). Besides offering delicious grilled fish and sushi, La Huella is the place to see and be seen. Reserve a table for lunch or dinner –

preferably out on the porch – as soon as you can to avoid missing out on the experience.

Off the beach, near the plaza, there's the more low-key **Lucy** (Las Garzas y Las Golondrinas, 00 598 448 62090, $$$). This is a tea house and casual spot for a quick bite. Food-lovers should head 45 minutes inland to the tiny town of Garzón, an ex-railway village where Argentinian celebrity chef Francis Mallman has a wonderful restaurant and hotel called **Garzón** (Garzón's central plaza, 00 598 441 02811, www.restaurantegarzon.com, $$$$).

Where to stay

If you think it's tough finding a table in José Ignacio, good luck finding a bed. With strict zoning laws limiting hotel operations, there are only a few dozen rooms on the entire peninsula. What to do? Well, you could just visit the area for day trips. Or rent a house for thousands of dollars (see local real estate listings) or contact **Oasis Collections** (in BA 4777 3692, www.oasispunta.com) which has places along this stretch of coast. But if you can book in advance, try **La Posada del Faro** (Calle de la Bahía, 00 598 448 62110, www.posadadelfaro. com, $$$$), the peninsula's top spot. With its bright, airy rooms equipped with fireplaces and terraces, La Posada del Faro is unfailingly chic, even though it's showing its age slightly. Bonus: there's a wet bar in the swimming pool.

Resources

Centro Información Turística
Parada 1, Calle 31, La Mansa (00 598 42 440514). **Open** *Dec-Feb* 8am-10pm daily. *Mar-Nov* 11am-6pm daily.

Getting there

By air **Aerolíneas Argentinas** (*see p250*) and **BQB Líneas Aéreas** (www.flybqb.com) fly several times daily from Buenos Aires to Punta del Este (50mins). Flights depart from BA's Aeropuerto Jorge Newbery and arrive at Punta's Laguna del Sauce airport, 16km (10 miles) outside the city centre.
By boat & road **Buquebus** (*see p249*) runs three fast boats a day to Colonia (1hr) and Montevideo (3hrs). Buses then take you to Punta, four hours from Colonia and two from Montevideo. The combined boat and bus service costs around US$90-$155 one-way. **Seacat** (*see p249*) and **Colonia Express** (*see p249*) also links Colonia with Punta del Este. Boats reach Uruguay in 1hr; you can then take a transfer by bus to Punta del Este. One-way rates including bus service cost from US$40 with Seacat and US$80 with Colonia Express.

ESCAPES & EXCURSIONS

Directory

Getting Around

ARRIVING & LEAVING

By air

Ezeiza (Aeropuerto Ministro Pistarini)
Ezeiza, Buenos Aires, 35km (22 miles) from city centre. Recorded flight information or operator, plus listings of airline telephone numbers 5480 6111 (English & Spanish), www.aa2000.com.ar.
Aeropuerto Ministro Pistarini, Buenos Aires's international airport, is more commonly known as Ezeiza. All international flights arrive and depart from here, except those between Buenos Aires and Uruguay and some from Chile. The airport has three interlinked terminals, A, B and C. Aerolíneas Argentinas uses Terminal B and C, while most other airlines operate out of Terminal A and some from C.

Allow 45mins for travel between downtown BA and Ezeiza, or 1hr 30mins during rush hour.

Australians, Americans and Canadians are required to pay a reciprocity fee upon arrival in Argentina (*see p263* **Visas**). This fee is enforced if you enter the country via Ezeiza and Aeroparque (*see right*), although not at other border crossings.

On landing in Ezeiza, go to the taxi desk in the arrivals hall and pre-pay a set fare of AR$200-$250 to city centre destinations. Reliable companies include **Manuel Tienda León** (4315 5115, www.tiendaleon.com.ar) and **Taxi Ezeiza** (5480 0066, www.taxiezeiza.com.ar). Several other *remise* companies accept advance calls for airport pick-ups. **Bilingual Airport Transfer** (4793 3496, www.bataxis.com) offers transfer services with English speakers.

Manuel Tienda León also operates a shuttle bus service to/ from the airport and its downtown office (Avenida Eduardo Madero s/n, Retiro). Buses leave every 30mins from the city centre, from 4am to midnight. From the airport there is a 24-hour service. Fares cost AR$65 one way, AR$124 return. There's free pick-up and drop-off at hotels, offices or homes in a defined area of the city centre; otherwise, journeys start and finish at the downtown office.

If you have more time than cash you can take the number 8 *colectivo* (city bus) for just AR$2, but allow at least two hours. For a quicker journey along the same route, look for the bus that says '*diferencial*' and costs AR$15. Bus 8 (make sure you take one that says Aeropuerto Ezeiza) runs to/from La Boca and Avenida de Mayo.

Aeroparque Jorge Newbery
Avenida Costanera Rafael Obligado, entre La Pampa y Sarmiento, Costanera Norte. Recorded flight information or operator, plus listings of airline telephone numbers 5480 6111 (English & Spanish), www.aa2000.com.ar. **Map** p287 N12.
Aeroparque Jorge Newbery, known simply as Aeroparque, is the arrival and departure point for all domestic flights, as well as those to and from the Uruguayan cities of Montevideo and Punta del Este and some from Santiago de Chile. It's located just 15mins from the city centre. **Manuel Tienda León** (*see left*) has a shuttle bus service to/from Aeroparque every 30mins (AR$27 one way), as well as *remise* services (around AR$85-$95 to the centre). There is also a taxi rank at the airport entrance. A taxi to the centre costs about AR$50-$60. Several city buses also serve the airport; the fare is AR$1.10-$1.25. Bus 37 Route D links Aeroparque with Recoleta.

By road

Estación Terminal de Omnibus
Avenida Ramos Mejía 1680, Retiro. Information 4310 0700. Subte C, Retiro/bus 93, 130, 152.
Buenos Aires's bus station is close to the Retiro train station (*see right*). Be wary of pickpockets in and around the terminal.

More than 80 long-distance bus companies operate here. They are grouped together by region (i.e. North-west or Patagonia), so it's easy to compare prices and times. There are services to every major destination in Argentina, and also to neighbouring countries.

For most destinations there are two levels of service, *común* and *diferencial* or *ejecutiva*. The latter has hosts or hostesses, includes food and has different types of seats. The most comfortable is

the *coche cama* – an almost fully reclining 'bed seat'. In high season (December to February, Easter week and July) it is worth buying your ticket in advance.

By sea

Regular boat services run between BA and Colonia and Montevideo in Uruguay (*see p248-252*), docking at the passenger port in Dársena Norte, a few blocks from the city centre at Avenidas Córdoba and Alicia Moreau de Justo. Cruise ships dock at Avenida de los Inmigrantes and Castillo, at the **Terminal Benito Quinquela Martín** (4319 9500).

PUBLIC TRANSPORT

Getting around BA is cheap and fairly easy. *Colectivos* (city buses) run frequently, cover the whole capital and offer 24-hour service, while the Subte – the small underground network – is a fast, but somewhat dingy, alternative.

Buses

There are 200 bus lines along a variety of *ramales* (routes) through every city barrio (neighbourhood). Service during the day is frequent. The *Guía T*, a handy guide to bus routes, can be bought for AR$10 from most newspaper stands.

Bus fares are AR$1.10-$1.25 for journeys within the capital. Say the price of the fare for your destination when you get on (if in doubt say *uno veinticinco* – the highest fare), then pay the fare in coins into the machine behind the driver (notes are not accepted). You can also pay by Sube card, which can be recharged at Subte stations and some kiosks. Pick up a card for AR$10 at locations listed here: www.sube.gob.ar; note that you'll need to show your passport.

Hold on tight while on board and be ready to yell if the bus starts to move while you're half on or off.

For lost property, *see p259*.

Underground

Buenos Aires's underground train network is called the Subte. It's the quickest and easiest way to get around the city during the day, though it can be very crowded during morning and evening peak hours – keep a close watch on your belongings. The service runs from 5am to 10.30pm (8am to 10pm on Sundays). Large parts of the city are not served by the network. A flat-rate ticket for all journeys, *un viaje*, costs AR$2.50 – pay at the *boletería* (ticket booth) or swipe your Sube card *(see Buses)*. Magnetic tickets for up to 10 Subte journeys can also be bought inside the stations.

The website www.metrovias. com.ar has regular updates about the service. LCD screens above station entrances give information about connections.

For lost property, *see p259*.

Trains

Trains connecting the northern suburbs with the city centre are more modern – and safer – than the badly maintained trains that serve the south, which leave from Constitución and are best avoided.

Retiro
Avenida Ramos Mejía 1358, Retiro. **Map** p285 H12.
Trains run north and west from Retiro, which is really three stations in one: Mitre, Belgrano and San Martín. From Mitre, **Trenes de Buenos Aires** (0800 3333 822, www.tbanet.com.ar) runs trains to Tigre, with connections to Capilla del Señor, San Isidro and Bartolomé Mitre in Olivos. From Belgrano, **Ferrovías** (4511 8833, www. ferrovias.com.ar) runs services to Villa Rosa. From San Martín, **Línea San Martín** (4311 9207, www.ugofe.com.ar) has a service to Pilar. Return fares range from AR$1.50 to AR$4.40.

Taxis & remises

Taxis in BA are reasonably priced and plentiful (except in rainy rush hours). However, visitors need to be wary of being taken for a long ride, or worst of all, being robbed by an unlicensed driver. Using only a radio taxi or a *remise* (licensed minicab) is recommended. You will need at least some Spanish to book a cab by phone, though staff in hotels and restaurants will usually be happy to help. If you have a smartphone, you can reserve a taxi through **SaferTaxi** (www.safertaxi.com). If you need to hail a cab in the street, try to stop a radio taxi (look for 'radio taxi' on

the doors or roof). Meters start at AR$7.30 (AR$8.70 after midnight). You are not expected to tip taxi drivers and they should give you change to the nearest AR10¢. Large bills are guaranteed to produce a sigh; keep small notes handy.

Taxis are black and yellow (radio cabs included), with a red *libre* (free) light in the front window. *Remises* look like other private cars and do not run on meters: agree a price before setting off. *Remises* are often less punctual than taxis. It's a good idea to make a second call, ten minutes before pick-up time, to check the *remise* is on its way.

For lost property, *see p259*.

Radio Taxi Pídalo *4956 1200*.
Radio Taxi Premium *4374 6666*.
Remises Via *4777 8888*.
Remises Recoleta Vip *4983 0544*.

DRIVING

Driving in Buenos Aires is best avoided. Walking or taking taxis are better options. If you do hire a car, be aware that speed limits on city streets – usually 40 or 60kmh – aren't always respected. Neither, you'll notice, are lane markings.

Car hire

You need to be over 21, with a driver's licence, passport and credit card to hire a car. Prices start at around AR$270 per day, depending on mileage. Major rental companies will allow you to take the car out of the country if you sign a contract in front of a public notary, which will set you back a few hundred pesos. You can often return the car to a different office within Argentina. Third party insurance (*seguro de responsabilidad civil*) is necessary, but it makes sense to take out fully comprehensive insurance.

Avis
Cerrito 1535, y Posadas, Retiro (4326 5542, www.avis.com.ar). **Bus** 17, 59, 102. **Open** 8am-8pm Mon-Sat; 9am-6pm Sun. **Credit** AmEx, DC, MC, V. **Map** p286 I11.
Baires Rent a Car
4822 7361, www.bairesrentacar. com.ar. **Credit** AmEx, MC, V.
Hertz Annie Millet
Paraguay 1138, entre Cerrito y Libertad, Tribunales (4816 8001, www.milletrentacar.com). **Subte** D, Tribunales/bus 10, 17, 59, 132, 152. **Open** 8am-8pm daily. **Credit** AmEx, DC, MC, V. **Map** p285 H11.

Breakdown services

Only members of automobile associations or touring clubs with reciprocal agreements with other regions (FiA in Europe and FITAC in the Americas) can use the breakdown services of the **Automóvil Club Argentino** (ACA, www.aca.org.ar). This includes members of the British AA and RAC. You can use this facility in Argentina for up to 30 days. You must present the membership credentials of your local club, showing the FITAC or FiA logo, to the mechanic.

Companies offering emergency assistance to drivers include **Estrella** (4922 9095, www. auxilioestrella.com.ar), which tows vehicles within Capital Federal or **JHD Auxilio Mecánico** (4613 5337, www.jhdauxiliomecanico. com.ar), which has assistance services within Capital Federal.

Automóvil Club Argentino (ACA)
Information and breakdown service 0800 888 9888, www.aca.org.ar.
FITAC members also get special deals on hotels and car rental.

Parking

Parking restrictions are indicated on street signs, but in general there is no driving or parking in the Microcentro area during working hours (and on some streets, there's no parking at any time). Parking is prohibited in the left lane on streets and avenues throughout the city, unless otherwise indicated.

Private garages (*estacionamiento privado* or *garaje*) are signalled by a large blue sign with a white letter 'E' in the middle. Parking costs around AR$10 per hour. Some barrios still have free on-street parking, though you'll probably be approached by an unofficial *guardacoche* (car-minder, possibly a child). You will be expected to pay a few pesos on your return.

CYCLING

Cycling in Buenos Aires can be a hazardous undertaking, even with the city's bike paths (*bicisendas*). However, pleasant cycling areas exist in Palermo and the Reserva Ecológica. For more on circuits and bike hire, *see p227*.

GUIDED TOURS

For guided tours of Buenos Aires, *see p42*.

DIRECTORY

Resources A-Z

ADDRESSES

Addresses begin with the street name, then the house or building number, followed by the apartment number. For directions, the cross street or the two streets either side of the building are given. Postal addresses should be written as follows:
Mickey MOUSE
Honduras 2738
Piso (floor) 2, Dept (flat) 34
1414 Buenos Aires
ARGENTINA

AGE RESTRICTIONS

The law says that to buy alcohol, cigarettes or have sex you must be at least 18; and you have to be at least 17 (16 with parental consent) to drive. In general, the law (or at least in the first three of those four cases), is broken.

ATTITUDE & ETIQUETTE

Meeting people

Argentinians are gregarious, friendly and usually interested in meeting foreigners. Tactile and physically demonstrative, most exchange a single right cheek-to-cheek kiss on first meeting – men as well as women. If you're meeting someone in a formal or business context, it's safer to shake hands.

Personal contacts are highly valued. In business, if someone is proving difficult to get hold of, a quick name-drop can help; or, better still, use a third party for an introduction. It does no harm – and in fact often does a lot of good – to lean on the foreign side of your business background.

It's best to start conversations with a *buen día* (before noon) or *buenas tardes* (afternoon) and a brief exchange of pleasantries, if your Spanish is up to it. You will find that most business people speak – and are happy to use – at least some English. Any kind of attempt to speak in Spanish tends to be very much appreciated.

In Argentina, punctuality for meetings is a phenomenon that is not widely observed. Out of politeness, as the foreigner, it is better if you are on time, but expect to be kept waiting, always.

Dress & manners

Argentinians are usually well presented and take pride in their appearance. In general, the dress code is best classified as smart casual and applies from the boardroom to the bedroom.

Argentina's contradictory quality is never more apparent than in the behaviour of its citizens. On the one hand, they are champions of door opening, seat proffering on public transport, friendly salutations and good manners; on the other, they are among the world's greatest perpetrators of shoulder barging and shameless queue jumping.

BUSINESS

When considering doing business in Argentina, you should first contact the commercial department of your embassy. It is also worth getting in touch with the centrally located Argentinian Chamber of Commerce **Cámara Argentina de Comercio** (Avenida Leandro N Alem 36, San Nicolás, 5300 9000, www.cac.com.ar).

Conventions & conferences

Many of Buenos Aires's major hotels offer comprehensive convention and conference facilities. The long established **Sheraton Hotel** in Retiro can accommodate up to 9,000 people in its 15 event rooms. A stone's throw from the Obelisco, the **Hotel Panamericano** has 16 rooms for between six and 1,000 participants, while the **Hilton Hotel** in Puerto Madero has extensive facilities for up to 2,000 delegates.

Couriers & shippers

DHL
Avenida Córdoba 783, entre Esmeralda y Maipú, Microcentro (0810 122 3345, www.dhl.com.ar). Subte B, Florida/bus 6, 26, 93, 130, 152. **Open** 9am-7pm Mon-Fri. **Credit** AmEx, DC, MC, V. **Map** p285 G11.
Call two hours ahead to arrange pick-up from your premises at no extra charge, from 9am to 5pm.

FedEx
Maipú 753, entre Avenida Córdoba y Viamonte, Microcentro (4393 6035, customer service 4630 0300, www.fedex.com/ar). Subte B, Florida/bus 6, 26, 93, 130, 152. **Open** 9am-7pm Mon-Fri. **Credit** AmEx, MC, V. **Map** p285 G11.
International door-to-door express delivery. Extra charge for home, office or hotel pick-ups.

UPS
Presidente Luis Saenz Peña 1351, entre Cochabamba y Constitución, Constitución (freephone 0800 222 2877, www.ups.com/ar). Subte E, San José/bus 60, 102, 129, 150. **Open** 10am-7pm Mon-Fri. **Credit** AmEx, MC, V. **Map** p285 E8.
International delivery for packages from 0.5kg to 50kg. Free pick-up.

Office hire & business centres

If you need use of a telephone, fax or internet, your best bet is one of the many *locutorios* (call centres) situated all across town (*see p262* **Telephones**). Charges are around AR$5 for an hour's internet use.

Most hotels, of course, have business centres, although the standard and number of computers available vary widely.

If you need something more permanent (or at least need to give that impression), there are several temporary offices in the city. Options include upmarket and expensive companies such as international outfit **Regus** (4590 2227, www.regus.com).

Areatres
Malabia 1720, entre El Salvador y Costa Rica, Palermo (5353 0333, www.areatresworkplace.com). Bus 15, 39, 55. **Open** 8.30am-8pm Mon-Fri. **Map** p287 M8.
Remote workers can stave off feelings of isolation by opting to rent desk space in this well-equipped office in Palermo, designed for freelancers looking for a flexible, modern environment in which to work and network. There's even a Starbucks next door.

Translators & interpreters

Estudio Laura Rosenzwaig
3rd Floor, Apartment C, Billinghurst 2467, entre Las Heras y Pacheco de Melo, Recoleta (4801 4536). Subte D, Bulnes/bus 10, 37, 59, 60, 102. **Open** 9am-6pm Mon-Fri. **No credit cards.** **Map** p286 K10.
Simultaneous translation for conferences and written translation work via fax or email.

Interhotel
1st Floor, Office M, Esmeralda 1056, entre Avenida Santa Fe y Arenales, Retiro (4311 1615, www.inter-hotel.com.ar). Subte C, San Martín/bus 45, 106, 152. **Open** 9.30am-6.30pm Mon-Fri. **No credit cards.** **Map** p285 G11.
Scientific and public translations.

USEFUL ORGANISATIONS

Ministerio de Relaciones Exteriores, Comercio, Internacional y Culto
Esmeralda 1212, y Arenales, Retiro (4819 7000, www.mrecic.gov.ar). Subte C, San Martín/bus 10, 17, 152. **Open** 9am-6pm Mon-Fri. **Map** p285 H11.

The public face of the government arm responsible for international business relations.
Dirección Nacional de Migraciones
Avenida Antártida Argentina 1355, Dársena Norte, Retiro (4317 0234, www.migraciones.gov.ar). Subte C, Retiro/bus 7, 9, 92, 100. **Open** 8.30am-1.30pm Mon-Fri. **Map** p285 G12.
For entry visas, student permits and work permits. Three-month business visas are also issued here.

CUSTOMS

Entering Argentina from overseas you can bring in the following without paying import duties: two litres of alcoholic drinks, 400 cigarettes, 5kg of foodstuffs, 100ml of perfume. If entering from a neighbouring country, these quantities are halved.

Those travelling to the UK may bring back 200 cigarettes, 2 litres of wine, 1 litre of spirits and 60ml of perfume free of charge. Duty-free goods totalling up to US$800 are allowed into the US.

DISABLED

Getting around

BA is not an easy city for those with mobility problems to get around. Pavements are in bad condition and there are often no drop-kerbs. Using the Subte is practically impossible, as few stations have lift access. An increasing number of *colectivos* (city buses) are *super-bajo* (ultra-low), and just about accessible for accompanied wheelchair users. Radio taxis and *remises* do what they can but are not specially equipped, and many lack the space to stash a wheelchair.
QRV – Transportes Especiales
(4306 6635, mobile 15 6863 9555) specialises in transport and trips for disabled passengers. Its minibuses are adapted for wheelchair users and are equipped with microphones and guides. A standard journey within the capital costs AR$120; call to check prices for city tours. Book 24 hours ahead.

Useful contacts

Red de Discapacidad (REDI)
4706 2769, www.rumbos.org.ar.
Eduardo Joly is a wheelchair user and director of this disabled persons' network, which can provide advice and useful information in Spanish.

DRUGS

Penalties for drug offences are severe in Argentina, and include lengthy imprisonment in local jails.

ELECTRICITY

Electricity in Argentina runs on 220 volts. Sockets take either two- or three-pronged European-style plugs. To use US electrical appliances, you'll need a transformer (*transformador*) and an adaptor (*adaptador*); for UK appliances, only an adaptor is required. Both can be purchased in hardware stores (*ferreterías*). Power cuts are occasional.

EMBASSIES & CONSULATES

Australian Embassy & Consulate
Villanueva 1400, y Zabala, Belgrano (4779 3500, www.argentina.embassy.gov.au). Bus 15, 29, 55, 59, 64. **Open** 8.30am-5pm Mon-Fri. *Visas* 9-11am Mon-Fri. **Map** p288 Q8.
British Embassy & Consulate
Luis Agote 2412, entre Avenida del Libertador y Las Heras, Recoleta (4808 2200, www.ukinargentina. fco.gov.uk). Bus 37, 60, 102. **Open** 8.30am-1pm Mon-Fri. *Visas* 9-11am Mon-Fri. **Map** p286 J11.
Canadian Embassy & Consulate
Tagle 2828, entre Figueroa Alcorta y Juez Tedín, Recoleta (4808 1000, www.argentina.gc.ca). Bus 67, 130. **Open** 8.30am-12.30pm, 1.30-5.30pm Mon-Thur; 8.30am-2pm Fri. *Visas* 8.45-10.30am Tue-Thur. **Map** p286 K11.
Irish Embassy
6th Floor, Avenida del Libertador 1068, entre Ayacucho y Avenida Callao, Recoleta (5787 0801, www.embassyofireland.org.ar). Bus 61, 62, 93. **Open** 9am-1pm Mon-Fri. **Map** p286 I12.
New Zealand Embassy & Consulate
5th Floor, Carlos Pellegrini 1427, entre Arroyo y Posadas, Retiro (4328 0747, www.nzembassy.com/ argentina). Subte C, Retiro/bus 10, 59, 130. **Open** 9.30am-12.30pm Mon-Fri. *NZ citizens* 9am-1pm, 2-5.30pm Mon-Fri. **Map** p285 H11.
United States Embassy & Consulate
Avenida Colombia 4300, entre Sarmiento y Cerviño, Palermo (5777 4533, argentina.usembassy.gov). Subte D, Plaza Italia/bus 37, 67, 130. **Open** 8.45am-5pm Mon-Fri. **Map** p287 M10.

EMERGENCIES

All available 24 hours daily.
Fire *100.*
For the fire brigade you can also
call 4383 2222 or 4304 2222.
Police *911 or 101.*
Also 4370 5911 in an emergency.
For tourist crime, *see p261.*
Defensa Civil *103 or 4956 2110.*
For gas leaks, power cuts, floods
and other major catastrophes.
Medical emergencies *107.*
To call an ambulance. For non-
emergencies, *see below* **Health**,
and for information on Hospitals
and Helplines, *see right.*
Emergencies at sea *106.*

GAY & LESBIAN

For more information on advisory
and cultural centres, as well as gay
accommodation options, *see pp200-
204* **Gay & Lesbian.** For HIV/
AIDS advice and information, see
below **Health.**
Grupo Nexo
4374 4484, www.nexo.org.
Useful multifaceted cultural centre,
offering counselling, information
and free HIV tests.

HEALTH

No vaccinations are required for
BA, though you should check with
your healthcare provider if you are
considering travel to other regions
of the country. The city's tap water
is drinkable. Argentina doesn't
have reciprocal healthcare
agreements with any other
countries; take out your own
medical insurance policy.

Accident & emergency

Ambulances are provided by
SAME (Sistema de Atención
Médica de Emergencia) – call
4923 1051 or 107. In case of
poisoning, call the **Centro de
Intoxicaciones del Hospital
Ricardo Gutiérrez** in Barrio
Norte at 4962 6666.
    The specialist burns hospital,
the **Hospital de Quemados**,
is at Avenida Pedro Goyena 369,
Caballito (4923 3022 or emergencies
4923 4082).
Hospital Británico
*Pedriel 74, entre Finnochietto y
Caseros, Barracas (4309 6500,
www.hospitalbritanico.org.ar).
Bus 59, 67, 100.* **Map** *p284 D7.*
Your best bet as an English speaker
is this private, modern hospital. An
appointment can be made to see an
English-speaking doctor. The

hospital has several locations, the
most central of which is in Barrio
Norte at Marcelo T de Alvear 1573
(4812 0040).
**Hospital de Clínicas
José de San Martín**
*Avenida Córdoba 2351, entre
Uriburu y Azcuénaga, Barrio Norte
(5950 8000, www.hospitaldeclinicas.
uba.ar). Bus 29, 61, 101, 111.*
Map *p286 I9.*
Buenos Aires's largest, most
centrally located public hospital. It
has departments for all specialities
and the city's main accident and
emergency unit. If you don't have
insurance, come here.
**Hospital de Niños
Dr Ricardo Gutiérrez**
*Sánchez de Bustamante 1399, y
Paraguay, Barrio Norte (4962
9232, 4962 9229). Bus 29, 92,
111, 128.* **Map** *p286 K9.*
Public paediatric hospital.

Contraception & abortion

The contraceptive pill and the
morning-after pill are both available
over the counter in pharmacies.
Condom machines are found in
the toilets of some bars, clubs and
restaurants and are available in
pharmacies, supermarkets and
kiosks. Abortion is currently
illegal in Argentina.

Dentists

For emergency dental treatment,
call the **Servicio de Urgencias**
at 4964 1259.
Drs Gustavo & Marisol Telo
*2nd floor, Apt B, Laprida 1621,
Barrio Norte (4828 0821,
www.dental-argentina.com.ar).
Subte D, Agüero/bus 39, 152.*
Open 10am-6pm Mon-Fri. **No
credit cards. Map** *p286 J10.*
Excellent surgery close to the city
centre. Services include cleaning,
cosmetic treatment, emergency
care, dental implants, crowns
and bridges. English spoken.
**Hospital Municipal de
Odontología Infantil**
*Don Pedro de Mendoza 1795,
entre Palos y M Rodríguez, La
Boca (4301 4834). Bus 29, 53,
64, 152.* **Map** *p284 A9.*
Dental attention for children,
available 24 hours a day.
Dr José Zysmilich
*1st Floor, Apt C, Salguero 1108,
entre Córdoba y Cabrera, Palermo
(4865 2322). Bus 26, 128.* **Open** 3-
7pm Mon, Wed, Fri. **Map** *p282 K5.*
English-speaking private dentist:
Dr Zysmilich is a member of the
American Dental Association.

Servicio de Urgencias
*Marcelo T de Alvear 2142, entre
Junín y Uriburu, Barrio Norte
(4964 1200). Subte D, Facultad
de Medicina, bus 12, 39, 60, 111,
152.* **Map** *p286 I9.*
Foreigners are welcome at this
university dental faculty but are
usually asked to pay a small fee.

Hospitals

For general medical needs, you can
see a doctor at any of the hospitals
listed in **Accident & emergency**,
see left.

Opticians

For a list of opticians, *see p177*
Shops & Services.

Pharmacies

There are always some pharmacies
open all night. Go to the nearest; if
it's not open, it will post details of
the nearest *farmacia de turno.*
Mega-pharmacy **Farmacity** (*see
p177*) has 24-hour branches located
across the city.

STDs, HIV & AIDS

Gay information service **Nexo**
(*see left*) offers free HIV tests and
a phoneline for people who are
HIV-positive: Línea Positiva
(4374 4484).
Pregunte Sida
0800 333 3444. 8am-10pm
Mon-Fri; 9am-6pm Sat, Sun.
Free HIV/AIDS helpline. Also
advice on general sexual health
issues and where to go for testing
or treatment.

HELPLINES

Although few helplines have
English-speaking staff, most will
find someone with at least a few
words – be ready with your phone
number in Spanish in case they
need to call back.
Alcohólicos Anónimos
4325 1813, www.aa.org.ar.
English-speaking groups meet
Monday to Friday at 7pm in the
Evangelical Methodist Church,
Corrientes 718, Microcentro.
**Centro de Orientación
a la Víctima**
4801 4444, 4801 8146.
Victim support.
**Comunidad Terapéutica
El Reparo**
4664 6641, www.elreparo.org.ar.
24-hour support for the drug
dependent. Some English spoken.

Teleamigo
4304 0061.
Phone support for people in crisis.

ID

By law everyone must carry photo ID. Checks are rare, but if you do get pulled over, you will be expected to show at least a copy of your passport or (photo) driving licence. Depending on how youthful you look, you may also be asked to produce ID to get into some bars and clubs.

INSURANCE

Argentina is not covered by any reciprocal health insurance schemes, so visitors from all countries are advised to buy comprehensive private insurance before they travel.

INTERNET

Downtown and in the more affluent neighbourhoods you'll rarely be more than a few blocks away from an internet café. Most have high-speed connections for about AR$5 an hour. *Locutorios* (call centres) are plentiful in the city and many offer internet access. Wireless access is popular in Buenos Aires, and you'll be able to connect for free in most hotels as well as many cafés, bars and restaurants; look out for the Wi-Fi signs.
For useful websites, *see p266* **Further Reference**.

LANGUAGE

Spanish is the language of Argentina, though it differs from the language you'll hear in Spain in a few key aspects. For the basics, *see pp264-265*. **Spanglish Exchange** (www.spanglish exchange.com) holds popular language exchange events around the city; if you're interested in learning in a more formal environment *see p261* **Study**.

LEGAL HELP

For legal help, contact your consulate or embassy (*see p257*) in the first instance.

LIBRARIES

Buenos Aires has no major English-language lending library, but the **Biblioteca Nacional** (*see p49*) has a reasonable reference section and the Hemeroteca in the basement

is a good resource for newspapers and magazines.

LOST PROPERTY

Keep a close eye on your belongings at all times. In general, if you've lost it, forget about it. Inside airports, try contacting the National Aeronautical Police to see if some honest soul has handed in your property: Ezeiza, 4480 2327; Aeroparque, 4514 1621. If you've lost something on public transport, call the operator, who should store lost property – but don't hold your breath.

MEDIA
Magazines

Gente
The best-selling weekly guide to the BA beau monde, with a straight-faced, almost reverential take on celebrity and media culture.
Los Inrockuptibles
Funky monthly mag on BA's music scene, with gig listings.
Noticias
Popular news weekly, juxtaposing provocative investigative specials and society nonsense.
Time Out insiders' guide to Buenos Aires
You've bought the book so, ahem, why not pick up the magazine as well? Published twice a year and available in all good bookshops and downtown kiosks.
Time Out Style BA
Our Spanish-language guide to the best of Buenos Aires with a focus on fashion, design and technology.
Wipe
A pocket-sized free monthly lifestyle and listings publication available in cafés, shops and hotels.

Newspapers

Argentina Independent
www.argentinaindependent.com
This English-language website includes articles on cultural, economic, political, social and environmental issues.
Buenos Aires Herald
English-language daily, read by expats and Argentinians. The Sunday edition includes articles from the New York Times. The classifieds are a good resource for finding private Spanish teachers.
Clarín
Mass-market daily that's fat with both local and international news. Somehow manages to be high-, middle- and low-brow at the same time and so sells loads.

La Nación
BA's grand old daily, beloved of the middle classes and conservative on culture, art and lifestyle. Better than Clarín for international news. Buy it on Friday for the entertainment listings supplement.
Página 12
Here the word on every article is *'opina'*, as every leftie in the city gives his or her opinion on subjects, squeezing in a bit of news here and there. The Sunday cultural supplement *Radar* is among the best. Also pick up the paper on Thursdays for a comprehensive guide to the weekend.

Radio

BA Cast
www.bacast.com
A weekly podcast in English and Spanglish aimed squarely at the expat community.
La Colifata
100.1FM in Barracas or at www.lacolifata.org
Psychiatric patients broadcast live from a mental hospital in Barracas.
FM de la Ciudad
92.7FM
Municipal service started in 1990 to ensure that tango, the essential soundtrack to Buenos Aires life, is available all day and all night.
Radio del Folklore
105.7FM
Get your fix of folky strumming and gaucho choirs.
Mega – Puro Rock Nacional
98.3FM
No chat, only music, and *rock nacional* at that.
Metrodance
95.1FM
By day, hip variety shows and news; by night and on weekends, dance and electronic music.
Rock & Pop
95.9FM
Brought *rock nacional* and rock culture in general to the fore.
La Tribu
88.7FM
Hip community radio station with an alternative stance on the issues of the day.

Television

These are the free-to-air channels available in Argentina; most hotels and homes also have cable and satellite channels.
América TV
Shows soaps, news, countless talk shows and home shopping programmes.

DIRECTORY

Canal 7
The only state-run TV channel. Programming is big on local culture and music.
Canal 9
Sex, scandals, sex, alien abductions and more sex are the hallmarks of BA's lowest of low-brow channels.
Canal 13
The most watched channel with the best series. Good nightly news.
Telefe – Canal 11
Big channel, fronted by big personalities like national treasure Susana Giménez.

MONEY

The Argentinian currency is the peso. After the old system, which pegged the peso to the US dollar at 1:1, was abandoned in January 2002, the currency was allowed to float freely and consequently devalue. At the time of writing its value was AR\$4.5 to one US dollar, and AR\$7.03 to one UK pound. At the time of going to press, unofficial inflation rates were claimed to be at 25 per cent or more.

The peso is divided into centavos. Coins are the silver and yellow-gold one-peso and two-peso coins, and the 50, 25, ten and five centavos. Bank notes come in denominations of 100 (purple), 50 (dark grey), 20 (red), ten (brown), five (green) and two (blue) pesos.

There are many fake notes and coins in circulation, so check your change carefully, especially in cabs. False bills are generally easy to detect, as the colours tend to lack the precision of authentic notes and the texture is plasticky. Fake coins are surprisingly commonplace; they're lighter in both colour and weight than legal tender.

Also avoid the illegal money changers (known as *arbolitos*, or little trees) on *calle* Florida. They are most likely to sting you with fake pesos and a low exchange rate.

ATMS

Most banks have 24-hour ATMs, signalled by a 'Banelco' or 'Link' sign. They distribute pesos only and usually charge a fee (US\$4). Some are only for clients of the bank in question, so look for a machine showing the symbol of your card company. Withdraw large sums discreetly and be careful picking a cab afterwards. Most foreign cards have a maximum withdrawal of AR\$1,000 at any time and some have even lower limits.

BANKS

It's extremely difficult to open an Argentinian bank account if you are a foreigner. Banks ask for endless paperwork, including wage slips and a local ID. To compound the situation, most won't accept a transfer unless you have an account.

To receive money, use **Forexcambio**, who can also cash foreign cheques or bankers' drafts, or **Western Union**. Charges vary according to the state of the market and the transfer amount, but average around US\$50.
Forexcambio
Marcelo T de Alvear 540, entre Florida y San Martín, Retiro (4010 2000, www.forexar.com.ar). Subte C, San Martín/bus 26, 61, 93, 52. **Open** 10am-4pm Mon-Fri. **Map** p285 G12.
Western Union
Avenida Córdoba 975, entre Suipacha y Carlos Pellegrini, Microcentro (freephone 0800 800 3030, www.westernunion.com). Subte C, Lavalle/bus 10, 59, 111. **Open** 9am-8pm Mon-Fri. **Map** p285 G12.

Travellers' cheques & bureaux de change

Travellers' cheques are often refused by businesses and can be difficult and expensive to change in banks. There are various bureaux de change in Microcentro around the intersection of Sarmiento and Reconquista streets that will change them. Commission is usually around four per cent and opening hours are approximately 9am-6pm.
American Express
Arenales 707, y Maipú, Retiro (4310 3000). Subte C, San Martín/ bus 10, 17, 70, 152. **Open** 9am-6pm Mon-Fri. **Map** p285 G12. Will change AmEx travellers' cheques without charge.

Credit cards

Credit cards are accepted in most outlets; photo ID is usually required. Visa (V), MasterCard (MC) and American Express (AmEx) are the most accepted cards. Diners Club (DC) is also valid in a number of places, but check first as staff are often unfamiliar with it.
Lost & stolen cards
American Express 0810 555 2639.
Diners Club 0810 444 2484.
MasterCard 4348 7070.
Visa 4379 3333.

Tax

Local sales tax is called IVA, aka *Impuesto a Valor Agregado*. It's a whopping 21 per cent, though as a rule it's always included on the bill or pricetag. The exception is hotel rates, which are generally listed without IVA in more expensive establishments. To find out how to claim back sales tax on your purchases, *see p155*.

OPENING HOURS

Opening hours are extremely variable, but here are some general guidelines:
Banks
Generally open 10am-3pm weekdays.
Bars
Most bars in Buenos Aires don't get busy until after midnight. Pubs, or evening bars, open around 6pm for happy hour (known as 'after office'), or 8pm in areas away from the centre, and most stay open till the crowds thin out.
Business hours
Ordinary office hours are 9am-6pm, with lunch from 1pm to 2pm.
Post offices
The **Correo Central** (Central Post Office; *see p261*) is open 8am-8pm Mon-Fri and 9am-1pm Sat. Other branch post offices are open weekdays from 10am to 6pm and some open on Saturdays from 10am to 1pm.
Shops
Most shopping centres open 10am-10pm, though there can be one hour's variation. The food court and cinemas stay open later. Shops on the street tend to open from 10am or 11am and close at around 7pm.

POLICE

Tourists needing to report a crime should contact the **Comisaría del Turista**, where English speakers will be able to help. Alternatively you can head to the police station in the neighbourhood in which the incident occurred; however we strongly recommend the tourist police as the first port of call. *See p258* for emergency telephone numbers and details.
Comisaría del Turista
Avenida Corrientes 436, entre San Martín y Reconquista, Microcentro (0800 999 5000). Subte B, Florida/ bus 10, 93, 99. **Open** 24hrs daily. **Map** p285 F11.
English-speaking staff are on hand to help tourists who've been robbed, ripped off or injured.

**Departamento Central
de Policía**
*Moreno 1550, entre Luis Sáenz
Peña y Virrey Cevallos, Congreso
(4370 5800). Subte A, Sáenz
Peña/bus 39, 86.* **Map** p285 F9.
This is the central police station,
but we still recommend you go
to the Comisaría del Turista.
Comisaría 2ª (San Telmo)
*Perú 1050, entre Carlos Calvo y
Humberto 1º, San Telmo (4307
0537). Bus 24, 30, 126, 152.*
Map p284 D9.

POSTAL SERVICES

Numerous competitors offer postal,
courier and express delivery
services, but Correo Argentino is
still the cheapest for domestic mail.
A letter weighing up to 20 grams
costs AR$2.50; from 20 to 150
grams costs AR$5. By airmail,
an international letter of up to 20
grams costs AR$9.50, from 20 to
150 grams is AR$28. Expect it to
take up to a fortnight (or more) to
arrive. Registered post (essential
for any document of value) costs
AR$31 for up to 150 grams
nationally, and from AR$45 to
send a letter of the same weight
internationally. There are Correo
Argentino branches throughout
the city, and many larger *locutorios*
(call centres) also offer some postal
services. If you're sending a package
over 2kg, head to the Correo
Internacional *(see below)* located
in front of the Retiro bus station.
  If you want to receive post in
Buenos Aires, get it sent directly
to your hotel or to a private address
if you have contacts here and then
cross your fingers: packages or
parcels of any value tend to go
astray. For couriers and shippers,
see p256. There is a *poste restante*
service at the Correo Central; it
costs AR$9 to collect each piece
of mail, which should be sent to:

Recipient's name
Sucursal Centro
C1000ZAA
Capital Federal,
Argentina.
Correo Central
*Sarmiento 151, entre LN Alem
y Bouchard, Microcentro (4891
9191). Subte B, LN Alem/bus 26,
93, 152.* **Open** 8am-8pm Mon-Fri;
9am-1pm Sat. **Map** p285 F11.
Correo Internacional
*Avenida Antártida Argentina,
y Avenida Comodoro Py, Retiro
(4316 1777). Subte C Retiro/bus
108, 126, 152.* **Open** 10am-5pm
Mon-Fri.

RELIGION

Argentina is a secular country;
the constitution insists on the
separation of church and state and
guarantees freedom of worship.
Roman Catholicism is the official
state religion. There are many
synagogues in Once, and many
evangelical gatherings that occur in
converted stores around BA. Here
are a few addresses of places of
worship. For a more complete list,
check the local Yellow Pages
(www.paginasamarillas.com.ar),
look under 'Iglesias, Parroquias y
Templos Religiosos'.
Anglican
*Catedral Anglicana de San Juan
Bautista, 25 de Mayo 282, entre
Perón y Sarmiento, Microcentro
(4342 4618). Bus 126, 130, 152.*
Service *English* 10am Sun. **Map**
p285 F11.
Buddhist
*Templo Budista Honpa-Hongwanji,
Sarandí 951, entre Carlos Calvo y
Estados Unidos, San Cristobal
(4941 0262). Subte E, Entre
Rios/bus 12, 37, 106, 168.*
Service 5pm Sun. **Map** p285 F7.
Roman Catholic
*Catedral Metropolitana, Avenida
Rivadavia, y San Martín,
Microcentro (4331 2845). Subte A,
Plaza de Mayo or D, Catedral or E,
Bolívar/bus 24, 29, 64, 86.*
Services *Spanish only* 8am, 11am,
12.30pm, 6pm Mon-Fri; 11am, 6pm
Sat; 10am, 11.30am, 1pm, 6pm Sun.
Map p285 F10.
Jewish
*Gran Templo de la Asociación
Comunidad Israelita Sefaradí,
Camargo 870, entre Gurruchaga
y Serrano, Villa Crespo (4855
6945). Subte B, Malabia/bus 15,
24, 57, 106, 110.* **Services** *(hours
change with seasons, call to
confirm)* 7.10am, 6.45pm Mon-Fri;
8.30am, 5.30pm Sat; 7.30am, 6pm
Sun.* **Map** p283 M3.
Muslim
*Centro Islámico Rey Fahd, Avenida
Bullrich 55, y Libertador, Palermo
(4899 0201). Subte D, Palermo/bus
39, 60, 130, 152.* **Map** p287 N10.
Presbyterian
*Iglesia Presbiteriana San Andrés,
Avenida Belgrano 579, entre
Bolívar y Perú, Monserrat (4331
0308). Subte E, Belgrano/bus 24,
29, 126.* **Services** *English* 10.30am
third Sun of the month. *Spanish*
7pm Sun. **Map** p285 E10.

SAFETY

Continued economic hardship in
Buenos Aires has been linked to

a rise in street crime, but with a
little common sense and a few basic
precautions, visitors should be able
to avoid trouble. Avoid pulling out
a wallet stacked with bills, and try
not to flash expensive jewellery
and cameras too obviously. Leave
non-essential cards and ID at home,
loop a leg through bag straps while
in restaurants, keep an eye on
belongings on public transport
(the Subte in particular) and always
use radio taxis. Check your notes
carefully, as forgeries abound. One
trick is for taxi drivers to accept
your hundred peso bill, switch it
surreptitiously, and hand you back
a forged bill saying they can't
change your money.
  Remember that while most
central areas are safe, more care
should be taken in the edgier
barrios of Constitución and La
Boca. Touristy San Telmo and
leafy Palermo can lull you into
a false sense of security, and
although violent crime is rare,
bag snatching, sadly, is not. If you
are actually threatened, hand over
your goods calmly: BA has a gun
problem. Football games can also
be dodgy. Distraction thefts are
common, such as where one person
sprays a mustard-like substance on
you while another 'kindly' offers to
clean it off, and then clears off with
your belongings.
  Street aggression is most
commonly of the verbal kind,
especially for women. The best
response is to ignore someone –
if he's really annoying, walk into
a shop to lose him.
  If you need to report a crime,
contact the **Comisaría del
Turista** *(see p260)* where English-
speaking staff are on hand.

SMOKING

Smoking is prohibited in all
enclosed public spaces including
restaurants, bars, shops and clubs,
as well as on public transport. In
many late-night bars and clubs the
ban is flagrantly ignored, but in
general you'll have to head outside
for a cigarette.

STUDY

Language classes

There are myriad institutes
offering Spanish classes in BA,
from outfits like **Ayres de
Español** (Gurruchaga 1851, 4834
6340, www.ayresdeespanol.com.ar),
Expanish (Juan D Perón 700,
www.expanish.com, 5252 3040),

DIRECTORY

Cetae Spanish School (Perú 267, 5272 1297, www.cetaespanish school.com) and **Academia Buenos Aires** (4th Floor, Hipólito Yrigoyen 571, 4345 5954, www. academiabuenosaires.com), all of which have individual as well as group classes. **LV Studio** (Darregueyra 2394, 4637 9442, www.lvstudioweb.com) offers varied activities like salsa nights, as does **VOS** (Marcelo T de Alvear 1459, 4812 1140, www.vosbuenos aires.com), which also has classes focusing on local speech. The University of Buenos Aires's **Laboratorio de Idiomas** (25 de Mayo 221, 4343 5981, www.idiomas.filo.uba.ar) has a Spanish for foreigners programme.

To organise an *intercambio* or language exchange, post your profile on **Conversation Exchange** (www.conversation exchange.com). Or check out the wildly popular language exchange events organised by **Spanglish** (www.spanishexchange.com), which take place in bars across town a few nights a week.

Universities

The state-run Universidad de Buenos Aires (UBA) is, in general, the most academically respected university. Study at UBA is free for Argentinians; prices for foreigners vary between faculties. Contact the *facultad* (faculty) that you are interested in for information about enrolment. Private universities tend to have better facilities and more reliable schedules (UBA's administration is notoriously disorganised).

UBA
1st Floor, Ayacucho 1245, entre Juncal y Arenales, Barrio Norte (4815 8309, www.uba.ar/ internacionales). Bus 10, 17, 39, 152. **Open** 9am-9pm Mon-Fri. **Map** p286 I10.
Contact the department for international relations if you want to study at the UBA. The **Centro Cultural Ricardo Rojas** (*see p191*) offers short-term art, cultural and language courses.
Universidad Argentina de la Empresa
Lima 717, entre Independencia y Chile, San Telmo (4000 7600, www.uade.edu.ar). Subte E, Independencia/bus 17, 59, 67, 105. **Open** 9am-9pm Mon-Fri. **Map** p285 E9.
A business school with agreements with universities in the US, Britain, Brazil and Germany, among others.

Universidad de Palermo
Avenida Córdoba 3501, y Mario Bravo, Palermo (4964 4600, www.palermo.edu). Bus 26, 36, 92, 128. **Open** 9am-9pm Mon-Fri. **Map** p286 K8.
This institution offers degrees and postgrad courses in all sorts of areas, from law to textile design.

Useful organisations

www.studyabroad.com
Information in English on studying around the world; includes details for Argentina.
Asatej
3rd Floor, Office 205, Florida 835, entre Avenida Córdoba y Paraguay, Microcentro (4114 7528, www.asatej.com). Subte B, Florida/bus 10, 26, 93, 130, 152. **Open** 10am-6pm Mon-Fri. **Map** p285 G11.
Student travel agency, with locations across town. ISIC cards are issued here.

TELEPHONES
Dialling & codes

All Buenos Aires landline numbers consist of eight digits. To call a mobile phone, 15 must be added to the front of an eight-digit number. From overseas, dial your country's international dialling code followed by 54 11 and the eight-digit number. To call mobile phones from overseas, dial 54 9 11 and leave out the 15. To dial overseas from BA, dial 00 then the country code and number (Australia 61, Canada 1, Ireland 353, New Zealand 64, UK 44, USA 1).

Useful numbers

Directory information 110
International operator 000

Mobile phones

Any unlocked tri- or quad-band GSM mobile phone will work in Buenos Aires; if you want a local number, pay-as-you-go SIM cards (*chips*) can be purchased in phone shops. The main mobile phone companies in BA are Claro, Movistar and Personal. You can top up your credit at kiosks.

Public phones & call centres

When they actually work, public phones are coin- or card-operated, sometimes both. Phonecards

(*tarjetas de llamadas*) can be bought from kiosks. Note that most public phones are broken.

BA is awash with *locutorios* (call centres), generally run by Telefónica or Telecom. Calls cost a few centavos more than from a public phone, but for a seat, air-conditioning and the guarantee that your last coin won't be gobbled, it's worth it. They usually offer fax services, internet access and sometimes post services.

TIME

The clocks have been known to go back and forward in a rather arbitrary manner, with some provinces not partaking in daylight saving, so the following time differences are not set in stone. Daylight saving time is not currently observed in Buenos Aires. Thus, the city is four hours behind GMT from March to October, and three hours behind GMT during the other months, but this may change in the future.

TIPPING

Leave ten to 15 per cent in a bar, restaurant, or for any delivery service. In hotels, bellboys expect AR$1.50-$2 for helping with your bags. Ushers in cinemas expect the same. When checking out, it's usual to leave a small tip for the maids.

TOILETS

You're probably more likely to be struck by lightning in Buenos Aires than to find a clean and functioning public toilet. However, most bars and restaurants – albeit grudgingly – offer evacuatory relief to the public. All shopping centres have public toilets, which are generally quite clean. And, of course, bathroom use is one of the few advantages conferred on the world by fast-food outlets.

TOURIST INFORMATION

The city tourist board website is www.bue.gov.ar, and has an English version.

The following are the official tourist information points:
Florida *Florida 100, y Bartolomé Mitre (no phone). Subte D, Catedral/bus 24, 140, 152.* **Open** 9am-6pm daily. **Map** p285 F10.
Puerto Madero *Dique 4, Alicia Moreau de Justo al 200*

(4313 4265). Bus 4, 130, 152. **Open** 9am-6pm daily. **Map** p285 F12.

Recoleta *Avenida Quintana y Ortiz (no phone). Bus 17, 67, 124, 130.* **Open** 9am-6pm daily. **Map** p286 J11.

Retiro *Terminal de Ómnibus, Avenida Antártida Argentina y Calle 10 (no phone). Subte C, Retiro/bus 92, 130, 152.* **Open** 7.30am-2.30pm Mon-Fri; 7.30am-5.30pm Sat, Sun. **Map** p286 H12.

San Isidro *Avenida Libertador, y Ituzaingó, San Isidro (4512 3209). Train Mitre or Tren de la Costa to San Isidro/bus 60, 168.* **Open** 8am-5pm Mon-Fri; 10am-6pm Sat, Sun.

For national tourist info, go to:
Secretaría de Turismo de la Nación *Avenida Santa Fe 883, entre Suipacha y Esmeralda, Retiro (4312 2232, 0800 555 0016).Subte C, San Martín/bus 59, 111, 132, 152.* **Open** 9am-5pm Mon-Fri. **Map** p285 G11.
Freephone information line *0800 999 2838* 8am-8pm Mon-Fri.

VISAS

Visas are not required by members of the European Community or citizens of the United States, Canada and Australia, although Argentina now enforces reciprocity fees upon Americans, Canadians and Australians, which must be paid upon arrival at either Ezeiza or Aeroparque airports. US citizens pay US$160 (valid for multiple entries for ten years), Australians US$100 (valid for a year for multiple entries), while Canadians pay US$75 per entry. Immigration grants you a 90-day visa on entry that can be extended by a quick exit out of the country – to Uruguay for example – or via the immigration service for AR$300. The fine for overstaying is also AR$300; if you do overstay, arrive at the airport early so you can pay the fine.
    More information about longer-stay visas for students or business travellers can be obtained from your nearest Argentinian Embassy.

WEIGHTS & MEASURES

Argentina uses the metric system for weights and measurements, though a few old measures still stand good in the countryside: horses are measured by *manos* (hands) and distances are sometimes measured by *leguas* (leagues).

WHEN TO GO

Climate

The summer months are December to March, and the winter season is July to October. The proximity to the Río de la Plata and the sea-level location make the city humid, so the summer heat and winter chill are felt more acutely.
    You'll also hear plenty about a local obsession, *sensación térmica*. This isn't the real temperature, but how hot it feels; so prepare yourself for a summer day and being told that it is 44ºC (111ºF)!
    Spring and autumn are ideal times to visit Buenos Aires – the weather is gorgeous and there's lots going on. November and April are the best months. At any time of year, be prepared for rain; heavy storms or a day or so of torrential downpour that can lead to flooding are common.

Public holidays

The following *feriados*, or public holidays, are fixed from year to year:
1 January (New Year's Day); **Jueves Santo** (Thursday before Easter); **Viernes Santo** (Good Friday); **1 May** (Labour Day); **25 May** (May Revolution Day); **9 July** (Independence Day); **8 December** (Day of the Immaculate Conception); **25 December** (Christmas).
For the following, the day of the holiday moves to the Monday before if it falls on a Tuesday or Wednesday, or to the Monday following if it falls from Thursday to Sunday:
2 April (Falklands/Malvinas War Veterans Day); **20 June** (Flag Day); **17 August** (San Martín Memorial Day); **12 October** (Columbus Day).

WOMEN

Argentinian men can be macho and flirtatious, but seldom behave agressively, making Buenos Aires one of the safest cities for female travellers in Latin America.
    A 24-hour freephone hotline, *0800 666 8537*, assists women in violent situations, with a network of organisations offering counselling and legal advice. The **Dirección General de la Mujer** *(7th Floor, Carlos Pellegrini 211, Microcentro, 4393 6466)* is a women's welfare commission.

WORKING IN BA

Finding work as an English teacher in Buenos Aires is not difficult, but opportunities dry up from December to February when everyone goes on holiday. Pay ranges from AR$30 to $60 per hour. It is best to contact an institute; these offer private or group classes as well as lessons to companies in Buenos Aires. Income can frequently fluctuate due to class cancellations. Provided you have your CELTA or TEFL qualification, English teachers can command between AR$60 and $100 per hour for private classes.
    Apart from mixing cocktails or bussing tables, most other job opportunities for foreigners are published on Craigslist.
    Most foreigners work on tourist visas, hopping to Uruguay and back every three months to renew their visa, though, strictly speaking, it's illegal.

THE LOCAL CLIMATE

Average temperatures and monthly rainfall in Buenos Aires.

	High (°C/°F)	Low (°C/°F)	Rainfall (mm/in)
Jan	30 / 87	20 / 69	79 / 3.1
Feb	29 / 84	19 / 66	71 / 2.8
Mar	26 / 80	17 / 63	109 / 4.2
Apr	23 / 73	14 / 57	89 / 3.5
May	19 / 66	10 / 51	76 / 2.9
June	16 / 61	8 / 46	61 / 2.4
July	15 / 59	7 / 45	56 / 2.2
Aug	17 / 63	9 / 48	61 / 2.4
Sept	19 / 66	10 / 51	79 / 3.1
Oct	23 / 73	13 / 55	86 / 3.4
Nov	25 / 78	16 / 61	84 / 3.3
Dec	28 / 83	18 / 65	99 / 3.9

DIRECTORY

Language

Porteños living and working in tourist areas usually speak some English and generally welcome the opportunity to practise it with foreigners. However, a bit of Spanish goes a long way, and making the effort to use even a few phrases will be greatly appreciated and respected.

As in other Latin languages, there is more than one form of the second person (you) to be used according to the formality or informality of the situation. The most polite form is *usted*, and though it's not used among young people, it may be safer for a foreigner to err on the side of politeness. The local variant of the informal, the *voseo*, differs from the *tú* that you may know from European Spanish. Both forms are given here, *usted* first, then *vos*.

PRONUNCIATION

Spanish is easier than some languages to get a basic grasp of, as pronunciation is largely phonetic. Look at the word and pronounce every letter, and the chances are you will be understood. As a rule, stress in a word falls on the penultimate syllable, otherwise an accent indicates stress. Accents are omitted on capital letters, though still pronounced. The key to learning Argentinian Spanish is to master the correct pronunciation of a few letters and vowels.

Vowels

Each vowel is pronounced separately and consistently, except in certain vowel combinations known as diphthongs, where they combine as a single syllable. There are strong vowels: a, e and o; and weak vowels: i and u. Two weak vowels, as in *ruido* (noise), or one strong and one weak, as in *piel* (skin), form a diphthong. Two strong vowels next to each other are pronounced as separate syllables (as in *poeta*, poet).

a is pronounced like the a in apple.
e is pronounced like the a in say.
i is pronounced like the ee in beet.
o is pronounced like the o in top.
u is pronounced like the oo in food.
y is usually a consonant; when it is alone or at the end of a word it is pronounced like the Spanish **i**.

Consonants

Pronunciation of the letters **f, k, l, n, p, q, s** and **t** is similar to English. **y** and **ll** are generally pronounced like the French '*je*', in contrast to the European Spanish pronunciation.

ch and **ll** have separate dictionary entries. **ch** is pronounced as in the English **ch**air.
b is pronounced like its English equivalent, and is not distinguishable from the letter **v**. Both are referred to as *be* as in English **b**et. **b** is **long b** (called *b larga* in Spanish), **v** is known as **short b** (*b corta*).
c is pronounced like the **s** in **s**ea when before e or i and like the English k in all other instances.
g is pronounced like a guttural English h like the ch in lo**ch** when before e and i and as a hard g like g in **g**oat otherwise.
h at the beginning of a word is silent.
j is also pronounced like a guttural English h and the letter is referred to as *jota* (similar to English hotter).
ñ is the letter n with a tilde and is pronounced like ni in o**ni**on.
r is pronounced like the English r but is rolled at the beginning of a word, and **rr** is pronounced like the English r but is strongly rolled.
x is pronounced like the x in ta**x**i in most cases, although in some instance it sounds like the Spanish j, for instance in **X**avier.

BASICS

hello *hola*
good morning *buenos días*
good afternoon *buenas tardes*
good evening/night *buenas noches*
OK *está bien*
yes *sí*
no *no*
maybe *tal vez/quizá(s)*
how are you? *¿cómo le va?* or *¿cómo te va?*
how's it going? *¿cómo anda?* or *¿cómo andás?*
Sir/Mr *Señor*; **Madam/Mrs** *Señora*
please *por favor*
thanks *gracias*; **thank you very much** *muchas gracias*
you're welcome *de nada*
sorry *perdón*
excuse me *permiso*

do you speak English? *¿habla inglés?* or *¿hablás inglés?*
I don't speak Spanish *no hablo castellano*
I don't understand *no entiendo*
speak more slowly, please *hable más despacio, por favor* or *hablá más despacio, por favor*
wait a moment *espere un momento* or *esperá un momento*
leave me alone (quite forceful) *¡déjeme!* or *¡dejame!*
have you got change? *¿tiene cambio?* or *¿tenés cambio?*
there is/there isn't *hay/no hay*
good/well *bien*
bad/badly *mal*
small *pequeño/chico*
big *grande*
beautiful *hermoso/lindo*
a bit *un poco*; **a lot/very** *mucho*
with *con*; **without** *sin*
also *también*
this *este*; **that** *ese*
and *y*; **or** *o*
because *porque*; **if** *si*
what? *¿qué?*; **who?** *¿quién?*; **when?** *¿cuándo?*; **which?** *¿cuál?*; **why?** *¿por qué?*; **how?** *¿cómo?*; **where?** *¿dónde?*; **where to?** *¿hacia dónde?* **where from?** *¿de dónde?*
where are you from? *¿de dónde es?* or *¿de dónde sos?*
I am English *soy inglés* (man) or *inglesa* (woman); **Irish** *irlandés*; **American** *americano/ norteamericano/estadounidense*; **Canadian** *canadiense*; **Australian** *australiano*; **a New Zealander** *neocelandés*
at what time/when? *¿a qué hora?/¿cuándo?*
forbidden *prohibido*
out of order *no funciona*
bank *banco*
post office *correo*
stamp *estampilla*

EMERGENCIES

Help! *¡auxilio! ¡ayuda!*
I'm sick *estoy enfermo*
I need a doctor/policeman/ hospital *necesito un médico/un policía/un hospital*
there's a fire! *¡hay un incendio!*

ON THE PHONE

hello *hola*
who's calling? *¿quién habla?*
hold the line *espere en línea*
could you repeat that, please?

me lo puede repetir, por favor? or
me lo podés repetir, por favor?

GETTING AROUND

airport *aeropuerto*
station *estación*
train *tren*
ticket *boleto*
single *ida*
return *ida y vuelta*
platform *plataforma/andén*
bus/coach station *terminal de
colectivos/omnibús/micros*
entrance *entrada*
exit *salida*
left *izquierda*
right *derecha*
straight on *derecho*
street *calle*; avenue *avenida*
motorway *autopista*
street map *mapa callejero*
road map *mapa carretero*
no parking *prohibido estacionar*
toll *peaje*
speed limit *límite de velocidad*
petrol *nafta*; unleaded *sin plomo*

SIGHTSEEING

museum *museo*
church *iglesia*
exhibition *exhibición*
ticket *boleto*
open *abierto*
closed *cerrado*
free *gratis*
reduced *rebajado/con descuento*
except Sunday *excepto
los domingos*

ACCOMMODATION

hotel *hotel*; bed & breakfast
pensión con desayuno
do you have a room (for this
evening/for two people)? *¿tiene
una habitación (para esta
noche/para dos personas)?*
no vacancy *completo/no hay
habitación libre*; vacancy
desocupado/vacante
room *habitación*
bed *cama*; double bed *cama
matrimonial*
a room with twin beds *una
habitación con dos camas*
a room with a bathroom/
shower *una habitación con
baño/ducha*
breakfast *desayuno*; included
incluido
lift *ascensor*
air-conditioned *con aire
acondicionado*

SHOPPING

I would like... *me gustaría...*
Is there a/are there any?

¿hay/habrá?
how much? *¿cuánto?*
how many? *¿cuántos?*
expensive *caro*
cheap *barato*
with VAT *con IVA (21 per cent
valued added tax)*
without VAT *sin IVA*
what size? *¿qué talle?*
can I try it on? *¿me lo puedo
probar?*

NUMBERS

0 *cero*
1 *uno*
2 *dos*
3 *tres*
4 *cuatro*
5 *cinco*
6 *seis*
7 *siete*
8 *ocho*
9 *nueve*
10 *diez*
11 *once*; 12 *doce*; 13 *trece*; 14
catorce; 15 *quince*; 16 *dieciséis*; 17
diecisiete; 18 *dieciocho*; 19
diecinueve; 20 *veinte*; 21 *veintiuno*;
22 *veintidós* 30 *treinta*
40 *cuarenta*
50 *cincuenta*
60 *sesenta*
70 *setenta*
80 *ochenta*
90 *noventa*
100 *cien*
1,000 *mil*
1,000,000 *un millón*

DAYS, MONTHS & SEASONS

morning *la mañana*
noon *mediodía*
afternoon/evening *la tarde*
night *la noche*
Monday *lunes*
Tuesday *martes*
Wednesday *miércoles*
Thursday *jueves*
Friday *viernes*
Saturday *sábado*
Sunday *domingo*
January *enero*
February *febrero*
March *marzo*
April *abril*
May *mayo*
June *junio*
July *julio*
August *agosto*
September *septiembre*
October *octubre*
November *noviembre*
December *diciembre*
spring *primavera*
summer *verano*
autumn/fall *otoño*
winter *invierno*

OTHERS

Argentina is Spanish-speaking. But as anyone arriving from Spain or Mexico can attest, the expressive, Italian-laced street slang of Buenos Aires known as *lunfardo*, can, at times, make communicating a confusing if not comical experience.

Talking among friends, porteños will start every few sentences with *'che'* ('hey, you' or 'mate') in the monotonous way Southern California skateboarders say 'dude'. Of course, the most famous *'che'*, and everybody's buddy, was Ernesto 'Che' Guevara.

Some local terms are so out of whack with traditional Spanish that using them incorrectly runs a risk of public ridicule. For example, in Mexico when you ask for a *paja*, you'd be given a straw, whereas to do the same in Argentina would be to confess you want a wank. Meanwhile, the Spanish verb *coger* (to take, or catch, as in a bus) means to fuck in Buenos Aires, inappropriate no matter what you think of public transport. Better to *tomar* a bus instead.

The real fun begins, though, when you start sifting through the more than 1,000 *lunfardo* words and expressions with which porteños liven up even the most mundane conversation. Many of them have their origins in the tango underworld at the beginning of the 20th century, but now are used even by presidents to get messages across in a typically straight-shooting manner. A few choice words or expressions you might hear only in Argentina (and Uruguay) are included below.

LOCAL SLANG

Although many words used in local slang have a macho connotation, as in *boludo* or *pelotudo* (big balls, used as an insult or to kid a friend), they also, somewhat illogically, can take a feminine form as in *boluda* or *pelotuda*.

work *laburo*
cool *piola*
police, jail *cana*
man, guy *chabón*
girl, chick *mina*
cigarette *faso* or *pucho*
sweet talk, bullshit *chamuyar*
crazy *chapita*
incapacitated by drugs *limado*
beer *birra*
large quantity (as in money)
bocha
money *guita*

DIRECTORY

Further Reference

BOOKS

Fiction & literature

Jorge Luis Borges *Selected Poems* Buenos Aires conjured up through the exquisitely crafted words of Argentina's literary hero.
Julio Cortázar *Hopscotch* The king of experiment's masterpiece.
Graham Greene *The Honorary Consul* Captures the conflicting currents of northern Argentinian society in the 1970s.
José Hernández *Martín Fierro* Epic 19th-century poem following a persecuted gaucho.
Alejandro López *Die Lady Die* Cross-dressing and cumbia feature in this picaresque tale of a Ricky Martin-obsessed provincial girl.
Tomás Eloy Martínez *Santa Evita* A gripping tale of the afterlife of Eva Perón's corpse.
Manuel Vázquez Montalbán *The Buenos Aires Quintet* A detective tries to find a relative in the city of the disappeared.
Ernesto Sábato *The Tunnel* The definitive existentialist portrait of Buenos Aires, with plenty of gloom and urban alienation.
Domingo Faustino Sarmiento *Facundo: Or, Civilization and Barbarism* A subjective assessment of the country during the era of Rosas and the provincial caudillos.

Non-fiction

Jimmy Burns *The Land that Lost Its Heroes: How Argentina Lost the Falklands War* The essential analysis of *that* conflict.
S Collier, A Cooper, MS Azzi and R Martin *¡Tango!* A definitive guide to tango in English.
Ronald Dworkin (introduction) *Nunca Más: The Report of the Argentine National Commission on the Disappeared* The accounts of torture and murder perpetrated by the 1976-83 dictatorship.
Robert Farris Thompson *Tango: the Art History of Love* Thompson traces the aetiology of those twisting thighs, not to Europe, but to sub-Saharan Africa.
Miranda France *Bad Times in Buenos Aires: A Writer's Adventures in Argentina* Insightful travelogue featuring shrinks, sex and machismo.

Uki Goñi *The Real Odessa* How Perón helped his Nazi mates find homes in Argentina after the war.
Diego Armando Maradona *El Diego* His own inimitable words.
Gabriela Nouzeille and Graciela Montaldo (eds) *The Argentina Reader* Great collection of texts from 16th-century journals to sociological analyses of football.
VS Naipaul *The Return of Eva Perón* Old-style travel writing, full of sharp political observations on Argentina in the 1970s.
Richard W Slatta *Gauchos and the Vanishing Frontier* Puts the cowboys in their historical context.
Jason Wilson *Buenos Aires: A Cultural and Literary Companion* Open your eyes to the roots and remains of literary greats.

FILM

Bombón el Perro *dir Carlos Sorín (2004)* A warm take on the foibles of the human condition.
Buenos Aires Vice Versa *dir Alejandro Agresti (1996)* Plot-driven Ken Loach-like work.
Derecho de Familia *dir Daniel Burman (2006)* Comedy drama about the trials of fatherhood.
El Día que Me Quieras *dir John Reinhardt (1935)* A classic: Gardel goes to Hollywood.
Eva Perón *dir Juan Carlos Desanzo (1996)* Esther Goris stars in this local, no-frills biopic.
Evita *dir Alan Parker (1996)* Madonna, Antonio Banderas... and Jimmy Nail.
Iluminados por el Fuego *dir Tristán Bauer (2005)* Award-winning drama about a Falklands War veteran who returns to the islands after one of his comrades commits suicide.
La Niña Santa *dir Lucrecia Martel (2004)* The story of the sexual awakening of a 16-year-old Catholic choir girl.
Nueve Reinas *dir Fabián Bielinsky (2000)* Con-artists try to make a fast buck on BA's streets.
Pizza, Birra, Faso *dir Adrián Caetano and Bruno Stagnaro (1998)* Down and out in Buenos Aires with a gang of street urchins.
El Secreto de sus Ojos *dir Juan José Campanella (2009)* Crime thriller and love story which won the 2010 foreign-language Oscar.

MUSIC

Bajofondo Tango Club A brilliant fusing of electronic beats with tango classics.
Charly García *Piano Bar* A solo work, considered by many to be the *porteño* rock icon's best.
Carlos Gardel *20 Grandes Éxitos* An absolute gem; the finest voice in tango and every track is a classic.
León Gieco *De Ushuaia a La Quiaca* A rocker's anthropological adventure in regional folk music.
Carlos Libedinsky *Narcotango* Tango electronica for dancers, dark bars and horizontal coupling too.
Manal *Manal* The first, and perhaps, best blues disc in Spanish.
Daniel Melingo *Tangos Bajos* Tom Waits meets the tango traditions of Edmundo Rivero.
Miranda *Sin restricciones* The album that catapulted the masters of catchy pop into the big time.
Astor Piazzolla *Buenos Aires: Zero Hour* Subtle, stirring tango from the postmodern maestro.
Soda Stereo *Canción Animal* Finest hour from the stadium-filling trio who conquered Latin America.
Mercedes Sosa *Mujeres argentinas* The young voice of folk legend 'la Sosa'.
Sui Generis *Obras Cumbres* A double album of rock-folk tracks from the legendary teaming of Charly Garcia and Nito Mestre.
Yerba Brava *Corriendo la coneja* One of the best *cumbia villera* albums – lewd, crude and shrewd.
Atahualpa Yupanqui *El payador perseguido* Master work from the folk poet and guitarist.

WEBSITES

www.argentinesoccer.com Everything you need to know about the national obsession.
www.bue.gov.ar The city government's site, featuring details of cultural events.
www.whatsupbuenosaires.com Hip recommendations for eating, shopping, drinking and clubbing.
www.guiaoleo.com.ar Listings for almost every restaurant in town.
www.landingpadba.com All you need to know from the moment you step off the plane.
therealargentina.com Articles on wine, travel, culture and food.

Content Index

INDEX

INDEX

Venue Index

INDEX

Advertisers' Index

Please refer to the relevant pages for contact details.

INDEX

Maps

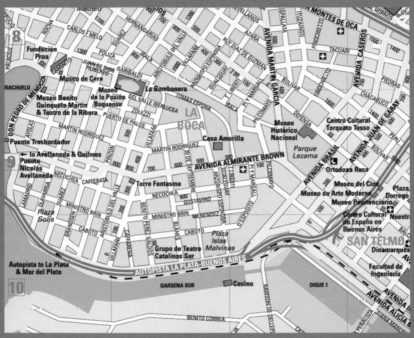

Major sight or landmark	▭
Railway Station	▭
Subte Station	●
Park	▭
Hospital	✚
Area .... CONSTITUCION	▭
Avenue	▭
River	▭
Church	✚
Airport	✈
Highway	▬
Pedestrian road	▭

Street Index

STREET INDEX

STREET INDEX

Subway

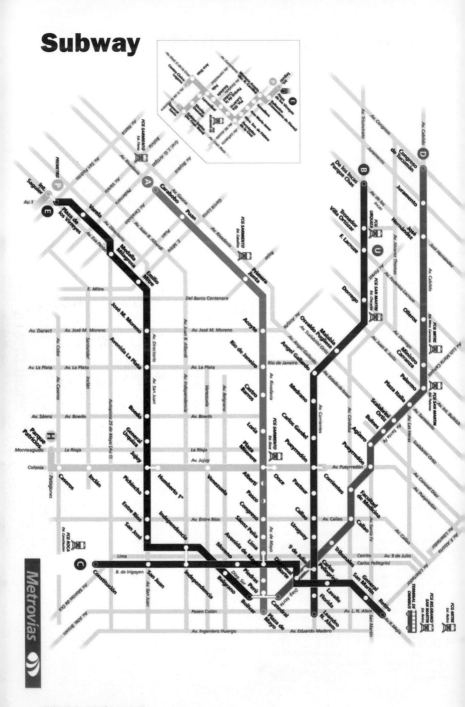

Escapes & Excursions

SANTA FE
PROVINCE

Santa Fe

Paraná

ENTRE RIOS
PROVINCE

Embalse Salto Grande

Concordia
Salto

Santana
do Livramento
Rivera

URUGUAY

Colón
Paysandú

Rosario

Gualeguaychú

Rio Paraná

San Nicolás
de los Arroyos

14

Fray
Bentos

Mercedes

Colón

San Pedro

12

San Antonio de Areco

Carmelo

Zárate

Carmen de Areco

Capilla del
Señor

7

San Andrés
de Giles

9

Campana

(Arg.)

Belén de Escobar

Colonia del Sacramento

Canelones

Minas

Rocha

Junín

Pilar

Tigre

1

La Paloma

Mercedes

Luján

Ciudad de
BUENOS AIRES
See p272-3

1

Piriápolis

Maldonado

Chivilcoy

LA PLATA

RIO DE LA PLATA

MONTEVIDEO

Punta del Este

Lobos

Límite del lecho y subsuelo

San Miguel
del Monte

Chascomús

Saladillo

3

Las Flores

BUENOS AIRES
PROVINCE

11

Límite exterior del Río de la Plata

Límite lateral marítimo argentino-uruguayo

Azul

San Clemente del Tuyú

Olavarría

Tandil

11

Pinamar

ARGENTINA

Villa Gesell
Mar de
las Pampas

Laprida

2

Mar Azul

Mar del Plata

VENEZUELA
GUYANA
COLOMBIA
SURINAM
GUAYANA
FRANCESA
ECUADOR

PERU

BRAZIL

BOLIVIA

Tres Arroyos

11

Miramar

SOUTH
ATLANTIC
OCEAN

YPARAGUAY

Puerto Iguazú

3

Necochea

URUGUAY
Ciudad de
Buenos Aires

Monte Hermoso

ARGENTINA

0   100 miles

CHILE

0   200 km

© Copyright Time Out Group 2012

0   1000 miles
0   1000 km

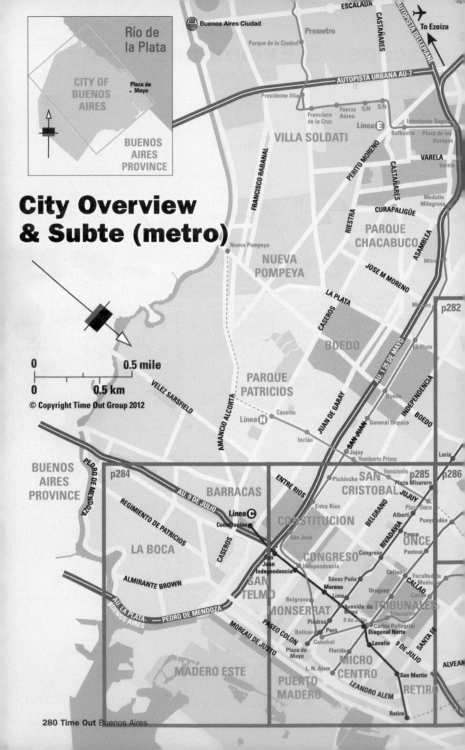

City Overview
& Subte (metro)

Río de
la Plata

Buenos Aires Ciudad

CITY OF
BUENOS
AIRES

Plaza de
Mayo

BUENOS
AIRES
PROVINCE

0   0.5 mile
0   0.5 km
© Copyright Time Out Group 2012

BUENOS
AIRES
PROVINCE

ESCALADA
CASTAÑARES
To Ezeiza

Premetro
Parque de la Ciudad

AUTOPISTA URBANA AU-7

Presidente Illia

Francisco
de la Cruz   Fuerza
Aérea   S/N   S/N
Línea E   Balbastro   Intendente Saguier
Plaza de los
Virreyes

VILLA SOLDATI

PERITO MORENO

CASTAÑARES

VARELA
Varela

Medalla
Milagrosa

CURAPALIGÜE

RIESTRA

PARQUE
CHACABUCO

ASAMBLEA

Mitre

FRANCISCO RABANAL

Nueva Pompeya

JOSE M MORENO

NUEVA
POMPEYA

LA PLATA

CASEROS

BOEDO   La Plata

AU 23 DE MAYO

p282

PARQUE
PATRICIOS

AMANCIO ALCORTA

VELEZ SARSFIELD

Línea H   Caseros

Inclán

JUAN DE GARAY

Boedo

INDEPENDENCIA

BOEDO

San Juan   General Urquiza

Jujuy
Humberto Primo

SAN JUAN

Loria

BUENOS
AIRES
PROVINCE

PEDRO DE MENDOZA

p284

AU 9 DE JULIO

BARRACAS

REGIMIENTO DE PATRICIOS

LA BOCA

ALMIRANTE BROWN

CASEROS

AU LA PLATA   PEDRO DE MENDOZA

BUENOS AIRES

ENTRE RIOS

Línea C
Constitución

Entre Ríos

San José

Pichincha   Venezuela

SAN
CRISTOBAL

Plaza Miserere
JUJUY

CONSTITUCION

BELGRANO

Alberti

RIVADAVIA

p285   p286

Pueyrredón

Pasco

ONCE

Pasteur

BARRACAS

MOREAU DE JUSTO

PASEO COLON

San
Juan
Independencia   Independencia

SAN
TELMO

MONSERRAT

Belgrano
Piedras
Perú

Bolívar
Catedral

Plaza de
Mayo

Florida

L. N. Alem

CONGRESO   Congreso

Moreno
Lima

Avenida de
Mayo
9 de Julio

Carlos Pellegrini
Diagonal Norte

Lavalle

9 DE JULIO

MICRO
CENTRO

LEANDRO ALEM

San Martín

Callao

Sáenz Peña

Uruguay

CALLAO
Callao

TRIBUNALES
Tribunales

SANTA FE

RETIRO

ALVEAR

Facultad de
Medicina

PUERTO
MADERO

MADERO ESTE

Retiro

280 Time Out Buenos Aires

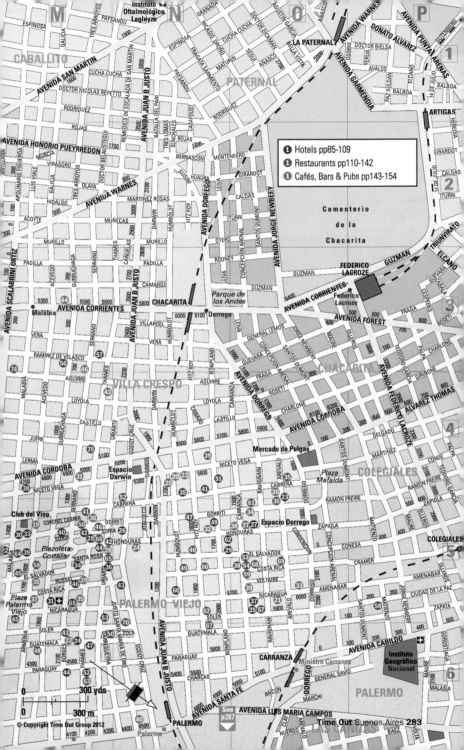

© Copyright Time Out Group 2012

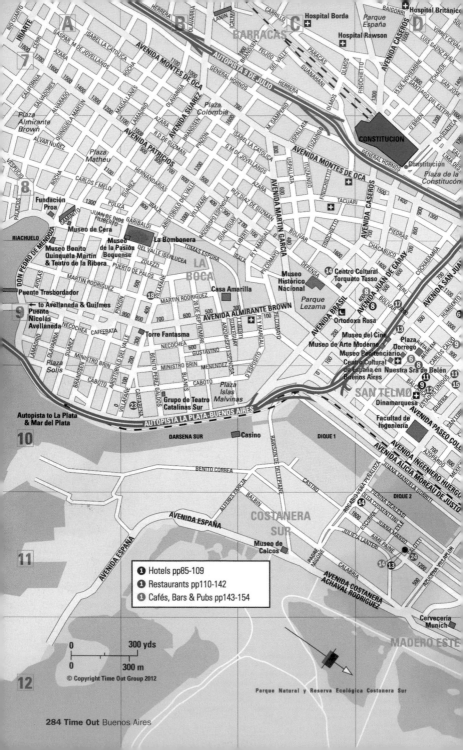

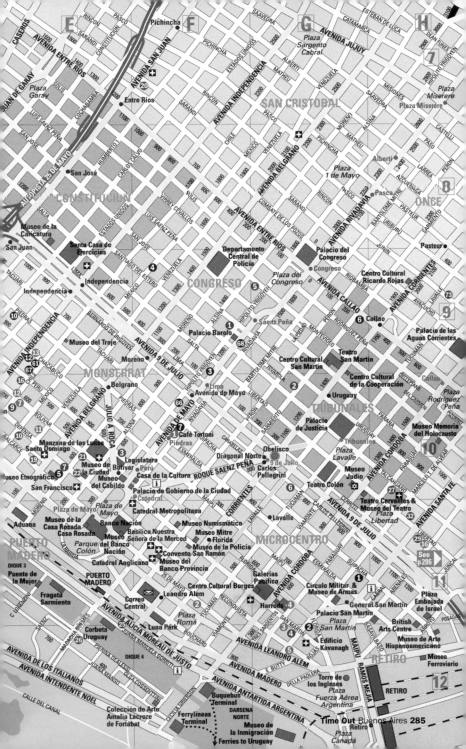

HIPÓLITO YRIGOYEN

AGUERO

Plaza
Almagro

SALGUERO

Medrano

K

PALESTINA

PRINGLES

ARGANARAZ

L

4400

AVENIDA RIVADAVIA

BARTOLOMÉ MITRE

ANCHORENA

GALLO

AVENIDA CORRIENTES

MARIO BRAVO

BULNES

HUMAHUACA

MEDRANO

GUARDIA VIEJA

BAUCH

LAVALLE

TUCUMÁN

ROCAMORA

ACHANDE FIGUEROA

CABRERA

GORRITI

HONDURAS

MASON

CABRERA

4100

4000

4200

PRINGLES

LAVALLE

See
p 282

Plaza
Miserere

Ciudad
Cultural
Konex

ABASTO

Carlos Gardel

Museo de los Niños

BILLINGHURST

SÁNCHEZ DE BUSTAMANTE

AVENIDA CÓRDOBA

JERÓNIMO SALGUERO

BULNES

GORRITI

HONDURAS

EL SALVADOR

COSTA RICA

GUATEMALA

SOLER

4200

4100

3900

4000

AVENIDA SCALABRINI...

11 DE SEPTIEMBRE

CASTELLI

SARMIENTO

VALENTÍN GÓMEZ

3100

Abasto

ZELAYA

AGUERO

GALLO

3300

SOLER

DEL SIGNO

JULIÁN ÁLVAREZ

ONCE

ECUADOR

BOULOGNE SUR MER

Museo Casa Carlos Gardel

ANCHORENA

3000

3700

PARAGUAY

MANSILLA
REP
DOMINICANA

CHARCAS

Plaza
Güemes

Basílica del
Espíritu Santo

SCALABRINI
ORTIZ

Pueyrredón

LAVALLE

VIAMONTE

JEAN JAURÈS

LAPRIDA

AVENIDA CORONEL DÍAZ

JERÓNIMO SALGUERO

JULIÁN ÁLVAREZ

Congregación
Sefardí

Pasteur

AZCUÉNAGA

PASO

SAN LUIS

Plaza
Monseñor
De Andrea

PARAGUAY

Hospital
de Niños

VIDT

ANASAGASTI

BERUTI

Facultad de Ciencias
Económicas

TUCUMÁN

LARREA

MANSILLA

Museo Xul Solar

Museo Casa de
Ricardo Rojas

GÜEMES

BULNES

ARENALES

SCALABRINI ORTIZ

Plaza
Houssay

Hospital de Clínicas

Facultad de Medicina

CHARCAS

2600

2700

2800

2900

Agüero

3200

AVENIDA SANTA FE

3400

3500

3600

Facultad de
Ciencias Sociales

AVENIDA SANTA FE

Alto Palermo

ARENALES

BERUTI

Palacio de
las Aguas
Corrientes

MARCELO T DE ALVEAR

RIOBAMBA

Facultad de
Ciencias Médicas

2300

Pueyrredón

BERUTI

BARRIO
NORTE

PALERMO

JUNCAL

Plaza
Rodríguez
Peña

PACHECO DE MELO

AZCUÉNAGA

LARREA

URIBURU

Hospital
Alemán

SÁNCHEZ DE BUSTAMANTE

FRENCH

Parque
Las Heras

AVENIDA SANTA FE

JUNÍN

AYACUCHO

59

PEÑA

2500

JUNCAL

AUSTRIA

SANTA FE DE BOLIVAR

BILLINGHURST

AVENIDA CORONEL DÍAZ

Hospital
Fernández

Museo de Arte
Popular José
Hernández

ARENALES

MONTEVIDEO

16

PACHECO DE MELO

Facultad de
Ingeniería

CASTILLO

Plaza
Mitre

2000

GUTIÉRREZ

AGUERO

33

Hospital
Rivadavia

ORTIZ DE OCAMPO

CERVIÑO

SEGUÍ

Museo de
Motivos
Argentinos

PARANÁ

Espacio
Fundación Telefónica
Plaza
Vicente López

RECOLETA

AVENIDA LAS HERAS

COPÉRNICO

Biblioteca
Nacional

PAGANO

Museo de
Arte Decorativo

ORTIZ DE OCAMPO

PALERMO
CHICO

Museo de
Arte Decorativo

URUGUAY

JUNCAL

VICENTE LÓPEZ

30

34

AVENIDA CALLAO

JUNÍN

AYACUCHO

1700

1800

See
p 285

GUIDO

QUINTANA

RODRÍGUEZ PEÑA

15

AVENIDA PUEYRREDÓN

Cementerio
de la
Recoleta

NEWTON

Plaza
Rubén
Darío

AGUADO

Plaza
República de Chile

ELIZALDE

MALBA

GUIDO

QUINTANA

18

Nuestra Señora del Pilar

Centro
Cultural
Recoleta

Plaza
Francia

TAGLE

Plaza
Uruguay

Canal 7

Malba

LIBERTAD

MONTEVIDEO

19

ALVEAR

AVENIDA ALVEAR

16

SCHIAFFINO

Palais de Glace

ROMERO

Museo Nacional
de Bellas
Artes

AVENIDA FIGUEROA ALCORTA

Floralis
Genérica

SEVILLA

Paseo
Alcorta

PARERA

17

POSADAS

20

COUTURE

GONZÁLEZ

Plaza
Naciones
Unidas

AUSTRIA

JUEZ TEDÍN

SALDÍAS

Patio
Bullrich

800

AVENIDA DEL LIBERTADOR

Parque Thays

Museo de
Arquitectura

Centro Municipal de
Exposiciones

Centro
de
Exposiciones
Costa
Salguero

❶ Hotels pp85-109

❶ Restaurants pp110-142

❶ Cafés, Bars & Pubs pp143-154

VILLA 31

RETIRO

AUTOPISTA ILLIA

AVENIDA CASTILLO

CALLE 7

COSTANERA RAFAEL OBLIGADO

PASEO COSTANERO

🏛 Buenos Aires Ciudad

286 Time Out Buenos Aires

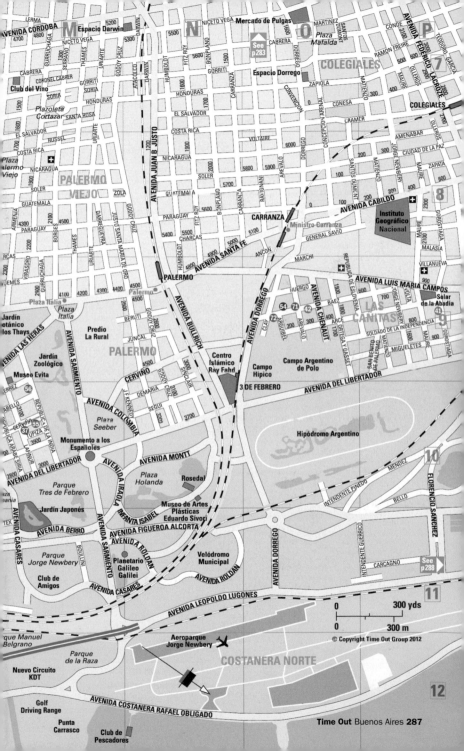

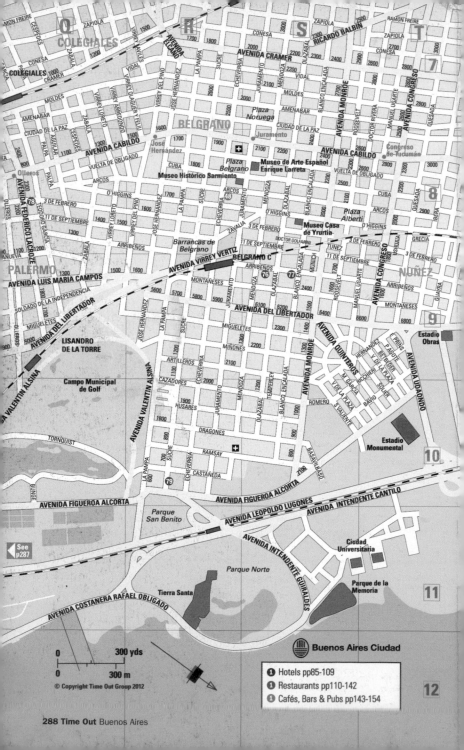

Q COLEGIALES

R AVENIDA CRAMER

S RICARDO BALBIN

T 7

BELGRANO

Plaza
Noruega

AVENIDA CABILDO

Museo de Arte Español
Enrique Larreta

Plaza
Belgrano

Museo Histórico Sarmiento

José
Hernández

CUBA

AVENIDA CABILDO

Congreso
de Tucumán

8

Plaza
Alberti

Museo Casa
de Yrurtia

Barrancas de
Belgrano

AVENIDA VIRREY VERTIZ

BELGRANO C

AVENIDA DEL LIBERTADOR

NUÑEZ

PALERMO

AVENIDA LUIS MARIA CAMPOS

9

LISANDRO
DE LA TORRE

AVENIDA QUINTEROS

Estadio
Obras

AVENIDA MONROE

Campo Municipal
de Golf

AVENIDA VALENTIN ALSINA

AVENIDA UDAONDO

Estadio
Monumental

10

AVENIDA FIGUEROA ALCORTA

Parque
San Benito

AVENIDA FIGUEROA ALCORTA

AVENIDA LEOPOLDO LUGONES

AVENIDA INTENDENTE CANTILO

AVENIDA INTENDENTE GUIRALDES

Ciudad
Universitaria

See
p287

Parque Norte

Tierra Santa

Parque de la
Memoria

11

AVENIDA COSTANERA RAFAEL OBLIGADO

0   300 yds

0   300 m

© Copyright Time Out Group 2012

🏛 **Buenos Aires Ciudad**

❶ Hotels pp85-109
❶ Restaurants pp110-142
❶ Cafés, Bars & Pubs pp143-154

12